# THE HUMANITY OF PRIVATE LAW

## PART II: EVALUATION

Part II of *The Humanity of Private Law* charts a new course for English private law in the twenty-first century. Part I set out the vision of human flourishing that English private law has in mind in seeking to promote its subjects' flourishing. Part II argues in favour of a very different account of what human flourishing involves, and explains what private law would look like were it to base itself on this alternative vision of the nature of human flourishing.

This volume:

- sets out and evaluates different models of what human flourishing involves;
- argues in favour of the view that human flourishing involves being engaged in a quest to lead a truthful life;
- explains in what ways a private law that sought to foster this distinctive vision of human flourishing would be different from English private law in its current state, in particular with regard to: (i) tackling fraud; (ii) promoting freedom of speech; (iii) preserving attention capacities; (iv) protecting people from being subjected to degrading or hateful treatment; and (v) enabling people to make a fresh start in their lives; and,
- considers whether and when it would be legitimate for the courts to transform English private law in the ways suggested in this volume

Part II of *The Humanity of Private Law* is a radical and prophetic book that is essential reading for anyone who is interested in understanding the contribution private law can make to our living in a society that promotes the flourishing of all its members.

# The Humanity of Private Law

## *Part II: Evaluation*

Nicholas J McBride

·HART·

OXFORD · LONDON · NEW YORK · NEW DELHI · SYDNEY

HART PUBLISHING

Bloomsbury Publishing Plc

Kemp House, Chawley Park, Cumnor Hill, Oxford, OX2 9PH, UK

1385 Broadway, New York, NY 10018, USA

HART PUBLISHING, the Hart/Stag logo, BLOOMSBURY and the Diana logo are
trademarks of Bloomsbury Publishing Plc

First published in Great Britain 2020

A catalogue record for this book is available from the British Library.

A catalogue record for this book is available from the Library of Congress.

| ISBN: | HB: | 978-1-50991-199-8 |
|---|---|---|
| | ePDF: | 978-1-50991-201-8 |
| | ePub: | 978-1-50991-200-1 |

Typeset by Compuscript Ltd, Shannon

To find out more about our authors and books visit www.hartpublishing.co.uk.
Here you will find extracts, author information, details of forthcoming events
and the option to sign up for our newsletters.

To Ines and Luca

*A l'alta fantasia qui mancò possa;*
*ma già volgeva il mio disio e 'l velle,*
*sì come rota ch'igeualmente è mossa,*
*l'amor che move il sole e l'altre stelle.*

# PREFACE AND ACKNOWLEDGEMENTS

Part I of *The Humanity of Private Law* began by quoting Richard O'Sullivan KC as saying in 1950 that 'The Common Law of England is one of the great civilising forces in the world.'[1] Writing 45 years later, and after listing a long series of moral disasters that afflicted British society in the second half of the twentieth century, Anne Glyn-Jones concluded that we live in a civilisation 'which has run its course, which is morally, aesthetically and spiritually bankrupt.'[2] Both views cannot be right. If they were, then it would have to be the case that the common law was one of the great civilising forces in the world *and* the inheritance of the common law's civilising effect was completely squandered in less than half a century. This seems too implausible to be true. Either O'Sullivan was wrong and the common law was not as beneficial as he supposed; or Glyn-Jones was wrong and our civilisation is not in as bad shape as she feared.

As between O'Sullivan and Glyn-Jones, I think Glyn-Jones is closer to the truth and would, in correction of O'Sullivan, say that 'The Common Law of England *sought* to be one of the great civilising forces in the world.' It did so by seeking to promote the flourishing of its subjects (while maintaining the conditions of its own legitimacy). However, the common law's attempt to carry out this project was fundamentally flawed because – as I will attempt to show in the following pages – it adopted a flawed view of what human flourishing entails.

In Part I, I called this view, the 'RP': the picture of human flourishing that most reflective people in modern Western liberal societies would endorse, not least because it is the picture that they receive from the culture in which they live. According to the RP, someone (S) is flourishing if S: (1) is in good health; (2) is well-educated; (3) is practically reasonable; (4) identifies with the way S's life is going; (5) has friends and a life partner that S cares about, and those friends and life partner are flourishing as well; (6) cares about S's own flourishing; (7) has at least one 'desire of the heart' to pursue some meaningful cause or project; (8) has mastered at least one trade and game that involves some degree of skill; (9) has opportunities to be creative; (10) is free of anxieties about S's future flourishing being impaired; (11) lives in a 'caring society' that seeks to foster the flourishing of all its members; and (12) does not depend on the suffering of others in order to flourish. If (1)–(12) are true of S we can say that S is flourishing according to the picture of human flourishing provided us by the RP – or, more succinctly, that S is RP-flourishing.

Part I claimed that English private law seeks to help us live an RP-flourishing life, a life characterised by the enjoyment of goods (1)–(12). Part II will argue, however, that the idea that human flourishing consists in the enjoyment of this combination of goods is illusory.

---

[1] O'Sullivan, *The Inheritance of the Common Law* (Hamlyn, 1950), 3.
[2] Glyn-Jones, *Holding Up a Mirror: How Civilisations Decline* (Imprint Academic, 1996), 506.

Moreover, the fact that our civilisation is founded – via institutions like private law – on a false picture of the nature of the human flourishing is the root cause of the legions of chickens coming home to roost that Glyn-Jones catalogued so exhaustively. The first three chapters of Part II seek to make out this argument.

Chapter 8[3] measures the RP against four postulates about human flourishing – propositions about human flourishing which I cannot prove to be true, but which I think we have good reason to accept – and finds it wanting. Instead, Chapter 8 sets out a quite different understanding of what human flourishing involves, based not on what you *have* in your life but on the *direction* in which your life is heading. I will argue that this 'journey model' of human flourishing has a much greater chance of satisfying our four postulates about human flourishing than any other model. Chapters 9 and 10 will flesh out the alternative vision of what human flourishing entails that was sketched in Chapter 8. Chapter 9 argues that human flourishing involves *someone's being engaged in a quest to lead a truthful life* (what I will call, more succinctly, 'QTL-ing'). Chapter 10 vindicates Chapter 9's claim that human flourishing consists in QTL-ing by testing it against the view of human nature that was introduced at the end of Part I: that we are the beings that are aware (or are capable of being aware) that we participate in Being.[4]

Chapter 11 turns back to private law and asks what would private law look like if it were based on the view that human flourishing consists in QTL-ing? The unsurprising answer is: very different. The most obvious difference will be over what kind of harms private law seeks to protect its subjects from suffering. A private law that seeks to foster RP-flourishing will seek to protect people from suffering the loss of goods such as health, wealth, and property. A private law that identifies human flourishing with QTL-ing will be far more concerned with protecting people's ability to interact properly with reality, and will as a result seek to protect people's attention capacities, self-image, and attitudes towards other people from being damaged or distorted. A private law that is concerned to promote QTL-ing will also be far more concerned to protect people's freedom of speech than our RP-flourishing-centric private law has proved to be.

Chapter 12 concludes by asking – should the rules and doctrines of private law be altered so that they give effect to the more authentic vision of human flourishing set out in this book? Unlike many other private law scholars, who would like to see their vision of private law implemented today, if not yesterday, I will answer this question in the negative, for the time being. The reason for my reticence is rooted in the fact that you can only be *helped*, and not *made*, to flourish as a human being – flourishing as a human being is like reading, sleeping or eating: it is ultimately something you have to do *yourself*. In the same way, you cannot be helped to flourish as a human being according to a vision of human flourishing that you do not yourself accept. This creates a fundamental democratic limit on what vision of human flourishing private law can base itself on: it can only base itself on the vision that is accepted by a large majority of its subjects. And it is obviously the case that the vast majority of the subjects of English private law do *not* identify human flourishing with QTL-ing, but instead identify it with the RP.

---

[3] The chapter numbers follow on sequentially from those in Part I.
[4] McBride, *The Humanity of Private Law, Part I: Explanation* (Hart Publishing, 2019), 262–65.

It follows that a renewal of private law along the lines proposed in this book must await a more fundamental renewal of people's views as to what human flourishing involves. If we are to avoid proving Glyn-Jones right, the need for us to think again as to what it means to live a good life is urgent, and our only hope of being part of the first civilisation in history that took itself to the precipice of ruin and turned back, rather than throwing itself over the edge. This book will have achieved its purpose if it improves the odds of our undergoing such a revolution in the head, as well as providing readers a glimpse of what English private law might look like in future should we find our way out of the dark woods in which we have lost ourselves.

The intellectual debts I have incurred and drawn on in working on this project on the humanity of private law have already been acknowledged in *The Humanity of Private Law, Part I*. However, I would like to acknowledge the especial and providential assistance that attending Thomas D'Andrea's reading group on 'The Metaphysics of Being' provided me in writing this volume. Tom helped to introduce me to a huge range of thinkers of whom I was previously only dimly aware, and whose influence will be obvious to anyone who reads this book, especially Chapter 10. I would also like to acknowledge the invaluable research assistance provided by Zoe Adams in preparing Chapter 8. I am also grateful to everyone at Hart Publishing for their help in bringing this book to publication, especially Sinead Moloney, Tom Adams, and Helen Kitto.[5] As always, my debt to my best friend Isabel and her two children, Ines and Luca, who are the dedicatees of this volume, is beyond words. Happily, and again perhaps providentially, the cover photo for this book (like the previous volume, of Rouen Cathedral)[6] fits the themes of this book – identifying human flourishing with a search or a quest – like a glove,[7] and features a young child who looks so much like Ines that, on seeing the cover, Luca indignantly demanded to know why he was not in the picture. It is my dearest hope that this book will help them, and others their age, find their way to an existence that more closely embodies authentic human flourishing than the kinds of existence sustained by our current social order.

---

[5] It should be noted that all references to sources on the Internet in this book are up to date as of 1 September 2019.

[6] As to why Rouen Cathedral, see McBride, *The Humanity of Private Law, Part I: Explanation* (n 4), 30, n 136.

[7] We will come across the philosopher Martin Heidegger frequently in this book, particularly in Chapter 10. When Heidegger knew he was dying, he asked Bernard Welte, the priest of the Archdiocese of Freiburg and a former student of Heidegger's, to preach a sermon at his graveside on the theme of 'Ask and you will receive, seek and you will find, knock and the door will be opened to you' (Luke 11:9): Richardson, *Heidegger: Through Phenomenology to Thought*, 4th ed (Fordham UP, 2003), 649–50. The sermon – Welte, 'Seeking and Finding: The Speech at Heidegger's Burial' – may be found in Sheehan (ed), *Heidegger: The Man and the Thinker* (Precedent Publishing, 1981).

# TABLE OF CONTENTS

# ABBREVIATIONS AND KEY TERMS

| | |
|---|---|
| (P1) | The first postulate of human flourishing: that human flourishing is within the reach of any human being and is not something that can only be enjoyed by a privileged elite. |
| (P2) | The second postulate of human flourishing: that anyone's flourishing can be harmed by a wide range of different events. |
| (P3) | The third postulate of human flourishing: that human flourishing is a good thing, everywhere and anywhere it exists. |
| (P4) | The fourth postulate of human flourishing: that human flourishing is self-sustaining across time and across persons. |
| QTL-flourishing | Living a life that is flourishing because it involves being engaged in a quest to lead a truthful life. |
| QTL-ing | Engaging in a quest to lead a truthful life. |
| RP | The picture of human flourishing that is widely accepted by *reflective* people in modern Western liberal societies, and is *received* in that it is promoted by the culture of those societies. |
| RP-flourishing | Living a life that is flourishing according to the RP. |

# TABLE OF CASES

# 8

# Human Flourishing II – Models and Postulates

In this chapter, I want to undermine the picture of human flourishing that I called the 'RP' in Part I of this project and which, I claim, English private law employs in seeking to promote the flourishing of all its subjects.

I will set out three different models of human flourishing, that I will call the 'Possessions Model', the 'Service Model', and the 'Journey Model'. The RP adopts the Possessions Model of human flourishing. I will argue that of these three models of human flourishing, the Service Model is incoherent and should be discarded, with the result that the only two plausible models of human flourishing that are on offer to us are the Possessions Model and the Journey Model. In order to determine which of these models we should adopt, I will set out four propositions about the nature of human flourishing. These propositions are postulates about human flourishing: we cannot prove these propositions are true but we should nevertheless assume they are true. I will argue that only the Journey Model is compatible with our four postulates about human flourishing, and that we should therefore reject any picture of human flourishing – including the RP – that does not fit the Journey Model of human flourishing.

## 1. Three Models

The difference between the three models of human flourishing that we will be discussing in this chapter can be simply summed up. The Possessions Model identifies human flourishing with what goods you possess. The Service Model identifies human flourishing with what work you do. The Journey Model identifies human flourishing with what direction your life is going in.

On the Possessions Model, whether you can be said to be flourishing or not depends on whether or not you possess certain goods. The vision of human flourishing that we have been calling the RP is an example of a Possessions Model. According to the RP, whether or not you can be said to be flourishing depends on whether you possess the 14 or so goods that constitute human flourishing according to the RP – having good health, not being muddled or confused, being practically reasonable, caring about various things, enjoying some degree of mastery of some at least one trade and game requiring some degree of skill, being creative, enjoying various external goods (such as private property, a reasonable level of income, and a decent environment), living in a caring society, and so on. But there are plenty of other visions of what human flourishing involves that also fit the Possessions Model. So a hedonist vision of human flourishing, according to which you can be said to be flourishing if your life is more pleasurable than not, fits the Possessions Model; as does a desire-fulfilment vision of human flourishing, according to which flourishing as a human being involves being someone whose (rational) desires are fulfilled.

The Service Model identifies human flourishing with one's working to advance or achieve some worthy cause or project. It is the Service Model of human flourishing that people are likely to have in mind if they identify figures like Martin Luther King, or Mahatma Gandhi, or Mother Teresa with human flourishing. According to the RP, figures like these cannot count as flourishing because they had to give up so much of what counts towards a flourishing life in giving themselves over to the cause of alleviating injustice, or poverty and sickness. On this view, the greatness of figures like MLK or Gandhi or Mother Teresa lay in their willingness to *sacrifice* themselves for others, and a Possessions Model of human flourishing like the RP helps us make sense of the scale of the sacrifice these great figures made in leading the lives they did, particularly in exposing themselves to physical hardship and loneliness. On the Service Model of human flourishing, this is the wrong way to look at people like MLK or Gandhi or Mother Teresa. Instead of seeing them as people who gave up on their own flourishing in order to alleviate injustice, or poverty and sickness, we should see them instead as figures who flourished as human beings in giving themselves over, completely and utterly, to working for those kinds of causes. If we also want to flourish as human beings, we should follow their example, set aside our petty creature comforts, and dedicate our lives to working for causes as worthy and noble as those pursued by MLK or Gandhi or Mother Teresa.

The Journey Model identifies human flourishing with the direction of travel that your life is taking. On the Journey Model, we should see a human being as a *homo viator* – someone who is travelling somewhere; and where you are travelling at any one time determines whether or not we can say that you are flourishing as a human being.[1] For example, consider two people, Peter and John. By all the standards set by the RP for determining whether someone is flourishing or not, Peter counts as living a flourishing life – he has a good job and is good at his job, has lots of money in the bank and lots of friends, has just celebrated his 10 year wedding anniversary, and so on. But tonight, at a party, Peter has been prevailed upon to try crack cocaine for the very first time. John is someone who has been addicted to crack cocaine for two years. According to the RP, we could not say that John leads a flourishing life – his addiction means that he has lost his home, his job and his family. He lives on the streets in squalor, begging for money from strangers, which he uses to feed his addiction. But tonight, with the assistance of his one remaining friend who cares about him, John – having hit rock bottom, and sickened by his life – is checking into a rehab clinic. Tonight, both Peter and John are turning around the direction of their lives, and that

---

[1] For a very clear statement of a Journey Model of human flourishing, see CLR James' *Beyond a Boundary* (Yellow Jersey Press, 2005), 149: 'Time would pass, old empires would fall and new ones take their place, the relations of countries and the relations of classes had to change, before I discovered that it is not quality of goods and utility which matter, but movement; not where you are or what you have, but where you have come from, where you are going and the rate at which you are getting there.' (In the original edition of *Beyond a Boundary* (Hutchison, 1963), these words are on pp 116–17.) Alasdair MacIntyre observes that 'James' account of what he had learned has both some notably Aristotelian features and some features that put him very much at odds with Aristotle. It is not a Platonic nor a Stoic nor a Kantian nor a Benthamite nor an Hegelian account. And it puts all those rival accounts in question': MacIntyre, *Ethics in the Conflicts of Modernity* (CUP, 2016), 295–96.

change in direction allows us – according to the Journey Model of human flourishing – to say that Peter is *not* flourishing as a human being, while John *is*. Peter's life has just started going in the wrong direction, while John's life is finally going in the right direction. For the Journey Model of human flourishing, direction is all – whether or not we can say that you are flourishing as a human being does not depend on where you are now (as it does on the Possessions Model or the Service Model), but on where you are going.

## 2. Problems with the Service Model

The Service Model tells us that human flourishing consists in working to achieve some worthy or noble cause. Immediately, we can see two problems with the Service Model.[2]

First, what if the cause in question (call it 'C') is achieved? If the Service Model is correct, then those whose flourishing depended on their working to achieve C (a cure for AIDS, an end to world poverty, an end to racial discrimination …) can no longer flourish because there is nothing more for them to do. According to the Service Model, the people who were working to achieve C were flourishing when they were doing this, but now that C has been achieved, their lives are now destined to go badly.

This seems like a strange result, but the lives of activists who give everything they have to achieve a particular cause (again, call it 'C') testifies to its truth. They identify so profoundly with the work they do in pursuing C that were C ever to be achieved, they would undergo an identity crisis.[3] They would be in the same position as the people in Constantine P Cavafy's poem 'Waiting for the Barbarians'. When told that 'night has fallen and the barbarians have not come. And some who have just returned from the border say there are no barbarians any longer', the people reply, 'And now, what's going to happen to us without barbarians? They were, those people, a kind of solution.'

It is for this reason that real-life activists working for C (whatever C is) typically can never accept that C might have been achieved, with the result that every time it is suggested that C has been achieved and there is nothing more for them to do, they refuse to accept this and invent new battles to fight in the cause of achieving C. However, there is something pathological about this way of living, and it is hard to see how someone who can never accept that their life's work has been achieved can be said to be flourishing. Insofar as adoption of the Service Model of human flourishing creates this pathology, it should be rejected.

Second, this pathology might be avoided if the cause, or causes, that one has to dedicate one's life to in order to be said to be flourishing under the Service Model can never be completely achieved. For example, there is every prospect that someone who dedicates their life to alleviating human suffering in the world will never run out of things to do. However, dedicating our lives to addressing an evil that can never be completely eliminated is terribly dangerous. We would more than likely end up, in Charles Taylor's phrase, 'in a

---

[2] For further discussion of the points made here, see Teichmann, *Nature, Reason, and the Good Life: Ethics for Human Beings* (OUP, 2014), 143.

[3] This is one explanation of the mental breakdown that John Stuart Mill suffered at the age of 20, triggered by his asking himself, 'Suppose that all your objects in life were realized; that all the changes in institutions and opinions which you are looking forward to, could be completely effected at this very instant: would this be a great joy and happiness to you?' and realising that the answer was 'No!': Mill, *Autobiography* (1865), chapter V.

perpetual flaming rage', adopting more and more extreme measures to 'hammer[] the really bad guys ... who are making the world worse, and who ... need[] to be conquered or eliminated. We make a feast of our righteous anger'. And, Taylor observes, 'This is the moment when we're readiest to allow ourselves the worst atrocities. And not even notice it, at least at the time.'[4] Bernard Williams agrees: 'When the hope is to improve humanity to the point at which every aspect of its hold on the world can be justified before a higher court, the result is likely to be ... self-hatred and self-contempt when you recognize that you will always fail. The self-hatred, in this case, is a hatred of humanity.'[5] *Likely* to be – but not if you can (Charles Taylor again, invoking Dostoevsky):

> [Escape the] terrible dialectic whereby a love for humanity, a love so strong and so horrified by the evil in this world that it cannot be separate itself from that evil, has in the first stage a kind of impotence in action, and then needing in some way to do something, to go somewhere, turns into violent action.[6]

The only way to do this, Taylor/Dostoevsky argues, is to love human beings *unconditionally*. This unconditional love for humanity will prevent you from despising human beings who do not live up to your noble goals for them, seeking more and more intrusive ways of controlling them, and destroying those who cannot be controlled.[7] However, the need to cultivate this remarkable, God-like, love for humanity as a whole, which mirrors the love a good parent feels for his or her children, will be beyond virtually everyone. The result is that someone who seeks to live up to the Service Model of human flourishing by pursuing a noble cause – like alleviating suffering in the world – that can never be fully achieved will almost certainly end up, at best, bitter and frustrated, and at worst, a moral monster. Given this, it is hard to see how anyone could recommend the Service Model to someone seeking to understand what human flourishing involves.

These points aside, there is a deeper problem with the Service Model of human flourishing. The most plausible version of the Service Model involves seeing flourishing as bound up with working to improve the lives of one's fellow human beings.[8] However, this picture of human flourishing founders on what is called the 'altruists' dilemma'.[9]

Suppose that the only thing that *I* want to do is help *you* do what *you* want to do. And the only thing that *you* want to do is help *me* do what *I* want to do. We have a problem: unless one of us has some kind of independent desire that does *not* involve helping the other to do what they want to do, 'there is nothing either of us can do.'[10] The same kind

---

[4] Taylor, 'Perils of moralism' in his *Dilemmas and Connections: Selected Essays* (Harvard UP, 2011), 363.

[5] Williams, 'The human prejudice' in his *Philosophy as a Humanistic Discipline* (Princeton UP, 2006), 152.

[6] Taylor, 'Dostoevsky and terrorism' (1996) 4 *Lonergan Review* 131, 144.

[7] Ibid, 150.

[8] For an example of such a view, see Kreeft, *Jacob's Ladder: 10 Steps to Truth* (Ignatius Press, 2013), chapter 4 ('Love'), invoking (at 63) the examples of Martin Luther King and Mother Teresa in support of the view that 'love is the secret of happiness not just for you, for individuals, but for the whole world.' Martin Luther King took much the same position in his *Strength to Love* (Fortress Press, 2010), 26–27: 'The true measure of a man is not where he stands in moments of comfort and convenience but where he stands at times of challenge and controversy. The true neighbour will risk his position, his prestige, and even his life for the welfare of others. In dangerous valleys and hazardous pathways, he will lift some bruised and beaten brother to a higher and more noble life.'

[9] See de Sousa, *Love: A Very Short Introduction* (OUP, 2015), 42.

[10] Ibid.

of problem afflicts the most plausible version of the Service Model. Suppose that, inspired by the example of people like Mother Teresa, you adopt the view that you can only say that your life is flourishing if you dedicate it to improving other people's lives. In other words, you take the view that human flourishing involves helping other people to flourish. But this view suffers from a fatal flaw. If you dedicate your life to helping other people to flourish – what does *their* flourishing entail? If you were consistent, you would have to say, 'Helping other people to flourish'. However, saying this involves descending down an infinite rabbit hole. The initial view that your flourishing involves helping other people to flourish turns into the view that your flourishing involves helping other people to help other people to flourish. And *that* view then turns into the view that your flourishing involves helping other people to help other people to help other people to flourish. And so on *ad infinitum*.[11]

The Service Model simply does not work if it confines itself to the simple-minded view that your flourishing involves helping to make other people's lives better. For the Service Model to work, flourishing cannot *just* be about helping other people to flourish – it has to involve something else that will stop the Service Model entering into an infinite regress.[12] One way of doing that is to say that human flourishing involves (a) having certain basic needs satisfied, and (b) working to ensure that other people's basic needs are satisfied as well. If we say this, we keep the idea, crucial to the Service Model, that your flourishing depends on your being dedicated to some worthy cause, but we don't enter into the infinite regress that the pure Service Model – which says that you will only flourish as a human being if you dedicate yourself to making other people's lives better – puts us in. Once we know what the 'basic needs' referred to in (a) and (b) are, we know what our flourishing entails – having those needs satisfied in our own life *and* working to ensure that those basic needs are satisfied in other people's lives as well.

However, it seems too demanding to say that you cannot be said to be flourishing as a human being if certain basic needs of yours are satisfied *but* you are *not* working to ensure that those basic needs are satisfied in other people's lives as well. What if you have no opportunity to work to do this, because everyone else's basic needs are *already* satisfied? It would seem more plausible to say that human flourishing involves (a) having certain basic needs satisfied, and (b)* *being ready* to work to help ensure that other people's basic needs are satisfied should the need arise.[13] However, if we say this, then we are essentially adopting a Possessions Model of human flourishing, under which your flourishing depends on your being in a certain state – that of having certain basic needs satisfied, and having the disposition to help ensure that other people's basic needs are satisfied as well should the need arise.

---

[11] Putting the point more mathematically, if you say that F = helping people to F, then you get F = helping people to (help people to F), which then yields F = helping people to (help people to (help people to help people to F)), and so on without any limit.

[12] To the same effect, see Pieper, *Happiness and Contemplation* (St Augustine's Press, 1998), 92–93, denying that we can 'offer a positive "yes"' to the idea that 'love [is] the ultimate fulfilment of life' 'because love must aim at something other than itself.'

[13] Cf. the last line of John Milton's poem 'When I Consider How My Light Is Spent' (c. 1655): 'They also serve who only stand and wait.'

The same collapse of the Service Model into some other model of human flourishing occurs if we attempt to get out of the infinite regress that the pure version of the Service Model places us in by saying that you will flourish as a human being if: (a) your life is heading in the right direction, and (b) you are working to help to ensure that other people's lives are heading in the right direction as well. The same moves that were made in the previous paragraph can be made here to lead us to adopt the less demanding position that we can only say that you are flourishing as a human being if: (a) your life is heading in the right direction, and (b)* you stand ready to help ensure that other people's lives are heading in the right direction as well should the need arise. As (b)* refers to your orientation or attitude towards other people in your life, (a) and (b)* together can be seen as components of a Journey Model of human flourishing, and the Service Model of human flourishing is simply left behind.

So whether or not the Service Model of human flourishing is (as I think it is) dangerous and ultimately self-defeating, it suffers from a more fundamental problem. The most attractive version of the Service Model – according to which human flourishing involves working to improve the lives of other human beings – is, on the face of it, incoherent. And insofar as it can be made coherent, this can only be done by collapsing it into a version of a Possessions Model or Journey Model of human flourishing. Given this, we can dispense with the Service Model as a plausible picture of what human flourishing involves. The real fight is between the Possessions Model and the Journey Model. Do we assess human flourishing by what you've got or where you are going?

## 3. Four Postulates

In order to answer these questions, I want to call in aid four propositions about human flourishing. None of these propositions is uncontroversial: it is possible to reject one or more of them, and there have been philosophers who have rejected one or more of these propositions in the past. And there is no way, so far as I can see, to *prove* that everyone *should* accept that *all* of these propositions are correct. To do so would almost certainly involve appealing to the correctness of a certain view of human flourishing, when the whole point of invoking these propositions is to help us to determine which view of human flourishing is correct. However, we have no reason to think that it is *unreasonable* to make the leap of faith of assuming that the following four propositions about human flourishing are true, and adopting them as starting points for evaluating a particular model of human flourishing. These four propositions therefore amount to *postulates* – statements about human flourishing that we are going to *assume* are true, for the purposes of thinking about human flourishing and evaluating different accounts of what human flourishing involves.

In this section, I will set out the four propositions, and say something in favour of the view that assuming that each of these propositions is correct is not an unreasonable thing to do. In the following sections, I will then show that only the Journey Model provides us with a way of thinking about human flourishing that is compatible with all of these propositions being correct. If the Possessions Model is correct, then one or more of the four propositions set out in this section would be incorrect. Fans of the Possessions Model may well say,

'So much the worse for your four propositions.' But I take my stand – and do not think it unreasonable to do so – on these four propositions being correct and their providing us with a good starting point for determining which model of human flourishing is correct.

## Universality

The first proposition is:

(P1) Human flourishing is within the reach of any human being and is not something that can only be enjoyed by a privileged elite.

(P1) is appealing because of its *egalitarianism*. Simone Weil wrote that:

> At the bottom of the heart of every human being, from earliest infancy until the tomb, there is something that goes on indomitably expecting, in the teeth of all experience of crimes committed, suffered, and witnessed, that good and not evil will be done to him. It is this above all that is sacred in every human being.[14]

(P1) tells us that *none of us* are deluded in having this expectation – under favourable circumstances, it is possible[15] for *every* existing human being to flourish at the same time, and no-one's flourishing need be bought at the expense of another's suffering.[16]

(P1) also helps us understand why *hating* other people results in one's harming oneself. When you hate someone else (call them 'X'), you are basically taking the position that you cannot flourish as a human being if X is flourishing: your flourishing is dependent on X suffering harm, and perhaps even being destroyed.[17] (P1) tells you that you are wrong to think this: it *cannot* be that your flourishing is dependent on X's not flourishing. So any time you spend thinking about X, and wishing for X's downfall, and perhaps working to bring that about, is wasted time[18] – it cannot contribute one bit to the measure of your flourishing.[19]

Appealing though (P1) is, it should be noted that it is easy to think of counter-examples that bring into question (P1)'s correctness. Raymond Gaita describes working on a psychiatric ward where the patients' conditions were so desperate that they were treated with

---

[14] Weil, 'Human personality' in Weil, *An Anthology* (Penguin, 2005), 71.

[15] Of course, under unfavourable circumstances, A's flourishing can come into conflict with B's flourishing (for example, where to save his life, A has to harm B); or A cannot flourish whatever he does (for example, where A is threatened with harm unless he harms B, someone A cares about – whatever A does, A's flourishing will end up being impaired); or A and B cannot flourish whatever they do (the same facts as before, except B cares for A as well as A cares for B – whatever A does, both A and B will end up suffering some kind of harm).

[16] Cf. Cottingham, *On the Meaning of Life* (Routledge, 2002), 69, condemning the idea that only a certain percentage of human beings will be able to lead a 'meaningful life' as 'both psychologically indigestible and ethically repugnant.'

[17] See McBride, *The Humanity of Private Law, Part I: Explanation* (Hart Publishing, 2019), 87, fn 34.

[18] Cf. Richard Kraut's reference to the 'burdensomeness' of living a life 'filled with anger, hatred, and jealousy': Kraut, *What is Good and Why* (Harvard UP, 2007), 161.

[19] Ibid, 188–89.

contempt or condescending pity by their nurses and doctors. The ward was visited one day by a nun whose treatment of the patients on the ward – 'the way she spoke to them, her facial expressions, the inflexions of her body' – 'revealed that even such patients were ... the equals of those who wanted to help them'.[20] But Gaita insists that the afflicted patients were *not* equals in terms of their capacity to flourish as human beings:

> Later, reflecting on the nun's example, I came to believe that an ethics centred on the concept of human flourishing does not have the conceptual resources to keep fully amongst us, in the way the nun had revealed to be possible, people who are severely and ineradicably afflicted. Only with bitter irony or unknowing condescension could one say the patients in that ward had any chance of flourishing. Any description of what life could mean to them invited the thought that it would have been better for them if they had never been born.[21]

Gaita's example poses a substantial challenge to (P1). How can we say that people who were disabled in the way that Gaita's patients were can flourish as human beings? And if we say that they can, then are we not in danger of saying that suffering the kind of disabilities that they suffered from is not such a bad thing? Any account of human flourishing that seeks to be compatible with (P1) must take on *Gaita's Challenge*.

## Loss

The second proposition is:

(P2) Anyone's flourishing can be harmed by a wide range of different events.

Some thinkers who endorse (P1) do so by defining human flourishing so narrowly, and placing the conditions of X's flourishing so completely under X's control, that no one but X can prevent X from flourishing. In this way, flourishing is placed within the reach of any human being who wishes to flourish. So, for example, Socrates – just after having been sentenced to death by the Athenian assembly in 399 BC – argued that 'a *good* man cannot be harmed either in life or in death'.[22] As Martha Nussbaum observes,

> Let us be clear about what this means. It means that virtue all by itself is sufficient – not just for feeling satisfied, but for having a life that is good, complete, choiceworthy, lacking in nothing. Other things, if present, can make the life a little better, but they are worth nothing without virtue, and they are no big deal if virtue is present, since full-fledged [flourishing] is already at hand.[23]

And the Stoic Epictetus – who was born a slave, and was disabled (perhaps intentionally by his slave master) in one of his legs – teaching about 500 years after Socrates' death, urged his followers 'To make the best of what is in our power, and take the rest as it naturally

[20] Gaita, *A Common Humanity: Thinking About Love and Truth and Justice* (Prakash, 2004), 18–19.
[21] Ibid, 19.
[22] Plato, *Apology*, 41d (emphasis added).
[23] Nussbaum, *Philosophical Interventions: Reviews 1986–2011* (OUP, 2012), 99 (reviewing Vlastos, *Socrates: Ironist and Moral Philosopher* (CUP, 1991), and focussing in this part of the review on Vlastos' essay 'Happiness and virtue in Socrates' moral theory' (ibid, 200–32)).

happens.'[24] For 'things outside the sphere of choice are neither good nor bad, and all things within the sphere of choice are in our own power.'[25] So only 'a man's own judgments [can] disturb him'[26] by making him value things that are outside his control, instead of only putting value on how he disposes of the things that are in his control:

> It is according to this plan of action that a man should chiefly exercise himself. Go out at the break of dawn, examine whomsoever you see or hear, and then answer, as if to a question. What have you seen? A handsome person? Apply the rule. Is this within the sphere of choice or outside it? Outside it. Throw it away. What have you seen? One grieving for the death of his child? Apply the rule. Death is outside the sphere of choice. Throw it aside. A consul met you? Apply the rule. What kind of thing is a consulship? Within the sphere of choice or outside it? Outside it. Throw this aside too. It does not stand the test. Fling it away. It is nothing to you.[27]

(P2) says that Socrates and Epictetus were wrong and affirms 'the fragility of goodness', in Martha Nussbaum's striking phrase.[28] Most people would agree with (P2), and disagree with Socrates and Epictetus.[29] The fact of love – and the experience of the wounds that one suffers when a loved one suffers – is enough on its own to undermine the idea that nothing that is outside your control can affect your flourishing.

However, if we assume that both (P1) and (P2) are correct, then any account of human flourishing is made to walk a very difficult tightrope. If the account makes flourishing dependent on a lot of conditions being satisfied, it will comply with (P2) but put itself in danger of violating (P1). If, on the other hand, the account makes flourishing dependent on just a few conditions being satisfied, it will comply with (P1) but put itself in danger of violating (P2).

## Value

The third proposition is:

(P3) Human flourishing is a good thing, everywhere and anywhere it exists.

Any account of human flourishing describes a horizon of value within which we can say that α is good *for* a particular person S (where α contributes to S's flourishing) and β is bad *for* S (where β detracts from S's flourishing).[30] And more generally it is part of the definition

---

[24] Epictetus, *The Discourses*, I.1.17.

[25] Ibid, II.13.10.

[26] Ibid, I.19.8.

[27] Ibid, III.3.14.

[28] Nussbaum, *The Fragility of Goodness* (CUP, 1st ed, 1986; revised ed, 2001).

[29] Cf. Pieper, *Happiness and Contemplation* (n 12), observing (at 26–27) of attitudes such as Socrates' and Epictetus' 'the keener eye will not fail to observe behind all the brave banners and heroic symbols the profound nonhumanity, the submerged anxiety, the senile rigidity, the tension of such an attitude.'

[30] As we saw in McBride, *The Humanity of Private Law, Part I* (n 17), 83, n 2, there are some thinkers who take the view that human flourishing creates an *exclusive* horizon of value for a particular agent S, with the result that the *only* way we can tell whether something is good or bad *for* S is to assess its effect on S's flourishing. I disagree: α can be good for S even though it will have no effect on S's flourishing, as S is already flourishing in the absence of α.

of flourishing that S's flourishing is good *for* S – in that, by definition, S can only be said to be flourishing if S's life is going well – and S's non-flourishing is bad *for* S in that S's life is, by definition, going badly if S is not flourishing.

None of this is relevant to (P3), which asserts that there is something special or significant about human flourishing which means that it is to be counted as a good thing, everywhere and anywhere it exists, in a way that we could not say – for example – that the flourishing of dinosaurs on the Earth 100 million years ago was a good thing. While many people would accept that this is true, Richard Kraut is skeptical as to whether it even makes sense to say something like (P3). In his important book *Against Absolute Goodness*, Kraut argues that 'we have no reason to hold that … some things have the property of being, quite simply, good.'[31] Kraut considers a number of potential counter-examples of 'absolute goods' that people might offer to his thesis: (1) beauty; (2) life; (3) the birth of a child; (4) biodiversity; (5) humanity. In response, Kraut argues:

(1)   In judging that it would be better if the universe were beautiful rather than ugly simply because a beautiful universe is better than an ugly universe, we 'do not need [to rely on] the further evaluative judgment that beauty is a good thing and ugliness is a bad thing.'[32] Thinking that a beautiful universe is better than an ugly universe because 'the beautiful [universe] has the property of being absolutely good, and the ugly world has the property of being absolutely bad' is as mistaken as thinking that 'six is a larger number than five' because six has the property being a large number and five has the property being a small number.[33] The truth is that 'comparative judgments do not need to rest on noncomparative judgments. To say that one state of affairs is better than another is to make a comparative statement. We should not assume that it must rest on the premise that there is such a thing as absolute goodness or absolute badness.'[34]

(2)   The idea that suicide is always wrong because in committing suicide 'we will have destroyed something that is, in all circumstances, a good thing' is implausible. 'The more plausible position' is that suicide is justified 'if one foresees that one's sincere moral efforts will accomplish little or nothing that is good *for* others or good *for* oneself … and if one is justifiably confident that one will continue to be deeply unhappy for the rest of one's life.'[35]

(3)   'The production of absolute goodness is not something to be thrown into the balance of considerations, as one factor among others, when we make decisions about whether to have children.'[36] Rather, bringing a child into the world is unjustified if the life of the child is 'likely to have little or nothing in it that is good for the child,'[37] while a couple who choose not to have children who could have lived rich and fulfilled lives in order to avoid a minor inconvenience to themselves have acted regrettably because they have failed for no very

---

[31] Kraut, *Against Absolute Goodness* (OUP, 2011), 8.
[32] Ibid, 101.
[33] Ibid, 101–02.
[34] Ibid, 102–03.
[35] Ibid, 129 (emphasis in original).
[36] Ibid, 132.
[37] Ibid, 131.

good reason to do what *would have been* good *for* the children that they would have had, had they decided to have children.[38]

(4)  'It is not true that biodiversity is, quite simply, a good thing.' The extinction of a species is normally to be regretted because 'never again will there by creatures of this type, and so never again will good lives – lives good for those creatures – exist.' But 'we would have reason to be glad about the extinction of a species, if we could be confident that the members of that species would otherwise have had painful lives in which nothing good for them could be experienced.'[39]

(5)  People 'have a greater value than other living things' but 'no light is shed [on why this is] by employing the concept of absolute goodness':[40]

> to speak meaningfully about the distinctive value and preciousness of human life, we do not need to make use of the concept of absolute goodness. We can instead compare what is good for us and what is good for other sorts of living things and meaningfully say that the things that are good for us – love, friendship, civility, respect, music, poetry, science, philosophy – exemplify the relation of being good for someone more fully than do the things that are good for wasps, mice, or mosquitoes. What is best for them is not as good for them as the best things in human life are good for us. If we have to choose between the two, there are reasons to work for the good of our own species rather than that of another.[41]

So a pilot who is faced with a choice between crashing a plane in a city or a forest should choose the forest 'because she ought to bring about as little harm as possible. She must choose between harming birds and harming human beings, and … when normal human lives are cut short, the harm done is great in comparison with the harm done when the lives of normal birds are cut short.'[42]

We can bring (P3) into line with Kraut's critique of the concept of absolute goodness if we read (P3) as saying *all* of the following, and I intend (P3) so to be read. *First*: a universe in which human beings flourish is better than a universe in which no human beings (and no beings with capacities similar to human beings) flourish. *Second*: we all have reason to wish that all currently existing human beings lead flourishing lives. *Third*: a couple who are capable of bringing a human being into the world have reason to do so (and we all have reason to wish that they do so) if that human being is likely to lead a flourishing life. *Fourth*: we all have reason not to sacrifice the flourishing of a human being (whether currently existing or existing in the future) even if doing so is necessary to secure the flourishing of a non-human being.

None of these things were true of dinosaurs at the time dinosaurs existed on Earth, but (P3) says that they are true of human beings. Assuming – as most people do – that (P3) is

---

[38] Ibid, 134.
[39] Ibid, 138–39.
[40] Ibid, 150.
[41] Ibid, 155.
[42] Ibid, 156.

correct in making these claims for human beings, any account of human flourishing has to be compatible with these claims.

## Continuity

The fourth proposition is:

(P4) Human flourishing is self-sustaining across time and across persons.

(P4) rests on a number of different claims about human flourishing, all of which have to be true for (P4) to be true. *First*: someone who is flourishing will not feel suicidal, and will seek to ensure that he or she will continue to flourish in the future. *Second*: someone who is flourishing will seek to contribute to the flourishing of other people generally (both people who currently exist and people who will exist in the future), and not just people that he or she cares about. *Third*: someone who is flourishing regards the continued existence of the aretaic community[43] that fostered his or her own flourishing, and the continued existence of aretaic communities generally, as more important than his or her continued flourishing.

If these three claims are true, then (P4) will be true: an aretaic community will, by promoting the flourishing of its members, ensure that the members of that community are motivated: (1) to live long, (2) to contribute to their own and others' flourishing, (3) to defend the community against threats to its existence, to the point of dying for the community, and (4) to assist other communities that contribute to their members' flourishing in defending them against threats to their existence.

In this way, human flourishing becomes self-sustaining across time and across persons: it contains within itself the materials needed to ensure that any generation of flourishing individuals will endure and will in time be succeeded by another generation of flourishing individuals. If, by contrast, any of the three claims set out above are not true, then (P4) will not be true: a flourishing person, or an aretaic community, will easily be snuffed out when the person or community in question encounters adversity, with the result that the continued existence of a flourishing person, or a community that fosters human flourishing, is just a matter of luck.

If (P4) is true, then we can take the fact that these three claims apply to a particular individual as marking them out as an example of human flourishing. Given this, it is interesting to read Pericles' Funeral Oration, which was delivered over the Athenian war dead in the first year of Athens' war with Sparta (in 431BC).[44] In seeking to rally the Athenians for the struggle ahead, the Athenian leader Pericles argued that the Athenians were exemplars of human flourishing precisely because all three of the claims that underlie (P4) were true of them.

With regard to the first claim, Pericles asserted that *Athenians lead an enviable existence that they are prepared to defend*: 'at Athens, we live exactly as we please, and yet are just as ready

---

[43] That is, a community that seeks to promote the flourishing of its members: see McBride, *The Humanity of Private Law, Part I* (n 17), 99.

[44] The Funeral Oration is set out in Thucydides, *The Peloponnesian War*, II.35–46.

to encounter every legitimate danger';[45] 'we provide plenty of means for the mind to refresh itself from business. We celebrate games and sacrifices all the year round, and the elegance of our private establishments forms a daily source of pleasure ... while the magnitude of our city draws the produce of the world into our harbour, so that to the Athenian the fruits of other countries are as familiar a luxury as those of his own.'[46] 'We cultivate refinement without extravagance and knowledge without effeminacy; wealth we employ more or use than for show, and place the real disgrace of poverty not in owning to the fact but in declining to struggle against it ... In generosity, we are equally singular, acquiring our friends by conferring not by receiving favours.'[47] 'I doubt if the world can produce a man, who where he has only himself to depend upon, is equal to so many emergencies, and graced by so happy a versatility as the Athenian.'[48]

With regard to the second claim, Pericles asserted that *Athenians seek to contribute to the flourishing of others generally*: 'we are a pattern to others than other than imitators ourselves.' Athens 'favours the many instead of the few; this is why it is called a democracy.'[49] 'We throw open our city to the world, and never by alien acts exclude foreigners from any opportunity of learning or observing.'[50] '[A]s a city we are the school of Hellas.'[51]

With regard to the third claim, Pericles asserted that *Athenians place the highest priority on the survival of Athens*:

> none of these [the Athenian war dead] allowed either wealth with its prospect of future enjoyment to unnerve his spirit, or poverty with its hope of a day of freedom and riches to tempt him to shrink from danger. No, holding that vengeance upon their enemies was more to be desired than any personal blessings, and reckoning this to be the most glorious of hazards, they joyfully determined to accept the risk ... So died these men as became Athenians. You, their survivors, must determine to have as unaltering a resolution in the field, though you may pray that it may have a happier issue.[52]

All of these factors, Pericles argued, combined to form 'the road by which we reached our position' whereby the Athenians' ancestors 'dwelt in the country without break in the succession from generation to generation, and handed it down free to the present time by their valour ... And our own fathers ... added to [our] inheritance the empire which we now possess, and spared no pains to be able to leave their acquisitions to us of the present generation.'[53]

Thucydides' description of life in Athens only a year after Pericles' speech, when Athens was ravaged by plague[54] – a plague that killed Pericles – might be taken by some as exposing

---

[45] Ibid, II.39.
[46] Ibid, II.38.
[47] Ibid, II.40.
[48] Ibid, II.41.
[49] Ibid, II.37.
[50] Ibid, II. 39.
[51] Ibid, II.41.
[52] Ibid, II. 43.
[53] Ibid, II.36.
[54] Ibid, II.53–54: 'Men now coolly ventured on what they had formerly done in a corner, and not just as they pleased, seeing the rapid transitions produced by persons in prosperity suddenly dying and those who had before had nothing succeeding to their property. So they resolved to spend quickly and enjoy themselves, regarding their lives and riches as alike things of a day. Perseverance in what men called honour was popular with none, it was so

Pericles' Funeral Oration to be a piece of wishful thinking. Reading Thucydides might lead us to believe that the three claims that underlie (P4) are untrue, and therefore the fact that these three claims are true of a particular individual tells us nothing about whether they are flourishing as a human being. Instead, the reality is – Thucydides teaches us – that people who enjoy a flourishing existence are *not* particularly motivated to protect their way of life in the face of adversity but are instead all too ready when hard times come to give up on their flourishing existence in favour of something easier. Moreover, the outcome of the Peloponnesian War – final defeat to Sparta about 25 years after Pericles' speech – might incline us to question whether aretaic communities do better than any other kinds of communities at protecting themselves from being defeated and disbanded by their enemies.

One possible response to these points would be to say that while Pericles was right to think that flourishing individuals, and an aretaic community, would sustain themselves over time, Athenians in the 5th century BC were *not*, in fact, exemplars of human flourishing, and Athens was not an aretaic community – with the result that their continued existence was simply a matter of luck, which eventually ran out. However, the more relevant response for our present purposes is that (P4) does *not* assert that a person's flourishing or the existence of an aretaic community can *never* be undone by adversity, and particularly the kind of adversity that is represented by plague or total war. (P4) merely argues in favour of the more moderate view that when faced with adversity, a flourishing person or an aretaic community will find the resources within themselves to put up *substantial* resistance to their being overcome by adversity and will *usually* find a way of sustaining themselves through that period of adversity.

Interpreted in this more moderate way, I take my stand, as Pericles did, on the view that (P4) is correct, as are the three claims on which (P4) rests.

## Applying the Postulates

With these four postulates in place, we are now in a position to assess the plausibility of our two remaining models of human flourishing: the Possessions Model and the Journey Model. I will argue that the Possessions Model, and in particular the version of the Possessions Model represented by the RP, fares particularly badly when measured up against these four postulates about human flourishing. The Possessions Model is unable to walk the tightrope thrown up by the combination of (P1) and (P2). A very complex version of the Possessions Model such as the RP easily satisfies (P2) but violates (P1). And, as we have seen, a much simpler version of the Possessions Model such as that endorsed by thinkers like Socrates and Epictetus satisfies (P1) but violates (P2). Moreover, it is unlikely that any version of the Possessions Model – and, in particular, the RP – can satisfy (P4). By contrast, it is *possible* for a Journey Model of human flourishing to satisfy all of (P1)–(P4). Whether it does or not depends on the particular version of the Journey Model that we are considering. The task of the following chapter will be to set out a particular version of the Journey Model which is both plausible, and which satisfies all of (P1)–(P4).

---

uncertain whether they would be spared to attain the object; but it was settled that present enjoyment, and all that contributed to it, was both honourable and useful.'

# 4.  Problems with the Possessions Model

## The Tightrope

We have already seen that if we accept the above four postulates about human flourishing, then any account of human flourishing must be compatible with *both* (P1) *and* (P2) being true. It must be true that human flourishing is within the grasp of any human being (which is the claim (P1) makes) *and* true that human flourishing can be harmed by a wide range of events (which is the claim (P2) makes).

And we have also already seen that the account of human flourishing that was endorsed by thinkers such as Socrates and Epictetus – which makes human flourishing dependent on one's being internally virtuous in one's dispositions and attitudes towards events – falls off the tightrope set up by (P1) and (P2) at the (P2) end of the tightrope. If Socrates and Epictetus are right, (P1) would be true, but it is hard to see how a wide variety of events could impair someone's flourishing as a human being. (On Socrates' and Epictetus' account, one could see how a wide variety of events might *prevent* someone *becoming* a flourishing person – being born in a vicious society, or being so indigent that one cannot live without performing vicious acts, would be two such events – but one cannot see how, on those accounts, someone who is *already* flourishing could have their flourishing impaired by a wide variety of events.)

Another account of human flourishing that falls off the (P1)–(P2) tightrope at the (P2) end *may* be John Finnis' account of human flourishing, as presented in writings such as his masterwork *Natural Law and Natural Rights*. Finnis argues that flourishing involves one in participating in a number of 'basic goods' such as life, knowledge, play, marriage, friendship, practical reasonableness, and so on. However, Finnis introduces one qualification to this:

> Some scholars may have little taste or capacity for friendship, and may feel that life for them would have no savour if they were prevented from pursuing their commitment to knowledge. None the less, it would be unreasonable for them to deny that, objectively, human life … and friendship are good in themselves. It is one thing to have little capacity and even no 'taste' for scholarship, or friendship, or physical heroism, or sanctity; it is quite another thing, and stupid or arbitrary, to think or speak or act as if these were not real forms of good.[55]

This suggests that someone who has *no capacity* to participate in a particular basic good might still be counted as flourishing *so long as* he still recognises that that good is a good, and would be open to participating in that good if the opportunity for doing so offered itself. So someone who has been unlucky in love and has not been able to find a life partner should not on that account be held not to be flourishing, so long as they are still open to the possibility that they might meet that kind of happiness in future. On the other hand, someone who has been unlucky in love and is led by their failure to revenge themselves on the world by scorning the company and advances of potential future life partners cannot be said to be flourishing: their refusal to open themselves to the possibility of finding love in the future involves them in refusing to acknowledge that that love counts as a basic good.[56]

---

[55] Finnis, *Natural Law and Natural Rights* (1st ed, 1980; 2nd ed, 2001; OUP), 105.
[56] Ibid, 118.

On this reading,[57] Finnis' account of human flourishing is compatible with (P1) being true – everyone, no matter what their circumstances, is capable of flourishing as a human being. But Finnis' account seems incompatible with (P2). A Job whose misfortune results in him losing his family, property, and health[58] would still be counted as flourishing on this reading of Finnis' account of human flourishing. While circumstances mean that Job is no longer capable of participating in some of the basic goods that Finnis identifies, he is still capable of participating in the others (most notably, life itself) and is open to participating in the goods he currently has no capacity to participate in – indeed, he is so open that he complains grievously of not being allowed to participate in those goods. But it would be hard to say that Job is flourishing in the circumstances in which he finds himself – not even Job's three friends, who come to see how he is, attempt to argue that he is still in good shape, despite what has happened to him. And if we do say, on the basis of this reading, that Job is still flourishing despite everything, then (P2) would seem to be untrue: there is very little that could impair the flourishing of someone who is already flourishing.

While the account of human flourishing that was discussed in Part I of this project, and which we have been calling the 'RP', was built on top of Finnis' account of human flourishing, the particular claim about human flourishing that we have been discussing here – and which would prevent Finnis' account from being compatible with (P2) – was not made part of the RP. So there is no danger of the RP being dismissed on the basis that it is incompatible with (P2). It is clear from the complexity of the account of human flourishing that the RP offers us that there are a wide variety of events that could impair the flourishing of someone who, before those events occurred, could be said to be flourishing according to the RP. The suffering of a loved one is an obvious example of one such event. The real threat to the RP is whether its complexity makes it incompatible with (P1) – the idea that human flourishing is within the grasp of any human being. So let's turn to that claim.

What does it mean to say that human flourishing is within the grasp of any human being? There are two possible readings:

(A)   Human flourishing is merely a matter of having the appropriate will. Someone who has the right kind of desires cannot be stopped from flourishing as a human being, no matter what their circumstances might be.

(B)   Anyone can flourish under reasonably favourable circumstances, and it is possible to imagine a world where everyone could enjoy the reasonably favourable circumstances that would enable them to flourish.

The RP is incompatible with (A). If the RP is the correct account of what human flourishing involves, then (A) is untrue – under the RP, human flourishing is not just a matter of having the right kind of desires but involves so much more than that. But is the RP compatible with (B)? If it is, then we can say that the RP successfully walks the tightrope between (P1) and (P2), so long as we are willing (and there seems no reason why we should not be) to interpret (P1) as saying what (B) does.

---

[57] The qualifier 'On this reading' is necessary, because it is not clear (and perhaps unfair) on the basis of the one quotation above to ascribe confidently to Finnis the position being discussed here.

[58] Job 1–2.

In determining whether the RP is compatible with (B), we need to say something about what 'reasonably favourable circumstances' means. It would be unreasonably demanding to think that circumstances will be reasonably favourable for flourishing if they make it *very likely* that someone in those circumstances will flourish. Equally, it would be unreasonably *un*demanding to think that circumstances will be reasonably favourable for flourishing if someone in those circumstances merely has *a chance* of flourishing. The most sensible position would seem to be that circumstances will be reasonably favourable for flourishing if it is *more likely than not* that someone in those circumstances will flourish as an individual. On this reading, (B) is claiming that –

(C)   It is possible to imagine a world where every single individual has a more than 50–50 chance of flourishing as a human being.

Is the RP consistent with (C)? Is it possible to imagine a world where every single individual has a more than 50–50 chance of flourishing as a human being if the RP amounts to a correct account of what it is to flourish as a human being? The following considerations incline me to think that the answer to this question is 'No' and that therefore the RP is incompatible with (C)'s being true. In what follows, I will use the phrase 'RP-flourishing' to describe the case where someone lives a life that is flourishing according to what the RP tells us human flourishing involves.

(1)   It is obvious that the world in which we live in now is *not* one where every single individual has a more than a 50–50 chance of RP-flourishing.[59] While RP-flourishing is well within the grasp of many people living in the affluent West, there are obviously huge areas of the world containing millions of people who do not enjoy a decent chance of RP-flourishing. Either their lives amount to nothing more than a daily struggle to exist, or they lead lives of mindless functionality with no opportunities for creativity or the formation of the sort of cares and loves and desires of the heart that are crucial to RP-flourishing.

(2)   It is also strongly arguable that various features of the world in which we live now that help certain individuals to have more than a 50–50 chance of RP-flourishing *also guarantee* that certain other individuals will have less than a 50–50 chance of RP-flourishing. So the world in which we live now is one where it is simply not possible for everyone to have a more than 50–50 chance of RP-flourishing.

First, RP-flourishing is a resource-intensive activity – especially in the case of the old or disabled, who require substantial resources and assistance if they are to enjoy a more than 50–50 chance of RP-flourishing. It is doubtful, however, that there are enough resources in the world to give everyone, including the old and disabled, a fair chance of RP-flourishing.[60]

---

[59] Good accounts of the state of the world we are living in now can be found in Stiglitz's *Globalization and its Discontents* (Allen Lane, 2003) and *The Price of Inequality* (Norton, 2012).

[60] Cf. Sklair, *The Transnational Capitalist Class* (John Wiley, 2001), 209: 'it is fallacious to assume that "meeting needs", "improving quality of life", and "improving environmental performance" are part of the solution to the ecological crisis … They are parts of the problem, particularly in terms of distinguishing real needs from artificial needs and establishing universal norms for an ecologically sound quality of life.'

RP-flourishing ultimately depends on access to land, water, oil, gas, metals, and food; and while the twentieth century has seen huge gains in the ability to produce more and more food from the same amount of resources, the other resources are largely fixed and increasingly scarce.[61]

Moreover, the *way* in which a given country obtains access to these scarce resources can have negative effects on the RP-flourishing of people who live in countries that are rich in those resources. Suppose, for example, that *Silvania* is generally wealthy and powerful but is poor in a particular resource R which is crucial for RP-flourishing. *Silvania* accordingly wishes to secure *reliable* access to R from another country, *Ruristan*, which is rich in R. Given this, it is in *Silvania*'s interests to encourage elements (call them 'the *Barons*') within *Ruristan* to assume monopoly control over R and use their control over R to benefit both themselves and *Silvania*.[62] As a result, the interests of the general population of *Ruristan* in benefiting from *Ruristan*'s being rich in R, and using that fact to promote their own RP-flourishing, are downgraded and ignored by both *Silvania* and the *Barons*. In this way, the RP-flourishing of people who live in *Silvania* is promoted, but through mechanisms that guarantee that the general population living in *Ruristan* will see little chance of RP-flourishing themselves.[63]

Second, RP-flourishing depends on the existence of public and private bodies (call them '*Suppliers*') that are able to supply people with the goods they need in order to RP-flourish. These *Suppliers* need to be staffed and run, with the result that a society that is built round RP-flourishing has the potential to divide into two classes: (i) those who work to produce the goods needed for RP-flourishing and (ii) those who receive those goods. So long as people living in that society are simultaneously workers and receivers, there will be no class divide between (i) and (ii) as everyone will fall into both classes. However, forces within the *Suppliers* that tend to prioritise the efficient production of goods over all other considerations will result in their staff being required to give up more and more of their time and creativity in the interests of production, so that the abilities of all but the most privileged workers to RP-flourish will be fundamentally impaired.[64] At this point, a class divide will

---

[61] The fact that the governments of Western liberal societies can only nowadays provide the goods that they do through deficit financing shows, almost by definition, that there are not enough resources to provide for everyone's flourishing even in the affluent West, let alone anywhere else in the world.

[62] See Perelman, 'Myths of the market: economics and the environment' (2003) 16 *Organization & Environment* 168, 200: 'a rich natural resource base makes a poor country, especially a relatively powerless one, an inviting target – both politically and militarily – for dominant nations … [P]owerful nations will not risk letting such a valuable resource fall under the control of an independent government …'

[63] This state of affairs is normally referred to as the 'resource curse' on populations living in countries blessed with rich natural rources: see Rosser, *The Political Economy of the Resource Curse: A Literature Survey* (Institute of Development Studies, 2006) and Stevens, Lahn and Karooshy, *The Resource Curse Revisited* (Chatham House Research Paper, 2015). The classic real world example of this 'resource curse' in action is provided by the relationship between countries in the West and oil-producing countries elsewhere in the world: see, generally, Wenar, *Blood Oil* (OUP, 2016). The same situation also exists in relation to agriculture in developing countries where the 'overall conclusion is that food crops for local consumption have been substituted on a very large scale by feed crops for export consumption [by animals being reared for meat in the West]': Saurin, 'Organizing hunger: the global organization of famines and feasts' in Thomas and Wilkin (eds), *Globalisation and the South* (Palgrave Macmillan, 1997), 118.

[64] Elkington, *Cannibals with Forks: The Triple Bottom Line of 21st Century Business* (Capstone, 1997) and Savitz, *The Triple Bottom Line* (Jossey Bass, 2006) optimistically argue that it is possible for companies to achieve economic success and treat their employees (and the environment) well. Against this, Lane's exhaustive survey of *The Market Experience* (CUP, 1991) argues (at 305f) that this is only true where the company enjoys substantial protection

arise between (i) those who are made to give up on their own RP-flourishing in the interests of helping others to RP-flourish, and (ii) those who are not asked to give up on their own RP-flourishing in the interests of others.[65] Those who are unlucky enough to fall in class (i) will not enjoy a more than 50–50 chance of RP-flourishing; in fact, their chances of RP-flourishing will be minimal.

Third, economic pressures on the *Suppliers* to produce and supply the goods needed for RP-flourishing as efficiently as possible mean that the *Suppliers* will want to employ the workers needed to staff and run those *Suppliers* as cheaply as possible. Given this, David Harvey observes that 'it is mighty convenient … for [the *Suppliers*] to have to hand a vast reservoir of trained but unused labour power.'[66] If such a reservoir is not available within the country where the *Suppliers* operate, then the *Suppliers* will seek to outsource the satisfaction of their labour needs to countries (or people coming from countries) where such a reservoir *is* available,[67] or they will rely as much as possible on technology to circumvent the need to employ real people. Given this, the cost-effective staffing and running of the *Suppliers* will usually depend on large numbers of people being unemployed – whether in the country where the *Suppliers* operate, or somewhere else in the world, or both. However, being unemployed is normally incompatible with someone's RP-flourishing. It follows that for the *Suppliers* to be staffed and run in the most cost-effective manner possible, it must be the case that large numbers of people are *not* in a state where they are RP-flourishing.

(3)   It seems very likely that it is *not* possible for a very different world, structured in a radically different way from the world we live in, to exist in which everyone has a more than 50–50 chance of RP-flourishing. Marxism can be seen as an attempt to think of what such a different world might look like – one in which, in Marx's words, *everyone* can 'hunt in the morning, fish in the afternoon, rear cattle in the evening, [and] criticise after dinner'.[68]

---

from competitive forces, and that companies that have to fight for market share to survive are inevitably forced into disregarding the interests of their employees in terms of what they require their employees to do.

[65] Cf. Christopher Caldwell's powerful article 'The migrants of Calais', *Weekly Standard*, March 7, 2016 (readily available on the Internet), quoting the geographer Christophe Guilluy as asking (in Guilluy's *La France périphérique* (Flammarion, 2015)), 'Why would you *expect* Paris to have a middle class?' – that is, a class that both participates in producing the goods required for RP-flourishing, and has the opportunity to enjoy those goods themselves. Instead, Paris is increasingly becoming a city divided between an upper class dedicated to living a RP-flourishing lifestyle and a lower class that exists purely to service the needs of the upper class.

[66] Harvey, *Seventeen Contradictions and the End of Capitalism* (Profile Books, 2014), 79.

[67] See, generally, Foster, McChesney and Jonna, 'The global reserve army of labor and the new imperialism' (2011) 63(6) *Monthly Review*.

[68] Marx, *The German Ideology* (1846), Vol I, Part 1 ('Feuerbach: opposition of the materialist and idealist outlooks'), section 2 ('First premises of the materialist method'). It might be argued that Marx himself did not identify human flourishing with RP-flourishing – see Fromm, *Marx's Concept of Man* (Bloomsbury, 2013), 35: 'There is no greater misunderstanding or misrepresentation of Marx than that which is to be found … in the thought of Soviet Communists, the reformist socialists, and the capitalist opponents of socialism alike, all of whom assume that Marx wanted only the economic improvement of the working class, and that he wanted to abolish private property so that the worker would own what the capitalist now has.' However, the RP provides us with much more than a merely economic conception of human flourishing, and it is not clear whether Marx would have *refused* to say that someone who was RP-flourishing (in particular, by virtue of their (a) enjoying the good of creativity, and (b) not depending on anyone else's suffering for the good things in their life) was actually flourishing as a human being. For further discussion that tends to support the view that Marx identified human flourishing with something very like RP-flourishing, see Hughes, *Ecology and Historical Materialism* (CUP, 2000), 176–94, and Leopold, *The Young Karl Marx* (CUP, 2007), 223–45, 277–78.

However, the grim record of Marxism when put into practice shows that such a world cannot exist – any attempt to bring it into existence produces a world where *virtually no one* has any chance of RP-flourishing. The world in which we live now – subject to certain marginal modifications – is one which gives people generally the best chance of RP-flourishing,[69] but it is also one that falls far short of the ideal of being a world in which *everyone* has a more than a 50–50 chance of RP-flourishing.

(4)    Finally, there is the matter of *Gaita's Challenge*. Certain individuals are born with, or develop over the course of their life, such substantial disabilities that even with a huge investment in resources and assistance, RP-flourishing would seem to be beyond them. Either they are born without a 50–50 chance of RP-flourishing, or they suffer an injury that reduces their chances of RP-flourishing well below evens, and there is not much we can do to improve their odds. This fact on its own would bring the RP into conflict with (C).

Given the above, we have to conclude that the RP is incompatible with (C), and therefore (B), and therefore (because the RP is also incompatible with (A)) (P1). Either the RP is untrue in what it tells us human flourishing involves, or the claim that human flourishing is within the reach of any human being is untrue. Faced with this choice, I would reject the RP. Others might be tempted to hang onto the RP's account of human flourishing, and reject (P1). However, if the RP is incompatible with any of our other postulates about human flourishing, the case for rejecting the RP would then become very strong. I will now go on to argue that the RP is also inconsistent with (P4) (that human flourishing is self-sustaining over time and persons).

## Social Reproduction

As we saw above, (P4) rests on a number of different claims, all of which have to be true for (P4) to be true. The *first claim* is that someone who is flourishing does not feel suicidal, and seeks to ensure that he or she will continue to flourish in the future. The *second claim* is that someone who is flourishing will seek to contribute to the flourishing of other people generally (both people who currently exist and people who will exist in the future), and not just people that he or she cares about. The *third claim* is that someone who is flourishing regards the continued existence of the aretaic community that fostered his or her own flourishing, and the continued existence of aretaic communities generally, as more important than his or her continued flourishing.

None of these claims seem to apply to people who are RP-flourishing. Modern Western liberal societies are the best incubators of RP-flourishing that have yet to be discovered, and yet at the same time Western liberal societies do not seem particularly effective at ensuring that RP-flourishing is self-sustaining across time and across persons.

---

[69] A point made most vividly and strongly in McCloskey, *The Bourgeois Virtues: Ethics for an Age of Commerce* (Univ of Chicago Press, 2006), 24–25: 'actually existing capitalism, not the collectivisms of the left or of the right, has reached beyond mere consumption, producing the best art and the best people ... Modern economic growth has led to more, not less refinement, for hundreds of millions who would otherwise have been poor and ignorant – as were, for example, most of your ancestors and mine.'

First, surveys of causes of death carried out by the World Health Organisation[70] show that developed countries such as South Korea, Belgium, Japan, Finland, Sweden, France and the USA feature in the top 50 countries (out of 183) for suicide rates per 10,000 of population. Falling outside the top 50, but still in the top 100 are New Zealand, Austria, Ireland, Switzerland, Canada and Australia, the Netherlands, and Norway. Only three developed countries with Western liberal governments fall outside the top 100 – Germany (104), the UK (123, with a suicide rate of 7.52 in 2017, up from 6.28 in 2014), and Israel (144). The bottom 25 positions on the list, which is where one might have expected modern Western liberal countries to congregate, are instead dominated by countries in North Africa, the Caribbean, and the Middle East. One also wonders how much worse the figures for suicide rates in Western liberal countries would be were it not for the ready availability of psychiatric help in Western countries, as well as advanced life-saving medical facilities that can prevent many would-be suicides proving fatal.

Second, it is well-known that modern Western liberal countries score particularly badly when it comes to birth rates. The CIA World Factbook 2018 survey of 226 countries[71] shows that no such country comes in the top 100 countries for births per 1,000 of population. Monaco comes bottom with 6.5 births per 1,000 of population (down from 6.65 in 2015). Italy (216), Germany (213) are comfortably in the bottom 25 countries, with Spain (205) and Poland (202) just outside. The USA (157), Australia (165), the UK (167), and Canada (189) are all in the bottom half of countries ranked by birth rate. Low birth rates in modern Western liberal countries mean that all such countries fall hopelessly short of the 2.1 children per woman 'fertility rate' that is needed to avoid the populations of those countries falling into decline, with the same world survey showing the UK achieving a fertility rate of 1.88 in 2018; the USA, 1.87; and Canada, 1.60.

Third, on 9 February 1933, the Oxford Union held its most famous debate. The motion 'That this House will in no circumstances fight for its King and Country' was passed by 275 votes to 153. While considered shocking at the time, the unwillingness to fight to defend one's country shown by 65 per cent of the Oxford Union voters has now become the norm in modern Western liberal societies. In a 2015 WIN-Gallup poll on people's willingness to fight to defend their country,[72] only 27 per cent of respondents in the UK expressed themselves so willing, while 51 per cent said they would not fight to defend their country. In Western Europe as a whole, 25 per cent were willing to fight, while 53 per cent said they would not. The proportion of people who were willing to fight to defend their country – 44 per cent – was higher in the United States, but still did not reach a majority.

Some of these results can be explained as underscoring the incompatibility of the RP with (P1). A society that encourages people to adopt the view of human flourishing supplied by the RP is bound (if the arguments made in the previous section are correct) to have many people living in that society who are unable to live up to this view of what human flourishing involves. These people, feeling themselves to be 'losers' in life, may be unable to live with themselves and seek to bring their lives to an end.[73] However, there is no reason to think

[70] www.worldlifeexpectancy.com/cause-of-death/suicide/by-country.
[71] www.cia.gov/library/publications/the-world-factbook/docs/rankorderguide.html.
[72] www.ibtimes.co.uk/three-quarters-british-people-would-refuse-fight-their-country-1482801.
[73] Cf. the tragic case of Tony Nicklinson, who felt that his life had lost any meaning after he suffered a stroke at the age of 51 which rendered him 'locked in' his body – paralysed and unable to move anything except his head

that suicides in Western liberal societies are confined to those whose lives are *not* going well by the standards set by the RP. And the incompatibility of the RP with (P1) does not account for the phenomenon of low birth rates in modern Western liberal societies, or the unwillingness of those living in those societies to defend those societies from their enemies. What these things point to is a deep incompatibility between the RP and (P4), rooted in the fact that the RP identifies your flourishing as a human being with what things *you* have in *your* life.

First, some suicides in modern Western liberal societies among people whose lives *are* going well by the standards set by the RP can easily be accounted for on the basis that someone (call them 'S') who identifies their flourishing with living up to those standards and finds that they have been lucky enough to meet those standards could easily suffer an ongoing anxiety that their luck will turn and that they may not live an RP-flourishing existence in the future.[74] If S is unable to dismiss this anxiety,[75] their anxiety may become so powerful that it becomes overwhelming and deprives S of any enjoyment that S might have otherwise felt in living a life that counts as RP-flourishing. At that point, suicide might start looking like an attractive option to S. Had S adopted a different vision of human flourishing that places less emphasis on what things you have in your life, then S might well have felt less anxiety about losing the things that he/she had in his/her life and been able to enjoy life more.

Second, if you identify your flourishing with the things that you have in your life, then you are inevitably going to react badly to the prospect of any event that endangers the presence of those things in your life. Having children and going to war are two obvious examples of such an event. They each create huge potential for destroying a form of life that is RP-flourishing and give no assurance that the person living that life will be able to readjust and once again live an RP-flourishing life while looking after children or having to cope with the exigencies of war. For someone who is already living an RP-flourishing life, childlessness and supine surrender to one's country's enemies will always look like much the better option in terms of guaranteeing one's ability to continue leading an RP-flourishing life in the future.

Given these considerations, it seems that the RP, as a vision of human flourishing, is incompatible with (P4) – the idea that human flourishing is self-sustaining over time and

---

and eyes. Nicklinson's (unsuccessful) legal case, seeking the permission of the law to have someone help him kill himself, reached the UK Supreme Court in *R (on the application of Nicklinson) v Ministry of Justice* [2015] AC 657.

[74] In his *To Have or To Be?* (Bloomsbury, 2013), the psychologist Eric Fromm criticises people who identify their flourishing with what they have on the basis that 'Because I *can* lose what I have, I am necessarily constantly worried that I *shall* lose what I have. I am afraid of thieves, of economic changes, of revolutions, of sickness, of death, and I am afraid of love, or freedom, of growth, of change, of the unknown; I become defensive, hard, suspicious, lonely, driven by the need to have more in order to be better protected' (94–95) (emphasis in original). See also Marcel, *Homo Viator: Introduction to a Metaphysic of Hope* (Henry Regnery, 1951) (trans. Craufurd), 61: 'The more we allow ourselves to be servants of Having, the more we shall let ourselves fall a prey to the gnawing anxiety which Having involves, the more we shall tend to lose not only the aptitude for hope, but even I should say the very belief, indistinct as it may be, of its possible reality.'

[75] Gregg Easterbrook attempted to persuade people to do this in his *The Progress Paradox: How Life Gets Better While People Feel Worse* (Random House, 2003), observing that 'Deep-seated in the minds of Americans and Europeans … is a fear that the West cannot sustain its current elevated living standards and liberal personal freedom. We fear that the economy will collapse …' but arguing that this 'collapse anxiety' is unfounded because 'Practically everything is getting better' (ibid, 33–34). Of course, just five years after Easterbrook's book was published, the Western economies *did* almost collapse so 'collapse anxiety' is not so irrational. The better way of dealing with 'collapse anxiety' would be to adjust our views as to what 'getting better' actually means.

across persons. Either the RP must be given up, or we must give up our belief in (P4). Given that the RP is already incompatible with (P1) – the idea that human flourishing is within the reach of any human being – the case for giving up on the RP seems very strong. If there is an alternative, plausible vision of human flourishing that is not incompatible with any of (P1)–(P4), then we should endorse that vision, and reject the RP, acceptance of which would force us to give up on so much else of what we believe about human flourishing.

## Prospects for Other Possessions Models

As it is with the RP, so it is likely to be with any other Possessions Model of human flourishing. The possessiveness involved in adopting a Possessions Model of human flourishing means that any such model is likely to fall foul of (P4).

Of course, we could make a particular Possessions Model of human flourishing compatible with (P4) by building into it requirements that someone can only be said to be flourishing if (a) they are free of anxieties that would otherwise make existence a burden to them, and (b) they would strongly desire, when the occasion arose, to defend their community or to procreate. However, this patently artificial fix would result in an individual who was 'flourishing' according to our model experiencing internal tensions (suppressed anxiety, or conflicting emotions) that might incline us to disbelieve that any such individual could really be said to be flourishing. Moreover, such an adjusted model of human flourishing would come into conflict with (P1) – flourishing would be eternally beyond those who could not get free of their anxieties of 'losing it all' or who could not bring themselves passionately to desire to defend their community or to procreate.

Given this, any Possessions Model of human flourishing is unlikely to provide a promising basis for a convincing vision of what human flourishing involves. This leaves us with only the Journey Model of human flourishing left. Can that do any better?

# 5.   Advantages of the Journey Model

I think it can. I will finish this chapter by showing how the Journey Model of human flourishing *can* reconcile (P1), (P2), (P3), and (P4). But this only shows the *potential* for a Journey Model of human flourishing to fit the various postulates about human flourishing that we are assuming are true. The next chapter will realise that potential by sketching out a particular version of the Journey Model of human flourishing that is consistent with all of our postulates about human flourishing. But let's begin with a much more abstract statement about what the Journey Model has to tell us about the nature of human flourishing.

## Formal Outline

The Journey Model of human flourishing assesses someone's flourishing according to what direction someone's life is going in. If it is heading in the 'right' direction, then that person is flourishing. If a person's life is heading in the 'wrong' direction, or going round in circles and not going in any direction at all, then that person is not flourishing as a human being.

So for the Journey Model to work, human lives have to possess the potential for directionality – it must be possible for someone's life to be seen as heading in a particular direction. Fortunately for the Journey Model, this is possible, and is in fact normal for human beings. As Alasdair MacIntyre observes:

> We live out our lives, both individually and in our relationships with each other, in the light of certain conceptions of a possible shared future, a future in which certain possibilities beckon us forward and others repel us, some seem already foreclosed and others perhaps inevitable. There is no present which is not informed by some image of some future and an image of the future which always presents itself in the form of a *telos* – or of a variety of ends of goals – towards which we are either moving or failing to move in the present.[76]

Of course, there will be individuals for whom this isn't true:

> When someone complains – as do some of those who attempt or commit suicide – that his or her life is meaningless, he or she is often and perhaps characteristically complaining that the narrative of their life has become unintelligible to them, that it lacks any point, any movement towards a climax or a *telos*.[77]

But this is not a normal, or a healthy, state for a human being to be in – unless we can see our life as heading *somewhere*, we feel lost and disorientated, unable to see 'the point of doing any one thing rather than another at crucial junctures in [our] lives'.[78]

Let's call the particular 'somewhere' that our lives need to be heading in the direction of in order to count as flourishing under the Journey Model, 'G'. So in the diagram below, a, b and c are all flourishing as they are leading lives that are directed towards G, while d and e are not flourishing as their lives are not directed towards G, but are rather directed away from G. Finally, f is not flourishing either as her life is going in a circle, and therefore nowhere.

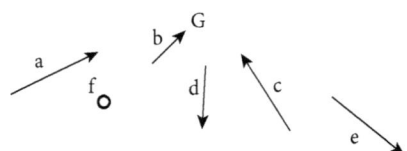

In MacIntyrean terms, a flourishing individual is on a 'quest' for G. This quest begins with an 'at least partly determinate conception' of what G is, but G can only be fully grasped by embarking on the quest because 'It is in the course of quest and only through encountering and coping with the various particular harms, dangers, temptations and distractions which provide [the] quest with its episodes and incidents that the goal of the quest is finally to be understood.'[79]

As the abbreviation 'G' might be taken as suggesting, is G *good*? One would have thought it must be. If anything deserves the title 'good', it is something that a human life ought to

---

[76] MacIntyre, *After Virtue*, 3rd ed (Bloomsbury, 2011), 250.

[77] Ibid, 252.

[78] Ibid.

[79] Ibid, 254. See also Magee, *Confessions of a Philosopher* (Weidenfeld & Nicholson, 1997), 556, reflecting on his own intellectual quest: 'I am on the way, journeying still, and no doubt will always be doing so, however long I may live. I do not even have much idea what it would be like to reach a destination, or what a destination would be like.'

be directed at moving towards and achieving – and that is what G is. However, it is important to note that G is *not* human flourishing. A life can fall well short of G and still count as flourishing on the Journey Model – to count as flourishing, someone's life just has to be *moving towards* G. If, as we have said already, human flourishing

> describes a horizon of value within which we can say that α is good *for* a particular person S (where α contributes to S's flourishing) and β is bad *for* S (where β detracts from S's flourishing).[80]

where does that leave G, in terms of G's goodness? I think we can say the following (assuming, of course, that the Journey Model of human flourishing is correct).

As we have seen, thinkers like Richard Kraut take the view that only those things that contribute to an individual's flourishing can be said to be good *for* that individual.[81] I disagree and take the view that some things can be good *for* an individual even though they do not contribute to that individual's flourishing, because they make an already flourishing existence *even better*.[82] If this is right, then we can say that it is possible that *achieving* G may be good *for* an individual because achieving G makes an already flourishing life (that is, a life that was moving towards achieving G) *even better*. On this view, someone who achieves G is not just 'doing well' in terms of how their life is going but is instead doing 'better than well'. This view seems sensible: if someone's life is going well merely by virtue of its being targeted at achieving G, it would make sense that their life will be taken to a higher plane of goodness – that their life will be going 'better than well' – if they actually achieve G.

So even though G is not to be identified with human flourishing (on the Journey Model of human flourishing), we can say that achieving G is good *for* any individual. And if we can say that, then we can make sense of Alasdair MacIntyre's otherwise puzzling remark that 'The good life for man is the life spent in seeking for the good life for man'.[83] The quest for G counts as a good life because one's flourishing consists in engaging in that quest; but the quest for G also amounts to a quest for a good life because in questing for G one is questing for something that will make one's life go not just well, but better than well.

All this assumes that the Journey Model is correct, but thinking about the goodness of G might lead us to conclude that the Journey Model is an unworkable model of human flourishing. Why can't we identify human flourishing with *achieving* G, and say that someone who has yet to achieve G cannot be said to be flourishing? On this view, none of a–f in the diagram above could be said to be flourishing. The only advantage a, b, and c have over d, e, and f is that a, b, and c have more of a *chance* of flourishing *in the future* as their lives are currently heading in the direction of G in a way that d, e, f are not.

In support of this objection to the Journey Model, recall that we said, in Part I of this project, that:

> if S's life is going well then S has *reason to be satisfied* with the way ... her life is going. In other words, S has no *need* to change ... her life – it is not *important* that S change ... her life – even though there will almost inevitably be ways in which S could change ... her life for the better.[84]

---

[80] See above, p 9. In his much later work *Ethics in the Conflicts of Modernity* (n 1), MacIntyre expands on this idea, identifying 'A good life [as] one in which an agent, although continuing to rank order particular and finite goods, treats none of these goods as necessary for the completion of her or his life, so leaving her or himself open to a final good beyond all such goods, as good desirable beyond all such goods' (at p 231).

[81] See McBride, *The Humanity of Private Law, Part I* (n 17), 83, n 2.

[82] Ibid.

[83] MacIntyre, *After Virtue* (above, n 76), 254.

[84] See McBride, *The Humanity of Private Law, Part I* (n 17), 83 (emphasis in original).

If S's life is heading in the direction of G, and achieving G is good for S, how can we say that S has reason to be satisfied that her life *merely continue* to head in the direction of G and thus – by definition – *never arrive* at achieving G? How can it be reasonable for someone to be content always to travel and never arrive at their destination?[85]

However, it is possible that S will be doomed to fail in the quest for G unless S adopts the attitude that she is content merely to travel in the direction of G, and refuses to concern herself with the issue of whether or not she will ever actually arrive at her destination. The idea that S is engaged in a *quest* for G, where S comes to a full understanding of the nature of G and is able to grasp G 'only through encountering and coping with the various particular harms, dangers, temptations and distractions which provide [the] quest with its episodes and incidents'[86] helps to make sense of why adopting this kind of attitude may be essential to S's succeeding in achieving G.

First, as S can only have a rough idea of what achieving G might be like when S starts out on his or her quest, and can only know that he or she has achieved G once he or she has achieved it, it would be pointless for S to spend time worrying about whether or not she has achieved G. Her energies would be better employed on seeking to ensure that she merely keeps on going in the direction of achieving G, and let G creep up on her, rather than seeking to ensure that she actually achieves G.[87]

Second, it is possible that G is *deep*, so that two people can achieve G, but one may do so to a much lesser extent than the other. (In the same way, someone who has achieved Grade 8 in playing the violin and the first violinist of the Berlin Philharmonic can both play the violin but the first violinist's abilities to play the violin are much greater than the Grade 8 violinist.) Given this, it would be unwise for S to make achieving G her goal as doing so might result in her resting content with achieving G at a very shallow level, rather than plumbing the depths that G contains. It is only if S is content merely to head in the direction of G, wherever that takes her, that she will be able to grasp G as fully as she is capable of grasping it.

Given these considerations, if S is engaged in a quest for G, it is possible that S will do best in that quest if she adopts the attitude that she is content to travel in the direction of G and is unconcerned as to whether or not she ever actually achieves G. So there may be nothing unreasonable in S's adopting the stance that her life will be going well so long as she is heading in the direction of G, while acknowledging that her life will be going better than well should she ever happen to achieve G. Whether this is in fact the case will depend on what G is. As we will see in the next chapter, when I set out an account of what G is, it does

---

[85] John Gardner's reflections on whether we have a reason to *try* to achieve some good, as opposed to a reason to *succeed* in achieving that good indicate the answer to these questions is 'We can't, and it's not': see his 'Obligations and outcomes in the law of torts' in Cane and Gardner (eds), *Relating to Responsibility* (Hart Publishing, 2001) and 'The wrongdoing that gets results' (2004) 18 *Philosophical Perspectives* 53.

[86] MacIntyre, *After Virtue* (n 76), 254.

[87] It is a notable trope of quest narratives that the hero of the quest only succeeds in finding the object of the quest accidentally, or without conscious effort – it is almost as though any deliberate attempts by the hero to achieve the object of the quest directly have the effect of pushing the object of the quest further away. See, for example, Book XIII of Homer's *Odyssey*, where Odysseus is sleeping when his hosts, the Phaeacians, land ashore his kingdom Ithaca, and they carry him still sleeping onto the beach and leave him there; or the Third Act of Richard Wagner's opera *Parsifal* where Parsifal stumbles into the part of the forest where the very person he has been looking for happens to be.

prove to be the case that S can only achieve G if she focuses on heading in the direction of G and does not concern herself with whether or not she has achieved G or will ever achieve G. But for the time being, we can simply note that at a formal level, we have no reason to think that the Journey Model is *necessarily* unworkable as a model of human flourishing.

## Compatibility with the Postulates

Having set out this formal outline of the Journey Model of human flourishing, we can now show how the Journey Model of human flourishing *might* be compatible with our four postulates of human flourishing.

(1) *Universality*. A Journey Model of human flourishing will be compatible with (P1) – the postulate that human flourishing is within the grasp of any human being – so long as, under favourable circumstances: (a) it is possible for any human being's life to be directed towards G, and (b) it is possible for all human lives to be directed towards G at the same time. Whether (a) and (b) *are* true will depend on what G is, but as presently informed we have no reason to think that (a) and (b) *cannot* both be true. For example, orienting one's life in the direction of G would not seem to be anywhere near as resource-intensive an activity as RP-flourishing, with the result that the Journey Model of human flourishing does not create the same problems over competition for resources that the RP does. So – so far as we know at the moment – it is *possible* that the Journey Model of human flourishing is compatible with (P1).

(2) *Loss*. A much bigger challenge for the Journey Model is to show that it is compatible with (P2) – the idea that someone's flourishing is not entirely under their control and can be harmed by a wide variety of events. At first sight, the Journey Model seems *in*compatible with (P2) in that the direction in which S's life is going always seems to be something that is under S's control. So, on the Journey Model, S is always capable of flourishing, whatever seemingly dreadful things happen to S. Invoking the words of W E Henly's poem *Invictus* (1875), S will always be able to say,

> In the fell clutch of circumstance
> I have not winced or cried aloud
> Under the bludgeonings of chance
> My head is bloody, but unbowed …

> It matters not how strait the gate,
> How charged with punishments the scroll,
> I am the master of my fate:
> I am the captain of my soul.

However, it *is* possible to see ways in which S's quest for G can be knocked off course without S being able to do anything to prevent this happening, and therefore possible to see how the Journey Model of human flourishing might be compatible with (P2).

One stock example we have been using of an event that will invariably damage S's flourishing – and which S may have no control over – is a loved one's being harmed. The Journey Model of human flourishing is able to account for how such an event can work to damage S's flourishing. Assume that S and a loved one, T, are both flourishing according to the Journey Model of human flourishing – both are on a shared quest for G. But something goes wrong with T: T abandons the quest and turns off to other pursuits. In this situation, S *could* cut T loose and push on alone towards G. But this is hardly likely to be the case. S's love for T means that S will *have* to abandon (temporarily) her own quest for G and embark on a new quest to reach T and see whether T can be persuaded to rejoin the quest for G. But while S is doing this, S cannot be said to be flourishing herself.

It is easy to think of other examples of events that are *inherently diverting* – events over which S might have no control, but will inevitably divert S from the quest for G and thereby impair S's flourishing. For example, if S is forced by circumstances to spend all her time trying to secure her continued existence, S will not have any time for anything else like questing after G. So putting S in a position where S has to spend all her time fighting to survive will inevitably be inconsistent with S's flourishing, even on the Journey Model of human flourishing.[88] Similarly, if S suffers a serious injury, such as the head wound referred to in Henly's poem. Such injuries need to be treated and time spent recovering from them. They might also have long-term ramifications that need to be coped and dealt with. So injuries are inherently diverting: they cannot but cause someone who suffers from them to abandon (at least temporarily) any quest for G that they were embarked on while they try to recover from, and cope with, the injury that they have suffered.

(3) *Gaita's Challenge.* Having shown how the Journey Model of human flourishing may be compatible, at a formal level, with (P2), we now have to check back and see whether we have thereby committed ourselves to any positions that might imply that the Journey Model is *in*compatible with (P1). In particular, we need to begin to take on *Gaita's Challenge* – how can we say that human flourishing is within the grasp of people suffering from very severe disabilities without making light of, or diminishing, the fact of those disabilities?

I think the Journey Model of human flourishing allows us to make the following preliminary response to *Gaita's Challenge*. Anything (call it 'X' for short) that makes it *harder* for someone ('S') to engage effectively in a quest for G must be counted as a bad thing, even if X does not make it *impossible* for S to engage in a quest for G. So where a disability makes it harder for S to engage in a quest for G, then the existence of that disability is a matter of regret even if the existence of that disability does not make it impossible for S to engage in a quest for G.

*If* it is the case that there are *no* disabilities that would make it impossible for S to engage in a quest for G, but there are *some* disabilities that would make it harder for S to engage in a quest for G without help and assistance to overcome the effect of those disabilities, then I think the Journey Model can meet *Gaita's Challenge* – we *can* say (compatibly with (P1)) that flourishing is not out of the reach of someone suffering from the kind of disabilities Gaita encountered on the psychiatric ward where he worked, without in any way making light of those disabilities or regarding them as irrelevant to one's prospects for flourishing.

---

[88] Cf. Raz's example of the 'Hounded Woman' in his *The Morality of Freedom* (OUP, 1986), 374: 'A person finds herself on a small desert island. She shares the island with a fierce carnivorous animal which perpetually hunts for her. Her mental stamina, her intellectual ingenuity, her will power and her physical resources are taxed to their limits by her struggle to remain alive. She never has a chance to do or even to think of anything other than how to escape from the beast.'

Whether it *is* the case that there are *no* disabilities that would make it impossible for S to engage in a quest for G, while there are *some* disabilities that would make it harder for S to engage in a quest for G without some form of help to deal with those disabilities, depends on what G is – and that is the subject of the next chapter. Until we know what G is, all we can say is that it is *possible* that the Journey Model of human flourishing is compatible with (P1) and can also meet *Gaita's Challenge*. In the next chapter, I hope to show that this possibility is actually realised.

(4) *Value*. If the Journey Model of human flourishing were correct, then it would be true by definition that questing for G, and achieving G, is good *for us*. But whether it is true that questing for G is 'good' in the wider sense suggested by (P3) – which asserts, among other things, that a universe that has beings in it like us who quest for G is better than a universe that does not have such beings in it – depends on what G is. Nothing more can therefore be said on this issue until the next chapter, but for the time being we can simply note that we have no reason to think that the Journey Model of human flourishing is incompatible with (P3) being true.

(5) *Continuity*. A similar point applies to whether the Journey Model of human flourishing is consistent with (P4). Whether the Journey Model is consistent with the idea that human flourishing is self-sustaining over time and across persons depends on whether people who are engaged on a quest for G enjoy the kind of resilience and the desire to share what they have with others that would make the quest for G self-sustaining over time and across persons. And that in turn depends on what kind of thing G is. But we can note at this point that the Journey Model does not suffer from the *possessiveness* that brings the RP, and any other Possessions Model of human flourishing, into conflict with (P4).

After all, every journey has to end somewhere and the journey of a human being through life must finally end in death. While someone who is on a quest for G will – as (P4) indicates they will – seek to put off the moment of their death as long as possible, they will also recognise that their quest may bring them to their final end sooner than they would like. When that happens, they will have a choice – to abandon their quest and the fate it has taken them to, or to stick with the quest and embrace their fate. Their flourishing will depend on them doing the second and not the first (at least if the Journey Model of human flourishing is correct). So adopting the Journey Model of human flourishing allows someone to reconcile themselves with death, as a price that they might be called upon to pay for their flourishing, in a way that someone who adopts the RP or some other Possessions Model of human flourishing could never be reconciled.[89] This means that someone who adopts the Journey Model of human flourishing has the potential to be more resilient in the face of mortal danger than someone who adopts a Possessions Model of human flourishing. It is therefore easier to see how (P4) *could* be true under a Journey Model of human flourishing than under a Possessions Model of human flourishing.

---

[89] Cf. Charles Taylor's observation in 'A Catholic modernity?' in his *Dilemmas and Connections: Selected Essays* (n 4), at 176, that there is a 'widespread inability' in our culture 'to give any human meaning to suffering and death, other than as dangers and enemies to be avoided or combated.'

## Journey to Where?

Having shown at a formal level that it is *possible* that the Journey Model of human flourishing is consistent with our four postulates about human flourishing, we now have to show that the Journey Model is *in fact* consistent with those four postulates. And for that, we need to arrive at some conclusions as to what G is. Given that I have been using the abbreviation 'G' to describe what it is that (according to the Journey Model) our flourishing involves our questing after, some might wonder whether G is *God*?[90] St Augustine's great statement to God on the first page of his *Confessions* that 'You have formed us for Yourself, and our hearts are restless until they find their rest in You' might lead us to think that G *is* God.[91] However, this is a possibility that I don't think we need to entertain in order to come up with a plausible account of what G might be. Instead, in the next chapter I will make a much more modest suggestion as to what G is. My suggestion is that G is *living a truthful life*, and that our flourishing involves our embarking on a quest to realise in our own lives the 'still powerful ideal that [we] should live without lies.'[92] It is to this ideal that I now turn.

---

[90] Alasdair MacIntyre leaves us in little doubt that on his particular Journey Model of human flourishing (summed up above, n 80), G *is* God, observing that G is to be found where 'the enquiries of politics and ethics end … [and] natural theology begins' (*Ethics in the Conflicts of Modernity* (n 1), 315).

[91] Interestingly, Germain Grisez – whose work on the basic human goods underlies John Finnis' vision of human flourishing and who therefore might be taken as supporting a Possessions Model of human flourishing – dismisses this statement of Augustine's (or, rather, St Thomas Aquinas' arguments in favour of this statement) as a 'blunder' in his 2005 Aquinas Lecture 'The restless-heart blunder' (the lecture is readily available online). I am grateful to Thomas D'Andrea for bringing this lecture to my attention.

[92] Williams, *Shame and Necessity* (Univ of California Press, 1993), 166.

# 9

# Truth and the Journey Model

## 1. Intimations of the Truth

Like the sun peeping through the clouds, we have occasionally gotten a glimpse of the links between truth and human flourishing in our previous discussions of the nature of human flourishing.

(1)   We twice had occasion to observe that someone (in the first example, someone who did not care about their own flourishing,[1] and in the second, a member of a privileged class who turned a blind eye to the way his government was persecuting members of a different class)[2] who was 'in flight from the real' could not be said to be flourishing as a human being.

(2)   In a footnote,[3] we observed that under the 'love test' for determining what human flourishing involves, someone who was hooked up to Robert Nozick's 'experience machine' – with the result that they lived in a permanent or semi-permanent dream state, imagining themselves to be enjoying all sorts of wonderful experiences – could not be said to be flourishing as a human being.

The original lesson that Nozick took from considering whether or not someone should plug into the experience machine was that 'we want to *do* certain things, and not just have the experience of doing them' and that 'we want to *be* a certain way, to be a certain sort of person' and not the kind of 'indeterminate blob' that we would be if we were plugged into the experience machine.[4] Writing 15 years later, Nozick thought that the experience machine thought experiment taught us that:

> We care about more than just how things feel to us from the inside; there is more to life than feeling happy. We care about what is actually the case. We want certain situations we value, prize, and think important to actually hold and be so. We want our beliefs, or certain of them, to be true and accurate; we want our emotions, or certain important ones, to be based upon facts that hold and to be fitting. We want to be importantly connected to reality, not to live in a delusion. We desire this not simply in order to more reliably acquire pleasures or other experiences … Nor do we want the added pleasurable feeling of being connected to reality. Such an inner feelings … also can be provided by the experience machine. What we want and value is an actual connection with reality.[5]

---

[1] McBride, *The Humanity of Private Law, Part I: Explanation* (Hart Publishing, 2018), 89.
[2] Ibid, 104.
[3] Ibid, 87, n 34.
[4] Nozick, *Anarchy, State and Utopia* (Basic Books, 1974), 43 (emphasis in original).
[5] Nozick, *The Examined Life* (Simon & Schuster, 1989), 106.

That our flourishing as human beings can be destroyed if we become detached from reality is easily confirmed by considering that:

> We would not wish for our children a life of great satisfactions that depended upon deceptions they would never detect: although they take great pride in artistic accomplishments, the critics and their friends too are just pretending to admire their work yet snicker behind their backs; the apparently faithful mate carries on secret love affairs; their apparently loving children really detest them; and so on. Few of us upon hearing this description would exclaim, 'What a wonderful life! It feels so happy and pleasurable on the inside.' That person is living in a dream world, taking pleasure in things that aren't so.[6]

(3)   In the two previous chapters in which we have discussed what human flourishing involves,[7] we did not once consider the possibility that human flourishing involves *believing* that one's life is going well. And nor has anyone else, so far as I know. At first sight this omission is very puzzling. It would be possible to take the view that you are flourishing as a human being if *either* A *or* B is true of you, where A is filled out by reference to whatever account of human flourishing one prefers and B is 'you believe your life is going well'. But no one seems to take such a view – you can only be said to be flourishing as a human being if A is true of you; B seems not to be an option. The fact that we do not even consider that B might provide us with a way of flourishing as human beings seems to suggest a deep connection between truth and human flourishing – someone who is deceived about what human flourishing involves cannot still be said to be flourishing just because they happen to believe that their life is going well.

These intimations about the nature of human flourishing – together with the support provided in the previous chapter for thinking that a Journey Model of human flourishing is the most promising model on offer of what human flourishing involves – suggest that we should seriously consider that human flourishing involves our being engaged in 'a quest to apprehend or be conscious of reality – or, if we may speak redundantly, to apprehend reality truly.'[8] That human flourishing involves a quest to lead a truthful life is not a new thought: it has been endorsed in the past by thinkers such as Simone Weil,[9] Josef Pieper,[10]

---

[6] Ibid, 105–06. Cf. Sumner, *Welfare, Happiness, and Ethics* (OUP, 1996), who argues (at 156–61) that being deceived about the faithfulness of one's partner does not necessarily impair one's happiness – whether it does or does not depends on how you would feel about your partner's affairs were you informed about them. Sumner's views are considered further below (pp 69–70), where I deal with objections to the account of human flourishing advanced in this chapter.

[7] McBride, *The Humanity of Private Law, Part I* (n 1), Chapter 2; and Chapter 8, above.

[8] Gamwell, 'On the Loss of Theism' in Antonaccio and Schweiker (eds), *Iris Murdoch and the Search for Human Goodness* (Univ of Chicago Press, 1996), 174.

[9] See Chenavier, *Simone Weil: Attention to the Real* (Univ of Notre Dame Press, 2012), 2: 'This is how Weil defined the "interior necessity" which guided her: "For me personally life had no other meaning, and fundamentally has never had another meaning, than waiting for truth" (*Ecrits de Londres*, 213).'

[10] See Pieper, *Happiness and Contemplation* (St Augustine's Press, 1998), 9 ('To be a human being is to want to know'), 47 ('We want to know the truth at any cost, even if the truth should be frightful'), and 58 ('the fulfilment of existence takes place in the manner in which we become aware of reality; the whole energy of our being is ultimately directed toward attainment of insight. The perfectly happy person … this person is the one who sees … [H]appiness … consists in this seeing').

Thomas Merton,[11] and Iris Murdoch.[12] However, none of those thinkers presented us with a systematic account of what the life of someone who is engaged in a quest to lead a truthful life might look like, so as to allow us to assess whether engaging in such a quest could be said to be the key to human flourishing. In Section 2 of this chapter I will set out such an account, and in Section 3 I will argue that this account, combined with the postulates about the nature of the human flourishing set out in the previous chapter, gives us good reason to think that human flourishing does indeed consist in engaging in a quest to lead a truthful life. Section 4 will conclude by considering some objections that might be made to such a claim.

## 2. The Truth-Seeking Life

The nature of a quest – the fact that we cannot fully grasp the nature of what it is that we are questing for without embarking on, and succeeding in, the quest – prevents us from describing what a quest to lead a truthful life looks like in terms of our moving closer and closer to a particular and determinate goal that can be described in advance. For all we know, what a truthful life would be for *you* may be very different from what a truthful life would be for *me*. However, it seems *un*likely that what is involved in engaging in a *quest* to lead a truthful life will be very different for *you* than it would be for *me*. To engage in such a quest would seem *always* to require one to be blessed with certain virtues (I will call these 'truth-seeking virtues'), to engage in certain activities (I will call these 'truth-seeking activities'), and to live in a community that fosters the existence of such virtues and activities among its members (I will call this a 'truth-seeking community'). It seems to follow that someone who lives in a truth-seeking community, engages in truth-seeking activities, and possesses the truth-seeking virtues is successfully engaged in a quest to lead a truthful life; and that if we can understand what these virtues and activities are, and what kind of community can claim to be a truth-seeking community, then we will understand what is involved in engaging in a quest to lead a truthful life and therefore (if the main claim of this chapter is correct) what it is to flourish as a human being.

## A Sense of Reality

The first truth-seeking virtue would seem to be a *sense of reality* – that is, an awareness that the world is such that it will not 'submit to our wishes', that it is 'on the contrary unyielding

[11] See Merton, *The Ascent to Truth* (Burns & Oates, 1951), 7: 'Our nature imposes on us a certain pattern of development which we must follow if we are to fulfil our best capacities and achieve at least the partial happiness of being human. This pattern … can be stated very simply, in a single sentence: *We must know the truth, and we must love the truth we know, and we must act according to the measure of our love*' (emphasis in original).

[12] See Murdoch, *The Sovereignty of Good* (Routledge, 2001), 37: 'I would suggest that at the level of serious common sense and of an ordinary non-philosophical reflection about the nature of morals it is perfectly obvious that goodness is connected with knowledge: not with impersonal quasi-scientific knowledge of the ordinary world, whatever that may be, but with a refined and honest perception of what is really the case, a patient and just discernment and exploration of what confronts one, which is the result not simply of opening one's eyes but of a certainly perfectly familiar kind of moral discipline.' See also Widdows, *The Moral Vision of Iris Murdoch* (Ashgate, 2005), 89: 'For Murdoch … the moral life is essentially a pilgrimage from illusion to reality, going on in the moment-to-moment judgments of daily life.'

and even hostile to our interests', and is 'not under our direct and immediate control'.[13] It is this fact – the fact of the 'world's being resistant to our will'[14] – that 'is the origin of our concept of reality, which is essentially a concept of what limits us, of what we cannot alter or control by the mere movement of our will.'[15] A quest to lead a truthful life would make no sense to someone who did not have a sense of reality, as such a person would be incapable of acknowledging that there was such a thing as truth. Pontius Pilate asked, 'What is truth?'[16] and so might anyone who possessed sufficient political power that they could bend and manipulate as they pleased the world in which they operated. Such a person would not have much use for a sense of reality – an imagination for possibilities would be far more important to them. By contrast, someone who possesses a sense of reality accepts that they operate under constraint – they accept that not everything is under their control, and nor would they want everything to be under their control.

It follows that a community that places a great deal of emphasis on enhancing and expanding people's abilities to control their surroundings and their circumstances cannot be said to be a 'truth-seeking community' and would instead be hostile to the notion of truth, and the sense of constraint that comes with that notion. We do not need to look far for an example of such a community: we live right in the middle of one.[17] One of the defining features of Western liberal societies is the emphasis such societies place on protecting and enhancing people's autonomy, and the hostility displayed in such societies towards the existence of constraints on what people can do. Such societies have a proclivity for 'magical thinking' – both in terms of thinking of ways in which we can 'render objects plastic to [our] will[s] without ... getting too entangled with them'[18] and, where that is not possible, in terms of wishing away the problems created by the intractability of nature by acting as though those problems do not exist:

> when dumb nature is understood to be threatening to our freedom as rational beings, it becomes attractive to construct a virtual reality that will be less so, a benignly nice [world] where there is no conflict between the self and the world; no contingency that hasn't been [already] anticipated ...[19]

Whatever a truth-seeking community looks like, then, we do not live in one.

If the first truth-seeking virtue is a sense of reality, does that suggest anything about what sort of activities are truth-seeking? It is likely that a sense of reality can only be sustained

---

[13] Frankfurt, *On Truth* (Alfred A Knopf, 2015), 99.

[14] Williams, *Truth and Truthfulness* (Princeton UP, 2002), 125.

[15] Frankfurt, *On Truth* (n 13), 99.

[16] John 18:38.

[17] Cf. Rieff, *My Life Among the Deathworks* (Univ of Virginia Press, 2006), at 177, contrasting a 'second world' (pre-twentieth century) culture where happiness was conceived as 'obedience to commanding truths' which has now been 'superseded by the third world [twentieth century] sense of happiness as freedom from commanding truth.' See also 184: 'The self-dispossession of the world of commanding truths is the project of modern culture. We all know the commanding truths, but to say it is a bore to the children of the third [twentieth century] culture.' Also Merton, *No Man is an Island* (Burns & Oates, 1955), 170: 'the whole word has learned to deride veracity or to ignore it. Half the civilized world makes a living by telling lies. Advertising, propaganda, and all the other forms of publicity that have taken the place of truth have taught men to take it for granted that they can tell other people whatever they like provided that it sounds plausible and evokes some kind of shallow emotional response.'

[18] Crawford, *The World Beyond Your Head: How To Flourish in an Age of Distraction* (Viking, 2015), 73.

[19] Ibid, 77. Matthew Crawford (at 71–72) instances the TV program *Mickey Mouse Clubhouse*, on the Disney Junior Network, as encouraging this sort of thinking from a very early age. Each episode of *Clubhouse* presents four problems which are solved simply 'by saying "Oh Tootles!" This makes the Handy Dandy machine appear, a computerlike thing that condenses out of the Cloud and presents a menu of four "Mouseke-tools" on a screen', where each tool is tailormade to solve one of the problems presented in the episode.

among people who are engaged in activities that require one to have a sense of reality – that constantly confront someone engaging in those activities with the need to acknowledge that there are some things outside their control. Matthew Crawford's first book was called (in the UK) *The Case for Working With Your Hands*[20] and it is undoubtedly the case that physical work presents us with the best example of an activity that cannot be engaged in successfully unless one brings to that activity a sense of reality – an awareness that what you are working with is not infinitely or easily manipulable. It is no surprise, then, that many of the thinkers already cited as having identified human flourishing with engaging in a quest to lead a truthful life should place special emphasis on people's engaging in physical work.[21]

The polar opposite of physical work, in this respect, is an *interpretative* activity – that is, an activity that involves interpretation. It is, then, no accident that Bernard Williams' very last book, on *Truth and Truthfulness*, was inspired in part by his worry that 'the constraints on interpretation (I mean, on any large scale, not at the level of words, sentences or even individual works) [are] so problematic in the humanities that a sophisticated inquirer will find it hard to sustain … a sense of straightforward discovery'.[22] If there are no limits on how a given text or series of events can be interpreted, then among interpreters a sense of reality – a sense of acting under some kind of constraint – will dissolve, and the notion of truth will become problematic for interpreters. This raises the disturbing prospect that insofar as the practice of law involves interpretation, there is some inconsistency between engaging in the practice of law and engaging in a quest to lead a truthful life.

Even more disturbingly, the fact that it is hard to characterise interpretative activities as truth-seeking may lead us to doubt whether *human beings* are capable of being truth-seeking animals. This is because one of the defining features of human beings is that they understand the world using what Bernard Williams called *thick ethical concepts*. Williams' examples of thick ethical concepts that *we* use in making sense of the world were: '*coward, lie, brutality, gratitude* …'[23] Thick ethical concepts, Williams explained, straddle the is-ought divide in that when they apply they are both 'world-guided and action-guiding'.[24] A thick ethical concept is world-guided because it 'may be rightly or wrongly applied' and people using the concept 'can agree that it applies or fails to apply to some new situation.'[25] While there might on occasion be some disagreement as to whether or not the concept applies in a particular case 'this does not mean that the use of the concept is not controlled by the facts or by the users' perception of the world.'[26] A thick ethical concept is, at the same

---

[20] Crawford, *The Case for Working With Your Hands* (Viking, 2010).

[21] See Pieper, *Happiness and Contemplation* (n 10), 56: 'Is not the man who labors constructively, the plowman, the gardener, and above all the creative artist, considered the prototype of the happy man'; Weil, 'Human Person-ality' in *Simone Weil: An Anthology* (Penguin, 2005), 80: 'physical labour is a certain contact with the reality, the truth, and the beauty of this universe and with the eternal wisdom which is the order in it.'

[22] Williams, *Truth and Truthfulness* (n 14), 146.

[23] Williams, *Ethics and the Limits of Philosophy* (Fontana Press, 1985), 140 (emphasis in original). Other standard examples of thick ethical concepts that are in use in our culture today are: generous/mean, loveable/hateful, inspir-ing/disappointing, admirable/contemptible, wise/foolish, freedom/slavery, democratic/undemocratic, beautiful/ugly, interesting/boring, innocent/guilty, sacred/ordinary, work/leisure. The catalogue of thick ethical concepts in use in our culture does not remain static over time: thick ethical concepts like noble/shameful, holy/unholy, and chaste/unchaste seem to be on the wane in our culture, while concepts like cute, unhealthy, and jerk enjoy much more currency nowadays than they would have, say, 80 years ago.

[24] Ibid, 141.

[25] Ibid.

[26] Ibid.

time, action-guiding because when it applies 'this often provides someone with a reason for action, though that reason might be a decisive one and may be outweighed by other reasons …'[27] So, for example, suppose I think of a particular course of action *x* as being 'cowardly'. 'Cowardly' will both describe what *x* *is*, and will count against my doing *x* in my deliberating as to what to do. By contrast, if I thought of *x* as being 'courageous', that concept will again describe what *x* *is*, and will count in favour of my doing *x* in my deliberating as to what to do.

If, as I have just claimed, one of the defining features of our humanity is the fact that we use thick ethical concepts in making sense of the world and determining what to do,[28] then it is a basic feature of our humanity that we engage in interpretative activities – both in using thick ethical concepts to characterise particular courses of conduct and states of affairs, and in debating the meaning, significance and application of particular thick ethical concepts. But if it is hard to sustain a sense of reality when engaging in interpretative activities, and easy for such activities to descend into a farrago of self-serving impostures,[29] that would seem to indicate that there is a basic tension between our being human and our engaging in a quest to lead a truthful life.[30] This tension can only be resolved by living in a community that maintains within itself a lively understanding of the various thick ethical concepts that are in use in that community to make sense of the world and how the members of that community are to act in the world, and strong checks on people's subverting the use of those thick ethical concepts for their own purposes.

## Attention

We can group a number of truth-seeking virtues around the concept of *attention*: (1) focusing on reality for long enough to be able to come to grasp some element or aspect of that reality; (2) paying attention to reality with a mind that is clear of the kinds of preconceptions that might prevent one appreciating some element or aspect of that reality; (3) being open to the possibility that significant truths about the nature of reality might be communicated to you from the most unexpected sources. Let's consider each of these in turn.

---

[27] Ibid, 140.

[28] Cf. Frankfurt, 'Freedom of the will and the concept of the person' in his *The Importance of What We Care About* (CUP, 1988), identifying (at 16) 'having second-order volitions … as essential to being a person' where someone's wanting 'a certain desire to be his will' amounts to a 'second-order volition'. Building on Frankfurt's work, Charles Taylor argues that our capacity to form such second-order volitions depends on our being able to evaluate 'the qualitative *worth* of different desires' by classifying them in such categories as 'higher and lower, virtuous and vicious, more and less fulfilling, more and less refined, profound and superficial, noble and base': Taylor, 'What is Human Agency?' in his *Human Agency and Language: Philosophical Papers Volume 1* (CUP, 1985), 16 (emphasis in original). But classifying desires in this way involves us in making use of thick ethical concepts. So Frankfurt and Taylor's work on what it is to be a person or a human agent seems to support the position in the text that our humanity is crucially bound up with our using thick ethical concepts to make sense of the world and in deciding what to do.

[29] Cf. Plato's dialogue *Euthyphro*, which is concerned with clarifying the thick ethical concept of *piety*, and takes place between Socrates and a young man, Euthyphro, who is bringing charges of manslaughter against his own father. While Euthyphro insists that his actions are perfectly pious, it is hard to avoid the impression that he is really acting in his own interests in bringing the charges.

[30] This tension is fundamental to Nietzsche's work, which focuses relentlessly on the self-serving nature of many of our truth claims in the field of morality and ethics.

(1) *Focus*. All of the writers mentioned so far as supporting the idea of human flourishing as involving a quest to lead a truthful life emphasise the importance of sustained focus on reality as crucial to our ability to undertake such a quest successfully. In setting out a catalogue of human needs, Simone Weil insists 'that for every person there should be enough room, enough freedom to plan the use of one's time, the opportunity to reach ever higher levels of attention, some solitude, some silence.'[31] Iris Murdoch calls on us to 'attempt to turn most of our time from dead (inattentive, obsessed, etc.) time into live time.'[32] To do this, we have to adopt 'a disciplined way of living' which involves abandoning the 'anxious calculating distracted passing of time when the present is never really inhabited or filled' in favour of an existence where 'presents moments are lived attentively as truth and reality.'[33] 'So much of our lives', Murdoch observes, is 'passed and wasted "elsewhere", as with the tourist who does not *look* at the famous monument, but fiddles with his camera to get a good "view" which he can display later to his neighbours.'[34] Antonin Sertillanges compares the kind of focus required if one is 'to let the truth sink into one, to be quietly submerged by it, to lose oneself in it, not to think that one is thinking, nor that anything in the world exists but truth itself' to that shown by an 'animal in the forest, concentrated, watchful, crouching with his eyes on his prey.'[35]

The enemy of the kind of extended focus required to engage in a quest to lead a truthful life is *distraction*. Many different sources of distraction can be identified. Simone Weil protested against the way working conditions in factories prevent people working in those factories from focussing on reality, both because 'Everybody …is constantly harassed and kept on edge by the interference of extraneous wills … What man needs is silence and warmth; what he is given is an icy pandemonium'[36] and because factory work is so mindless that it 'is incompatible with [the kind of attention required to focus on reality] since it drains the soul of all save a preoccupation with speed.'[37] Matthew Crawford, writing 60 years after Weil, argues that we are now 'living through a crisis of attention' caused by the fact that 'Ours is now a highly mediated existence in which … we increasingly encounter the world through representations [that] are manufactured for us'[38] by companies that earn money by persuading us to attend to the representations that they are supplying.

Thomas Merton points to how a lack of *detachment* results in our losing the kind of extended focus needed to attend to reality: 'Lacking this detachment, we are subject to a thousand fears corresponding to our thousand anxious desires. Everything we love is uncertain: when we are seeking it, we fear we may not get it. When we have obtained it, we fear even more that it may be lost. Every threat to our security turns our work into agitation.'[39] But a perhaps more fundamental source of distraction is the fact that we *want* to be distracted. This point was first made by Blaise Pascal in his *Pensées*, which were assembled

---

[31] Weil, 'Human Personality' (n 21), 79.

[32] Murdoch, *Metaphysics as a Guide to Morals* (Chatto & Windus, 1992), 263.

[33] Ibid, 263.

[34] Ibid, 264. Cf. Zygmunt Bauman's essay 'From Pilgrim to Tourist – or a Short History of Identity' in Hall and du Gay (eds), *Questions of Cultural Identity* (SAGE Publications, 1996).

[35] Sertillanges, *The Intellectual Life* (The Catholic University Press of America, 1992), 133.

[36] Weil, 'Human Personality' (n 21), 79.

[37] Weil, 'Prerequisite to the Dignity of Labour' in Weil, *Simone Weil: An Anthology* (n 21), 275–76.

[38] Crawford, *The World Beyond Your Head: How To Flourish in an Age of Distraction* (n 18), ix.

[39] Merton, *No Man is an Island* (n 17), 97.

and published after his death in 1662. Pascal argued that it is a basic fact of human nature that a man 'does not know how to stay quietly in his room.'[40] Pascal argued that human beings are so unhappy, at base, that they want 'to be diverted from thinking of what they are, either by some occupation which takes their mind off [themselves], or by some novel and agreeable passion which keeps them busy, like gambling, hunting, some absorbing show, in short by what is called diversion.'[41] Some recent and startling proof of the truth of Pascal's claims was provided by experiments run in 2014 by the University of Virginia which showed that 67 per cent of men and 25 per cent of women would rather give themselves an electric shock than sit quietly in a room alone with their thoughts for 15 minutes.[42]

It follows that achieving the kind of extended focus needed to engage in a quest to lead a truthful life 'is not easy and demands a moral discipline'[43] in order to overcome the 'violent repugnance for true attention' that Simone Weil detected in our souls; a repugnance that is far stronger 'than the flesh has for bodily fatigue.'[44] It also requires that one *not* live in a community that is geared towards supplying people with the kind of endless distractions that they eagerly crave.

(2) *Clarity*. Iris Murdoch observes that just 'opening our eyes' does not necessarily enable us to 'see what confronts us … Our minds are continually active, fabricating an anxious, usually self-preoccupied, often falsifying veil which partially conceals the world.'[45] For example, Charles Taylor notes, 'the lustful, focusing as they do on their own bodily pleasure and excitement, are imperfectly able to notice and respond to the needs of the person whom they love or event to take in their full particularity. A person who is seen as a vessel of pleasure is not seen truly for what he or she *is*.'[46]

If our prolonged focus is going to enable us to grasp properly some aspect of reality, it needs to be cleaned of any distorting preconceptions that would prevent us from seeing what is in front of us. Murdoch supplies a famous example of this process of cleaning at work.[47] She imagines a mother ('M') feeling hostility towards her daughter-in-law ('D'), finding her 'unpolished and lacking in dignity and refinement.' M, in considering her feelings about D, reminds herself that 'I am old-fashioned and conventional. I may be prejudiced and narrow-minded. I may be snobbish. I am certainly jealous. Let me look again.' In looking again, 'gradually [M's] vision of D alters … D is discovered to be not vulgar but refreshingly simple, not undignified but spontaneous … not tiresomely juvenile, but delightfully youthful, and so on.'

The novelist David Foster Wallace makes the same point, arguing that 'Everything in my own immediate experience supports my deep belief that I am the absolute center of the

---

[40] Pascal, *Pensées* (Penguin Classics, 1995), [137].

[41] Ibid.

[42] www.sciencemag.org/news/2014/07/people-would-rather-be-electrically-shocked-left-alone-their-thoughts.

[43] Murdoch, *The Sovereignty of Good* (n 12), 63.

[44] Weil, 'Reflections on the Right Use of School Studies with the View to the Love of God' in Weil, *Waiting for God* (Harper Colophon, 1951), 111.

[45] Murdoch, *The Sovereignty of Good* (n 12), 82.

[46] Taylor, 'Iris Murdoch and Moral Philosophy' in Antonaccio and Schweiker (eds), *Iris Murdoch and the Search for Human Goodness* (n 8), 35 (emphasis in original).

[47] Murdoch, *The Sovereignty of Good* (n 12), 17–18.

universe, the realest, most vivid and important person in the existence' and that if we are aware of the distorting effects that this belief has on the way we look at other people we can choose *not* to operate on our 'default setting … [of] being deeply and literally self-centred, [interpreting] everything through this lens of self'[48] and instead see things differently, and possibly more accurately. So when stuck in a supermarket queue, instead of reflecting on 'how repulsive most of [the people in the queue] are and how stupid and cow-like and dead-eyed and nonhuman they seem … and how annoying and rude it is that people are talking loudly on cell phones in the middle of the line'[49] we can instead choose to reflect that 'this fat, dead-eyed, over-made-up lady who just screamed at her kid … – maybe she's not usually like this; maybe she's been up three straight nights holding the hand of her husband, who's dying of bone cancer …'[50]

(3) *Openness.* Wallace argues that if you achieve this kind of selflessness in your thinking, 'It will actually be within your power to experience a crowded, hot, slow, consumer-hell-type situation as not only meaningful, but sacred, on fire with the same force that lit the stars – compassion, love, the subsurface unity of all things.'[51] But to be able to do this – 'To see a world in a grain of sand / And a Heaven in a wild flower, / Hold infinity in the palm of your hand, / And Eternity in an hour …'[52] – one has to be open to experiencing epiphanies: 'the discovery of more universal and possibly profound significance in a situation of drab, everyday, goings-on, happenings so commonplace and trivial, quotidian, that one could hardly call them events (a word that already implies some kind of significance).'[53]

A famous literary example of an epiphany is provided by James Joyce's *Portrait of the Artist as a Young Man* (1916), where Stephen Dedalus observes a girl wading in Dublin Bay:

> Heavenly God! cried Stephen's soul, in an outburst of profane joy … Her image has passed into his soul for ever and no word had broken the holy silence of his ecstasy. Her eyes had called him and his soul had leaped at the call. To live, to err, to fall, to triumph, to recreate life out of life! A wild

---

[48] Wallace, *This Is Water: Some Thoughts, Delivered on a Significant Occasion, About Leading a Compassionate Life* (Little Brown, 2009), 44.

[49] Ibid, 77.

[50] Ibid, 89.

[51] Ibid, 93 (emphasis in original). See also the appendix to Wallace, *The Pale King* (Hamish Hamilton, 2011), where Wallace recommends (at 546) achieving selflessness by exposing yourself to 'crushing, crushing boredom', by paying 'close attention to the most tedious thing you can find (tax returns, televised golf), and, in waves, a boredom like you've never known will wash over you and just about kill you. Ride these out, and it's like stepping from black and white into color. Like water after days in the desert. Constant bliss in every atom.'

[52] Blake, 'Auguries of innocence' (1803).

[53] Barfoot, '"Milton silent came down my path": the Epiphany of Blake's Left Foot' in Tigges (ed), *Moments of Moment: Aspects of the Literary Epiphany* (Rodopi, 1999), 61. Cf. Murdoch, *Metaphysics as a Guide to Morals* (n 32), 496: 'On the road between illusion and reality there are many clues and signals and wayside shrines and sacraments and places of meditation and refreshment. The pilgrim just has to look about him with a lively eye. There are many kinds of images in the world, sources of energy, checks and reminders, pure things, inspiring things, innocent things attracting love and veneration', and Woolf, *A Room of One's Own* (1929), §6: 'What is meant by "reality"? It would seem to be something very erratic, very undependable – now to be found in a dusty road, now in a scrap of newspaper in the street, now a daffodil in the sun. It lights up a group in a room and stamps some casual saying. It overwhelms one walking home beneath the stars and makes the silent world more real than the world of speech – and then there it is again in an omnibus in the uproar of Piccadilly. Sometimes, too, it seems to dwell in shapes too far away for us to discern what their nature is. But whatever it touches, it fixes and makes permanent. That is what remains over when the skin of the day has been cast into the hedge; that is what is left of past time and of our loves and hates.'

angel had appeared to him, the angel of mortal youth and beauty, an envoy from the fair courts of life, to throw open before him in an instant of ecstasy the gates of all the ways of error and glory. On and on and on and on!

Similarly, Thomas Merton tells of an experience he had in 'Louisville, at the corner of Fourth and Walnut, in the center of the shopping district' of being

> suddenly overwhelmed with the realization that I loved all these people, that they were mine and I theirs, that we could not be alien to one another even though we were total strangers. It was like waking from a dream of separateness, of spurious self-isolation in a special world, the world of renunciation and supposed holiness ... This sense of liberation from an illusory difference was such a relief and such a joy to me that I almost laughed out loud ... [If] only everybody could realize this! But it cannot be explained. There is no way of telling people that they are all walking around shining like the sun.[54]

The poet Ruth Pitter, in her essay 'We cannot take less', reported having the same kind of experience when:

> I was sitting in front of a cottage door one day in spring, long ago; a few bushes and flowers round me, a bird gathering nesting material, the trees of the forest at a little distance. A poor place – nothing glamorous about it ... Suddenly everything assumed a different aspect – no, its true aspect. For a moment, it seemed to me, the truth appeared in its overwhelming splendour. The secret was out, the explanation given. Something that had seemed like total freedom, total power, total bliss – a good with no bad as its opposite – an absolute that had no opposite – this thing, so unlike our feeble nature, had suddenly cut across one's life and vanished.[55]

Antonin Sertillanges provides us with a list of potential epiphanies that are available to us, if we are open to them:

> Let a workshop speak to you not only of iron and wood, but of man's estate of work, of ancient and modern social economy, of class relationships. Let travel tell you of mankind, let scenery remind you of the great laws of the world; let the stars speak to you of measureless duration; let the pebbles on your path be to you the residue of the formation of the earth; let the sight of a family make you think of past generations; and let the least contact with your fellows throw light on the highest conception of man.[56]

The truth-seeking virtues that we are grouping together here under the heading 'attention' can only count as truth-seeking virtues if attention is rewarded with insight. For example, focus, clarity, and openness would not count as truth-seeking virtues among the prisoners in Plato's allegory of the cave.[57] The prisoners – representatives of unenlightened humanity – are held in place facing the back of a cave and watch shadows playing on the wall in front of them, shadows that are produced by the prisoners' captors moving figures in front of a fire that blazes behind the prisoners' backs. No amount of focus, clarity, and openness will help

---

[54] Merton, *Conjectures of a Guilty Bystander* (Image Books, 1968), 156–57.

[55] Quoted in King (ed), *Sudden Heaven: The Collected Poems of Ruth Pitter* (Kent State University Press, 2018), xix. Pitter's essay was unpublished but formed the basis of a 1961 BBC radio address entitled 'Hunting the unicorn' (reprinted in ibid, 381). In that talk, when alluding to this epiphany (which happened when she was 'no more than fourteen years old'), she reflected, 'Is it [her experience] ... a hint of something more real than this life – a message from reality – perhaps a particle of reality itself? If so, no wonder we hunt it so unceasingly, and never stop desiring it and pining for it. For our daily life seems ... largely unreal, and perhaps it is getting more so' (ibid, 383).

[56] Sertillanges, *The Intellectual Life* (n 35), 74.

[57] Plato, *Republic*, 514a–516b.

the prisoners get anywhere in understanding the truth of their position. For that, they need to get up and find their way out of the cave. So for the virtues that we have grouped under the heading 'attention' to count as truth-seeking virtues, it must be true that (a) the world is such that the truth about it can be understood through our paying attention to it; (b) we do not live in a community where we are systematically misled about the nature of the world and our place in it; and (c) we do not associate with people who mislead us about matters that are important to us.[58]

## Humility

Humility is a crucial truth-seeking virtue, for two reasons. First, a given person (S) can never be sure that he is in possession of the truth – S may have been misled by other people about the truth and, as we will see, S is more than capable of misleading himself about the truth. Second, the truth is *deep* – a full knowledge of the truth can only be acquired in stages, where each successive stage of understanding reveals the previous stage to have provided only a partial and inadequate understanding of the truth.[59] In order to move from one stage of understanding to another, S must have the humility to acknowledge that his current level of understanding is capable of being superseded by a deeper and richer level of understanding.

The virtue of humility entails: (1) that S be open to considering arguments that indicate that S's current beliefs are incorrect;[60] (2) that S revise his beliefs if the arguments that indicate that S's current beliefs are incorrect seem to be valid, and not grimly hang on to his beliefs in the teeth of those opposing arguments just because they happen to be *his* beliefs;[61] (3) that S acknowledges that his current beliefs may give him only a partial and inadequate understanding of the truth, and that it is possible (indeed, very likely) that there exists a deeper level of understanding which he does not yet possess that would both make sense of, and transcend, his current beliefs.[62] The virtue of humility does *not* entail: (4) that S adopt a skeptical attitude towards his current beliefs, with the result that S is not willing to say that

---

[58] Cf. Wood, *Blaise Pascal on Duplicity, Sin, and the Fall* (OUP, 2013), 84: 'Someone who is born into a society that inordinately values wealth … will be taught in thousands of near-imperceptible ways to love wealth and to pursue it at the expense of higher goods. Even if such a person becomes, say, a teacher instead of a banker, the love of wealth will continue to infect his choices and distort his relationships.'

[59] Cf. Murdoch, *Metaphysics as a Guide to Morals* (n 32), 320: 'The spiritual life is a long disciplined destruction of false images and false gods until (in some sense which we cannot understand) the imagining mind achieves an end of images and shadows …'.

[60] Cf. Wallace, *This is Water* (n 48), condemning (at 32) the kind of 'arrogance, blind certainty [and] closed-mindedness that's like an imprisonment so complete that the prisoner doesn't even know he's locked up.'

[61] Cf. Geach, *Truth and Hope* (Univ of Notre Dame Press, 2001), 39: 'acquiescing consciously in a detected inconsistency [in one's beliefs] is like cherishing a viper in one's bosom: it is to ensure that somewhere one's thinking will be at fault in a non-logical manner. We are tempted to such acquiescence by that grave intellectual vice which Quine has labelled the desire to *have been* right; we may wish for the advantage of accepting some newly discovered truth without the discomfort of frankly confessing and recanting old errors.'

[62] Cf. Sertillanges, *The Intellectual Life* (n 35), 125: 'Some minds quickly reach the point of being satisfied with a given amount of knowledge. They work in the beginning, then lose the sense of the void always waiting to be filled. They do not remember that we are always void of what we have not, and that, in a limitless field of discovery, we never have reason to say: let us stop here … To know, to seek, to know more and to start afresh to seek more, is the life of a man devoted to truth …'.

he believes his current beliefs are correct and is not willing to make arguments in favour of his current beliefs in the face of arguments that might be taken as indicating that his beliefs are incorrect.[63]

Two things follow from the importance of humility as a truth-seeking virtue. First, the quest to lead a truthful life can only be carried on in *dialogue* with other people. It is only by being exposed to other people's beliefs, and the arguments that they can make in favour of those beliefs, that you can test the quality of your own beliefs and have the opportunity of revising them if they prove to be faulty.[64] So someone who is engaged in a quest to lead a truthful life will seek to engage in activities that give him the opportunity to discover, and discuss, other people's beliefs on the matters that matter to him; and a truth-seeking community will seek to foster the existence of such activities, and will not seek to clamp down on such activities by, for example, restricting people's freedom of expression or placing limits on when people can associate together for the purpose of discussing matters of common interest to them.

Second, the fact that humility is a truth-seeking virtue accounts for, in part, why someone who is engaged in a quest to lead a truthful life will be content *merely* to engage in the quest, and will not concern themselves with whether they *succeed* in their quest. In other words, someone who is engaged in a quest to lead a truthful life will adopt the attitude described by Gotthold Lessing:

> If God held all truth concealed in his right hand, and in his left hand the persistent striving for the truth ... and should say 'Choose!' I should humbly take the left hand and say, 'Father, I will take the striving. For pure truth is for thee alone.'[65]

Lessing's choice is the one that the truth-seeking virtue of humility would dictate one make, as someone (S) who is concerned about *succeeding* in living a truthful life will be in grave danger of violating all of the nostrums (1)–(3), above, that are associated with the virtue of humility. The fact that it matters to S that he *succeed* in living a truthful life will make him

---

[63] Cf. Chesterton, *Heretics* (1905), chapter 20 ('Concluding Remarks on the Importance of Orthodoxy'): 'Man can be defined as an animal that makes dogmas. As he piles doctrine on doctrine and conclusion on conclusion in the formation of some tremendous scheme of philosophy and religion, he is, in the only legitimate sense of which the expression is capable, becoming more and more human. When he drops one doctrine after another in a refined scepticism, when he declines to tie himself to a system, when he says that he has outgrown definitions, when he says that he disbelieves in finality ... then he is by that very process sinking slowly backwards into the vagueness of the vagrant animals and the unconsciousness of the grass.'

[64] Cf. MacIntyre, 'The Idea of an Educated Public' in *Education and Values: The Richard Peters Lectures* (Univ of London Institute of Education, 1987), 24: 'it is a familiar truth that one can only think for oneself if one does not think by oneself. It is only through the discipline of having one's claims tested in ongoing debate, in the light of standards on the rational justification of which, and on the rational justification afforded by which, the participants in debate are able to agree, that the reasoning of any particular individual is rescued from the vagaries of passion and interest.'

[65] Lessing, *Anti-Goetze: Eine Duplik* (1778). For criticism of Lessing's choice, see Kuyper, *Scholarship: Two Convocation Addresses on University Life* (Acton Institute, 2014), 29–31. Kuyper explains Lessing's choice as being based on a desire to find out the truth *oneself*, rather than relying on anyone else – which desire he (rightly) thinks can have undesirable effects (not least in your being happy to spend time reinventing the wheel). However, my humility-based argument in favour of Lessing's choice is not vulnerable to Kuyper's objection – someone who is engaged in a quest to lead a truthful life will be very happy (and will in fact have little choice but) to rely on what others engaged in the same quest have learned. For a defence of Lessing's choice that *does* see it as based on the importance of seeking out the truth *oneself*, see Gelven, *What Happens To Us When We Think: Transformation and Reality* (State Univ of New York Press, 2003), 125.

resistant to: (a) listening to arguments that indicate that he has not succeeded in achieving his goal; (b) changing his life in response to valid arguments that indicate that he has not succeeded in achieving his goal; and (c) acknowledging that he may have actually only achieved a partial success in achieving his goal, and that a more and more complete achievement of that goal still awaits him.

If S is merely content to engage in the quest to lead a truthful life, and attaches no importance to his achieving that goal, then he will be much *less* likely to do any of (1)–(3) and will therefore be much *more* likely to succeed in leading a truthful life. This is an important result because, as we saw in the previous chapter, one can only plausibly say that someone is flourishing as a human being if they are engaged in a quest for some good G if they have good reason to be content merely to engage in that quest, and not to succeed in achieving the good G after which they are questing.[66] It seems that when it comes to the quest to lead a truthful life, such a quest cannot be achieved without the virtue of humility, and the virtue of humility cannot be maintained if it matters to the person (S) engaged in that quest that they succeed in that quest. The maintenance of that virtue depends on S's being merely content to engage in the quest to lead a truthful life, and paying no heed to whether or not he succeeds in achieving that quest.

## Honesty

While, as was observed earlier, we cannot say in advance what a truthful life will look like, we *can* say that leading a truthful life *will* involve being honest. So someone (S) who is engaged in a quest to lead a truthful life will, as part of that quest, strive to be honest. This truth-seeking activity seems to have two aspects. Honesty demands, first, that S be *realistic* – in other words, that S not deceive herself into thinking that something is true that is not in fact true. Second, honesty demands that S be *sincere* – in other words, that S not encourage other people to adopt beliefs that, to the best of S's knowledge, are false. So engaging in a quest to lead a truthful life would seem to involve striving to be (1) realistic in the way one forms one's beliefs, and (2) sincere in one's dealings with other people. Let's take each of these in turn.

(1) *Realism*. The question of how self-deception occurs is a difficult one, and has led some thinkers to deny that such a thing is possible as it seems to imply that S could induce herself to believe something that she knows is not true.[67] However, we can identify two mechanisms by which self-deception might occur.

First, S believes, or strongly suspects, that *x is* true, but also has a strong desire that it be the case that *x* is *not* true. Then some change of circumstances (C) occurs that results in S revisiting the question of whether *x* is true or not, and S convinces herself, on the basis of C's happening, that her initial belief, or strong suspicion, that *x* is true is unfounded, and that *x* is not in fact true. However, no one who did not wish that *x* were true would come to the conclusion that *x* is not true on the basis of C's happening. We can call this case of self-deception, *wishful thinking*.

---

[66] See above, p 26.
[67] For a good discussion of the topic see Wood, *Blaise Pascal on Duplicity, Sin, and the Fall* (n 58), chapters 5–6.

Second, S believes that *x* is not true, and is very happy to believe that *x* is not true. However, S also believes, or strongly suspects, that her belief that *x* is not true is based on incomplete information, and that were she to acquire more complete information, then she might have to revise her belief that *x* is not true. But because S is happy to believe that *x* is not true, S decides not to seek out any more information relevant to the issue of whether *x* is true or not. Had S done this, S would have realised that *x* is not true. We can call this case of self-deception, *turning a blind eye to reality.*

In both cases, S's deceiving herself is rooted in her having a strong desire that it be the case that *x* is not true. One way, then, that S could avoid deceiving herself is to cease having any desires as to what is the case – instead, she adopts a *que sera sera* mentality under which she is content to deal with whatever does happen to be the case. However, it seems unlikely that any human being could achieve this degree of impassibility. Given this, S can never reach her state where she can *guarantee* that her beliefs will not be affected by self-deception: as Stanley Hauerwas observes, 'To be is to be rooted in self-deception.'[68] The best S can do is to *try* to be realistic. That is, the best that S can do is adopt a policy of 'constant vigilance':[69] guarding against the possibility that her beliefs are affected by self-deception by constantly checking those of her beliefs that accord with the way she wishes the world would be to see whether they are affected by those wishes. Fortunately, *trying* to be realistic is all that S is required to do if she is to flourish as a human being, according to the picture of human flourishing being developed in this chapter.

(2) *Sincerity.* Sincerity is much easier to achieve, under the right circumstances – being insincere always involves a *choice* to be insincere given that insincerity involves encouraging people to adopt beliefs that you *know* or *strongly suspect* are incorrect. However, what if the circumstances are *wrong* and S feels impelled because of those circumstances to be insincere to someone?

Take, for example, the standard example of someone's lying to save someone else's life. Alasdair MacIntyre describes a case during World War II where a Dutch housewife took in a Jewish neighbour's child just before the neighbour 'was arrested and sent to a death camp … Confronted by a Nazi official who asked [the housewife] whether or not all the children living in her home were her own she lied.'[70] On the picture of human flourishing being developed in this chapter – where flourishing involves embarking on a quest to lead a truthful life – did the housewife in this case impair her flourishing through her lie? My view is that the housewife's flourishing *was* impaired in this case as a result of her lie, but to say the *housewife* impaired *her own* flourishing through her lie is to place the responsibility for the impairment in the housewife's flourishing in the wrong place. It is rather the Nazi official – and the murderous regime standing behind him – who impaired the housewife's flourishing by making it impossible for her to be sincere in her response to the official's question.

The same point can be made about Vaclav Havel's example (drawn from real life in communist-ruled Czechoslovakia) of 'The manager of a fruit and vegetable shop [who] places in his window, among the onions and the carrots, the slogan: "Workers of the world,

---

[68] Hauerwas, *Truthfulness and Tragedy* (Univ of Notre Dame Press, 1997), 95.
[69] Ibid.
[70] MacIntyre, 'Truthfulness and Lies: What Can we Learn from Kant?' in his *Ethics and Politics: Selected Essays Volume 2* (CUP, 2006), 135.

unite!'"[71] Havel observes that the manager does not really believe in the slogan, but only posts the slogan in the window in order to say, 'I, the greengrocer XY, live here and I know what I must do. I behave in the manner expected of me. I can be depended upon and am beyond reproach. I am obedient and therefore I have the right to be left in peace.'[72] On the view of human flourishing being developed in this chapter, Havel's greengrocer's insincerity prevents us from saying that he is flourishing as a human being.[73] This is so even though the greengrocer's insincerity is not his fault, and is instead the responsibility of the society he lives in, which places overwhelming pressures on him to post up slogans in his window that he does not believe.

So a community that makes it very difficult or impossible for its members to be sincere in the way they deal with each other is one that prevents its members engaging in a quest to lead a truthful life, and therefore (if the claims made in this chapter are correct) prevents its members flourishing as human beings. We might wish that this were not the case – that someone's flourishing could enjoy greater protection from the happenstance of what sort of community one grows up in – but not to admit that this *is* nevertheless the case would be to fall into the vice of wishful thinking and thereby endanger our own flourishing (so long, again, as the claims about the nature of human flourishing being made in this chapter are correct).

## Integrity

Havel observes of the greengrocer in his example that had he been instructed by his political masters to post up a slogan saying 'I am afraid and therefore unquestioningly obedient' – a statement that would be true – the 'greengrocer would be embarrassed and ashamed to put such an unequivocal statement of his own degradation in the shop window ...'.[74] Were the greengrocer in this alternative scenario to obey and post up the demeaning slogan, he would feel that he was not being *true to himself* in posting up the slogan, even though what the slogan says is completely true.

The 'self' that the greengrocer would not be true to in posting up the slogan would not be the 'self' that he actually is – someone who is under the thumb of his political masters – but the self that he would *like* to be – someone who, among other things, is courageous rather than cowardly.[75] It seems, then, that part of living a truthful life involves feeling that

---

[71] Havel, 'The Power of the Powerless' in Havel (ed), *The Power of the Powerless* (Routledge, 2009), 13.

[72] Ibid.

[73] See also Milosz, *The Captive Mind* (Penguin, 2001) – another work that emerged out of the experience of living under communism – describing (at 20) a writer, living under communism in Eastern Europe, who feels impelled – there being 'no other salvation on the face of the earth' – to write an article in praise of the ruling communist government (despite despising the Western communists who are blind to the faults of the communist governments in the East). Having written the article, the writer marvels 'at the ease with which [it was written]. In the last analysis, there was no reason for raising such a fuss. Everything is in order. He is past the "crisis". He does not emerge unscathed, however. The after-effects manifest themselves in a particular kind of extinguishment that is often perceptible in the twist of his lips. His face expresses the peaceful sadness of one who has tasted the fruit from the Tree of the Knowledge of Good and Evil, of one who knows he lies ...'.

[74] Havel, 'The Power of the Powerless' (n 71), 13.

[75] Cf, Marcel, *The Mystery of Being, Part I: Reflection and Mystery* (Harvill Press, 1950), 143: 'The self to which I have to be true is perhaps merely the cry that comes out to me from my own depths – the appeal to me to become that which, literally and apparently, I now am not.'

you *actually are* the person you would like to be. We can say that someone who has achieved this state of being possesses the quality of *integrity* (though others might use the terms 'authenticity'[76] or 'wholeness' to describe this quality). And we can also say that engaging in a quest to live a truthful life involves, in part, engaging in a quest to achieve this quality of integrity, where you can say that the person you are corresponds with the image of the person you would like to be.

How is this image arrived at? In constructing this image, we begin with a set of thick ethical concepts[77] that we have inherited and refined for ourselves, and that offer to help us both make sense of the world and decide what to do. So, for example, one of the thick ethical concepts that Havel's greengrocer will be familiar with is 'cowardly'. That concept picks out certain actions – such as posting up a slogan saying 'I am afraid and therefore unquestioningly obedient' – as being 'cowardly' and as therefore to be avoided. The person the greengrocer would like to be is someone *who acts in accordance with the thick ethical concepts that the greengrocer himself acknowledges as valid*. Such a person would, among other things, have an aversion to performing cowardly acts and would therefore refuse to put up a slogan saying 'I am afraid and therefore unquestioningly obedient' unless there was some good reason for doing so, which was not rooted in a desire to save his own skin.[78] The greengrocer knows this, and so knows that posting up the slogan 'I am afraid and therefore unquestioningly obedient' would amount to a betrayal of the person he would like to be. Hence his unwillingness to do this.

Of course, the person the greengrocer would like to be would not put up a slogan saying 'Workers of the world, unite!' either, and for the same reason – that doing so is cowardly. But Havel's greengrocer is able to put up *that* slogan without any threat to his integrity because the greengrocer has talked himself into thinking that putting up *that* slogan is *not* cowardly. As Havel observes, the slogan 'indicates a level of disinterested conviction … [which allows] the greengrocer to say, "What's wrong with the workers of the world uniting?" Thus the [slogan] helps the greengrocer to conceal from himself the low foundations of his obedience …'[79] So the problem with the greengrocer's putting up the slogan 'Workers of the world, unite!' – from the point of view of his engaging in a quest to lead a truthful life – is not that doing so involves a lack of integrity (it does not, because the greengrocer does not, in posting up *that* slogan, feel that doing so distances him from the person he would like to be) but, rather, the wishful thinking involved in thinking that the person the greengrocer would like to be would have no problem with posting such a slogan on the shop window.[80]

---

[76] This is Michael Lynch's preferred term (see his *True to Life: Why Truth Matters* (MIT Press, 2005)), arguing (at 126) that 'authenticity, being true to yourself, requires having the will you want to have – identifying with the desires that guide your action.'

[77] See above, p 35.

[78] So the greengrocer's ideal self would not hesitate to put up the slogan if, for example, his wife and children had been threatened with execution if he did not comply. It would be a nice question, in any case, whether complying in such circumstances could even be classified as a cowardly act.

[79] Havel, 'The Power of the Powerless' (n 71), 14.

[80] Were the greengrocer to be prevailed upon to post up a slogan saying 'I am afraid and therefore unquestioningly obedient', the same process of wishful thinking would undoubtedly set in, with the greengrocer convincing himself, by looking at what he had done from as many angles as possible, that the kind of person he would like to be would not, in fact, have any problem posting up such a slogan in his shop.

A lack of integrity, then, involves a *felt* disconnect on S's part between the kind of person S actually is and the kind of person that S would like to be – where the kind of person S would like to be is someone who does a good job of navigating the ethical map[81] that S carries around with her and that is created by the thick ethical concepts that S acknowledges as valid. It is this kind of felt disconnect that St Paul confessed to in his letter to the Romans: 'I do not understand myself. For what I want to do, I do not do; while what I hate, I do.'[82] Someone (S) who is engaged in a quest to lead a truthful life will strive to eliminate any gap that S perceives between the sort of person that S is at the moment and the sort of person S would like to be – and in doing this S will also strive *not* to fall into the trap of wishfully thinking that her initial impression was wrong and that S is actually *already* the kind of person that S would like to be.

## Love

So far we have catalogued three truth-seeking virtues ((1) a sense of reality, (2) attention (which is broken down into three truth-seeking sub-virtues: focus, clarity, and openness), (3) humility) and two truth-seeking activities ((4) striving to be honest; and (5) striving to be the kind of person one wants to be) as essential to someone's engaging in a quest to lead a truthful life. It seems doubtful that any of these virtues can be possessed, or any of these activities can be engaged in, for very long by someone (S) unless S also possesses a fourth truth-seeking virtue, which is love of the truth.

Without a love of the truth – defined by William Wood as 'an interpretive stance in which we want all our judgments to be determined by objective reality instead of our own desires'[83] – we would soon chafe and rebel against the constraints that a sense of reality places on what we can do and what we can be. We would trade truth for power, reality for possibility. Without a love of the truth, we would not have the patience to give reality the kind of extended, open, and clear-minded attention that would allow us to grasp and understand that reality.[84] Without a love of the truth, we would be content to *think* that we had understood the truth, instead of questioning ourselves constantly to see whether we have *actually* understood the truth. And without a love of the truth, we would be swallowed up by an all-too-human love of ease and comfort, and *that* love would impel us to engage in various forms of self-deception and deception of others,[85] and to do whatever will make for the easiest, most comfortable life for us rather than making the effort – an effort that is often arduous, and sometimes dangerous – to be the kind of person we would like to be.

---

[81] For the concept of an 'ethical map', see McBride, *The Humanity of Private Law, Part I* (n 1), 22.

[82] Romans 7:15.

[83] Wood, *Blaise Pascal on Duplicity, Sin, and the Fall* (n 58), 216.

[84] Cf. Murdoch, *The Sovereignty of Good* (above, n 12), 65: 'The direction of attention is, contrary to nature, outward away from self which reduces all to a false unity, towards the great surprising variety of the world, and the ability so to direct attention is love.'

[85] Cf. Merton, *No Man is an Island* (above, n 17), 175: 'In the end the problem of sincerity is a problem of love. A sincere man is not so much one who sees the truth and manifests it as he sees it, but one who loves the truth with a pure love.' See also the story told about Bertrand Russell by Peter Geach (in his *Truth and Hope* (n 61), at 56). Provided with a 'proof' of an axiom in mathematics that had been written by a colleague who was dying, and seeing that the proof was invalid, Russell refused to tell his dying colleague the consoling lie that the proof was valid – 'logic was sacred for Russell: about logic he absolutely would not lie.'

Love of the truth, then, lies at the heart of someone's being able to engage in a quest to lead a truthful life. But, it might be wondered, where does this love come from, when it exists? Is it (a) something that is natural to human beings; or is it (b) something that depends on a kind of mental conditioning for it to exist?

If (b) is the case, then that would cast overwhelming doubt on the claims being made in this chapter that human flourishing consists in engaging in a quest to lead a truthful life. If such a quest cannot be engaged in without possessing a quality that is fundamentally alien to human beings, it can hardly be the case that engaging in that quest is the very essence of human flourishing.

Blaise Pascal seemed to support (b) when he said that, 'Man is … nothing but disguise, falsehood and hypocrisy, both in himself and with regard to others. He does not want to be told the truth. He avoids telling it to others, and all these tendencies, so remote from justice and reason, are naturally rooted in his heart.'[86] However, I think Pascal's 'nothing', in the above quotation, is too pessimistic. I would concede that it is obviously the case that anyone who had to choose between comfort and truth, or power and truth, would feel a tug towards choosing the first option in that pair of choices. However, as Aristotle observed, 'All men by nature desire to know'[87] and anyone presented with the above choices would recognise in their heart that the second option – truth – is not to be passed up lightly, if at all.

In further support of (a), we can observe that the love of truth caters for, and responds to, two human needs: (i) the need to be free; and (ii) the need to achieve union with something or someone outside of oneself. On (i), Bernard Williams instances Primo Levi as taking refuge in science and manual pursuits such as mountaineering as an antidote to the 'the filth of fascism which polluted the sky' in 1939.[88] Williams observes that what Levi needed was to spend his time on 'something in which the effort was not arbitrary, and in which the struggle was not one against another will. Science is, in game-theoretical terms, not a two-party game: what confronts the inquirer is not a rival will, and that is a key to the sense of freedom that it can offer.'[89] Williams continues:

> To be free, in the most basic, traditional, intelligible sense, is not to be subject to another's will. It does not consist of being free from all obstacles. On the contrary, freedom has any value only if there is something you want to do, and if, moreover, the want you have is not one that you can change at will for another want. A central form of freedom, then, is not to be subject to another's will in working toward something you find worthwhile.[90]

Levi achieved this kind of freedom in his scientific inquiries: 'The sense of freedom that Levi found in [those] inquiries was grounded in their truthfulness: the "dictates" of nature are not the product of anyone's power.'[91]

On (ii), the pursuit of truth takes one out of oneself – what David Foster Wallace calls the state of being 'lords of our tiny skull-sized kingdoms, alone at the center of creation'[92] – and

---

[86] Pascal, *Pensées* (n 40), [978]. A more down-to-earth way of making the same point is provided by a line in the film *The Big Short* (2015): 'The truth is like poetry – and most people f – king hate poetry' (supposedly overheard in a bar in Washington DC).

[87] This is the very first line of Aristotle's *Metaphysics*.

[88] Williams, *Truth and Truthfulness* (n 14), 144.

[89] Ibid, 144–45.

[90] Ibid, 145.

[91] Ibid, 146.

[92] Wallace, *This is Water* (n 48), 117.

connects one with reality. For example, in his autobiography, the great cellist Pablo Casals confided that

> For the past 80 years I have started each day in the same manner. It is not a mechanical routine but something essential to my daily life. I go to the piano, and I play two preludes and fugues of Bach. I cannot think of doing otherwise. It is a sort of benediction on the house. But that is not its only meaning for me. It is a re-discovery of the world of which I have the joy of being a part. It fills me with awareness of the wonder of life, with a feeling of the incredible marvel of being a human being.[93]

By contrast, someone who 'effectively views himself as the center of the universe … treats external objects and other people either as obstacles to his projects or as means of achieving them. He cannot see the world as it truly is …'[94] and is unable as a result to achieve any kind of union with those external objects (in the way, for example, that a pianist feels fused with the piano that he is playing, and the music that he is playing on the piano) or those other people (in the way, for example, that friends or lovers feel themselves united together). So someone for whom the truth means nothing is unable to achieve any kind of meaningful connection with the things and people around him. As Adrienne Rich observed, 'The liar leads an existence of unutterable loneliness'[95] and

> The possibilities that exist between two people, or among a group of people, are a kind of alchemy. They are among the most interesting things in life. The liar is someone who keeps losing sight of these possibilities. When relationships are determined by manipulation, by the need for control, they may possess a dreary, bickering kind of drama, but they cease to be interesting. They are repetitious; the shock of human possibilities has ceased to reverberate through them.[96]

So there is nothing unusual, or inhuman, about the love of truth. It is, instead, the lack of a love of truth that is unnatural in terms of the kind of existence that it leads to – an existence the nature of which was never better expressed than by O'Brien in George Orwell's *Nineteen Eighty Four* (1948): 'We are not interested in the good of others; we are interested solely in power, pure power. We are different from the oligarchies of the past in that we know what we are doing … We know that no one ever seizes power with the intention of relinquishing it. Power is not a means; it is an end … The object of power is power.'

## External Goods

Engaging in the quest to lead a truthful life therefore requires that one possess four truth-seeking virtues, of which the love of truth is the most important.[97] However, much more

---

[93] Quoted in Gaita, *A Common Humanity* (Prakash, 2004), 219.

[94] Wood, *Blaise Pascal on Duplicity, Sin, and the Fall* (n 58), 217.

[95] Rich, 'Women and Honor: Some Notes on Lying' in her *On Lies, Secrets, and Silence: Selected Prose* (WW Norton, 1995), 191.

[96] Ibid, 193.

[97] To these four we might add two more: (1) *faith* that the world is such that attention to it will be rewarded with insight, and that the raw materials (for example, knowledge we have inherited of various thick ethical concepts) which we will use in our quest are not completely useless; and (2) *hope* that we will make some progress in our quest towards the goal of actually living a truthful life. However, these are not as important as the four treated in detail in the text.

than just these virtues is needed for someone to be able to engage in the quest to lead a truthful life. As we have seen already, engaging in such a quest is made difficult or even impossible if one lives in a community where: (a) you are plagued by distractions that make focussing for any period of time very difficult; or (b) you are systematically misled about the nature of the world and your place in it; or (c) severe limits are placed on your freedom of speech or ability to associate with other people; or (d) you have to lie in order to survive or make a living.[98] So engaging in a quest to lead a truthful life requires that (1) you live in a community where none of (a)–(d) are true.

Other external goods that someone (S) needs to be able to take advantage of in order to engage in a quest to lead a truthful life are: (2) a reasonable level of health and income; (3) peace of mind; (4) the time and space to reflect on reality – what Josef Pieper called the enjoyment of *leisure*: 'the preserve of freedom, of education and culture, and of that undiminished humanity which views the world as a whole';[99] (5) friendship with others who are willing to engage in a shared quest with S to lead a truthful life; (6) work that allows S to exercise the five truth-seeking virtues listed above, where work is regarded as more or less valuable depending on how far it allows S to exercise those five truth-seeking virtues, and is regarded as of no value at all insofar as it does not allow S to exercise any of the five truth-seeking virtues to any great extent; (7) an education that enables S to engage with 'the best which has been thought and said in the world', as well as the best artistic achievements, where 'best' means that which allows us to 'see things as they are';[100] (8) an upbringing that (i) provided S with an understanding of a range of thick ethical concepts, thereby enabling S to make sense of the world and decide what to do, (ii) encouraged S to question that understanding and improve on it where improvement seems possible; (9) acquaintance with a number of moral exemplars (contemporary, historical, or fictional) who exemplify both the ability to navigate the ethical map created by the thick ethical concepts that S inherited, and the ability to question and improve on those concepts.

## Further Requirements?

In setting out the vision of human flourishing that we have been calling the RP, we found it necessary to make various modifications to the vision of human flourishing provided to us by John Finnis, which provided the basis for the RP. These modifications required us to say that someone (S) can only be said to be flourishing if:

(1)   S cares about her own flourishing;
(2)   S has at least one 'desire of the heart' – that is, there is something that S cares about that is not her own flourishing and is not something that anyone would have to care about in order to count as flourishing;
(3)   S identifies with the life she is leading;

---

[98] See pp 44–45.
[99] Pieper, *Leisure: The Basis of Culture* (Ignatius Press, 2009), 53.
[100] Arnold, *Culture and Anarchy*, revised ed (1875).

(4) S is able to participate in the good of creativity;
(5) S lives in a political community that is also an aretaic community, a community that is concerned to promote the flourishing of all its members.[101]

Do we also need to incorporate these requirements into the vision of human flourishing that is being set out in this chapter? It seems unlikely that we need to make any special accommodation for these requirements if we understand human flourishing as involving one's engaging in a quest to lead a truthful life. It seems very likely that all of these requirements will be *automatically* satisfied in the case of someone who is engaged in such a quest.

Taking requirement (1) first (that S care about her own flourishing), it is hard to imagine that S would not care about her own flourishing if she were engaged in a quest to lead a truthful life given that one of the postulates about human flourishing that we are assuming is true – (P3) – is that 'Human flourishing is a good thing, everywhere and anywhere it exists'. If S did not care about her own flourishing, she would have to deny that (P3) is true, when taking such a stance – basically endorsing a lie (that human flourishing is not a good thing) – would seem to be incompatible with her ambition to lead a truthful life.

Requirement (2) insists that S's flourishing depends on her caring about a particular project or cause that other people do *not* have to care about if we are to count *those* people as flourishing. If S were engaged in a quest to lead a truthful life, it is hard to imagine that she would not satisfy this requirement. This is for two reasons. First, some of the truth-seeking virtues listed above cannot be developed outside the pursuit of particular projects or causes. In particular, the virtue of *attention* cannot be developed unless one *absorbs* oneself in particular projects or causes that demand that we attend to reality if they are to be successfully pursued. Second, the love of truth that S will bring to her quest to lead a truthful life will lead her to focus on realising the truth in a particular field of activity or inquiry. This will require her to care about that field of activity or inquiry, but obviously other people will not have to care about *that* field of activity or inquiry for *them* to be counted as flourishing.

It is hard to imagine that requirement (3) – that S identify with the life she is leading – will not be satisfied if S is engaged in a quest to lead a truthful life. Obviously, S's quest will have its disappointments – in particular, S is very likely to fail to be true to herself (the self she would like to be) in many situations, and will on such occasions echo St Paul's lament over his own failures. But S will still identify with the most basic fact of her life, which is the quest that she is engaged on to come closer and closer to leading a truthful life. And S's identification with this fact of her life will be reinforced by the fact that if she is to succeed in her quest, it is important that she focus on the quest rather than its outcome.[102]

It might be thought that requirement (4) – that S participate in the good of creativity – creates the greatest tension between the five requirements being discussed here and the vision of human flourishing being set out in this chapter. Creativity is associated with fluidity and possibility, while truth is associated with fixity and the here and now. However, it is hard to imagine that the kind of work that counts as 'best' under the vision of human flourishing being advanced in this chapter – work that encourages the development and exercise of the five truth-seeking virtues set out above – will not be extremely creative in nature.[103]

---

[101] See McBride, *The Humanity of Private Law, Part I* (n 1), 86–107.
[102] See above, pp 42–43.
[103] Cf. Simone Weil's condemnations of mindless factory work: above, text at n 37.

For example, craftwork is generally regarded as involving a large amount of creativity; and yet, as Richard Sennett observes, 'craftsmanship focuses on objective standards, on the thing in itself'[104] and that one of the rewards 'craftsmanship holds out for attaining skill [is that] people are anchored in tangible reality.'[105]

The same point applies to a creative activity like writing poetry, of which Jane Hirshfield remarks:

> Every good poem begins in language awake to its own connections – language that hears itself and what is around it … and knows more perhaps than even we do about who we are, what we are. It begins, that is, in the mind and body of concentration. By concentration, I mean a particular state of awareness: penetrating, unified, and focused, yet also permeable and open.[106]

She goes on to observe that 'Great art is thought that has been concentrated …: honed and shaped by a silky attention brought to bear on the recalcitrant matter of earth and of life.'[107] The links that Sennett and Hirshfield trace here between creativity and truth-seeking would seem to lie in this: activity that is directed at producing something (such as a child's daubs) that *could be anything* is mindless and does not really count as creative activity at all. Only activity that is directed at producing something that, when it is produced, possesses an inner truth that compels us to acknowledge 'It could never be any other way'[108] truly counts as creative in nature.

Finally, when it comes to requirement (5) – that S live in a political community that is also an aretaic community, dedicated to fostering the flourishing of *all* its members – it seems very likely that if S did not live in such a community, it would be very difficult for S to engage in the quest to live a truthful life for a sustained period of time. If she lived in a community that actively inflicted undeserved suffering on some of its members, S would be unable to live with the knowledge of that suffering for very long without: (i) going into denial about what is happening; (ii) taking refuge in fantasies that the persecuted members deserve what is happening to them; (iii) protesting against what S's government is doing. Doing (i) or (ii) would involve S abandoning her quest to lead a truthful life, and doing (iii) would probably result in S being deprived of some of the external goods needed by her to continue in her quest to lead a truthful life.

And if S lived in a community in which it was a matter of sheer luck whether someone flourishes or not, S – one of the lucky ones whose circumstances have allowed S to flourish – might well end up concluding that it is not just a matter of luck that S flourishes while others do not, and that S is in some way superior to those who have not been as fortunate as her. The difficulty that holding such a belief would create for S's seeking to live a truthful life is obvious. It follows that if S wishes to engage in a quest to lead a truthful life, that quest can

---

[104] Sennett, *The Craftsman* (Allen Lane, 2008), 9.

[105] Ibid, 21.

[106] Hirshfield, 'Poetry and the Mind of Concentration' in her *Nine Gates: Entering the Mind of Poetry* (Harper Collins, 1998), 3.

[107] Ibid, 5.

[108] The last words on The Beatles' *Sgt. Pepper's Lonely Hearts Club Band* album (1967). Cf. the fourth movement of Beethoven's sixteenth string quartet (the last complete piece of music he composed), under the opening chords of which Beethoven wrote, 'Muss es sein?' ('Must it be?'), and under the main theme of which he wrote, 'Es muss sein!' ('It must be!'); and the story of Michelangelo's response when he was asked what he was sculpting as he hammered away at a block of marble: 'There is an angel inside this block and I am setting him free.'

only be engaged in with any realistic prospect of success within a political community that is dedicated to encouraging and enabling *all* of its members to engage in the same quest that S is embarked on.

If, then, we adopt the vision of human flourishing set out in this chapter, there is no need to qualify that vision by specifying that someone (S) who is flourishing according to this vision will only truly count as flourishing if requirements (1)–(5) are *also* satisfied in S's case. If S is engaged in a quest to lead a truthful life, requirements (1)–(5) will, in all likelihood, *already* be satisfied in S's case, and there is therefore no need to withhold judgement on whether S is flourishing as a human being. Knowing that S is engaged in a quest to lead a truthful life is enough – at least if the vision of human flourishing set out in this chapter is correct.

## Summary

The table below sets out the essential elements that will be true of someone who is engaged in a quest to lead a truthful life, and who is therefore flourishing according to the vision of human flourishing set out in this chapter.

| Body | Mind | Heart | Activities | External Circumstances |
|---|---|---|---|---|
| (1) Life and good health. | (2) A sense of reality. <br><br>(3) Ability to focus on reality. <br><br>(4) Clear-minded; free of distorting prejudices <br><br>(5) Openness to epiphany. <br><br>(6) Humble. <br><br>(7) Enjoys peace of mind. | (8) Love of truth. <br><br>(9) Love of particular fields of activity or inquiry that encourage development and exercise of truth-seeking virtues. | (10) Does work that places strong emphasis on developing and drawing on, sense of reality. <br><br>(11) Strives to be realistic in viewing world. <br><br>(12) Strives to be sincere in dealings with others. <br><br>(13) Strives to be true to oneself – the self one would like to be – in deciding what to do. | (14) Lives in community where (a) protected from distractions that would destroy or disrupt ability to focus on reality; (b) not systematically misled about nature of world or one's place in the world; (c) enjoy a great deal of latitude in terms of freedom of speech and freedom of association; (d) no one is compelled to lie in order to seeking live or make a living. <br><br>(15) Enjoys a reasonable level of income. <br><br>(16) Enjoys the kind of leisure needed to reflect on reality. |

Let's say that someone who lives the kind of life described above is 'QTL-ing', where 'QTL-ing' is the present participle of the verb 'to QTL', and where 'to QTL' is short for 'to be engaged in a quest to lead a truthful life'. The question we now have to address is whether QTL-ing is the key to human flourishing. Establishing *that* is the task of the final two sections of this chapter.

## 3. Compatibility with the Postulates

This section will set out the case for taking the view that human flourishing consists in engaging in a quest to lead a truthful life – what we are calling 'QTL-ing'.

Making out the case involves an uphill struggle. When we first discussed the nature of human flourishing, we identified two tests that we could use to clarify our views about the nature of human flourishing: (1) the *satisfaction test* – if S's life lacked X, or Y was present in S's life, would S still have reason to be satisfied about how his life was going?; (2) the *love test* – if you loved S, would it be important to you that X was present in S's life, or that Y was absent from S's life?[109] However, these tests are of limited usefulness in this context as we are so mired in the vision of human flourishing that we are calling the 'RP' that it is very likely that we would judge that a S who was QTL-ing did *not* have reason to be content with how his life is going, and that if we loved S it would be important to us that S's life be significantly different from the way it is at the moment. Against this, and as a way of opening up our mind to the possibility that human flourishing consists in QTL-ing, we could observe two points:

(1) *Aristotle*. Aristotle argued that a flourishing life would be (i) sufficient,[110] and (ii) involve the exercise of capacities that are distinctively human.[111] (i) is just another way of putting the satisfaction test, and for the reasons just given is of limited usefulness to us. It is because of (ii) that Aristotle dismissed the view that human flourishing could consist in physical flourishing, or a 'life of perception', as plants can physically flourish, and animals can see things.[112] Instead, Aristotle settled on 'an activity of the soul which follows or implies reason'[113] as the key to human flourishing as such an activity is unique to humans, and cannot be engaged in by plants or animals. However, (ii) is even more strongly true of QTL-ing, and, indeed, in the tenth and final book of his *Nicomachean Ethics*, Aristotle settled on the life of a 'man who is contemplating the truth' as involving a higher form of flourishing than the life of a man who performs various noble deeds through acting courageously or magnanimously, as a life of contemplation requires fewer means than a life of noble deeds.[114]

(2) *Finnis*. John Finnis' account of human flourishing – which provided the springboard for the vision of human flourishing that we have been calling the RP – rejects the view, which underlies Aristotle's (ii), that 'knowledge of human nature ... [allows us] to understand human ... flourishing.'[115] Rather, such an understanding comes from reflecting on 'intelligible objects of human willing and action, objects which are the intelligible goods (called 'values' in this book).'[116] It will be recalled that there are seven of these 'basic goods': life,

---

[109] See McBride, *The Humanity of Private Law, Part I* (n 1), 86–87.
[110] Aristotle, *Nicomachean Ethics*, I.7, 1097b6–20.
[111] Ibid, I.7, 1097b25.
[112] Ibid, I.7, 1097b32–1098a1.
[113] Ibid, I.7, 1098a6.
[114] Ibid, X.8.
[115] Finnis, *Natural Law and Natural Rights*, 2nd ed (OUP, 2011), 416.
[116] Ibid, 416.

knowledge, skilful play and work, friendship, practical reasonableness, marriage, and harmony with all reality.[117]

In reflecting on the 'objects of human willing and action', even people who make bad choices have something to teach us about the nature of human flourishing. This is because many of those bad choices *are* directed at achieving an intelligible human good, but are flawed in some way. For example, Finnis argues that selfishness or cruelty can often be explained on the basis that, in the case of selfishness, 'the pursuit of a value … or of a standard material means to sustaining a value … becomes locked into a pattern of exclusiveness or inversion – producing selfish indifference to the inclusive realization of that same value in the lives of others, and to the intrinsic value of sharing goods in friendship' and, in the case of cruelty, '[it] may be found to be an inverted form of pursuit of the value of freedom and self-determination and authenticity: some people may make themselves "feel real" to themselves by subjecting others to their utter mastery.'[118]

Joseph Raz points out that 'In their actions people and other living beings can be attracted to good options without recognizing their value. They may, for example, seek warmth, shelter, protection from predators, food and water, both for themselves and others, because they are, as we might say, "hard wired" to do so.'[119] Raz goes on to say that human beings, being rational, more often act for reasons – that is, they perform actions that are 'taken because the agents believed that they have some value.'[120] However, it might be that we are 'hard wired' to *believe* that the basic goods identified by Finnis as the characteristic objects of our choices have some value.

If we are so 'hard wired', then the idea that human flourishing consists in QTL-ing could explain why this is. This is because all of the basic goods identified by Finnis have their part to play in a life centred around QTL-ing. And if we *are* 'hard wired' to believe that the basic goods identified by Finnis are valuable, because of the contribution they can make to QTL-ing, this would also account for the fact that it is only *certain forms* of these goods that we recognise as being valuable. And when we reflect on *what* forms of (say) friendship, or marriage, or knowledge, or play, we regard as valuable, the 'right' forms seem strongly to correlate with their ability to contribute to one's QTL-ing. For example, attaining some degree of proficiency in chess is generally regarded as valuable; attaining the same degree of proficiency in playing Grand Theft Auto is not. Learning to read Russian is generally regarded as valuable;[121] learning *pi* to 1,000 decimal places is not. The sort of friendship that William Pitt and William Wilberforce enjoyed is generally regarded as valuable; the sort of friendship that Adolf Hitler and Albert Speer had is not.

So it might be that the raw data of observations about human choices that form the basis of Finnis' account of human flourishing in fact support the idea that human flourishing consists in QTL-ing.

However, points (1) and (2) can do no more than open our minds to the possibility that human flourishing consists in QTL-ing. For a more convincing case, we need to establish

---

[117] See the list in ibid, 448.

[118] Ibid, 91.

[119] Raz, 'Value: A Menu of Questions' in Keown and George (eds), *Reason, Morality, and Law: The Philosophy of John Finnis* (OUP, 2013), 14.

[120] Ibid.

[121] Iris Murdoch's example: Murdoch, *The Sovereignty of Good* (n 12), 87.

that the proposition that human flourishing consists in QTL-ing is compatible with our four postulates about human flourishing.

## The Tightrope: (P1) and (P2)

Our first two postulates state:

(P1)    Human flourishing is within the reach of any human being and is not something that can only be enjoyed by a privileged elite.

(P2)    Anyone's flourishing can be harmed by a wide range of different events.

As has already been observed, these two postulates put up a tightrope that any defensible vision of human flourishing has to cross without falling off.[122] If one's vision of human flourishing is too easily satisfied, then there is a danger that (P2) will be violated. If one's vision of human flourishing is too ambitiously demanding, then (P1) may well be violated. Is the idea that human flourishing consists in QTL-ing able successfully to cross this tightrope, while at the same time meeting what we have been calling *Gaita's Challenge* – the need to be able to say that *no* disability shuts someone out of flourishing as a human being, without at the same time trivialising and making light of human disabilities?[123]

Beginning with the (P1)–(P2) tightrope, I believe that the idea that human flourishing consists in QTL-ing is consistent with both (P1) and (P2). Josef Pieper claims that QTL-ing is consistent with (P1) when he points out that:

> Anybody can ponder human deeds and happenings and thus gaze into the unfathomable depths of destiny and history; anybody can get absorbed in the contemplation of a rose or human face and thus touch the mystery of creation; everybody, therefore, participates in the quest that has stirred the minds of the great philosophers since the beginning.[124]

And, as we have just seen,[125] one of the reasons Aristotle gave for thinking that a life of QTL-ing was a higher form of human flourishing than a life involving the performance of noble deeds was that a life of QTL-ing required far less by way of resources than a 'noble' life. So it is unlikely that the idea that human flourishing consists in QTL-ing will founder on the same rock as the idea that human flourishing consists in RP-flourishing did: that RP-flourishing requires such an investment and organisation of resources that it is hard to believe that a society could be arranged in such a way as to allow *all* of the members of that society to RP-flourish.[126]

At the same time, what is involved in QTL-ing is not so narrow that (P2) will not be true of QTL-ing. We can easily envisage a wide range of events, outside the control of a particular person S, which could or will impair S's ability to QTL. We have already seen that the kind of society S lives in will be crucial to S's being able to QTL so that, for example, if the state of that society is such that S will have to lie in order to save his life or make a living

---

[122] See above, p 9.
[123] See above, p 8.
[124] Pieper, *Only the Lover Sings: Art and Contemplation* (Ignatius Press, 2000), 24.
[125] See above, p 54.
[126] See above, pp 17–20.

then QTL-ing will be beyond S. It is also easy to see how the kind of events canvassed in the last chapter as being possibly disruptive of human flourishing under a Journey Model of flourishing[127] – someone's being physically injured, or the non-flourishing of a loved one – might result in someone's capacity to engage in a quest to lead a truthful life being damaged.

S's being physically injured automatically switches S's attention onto himself to a much greater extent than would otherwise normally be the case, and gives S every excuse he needs to indulge in the all-too-human proclivity of regarding himself as being 'the absolute center of the universe, the realest, most vivid and important person in existence.'[128] Similarly, if S and a loved one, T, are embarked on a joint quest to lead a truthful life, and T turns off from the quest, choosing instead to lead a life full of chemical highs – a life akin to that led by someone on Nozick's 'experience machine' – that choice of T's could have a number of negative ramifications for S's own ability to QTL. Deprived of the help of the partner with whom he was engaged in a quest to lead a truthful life, and the check that partner provided on S's judgements as to what leading a truthful life might involve, S might himself lose his way. And, as was suggested in the previous chapter,[129] S might have to abandon his quest for the time being if he is to go after T and try to persuade her to re-engage in that quest with him.

With these points made, let's now turn to *Gaita's Challenge*. Does the idea that human flourishing consists in QTL-ing allow us to say (as (P1) demands that we say) that S's suffering from very severe disabilities does *not* prevent S from flourishing without, however, falling into the trap of diminishing or making light of those disabilities?

Let's consider, first of all, Raimond Gaita's contention that people suffering from the kind of severe disabilities that he came across in his work on a hospital ward were incapable of flourishing as human beings.[130] If we adopt the view that human flourishing consists in QTL-ing, we can see that even very severe disabilities are not incompatible with someone's flourishing as a human being. This is because everyone, no matter how desperate their condition, is capable of reaching out to, and grasping, some truths about themselves and their place in the world. Gaita's own story demonstrates this point: the nun that he witnessed caring for the patients on his ward *bore witness* to him, the other people working on the ward, *and the patients that she was treating* 'that even such patients were ... the equals of those who wanted to help them.'[131] In what respect were they equals?

The work of Jean Vanier, the founder of the worldwide network of L'Arche communities for people suffering from intellectual disabilities, suggests that the answer is – we are all loveable, we are all loved, we all need to be loved, we all need to love. And this is a lesson that *everyone* who makes up a L'Arche community learns: not just those people suffering from disabilities who *stay* in those communities, but also the people who *work* in those communities:

> At L'Arche ... the main emphasis is on welcoming people, caring for them, working and living in community with people suffering from intellectual disabilities who form part of the community.

---

[127] See above, pp 27–28.

[128] Wallace, *This is Water* (n 48), 36. Cf. Mel Brooks' joke: 'Tragedy is when I cut my finger. Comedy is when you fall into an open sewer and die.' We laugh because we recognise ourselves in the joke.

[129] See above, p 28.

[130] See above, p 8.

[131] Gaita, *A Common Humanity: Thinking About Love and Truth and Justice* (Prakash, 2004), 18–19.

This kind of life, lived in communion with people who are weak, is the source of healing and liberation for assistants as much as for those with disabilities ... As we share the same table and become friends with people suffering from intellectual disabilities, people who have suffered marginalization, we achieve unity, reconciliation and peace. We grow in divine tenderness.[132]

So everyone is capable of QTL-ing: even the most disabled are capable of grasping (if they are treated in accordance with the truth about them) that they are loveable, and loved, and are capable of acknowledging their need to be loved, and their need to love.

However, that *if* in the previous sentence shows why saying that even the most severely disabled people are capable of flourishing as human beings does *not* involve diminishing or making light of those people's disabilities. People with disabilities become a lot more dependent on other people for their flourishing than people without disabilities; and that degree of dependency means that people with disabilities are a lot more vulnerable to having their flourishing radically impaired than people who do not suffer from such disabilities. Being treated by *Cain* as though you are worth nothing is easy to ignore if *Cain* is a stranger that you meet on the street; much harder to shrug off if you are disabled and unable to look after yourself and *Cain* is your primary care-giver who you have to see every day.[133] It is true, as both Jean Vanier and Stanley Hauerwas have observed,[134] that *not* suffering from any kind of disability can impair one's capacity to QTL as *Abel*'s lack of disability can encourage *Abel* to indulge fantasies of being completely independent and invulnerable; fantasies that both alienate *Abel* from his own reality, and distance him from other people. However, whatever the dangers for their ability to QTL that perfect health poses for someone,[135] they are surely dwarfed by the dangers that are posed by suffering disabilities that mean one's self-image and understanding of the world are almost wholly dependent on how one is treated by the people who are charged with looking after your needs.

So if we accept that human flourishing consists in QTL-ing, I think we can meet *Gaita's Challenge*. Identifying human flourishing with QTL-ing allows us to say that even someone suffering from the most devastating disabilities is capable of flourishing as a human being, without in any way ignoring or making light of the disadvantages that the existence of those disabilities pose for them in terms of their prospects for flourishing.

---

[132] Vanier, *The Heart of L'Arche* (SPCK, 2013), 53.

[133] Cf. the story told by Stanley Hauerwas in Hauerwas and Vanier, *Living Gently in a Violent World* (InterVarsity Press, 2008), at 53, of visiting a nursing home in Indiana and seeing 50 people in 'the day room. Their clothes were stripped off, and they were often sitting in their own feces. That place was designed, I'm afraid, to produce in visitors the reaction, "These people would be better off dead."

[134] Vanier, *The Heart of L'Arche* (n 132), 85: 'Human beings are attracted by success, wealth, power and the limelight ... They reject the ugly and poor. By climbing up the social ladder ... [they] lose a sense of human solidarity, and cut themselves off from the poor. This rejection reveals the shadows, the prejudices and the great poverty of their hearts. But if they can begin to forge links with those who are rejected, they will set out on the road towards freedom'; Hauerwas, *Suffering Presence* (Univ of Notre Dame Press, 1986), at 184, reflecting that the disabled 'scare us so much [because] they remind us that for all our pretension we are as helpless as they are when all is said and done. Like them, we depend on others for our lives and for the simple things to make life liveable. We prefer to keep our dependence hidden, however, as we are under the illusion that ... we are in control of our existence.'

[135] It is to be noted that in the table setting out the conditions for QTL-ing, we only required that someone who was QTL-ing enjoy a *reasonable* degree of health; and even that is not necessarily required, as our reflections on disability show.

## The Value of Human Flourishing: (P3)

With our first two postulates about the nature of human flourishing satisfied by the idea that human flourishing consists in QTL-ing, let's now turn to the third, which states that:

(P3) Human flourishing is a good thing, everywhere and anywhere it exists.

We cannot show that the view that human flourishing consists in QTL-ing is compatible with (P3) merely by observing what everyone would concede: that it is good *for* people not to lead their lives in a state of muddle or confusion.[136] (Even people who deny that human flourishing consists in QTL-ing would concede this – they would simply argue that this simply establishes that not being muddled or confused on certain matters is an *element* in someone's flourishing.) To establish that the view of human flourishing being advanced in this chapter is compatible with (P3), we have to show that if it *were* the case that human flourishing consists in QTL-ing, then a number of things would follow.

(1)  A universe in which human beings QTL is better than a universe in which no human beings (and no beings with capacities similar to human beings) QTL.
(2)  We all have reason to wish that all currently existing human beings QTL.
(3)  A couple who are capable of bringing a human being into the world have reason to do so (and we all have reason to wish that they do so) if that human being is likely to QTL.
(4)  We all have reason not to sacrifice the QTL-ing of a human being (whether currently existing or existing in the future) even if doing so is necessary to secure the flourishing of a non-human being.

Can we make such ambitious claims for QTL-ing? (P3) requires that we do. If we cannot, then (P3) requires us to give up the idea that human flourishing consists in QTL-ing and invites us to locate human flourishing in some other state or activity that *would* allow us to make claims analogous to claims (1)–(4).

Let's begin with (1), the most fundamental claim. Can we say that a universe in which human beings engage in a quest to lead a truthful life is better than a universe in which no human beings engage in such a quest? The Russian author and dissident Alexander Solzhenitsyn gestured at such a claim when he quoted the Russian proverb '*One word of*

---

[136] For such observations, see Frankfurt, *On Truth* (n 13), 51–52 ('When we are engaged in active life, or when we attempt to plan and to manage our various practical affairs, we are undertaking to cope with *reality* ... The outcome of our efforts – as well as the value to us of those outcomes – will depend, at least in part, on the properties of the real objects and events with which we are dealing ... Insofar as truths possess instrumental value, they do so because they capture and convey the nature of these realities'); Craig, *Knowledge and the State of Nature* (OUP, 1995), 11 ('Human beings need true beliefs about their environment, beliefs that can serve to guide their actions to a successful outcome') and 131–32 (observing of someone who forms correct beliefs about what is happening 'without the slightest need or wish to intervene' in what is happening: 'Since ... it is a matter of complete indifference to him [what is happening] ... there is ... no reason ... why he should prefer [his] beliefs [as to what is happening] to be true rather than false' – the implication being that as soon as he cares about what is happening, 'he must come to value true beliefs'); Lynch, *True to Life* (n 76), 48 ('the less accurate I am in my beliefs about just my immediate environment, the less likely I am to succeed in my goals – including my goal of surviving').

*truth outweighs the whole world*'[137] and went on to say that 'on such a fantastic breach of the law of conservation of mass and energy are based my own activities and my appeal to the writers of the world.'[138] Michael Gelven makes the same gesture when he imagines two friends looking up at the stars. One remarks on how the vastness of space makes him feel puny and insignificant. The other agrees, but then says, 'Yet, here we are, thinking about the vastness, and that just makes *us* matter somehow, maybe even more than the greatness of the expanse itself.'[139] How can we make sense of such 'fantastic' statements, which seem to suggest that seeking to lead a truthful life is so important and significant that the nature of the universe is fundamentally transformed, and for the better, by someone's undertaking this quest?

We can begin to make sense of these statements if we acknowledge three points. The first point was made by Albert Einstein: 'What is most incomprehensible about nature is the fact that it is comprehensible.'[140] It is possible to understand reality, where 'understanding reality' means, fundamentally, being able to explain why reality is the way it is. The second point is that – so far as we know – human beings are the only animals in the universe who have the capacity to understand reality; in other words, we are the only animals who have the ability to explain why reality is the way it is. The third point is that, as St Paul observed, 'we see through a glass, darkly'[141] – although we have the capacity to understand reality, we are not born with very much understanding of reality. So in order to understand reality, we have to grow and develop as human beings. We are like a key to a locked box that is located thousands of miles away. If the box is to be unlocked, a journey has to be undertaken. We QTL when we embark on the journey that has to be undertaken if we are to realise our capacity to understand reality.

None of the above considerations establish that a universe in which people QTL is better than a universe in which no one is embarked on a quest to lead a truthful life. However, they give us good reason to think that *something* important would be achieved by people embarking on such a quest, and that the universe would therefore be a better place for people's embarking on that kind of quest. To say that *nothing* of any significance could be achieved by people's embarking on a quest to lead a truthful life is to commit to the view that there is *no reason at all* why (i) reality is comprehensible, (ii) we are uniquely able to understand reality; but (iii) in order to understand reality we have to grow and develop as human beings. It seems unlikely that these three things are just a coincidence. As Ophelia Benson and Jeremy Stangroom observe, even if we are just 'jumped-up apes in clothes', that gives us

> all the more reason to try to figure out the cosmos this jumped-up ape evolved in. How interesting if natural physical processes produced not only stars and planets and rocks and trees but also

---

[137] Solzhenitsyn, *One Word of Truth: The Nobel Speech on Literature 1970* (The Bodley Head, 1972), 27 (emphasis in original).

[138] Ibid.

[139] Gelven, *What Happens To Us When We Think* (n 65), 59 (emphasis in original). Cf. Pascal, *Pensées* (n 40), [200]: 'Man is only a reed, the weakest in nature, but he is a thinking reed. There is no need for the whole universe to take up arms to crush him: a vapour, a drop of water is enough to kill him. But even if the universe were to crush him, man would still be nobler than his slayer, because he knows that he is dying and the advantage the universe has over him. The universe knows none of this. Thus all our dignity consists in thought. It is on thought that we must depend for our recovery, not on space and time, which we could never fill. Let us then strive to think well; that is the basic principle of morality.'

[140] Quoted in Pieper, *Josef Pieper: An Anthology* (Ignatius Press, 1989), 94.

[141] 1 Corinthians 13:12.

animals that can understand the laws of those very processes. What a good reason to try. In other words, that's one answer to the question, 'Why does truth matter?' It matters because we are the only species we know of that has the ability to find it out.[142]

*What* might be achieved by our embarking on the journey that we need to make in order to understand reality is as mysterious to us as the nature of reality is to those who have not attempted that journey. This mystery is linked to the fact that we cannot know what a truthful life would look like unless we undertake the quest to live such a life.[143] But we can be optimistic that something of significance will be achieved by making the journey.

It might be objected to this that if we found the key to a locked box that was located thousands of miles away, there might be a reason why the key and the box have ended up so far away from each other – unlocking the box might be dangerous.[144] However, were that the case, both the key and the box – and if not the box, certainly the key – would have been destroyed. The fact that we *exist* gives us hope that there is a good reason for us to exist, and that that good reason is located in our unique ability to understand reality, and what would be achieved were we to attempt to make use of that ability.

A further objection might be made: QTL-ing involves a lot more than just trying to understand reality. The truth-seeking virtue of seeking to achieve integrity in one's life requires that someone (S) attempt to be true to the kind of person she would like to be, which will be someone who does a good job of moving through the world as it is defined by the thick ethical concepts that S accepts as valid. How can S's attempting to be true to the kind of person she would like to be count as being of such significance that we could say that a universe where someone like S attempts to do this is a better place than a universe where no one attempts to do this?

Once again, three observations can be made here, very similar to the ones that were made above about understanding reality. First, the world presents itself to human beings as endowed with ethical significance, and the thick ethical concepts used by human beings to interpret the world and decide what to do purport to explain in what ways the world is ethically significant. Second, human beings seem to be the only animals capable of guiding their actions by reference to an ethical understanding of the world. Third, it does not come naturally to human beings to do this – they have to grow and develop as human beings in order to bring their actions into harmony with their ethical understanding of the world. QTL-ing involves embarking on the journey that has to be undertaken if that kind of harmony is to be achieved.

Once again, it seems unlikely that it is just a coincidence that: (i) the world presents itself to human beings as being ethically significant; (ii) human beings are the only animals that are able to guide their actions according to that understanding of the world; but (iii) in order to do this, we have to grow and develop as human beings. It seems unlikely, given the conjunction of (i), (ii) and (iii) that embarking on the journey that we need to make in order to bring our actions into harmony with our understanding of the ways in which the world is ethically significant serves *no purpose at all*. It is far more likely that *something* will be

---

[142] Benson and Stangroom, *Why Truth Matters* (Continuum, 2006), 162.

[143] See above, p 24.

[144] Cf. Genesis 3:22, where Adam and Eve are expelled from the Garden of Eden because if they were allowed to stay there, they might be tempted to eat from the tree of life, and become immortal.

achieved by our embarking on that journey – in other words, by our QTL-ing – that allows us to say that the universe is a better place for our embarking on that journey that it would be if no one attempted the trip. What that *something* might be, it is hard to say – though I will offer my speculation in the following chapter. We can only know for sure what it is by making the journey.

We can bring these points about the nature of QTL-ing together by saying that when we QTL, we are engaged on a journey that, when completed, will allow us both to understand reality and to act in harmony with reality, and that we have every reason to think that something of importance is achieved by the mere fact of our engaging in that journey – something of such importance that we can say that a universe in which human beings QTL is a better place than a universe in which no one QTLs. If this is correct, then the view that human flourishing consists in QTL-ing is consistent with claim (1).

But what about claims (2), (3) and (4)? These claims are all claims about *how much* QTL-ing is desirable, and they all agree that *as much QTL-ing as possible* is desirable. A universe in which 10,000 human beings QTL is better than a universe in which 100 people QTL; a universe in which five billion human beings QTL is better than a universe in which five million human beings QTL. Are these claims supportable? A couple of arguments may be made in support of them.

First, QTL-ing is impossible except in dialogue with other people[145] and within communities that foster the conditions necessary for QTL-ing to happen.[146] It follows that the prospect of any one person's QTL-ing is vastly increased the more people there are who QTL. So *if* claim (1) is correct – that a universe in which one person QTLs is better than a universe in which no one QTLs – then it would seem to follow that claims (2), (3) and (4) are correct, as QTL-ing most reliably goes on in a universe where as many people as possible QTL.

Second, if it is not an accident that there exist in the universe beings who are capable of understanding, and acting in harmony with, reality, it also seems unlikely that it is not an accident that *all* human beings – not just a subset of the class of human beings – have the capacity to understand, and act in harmony, with reality. If this is not an accident, it seems there is some significance attached to as many human beings as possible undertaking the journey that they have to undertake if they are to understand, and act in harmony, with reality – in other words, it seems there is some significance attached to as many human beings as possible QTL-ing. If this is right, then claims (2), (3) and (4) would seem to be made out.

## The Continuity of Human Flourishing: (P4)

If the view that human flourishing consists in QTL-ing is consistent with our first three postulates about human flourishing, what about our fourth postulate:

(P4) Human flourishing is self-sustaining across time and across persons.

---

[145] See above, p 42.
[146] See above, pp 34, 36, 38, 45, 50, 52–53.

We have already seen that (P4) rests on a number of different claims about human flourishing, all of which have to be true for (P4) to be true. *First*: someone who is flourishing does not feel suicidal, and seeks to ensure that he or she will continue to flourish in the future. *Second*: someone who is flourishing will seek to contribute to the flourishing of other people generally (both people who currently exist and people who will exist in the future), and not just people that he or she cares about. *Third*: someone who is flourishing regards the continued existence of the aretaic community that fostered his or her own flourishing, and the continued existence of aretaic communities generally, as more important than his or her continued flourishing.

It is easy to see how the view that human flourishing consists in QTL-ing is consistent with all of these claims about human flourishing. This is because of the crucial importance of having a love of the truth for someone's being able to QTL.[147] As a result, someone who QTLs will be motivated: (i) to continue on with his journey to lead a truthful life for as long as possible; (ii) to contribute to the QTL-ing of other people generally; and (iii) to support the existence of communities that foster QTL-ing. So if human flourishing *does* consist in QTL-ing, all of the three claims that underpin (P4) will be true.

It might be objected that any community that is dominated by a concern to foster QTL-ing is doomed to collapse very quickly: a community made up of people who are simply concerned with understanding reality cannot last very long when so many practical tasks need to be performed for a community to sustain itself for very long. However, this objection is based on a misconception as to how many different professions and lines of work are consistent with someone's QTL-ing. As Antonin Sertillanges observes,

> A country priest who devotes himself to his parishioners, a doctor who turns away from study to give help in urgent cases, a young man of good family who adopts a calling to help his people and in doing so has to turn his back on liberal studies, are not profaning the gift that is in them, they are paying homage to the True … If they acted otherwise they would offend truth no less than virtue, since, indirectly, they would be setting living truth at variance with itself.[148]

Bernard Williams raises another possible objection to the view that (P4) is consistent with the view that human flourishing consists in QTL-ing. He observes that 'The search for an authentic life is always questionable, and it is not a secret that it can lead to ethical and social disaster.'[149] Williams identifies a number of different reasons why this is:

(1) there is no guarantee that what amounts to a truthful life for me is compatible with what amounts to a truthful life for you;[150]
(2) someone (S) who is engaged in a search to live an authentic life has the potential to be unsteady and unreliable in his dealings with others as he searches for the truth about himself among an ever-changing set of 'conflicting moods and short-term feelings',[151] and feels ever-greater 'hypocrisy, frustration, and bitterness'[152] when society, in an attempt at self-preservation, attempts to make him more 'steady';

---

[147] See above, pp 47–8.
[148] Sertillanges, *The Intellectual Life* (n 35), 26.
[149] Williams, *Truth and Truthfulness* (n 14), 205.
[150] Ibid, 183: 'however authenticity is expressed as an ideal, it is clear that its demands will not necessarily coincide with the demands of anyone else, or of anyone else's authenticity.'
[151] Ibid, 178.
[152] Ibid, 200.

(3) S will also be particularly prone to 'wishful thinking and self-deception';[153] for exam-
    ple, he may optimistically identify his authentic self with someone who is 'basically
    benevolent and well-disposed toward others'[154] and as a result condemn others who
    have, perhaps, a shrewder perception of S's personality as 'wicked, members of an evil
    conspiracy'[155] bent on defaming S.

Taking these points in reverse, it would seem that the cure for (3) is more QTL-ing – in
particular, the cultivation of the truth-seeking virtue of humility – and not the abandon-
ment of the quest to lead a truthful life. As far as (2) is concerned, Williams' model of the
'unsteady' self that is created by the attempt to lead an authentic life is *Lui* ('Him'), one of
the participants in Denis Diderot's 1774 dialogue *Rameau's Nephew*. However, *Lui* does not
seem a particularly good model of QTL-ing; there seems no reason why someone who *is*
QTL-ing should not be able to acknowledge the need to be steady and reliable in his dealings with others – to deny *that* would seem to involve one in denying an obvious truth,
and thereby endanger one's status as someone who is QTL-ing. Finally, point (1) seems to
overlook the point made above about the range of different professions and lines of work
that are compatible with someone's QTL-ing. Given this, it is hard to imagine that a community could *not* exist where every member of that community's QTL-ing was consistent with
everyone else's QTL-ing.

A final point can be made in favour of the compatibility of the view that human flourishing consists in QTL-ing with (P4)'s being true. Two of the institutions that have enjoyed
the longest continuous existence in the UK are the church, and the universities. Both those
institutions have, until lately, drawn their lifeblood from a love of the truth. That these two
things – these institutions' centuries-long existence, and their love of the truth – are *not*
connected is hard to imagine. The connection between the two is underscored when one
reflects that if these institutions are now rotting from within, their decision in the second
half of the twentieth century to give up on the pursuit and the love of truth – in the case
of church, in favour of 'moralistic therapeutic deism'[156] (seeing religion as an aid to feeling good about oneself and an encouragement to be nice to others), and in the case of the
universities, in favour of adopting an ironic, playful stance towards all truth-claims[157] –
seems likely to have something to do with their decline.

## Summary

This concludes the case made in this chapter *for* thinking that human flourishing consists in
QTL-ing. This view of human flourishing is not only plausible – in that it identifies human

---

[153] Ibid, 205.

[154] Ibid, 179 (instancing the example of Jean-Jacques Rousseau).

[155] Ibid, 180.

[156] See Smith and Denton, *Soul Searching: The Religious and Spiritual Lives of American Teenagers* (OUP, 2005).

[157] See, in particular, Rorty, *Contingency, Irony, and Solidarity* (CUP, 1991). For an attack on the adoption of such a
stance in the realm of the sciences, see Sokal, *Beyond the Hoax: Science, Philosophy and Culture* (OUP, 2008) (which
book carries the following lines (by Violeta Parra) after the title page: 'I do not play the guitar / for applause. / I sing
of the difference / between what is true and false. / Otherwise I do not sing').

flourishing with the exercise of capacities that are unique to human beings – but it is also consistent with all of our postulates about human flourishing. In the absence of any other account of human flourishing that does as good a job of being plausible and being consistent with our four postulates, we have every reason to endorse the view that human flourishing consists in QTL-ing. Despite this, objections can and have been made to this view. The final section of this chapter is devoted to those objections.

# 4.  Three Objections

Three objections can be, and have been, made to the position on human flourishing that has been taken in this chapter.

The first objection is that acknowledging the truth can make someone's (S's) life go worse. If this is true, then this would seem to undermine the view that human flourishing consists in QTL-ing, as it is hard to see on that view how acknowledging the truth could damage someone's flourishing as a human being.

The second objection is the flipside of the first – it argues that believing a lie can sometimes make S's life go better. This point, if made out, again seems to undermine the view that human flourishing consists in QTL-ing.

The third objection relies on a weaker claim than the second. The third objection observes that causing someone to live a lie (as in the case where S thinks she is happily married to a husband who is actually having a long-term affair with someone else) may not harm S's flourishing as a human being. Whether it does or not depends on how S would feel about the truth were it finally to be revealed. This argument seems inconsistent with the idea that human flourishing consists in QTL-ing, as that view would tend to indicate that being caused to live a lie automatically prevents one from QTL-ing, and therefore flourishing as a human being.

Let's now consider each of these objections in turn.

## The Harmfulness of Truth

In his book *How Should We Live?* John Kekes attacks 'ideal theories' of how we should live that set out 'an ideal that guides how everyone, always, everywhere should live.'[158] The last substantive chapter in the book is devoted to attacking the idea that truthfulness lies at the heart of human flourishing. While recognising 'the importance of truthfulness', he argues that 'there are also other important ideals that often conflict with truthfulness, and it is not a requirement of reason that such conflicts always be resolved in favour of truthfulness.'[159] In order to make this claim out, Kekes presents us with a sketch of someone he calls the 'Betrayed Woman'.[160]

---

[158] Kekes, *How Should We Live? A Practical Approach to Everyday Morality* (Univ of Chicago Press, 2014), 1.
[159] Ibid, 192.
[160] Ibid, 193.

The Betrayed Woman (let's call her 'Medea') abandoned what was quite a low-level career to marry and raise two children that she had with her husband. While the children were still young, Medea's husband had an affair, and instituted divorce proceedings against Medea so that he could live with 'his newfound lover'. The divorce left Medea alone to raise her two children – who also felt betrayed by their father's conduct – on an income that is barely enough to support the three of them. Medea is now approaching middle age, and her employment history and her children's needs are such that it is 'very difficult for her to get a decent, well-enough-paying job.' Medea is filled with rage at her situation, and her rage causes her to develop a violent temper and feelings of bitterness towards everyone, including her children. Life in the family home soon enters a downward spiral involving her becoming neglectful of everything, with the result that she feels even greater rage and despair about her situation.

Trying to face up to things, Medea realises that she has two options. She can 'continue to be truthful as she can about her condition and accept that there is no realistic prospect of improvement, that her rage is justified, and that she can only live on miserably one day at a time, without self-deception, false hopes, and the unwarranted expectation of a miracle.'[161] Or she can 'stop dwelling on the truth of her condition' and seek to improve things for herself by 'acting as if she were what she is not, namely, confident, in control of her life, courageously facing the odds against her, cheerful in the face of her misfortune, controlling her feelings, and doing what an admirable person that she is not would do if that person were in her ghastly condition.'[162] Kekes recommends that Medea take the second option, which requires her to 'ignore the truth about what she is in order to focus on becoming what she knows she is not.'[163]

What does the view that human flourishing consists in QTL-ing have to say about this situation? First, this view does a good job of diagnosing what Medea's problem is. Medea is not enjoying a flourishing existence because she lacks *integrity*, in the sense that she feels alienated from herself: she would like to be a person who is confident and in control of her life, but she is aware she is not. But worse, from the point of view of Medea's QTL-ing, she cannot see a way in which she can strive to become more integrated as a person. It is this sense of being blocked from being the kind of person she would like to be that is at the root of Medea's problems.

Second, in terms of diagnosing a solution for Medea's problems, Kekes' solution – just *be* who you want to be – seems heartless in that it ignores the fact that Medea *cannot* be the kind of person she wants to be. Kekes might say, 'That's precisely the point – if Medea is to feel better about her situation, she has to ignore the facts of her situation.' However ignoring the truth in this way is likely to bring about a further, and more devastating collapse, when reality intrudes into the fantasy world that Kekes is recommending Medea constructs for herself. A more promising way forward would be to invite Medea to think again about what sort of person she wants to be.

At the moment, Medea wants to be confident and in control of her life because the thick ethical concepts that dominate our culture attach a high degree of ethical significance to

---

[161] Ibid, 194.
[162] Ibid, 194–95.
[163] Ibid, 195.

those kinds of qualities. However, by choosing to give up her career in favour of getting married and raising children, Medea actually turned her back on the ideal of being in control of her life earlier on in her life, and aspired instead to be someone whose life was characterised by such qualities as trust, dependence, vulnerability, and responsibility. Now that the support that was provided for that life has been ripped out from under her, it is not surprising that Medea should abandon her aspiration to be the kind of person she wanted to be when she got married, and should seek instead to be someone who is completely self-sufficient and in control of her life – and should rage against the fact that her earlier choices mean that it is now not possible for her to be that kind of person.

If Medea is to flourish again, she needs to find a way of wanting to be the kind of person she *can* be given her situation, which is the kind of person she wanted to be when she got married. She needs to remind herself of what it was that attracted her to being that kind of person, and realise that that attraction still remains – her husband's betrayal does not mean that being someone whose life is all about trust, dependence, vulnerability, and responsibility is no longer the right choice for her. It may be that it is impossible for her to do this. If so, then it will not be possible for Medea to flourish (absent some unexpected change in her fortunes that allows her to achieve a position of self-sufficiency and control). But it may be that Medea will be able, as she did once before, to turn her back on the ideals of control and self-sufficiency and aspire to be someone who embraces vulnerability and the need to depend on others, while having others depend on her. So there is nothing in the situation presented by Kekes which seriously challenges the idea that human flourishing consists in QTL-ing; in fact, Kekes' hypothetical shows us that this view of human flourishing helps us to understand why we are not flourishing when we are not, and how we might achieve a flourishing existence.

## The Benefits of Lies

The first objection to the idea that human flourishing consists in QTL-ing argues that certain truths can be damaging to our flourishing and should therefore be avoided. The second objection argues that certain lies can actually promote our flourishing. So Alasdair MacIntyre observes, quoting from Albert O Hirschman's *Development Projects Observed*:[164]

> False beliefs are sometimes useful. Albert O Hirschman has argued compellingly, for example, that because we underestimate our own creativity, 'it is desirable that we underestimate to a roughly similar extent the difficulties of the tasks we face, so as to be tricked … into undertaking tasks that we can, but otherwise would not dare, tackle.'[165]

A real-life example of the supposed benefit of lies (or, at least, untruths) is provided by Steve Jobs, the co-founder of Apple Computer and the man responsible for Apple's revival from 1997 onwards into becoming the most valuable company in the world. Jobs' biographer,

---

[164] Hirschman, *Development Projects Observed* (Brookings Institute, 1967), at 83.

[165] MacIntyre, 'Truth As a Good: A Reflection on *Fides et Ratio*' in his *The Tasks of Philosophy: Selected Essays Volume 1* (CUP, 2006), 203. Cf. Lynch, *True to Life* (n 76), at 114, giving the example of a 'naïve mountain climber, whose false belief that the summit is attainable helps him get further up the slope than he might have otherwise been able to'.

Walter Isaacson, quotes a number of people who worked with Jobs as saying that Jobs would create a 'reality distortion field' where he would set people goals that would, to them, seem impossible to meet.[166] However, Jobs' insistence that the goals could be met overpowered his co-workers' disbelief, with the result that the 'impossible' goals were actually met. Steve Wozniak, the other founder of Apple Computer, is quoted by Isaacson as saying of Jobs, 'His reality distortion is when he has an illogical vision of the future, such as telling me that I could design the Breakout game in just a few days. You realise that it can't be true, but he somehow makes it true.'[167]

Do these examples show that 'surrounding ourselves with fantasy' can be beneficial? Two points can be made. First, where there is evidence that we suffer from an in-built cognitive bias in our thinking – of the type first explored by the behavioural scientists Daniel Kahneman and Amos Tversky[168] – there is no violation of truth involved in adopting a particular procedure to correct for that bias, so as to ensure that we are looking at things clearly.

For example, someone (S) who suffers from severe low-esteem is very likely to interpret other people's actions in a way that reinforces their low self-estimation: for instance, a colleague's walking past S without saying 'Hello' is very likely to be interpreted as a deliberate snub. In order to get closer to the truth of what other people think of him, S would be well-advised to adopt a rule that he will interpret other people's actions in the most optimistic way possible, even if that will sometimes result in S thinking that his colleague didn't say 'Hello' because he was too busy to talk when a deliberate snub *was* intended. If we do suffer from a cognitive bias that causes us to underestimate our creativity, then adopting something like Hirschman's correction for that bias would seem sensible, in order to get a correct view of the underlying truth of whether or not a particular project should be undertaken. Similarly, if Steve Jobs had been aware of this cognitive bias among his colleagues, it would have been sensible for him to adopt a rule that 'find out how long my colleagues think it will take to do a job and then insist in the face of anything they might say that they can do it in half the time' on the basis that his co-workers had an in-built tendency to underestimate their own abilities.

Second, where there is *no* evidence that we suffer from an in-built cognitive bias in our thinking, adopting false beliefs is extremely dangerous and liable to result in disaster. A mountain climber who – on the brink of exhaustion – encourages himself to keep going by telling himself 'the summit's only a few feet away' when in fact he cannot see the summit, may well end up dying on the mountain. And Steve Jobs' very patchy business record from 1980 to the mid-1990s may have been largely due to his tendency to be *too* optimistic in his beliefs as to what he and his co-workers were capable of doing.[169]

---

[166] See Isaacson, *Steve Jobs: The Exclusive Biography* (Little, Brown, 2011), chapter 11.

[167] Ibid, 107–08.

[168] See, generally, Kahneman, *Thinking, Fast and Slow* (Penguin, 2012).

[169] Cf. Schlender and Tetzeli, *Becoming Steve Jobs: The Evolution of a Reckless Upstart Into a Visionary Leader* (Sceptre, 2015). *Becoming Steve Jobs* describes how Jobs' business failures and the lessons he learned from them were essential to his later success. The authors observe (at 11) that the image of Steve Jobs as generating a 'reality distortion field' does not correspond with their personal experiences of what Jobs was like. It may be that by the time Jobs reassumed control of Apple, he had realised that generating reality distortion fields for his co-workers did more harm than good.

So adopting what seem like false beliefs only tends to be helpful when they either turn out to be true, or help us understand a deeper reality. So the helpfulness of adopting what seem like false beliefs does not bring into question the claim that human flourishing consists in QTL-ing.

## The Harmlessness of Lies

The third objection argues that while deceiving someone about their life may not be beneficial, it is not necessarily harmful either – as the view of human flourishing advanced in this chapter suggests it must be. Wayne Sumner discusses at length the example of a 'woman who for months or years has believed in, and relied on, the devotion of a faithless and self-serving partner.'[170]

Sumner – who shares Kekes' hostility to theories of human flourishing that would seek to determine for everyone what they have to do in order to flourish as human beings – argues that saying that the woman in his example (call her 'Penelope') is not flourishing while she is with her partner because 'any happiness based on illusion can make no intrinsic contribution to our well-being' is 'presumptuously dogmatic'.[171] Instead it should be up to Penelope to decide whether her partner's lies mean that her life is not going well. If her reaction to being told that her partner is consistently cheating on her would be to say, 'I thought everything was going so well, but now I can see that it was all a farce'[172] then we would conclude that Penelope's life is not going well, and that she is not therefore flourishing as a human being. However, if Penelope's reaction would be to say, '*c'est la vie*; at least he was charming and we had a lot of fun'[173] then we should not take into account the fact that Penelope's fun is based on a lie in determining how far we can say that Penelope is flourishing as a human being: if Penelope's partner's lies don't matter to Penelope, why should they matter to us?

Sumner's example assumes that the *only* thing that would prevent us from saying that Penelope is flourishing as a human being while she is with her partner is the fact that he is systematically lying to her about the nature of their relationship. However, if Penelope would react to the news of her partner's lies by saying '*c'est la vie ...*' then – on the view of human flourishing being advanced in this chapter – Penelope's partner's lies are *not* the only thing that should prevent us from saying that Penelope is flourishing as a human being. Penelope's hypothetical reaction shows that Penelope is not interested in leading a truthful life, but instead identifies her flourishing with having fun. It is *that* fact about Penelope, rather than the fact that her partner is lying to her, that should result in our saying that Penelope is not flourishing as a human being.

It follows that Sumner's example cannot touch the claims made in this chapter. If Penelope's partner's lies mean nothing to Penelope – at least compared with the memory of how their times together made her feel – then that shows she is not flourishing, according to the conception of human flourishing advanced in this chapter. And if Penelope's partner's lies make her feel like her time with him has been utterly wasted, the view that human

---

[170] Sumner, *Welfare, Happiness, and Ethics* (n 6), 156.
[171] Ibid, 159.
[172] Ibid, 160.
[173] Ibid, 161.

flourishing consists in QTL-ing explains why this is so – while Penelope has been with her partner, she has been living a lie and has not got anywhere near the goal of leading a truthful life.

By contrast, Sumner's theory of human flourishing would *not* say that Penelope is *right* to feel that her partner's lies mean that she has wasted her time with him; as Sumner observes, using italics to emphasise his words, '*there is no right answer to the question of what [Penelope's] reaction should be.*'[174] Penelope would probably disagree. She does not *just* feel that her time with her partner has been a waste. She has a *reason* for thinking that her time with her partner has been a waste. Her reason for thinking this is that she takes the view that a life based on a lie is not a flourishing one. The argument of this chapter has been that she is not wrong to take this view. Human flourishing, this chapter has claimed, consists in someone's being engaged in a quest to lead a truthful life and being made to live a life based on a lie makes engaging in such a quest impossible.

## Into the Deep

With this third objection to the view that human flourishing consists in QTL-ing despatched, it might be thought nothing more can be said in favour of this view. However, if truth is deep,[175] then so must be the truth about the nature of human flourishing. And so it proves. Part I of *The Humanity of Private Law* ended with the observation that (i) what is distinctive about human beings is that they are aware (or are capable of being aware) that they participate in Being.[176] The following chapter will reflect on whether proposition (i) supports or undermines the proposition that (ii) human flourishing consists in QTL-ing. In arguing that (i) supports (ii), we will achieve a much deeper understanding of the nature of human flourishing than we have been provided so far by the observations made in this chapter about the nature of QTL-ing.

---

[174] Ibid, 159.
[175] See above, pp 26, 41.
[176] McBride, *The Humanity of Private Law, Part I* (n 1), 265.

# 10

## The Approach of Being

We have already seen that John Finnis was unwilling to reach conclusions about the nature of human flourishing from propositions about human nature.[1] However, it would be strange if there were no link between our flourishing and our nature. It is that link I propose to explore in this chapter, taking as my starting point the end point of Part I of this project, where we arrived at the conclusion that human beings are 'the beings who are aware (or are capable of being aware) that [they] participate in Being.'[2] If we can show that such a view of human nature supports the view that human flourishing consists in engaging in a quest to lead a truthful life (or QTL-ing, for short), then the arguments in the previous chapters in favour of that view are considerably strengthened.

At first sight, the prospects seem to run strongly the other way – it might be thought that taking the view that human beings are aware[3] that they participate in Being is *in*compatible with either (i) the view that there is such a thing as human flourishing; or (ii) the view that human flourishing consists in QTL-ing. This is for two reasons.

First, as we will rehearse below, we arrived at this view of human nature at the end of Part I by relying on Arthur Schopenhauer's amendments of Kant's picture of reality. Schopenhauer concluded that reality as it really is – as opposed to reality as it appears to us – was undifferentiated. We called this undifferentiated reality 'Being', but Schopenhauer called it 'Will' because he, pessimistically, saw this undifferentiated reality as consisting in a blind, destructive *force*. On this view of reality, the nature of the universe we are living in seems to make human flourishing unimaginable: 'As flies to wanton boys are we to the gods. They kill us for their sport.'[4] But *if* flourishing is possible in such a dark universe, it certainly cannot be achieved through *truthfulness*, but rather by averting one's eyes from the surrounding darkness and taking refuge in fantasies that make life halfway tolerable.[5]

Second, far and away the greatest philosopher of Being in the twentieth century – and perhaps of all time – was Martin Heidegger. As a result, we will have reason to make substantial reference to Heidegger's thinking about Being below. However, there is something amoral about Heidegger's view of Being that makes it strongly akin to the capricious

---

[1] See above, p 54, n 115.

[2] McBride, *The Humanity of Private Law, Part I: Explanation* (Hart Publishing, 2018), 265.

[3] From now on, to save words, I will drop the qualifier '(or are capable of being aware)' – only reintroducing it when it is necessary to do so. But the qualifier should always be read as being present, even when absent.

[4] *King Lear*, Act IV, Scene 1.

[5] See Williams, *Truth and Truthfulness* (Princeton UP, 2010), 268: 'there are very compelling true accounts of the world that could lead anyone to despair who did not hate humanity' and remarking of the death of Kurtz in *Heart of Darkness* (1899), whispering 'The horror!', that the 'truth, the one that Kurtz saw at the last moment of his life, is not one that left to itself could keep anyone alive.' See also Murdoch, *Metaphysics as a Guide to Morals* (Chatto & Windus, 1992), 498: 'Someone may say, if you are always noticing images of God or Good or seeing spiritual ladders ... you are very lucky. Your view of spiritual refreshment as everywhere available is ridiculously optimistic, even sentimental. It seems to neglect how miserable we are, and also how wicked we are. The average inhabitant of the planet is probably without hope and starving. It is terrible to be human. It is *deinos*.'

Will that Schopenhauer saw as underlying the world. This led Iris Murdoch to condemn Heidegger's late, and most developed, thinking about Being as 'essentially demonic'.[6] She went on to observe that 'in the thinking of late Heidegger [Being] becomes a sinister historicised Fate, a posited entity about whose future "structure" or "intentions" we may speculate. (A player of games.)'.[7]

The amorality[8] of Heidegger's thinking about Being will surprise no one who is aware of Heidegger's willingness to treat with the Nazi regime in its early years in power in Germany, or the fact that he remained a member of the Nazi Party until the end of World War II.[9] But it should also provoke a worry that thinking of human beings as beings that are aware that they participate in Being will result in a vision of human flourishing that we cannot accept because it will be fundamentally amoral in nature. Such a vision would be incompatible with our third postulate about human flourishing – that 'Human flourishing is a *good* thing, every-where and anywhere that it exists.' An amoral vision of human flourishing could not satisfy that third postulate, and if that is what we are provided with by the above view of what it is to be human, then that view tends to indicate that there is no such thing as human flourishing.

Given these two points, the view that human beings are beings that are aware that they participate in Being will only support the view that human flourishing consists in QTL-ing if we can come up with a plausible account of Being that is not affected by Schopenhauer's pessimism or Heidegger's amorality. That is the task that will occupy the next section of this chapter.

# 1.  Being and Beings

## Lumpers and Splitters

As in other fields of inquiry, we can divide up thinkers about being into Lumpers and Splitters.[10] The world presents itself to us as split – as composed of an infinite variety of

---

[6] Ibid, 456. Murdoch included Nietzsche in this condemnation, and Nietzsche's philosophy was itself strongly influenced by Schopenhauer.

[7] Ibid, 471. See also 71 (and 75–76), accusing Schopenhauer and Heidegger of viewing life as 'a game and a jest' with the result that 'We live with the sense of hopeless, ruthless contingency, we are victims of chance.'

[8] William Barrett – no critic of Heidegger's – remarked of Heidegger's *Being and Time* (1927) that 'to attempt to read *Being and Time* as a phenomenology of the moral consciousness is to produce something grotesque and monstrous' (Barrett, *The Illusion of Technique* (Anchor Books, 1979), 274). Heidegger's attempt to interpret Aristotle's *Nicomachean Ethics* as anticipating his own philosophy of Being is completely demolished by Gonzalez, 'Beyond or beneath good and evil? Heidegger's purification of Aristotle's Ethics' in Hyland and Manoussakis (eds), *Heidegger and the Greeks* (Indiana UP, 2006). Gonzalez's critique culminates in the devastating observation that 'we have in Heidegger's reading of Aristotle's *Ethics* probably the most thorough distortion and misinterpretation of a Greek text in the history of philology.' As Gonzalez notes, his analysis puts in question Lawrence Hatab's attempt in *Ethics and Finitude: Heideggerian Contributions to Moral Philosophy* (Rowman & Littlefield, 2000) to construct an Heideggerian ethics, particularly where he does so (in chapter 4) by invoking Aristotle's ethics as a predecessor to Heidegger's.

[9] On which, see Ott, *Martin Heidegger: A Political Life* (Fontana Press, 1994); and Gessmann, 'Heidegger and National Socialism: He Meant What He Said' in Mitchell and Trawny (eds), *Heidegger's Black Notebooks: Responses to Anti-Semitism* (Columbia UP, 2017).

[10] The distinction was first drawn by Charles Darwin, in relation to the categorisation of organisms: lumpers would tend to see different organisms as belonging to the same species, while splitters would adopt a more cautious approach.

distinct beings, all the way down to the sub-atomic level. However, appearances can obviously be deceiving: just because appearances lead us to believe that $x$ is true, that does not necessarily mean that $x$ is actually true. A *Naïve Splitter* argues that when it comes to the world, we have no reason to think that its appearances are deceiving.[11] The fact that the world appears to be split gives us every reason to think that the world *is* actually split. On the other hand, a *Non-Naïve Splitter* thinks that there is an important distinction between the way the world appears to us and the way the world actually is: we cannot transcend the way we experience the world and penetrate to the reality of the way the world actually is. Despite this, the *Non-Naïve Splitter* maintains that the world as it actually is – the 'real' world – *is* split, so there is some correspondence between the way we experience the world and the way the world actually is. A *Lumper* agrees with the distinction that the *Non-Naïve Splitter* makes between the world as it appears to us and the world as it actually is, but maintains that the 'real' world – the world as it actually is – is not split, but One. The world appears to us to be split because the 'real' world manifests itself in split form.

A thinker like David Stove was a *Naïve Splitter*.[12] As we saw in Part I of this project, Immanuel Kant was a *Non-Naïve Splitter*.[13] He believed that things exist at a phenomenal and noumenal level. The phenomenal level corresponds with how a particular thing – such as a tree – is experienced by us. We experience a tree via our senses and a matrix of sensibilities that allow us to experience the tree as existing in space and time and in causal relationships with other things. The noumenal level corresponds with the tree as it actually is. We can never know the noumenal tree – the tree as it actually is – but can only experience it at the phenomenal level. However, reality at the noumenal level is just as split as reality appears to us to be split at the phenomenal level: for every tree that we see at the phenomenal level, there exists a noumenal tree, separate from all the other noumenal trees in existence.

As we also saw in Part I of this project, Schopenhauer, Kant's most devoted follower, argued that Kant's view involved a logical contradiction.[14] If things only *appear* to us to exist in space and time because of the way we are built to experience things, and therefore do not *actually* exist in space and time at the noumenal level, then reality at the noumenal level cannot be differentiated, or split. This is because the only way reality can be differentiated – or split – is in space and time. What makes the tree outside my window different from the tree outside yours is that they occupy a different space. What makes the kiss you gave me today different from the kiss you gave me yesterday is that they are separated in time. So at the noumenal level, reality must be One.[15]

---

[11] The word 'naïve' is not used here in any pejorative sense, but simply in the sense of taking things to be as they appear to be.

[12] See Stove, 'Judge's Report' in his *Cricket Versus Republicanism and Other Essays* (Quakers Hill Press, 1995), awarding the title of 'The Worst Argument In The World' to the argument that 'we cannot know things as they are in themselves' because 'We can know things only – as they are related to us; under our forms of perception and understanding; insofar as they fall under our conceptual schemes, etc'. See also Parts 1 and 2 of his essay 'Idealism: a Victorian Horror Story' in his *The Plato Cult and Other Philosophical Follies* (Blackwell, 1991) and *Against the Idols of the Age* (Routledge, 1999) respectively.

[13] McBride, *The Humanity of Private Law, Part I: Explanation* (n 2), 261–62.

[14] Ibid, 262.

[15] Subsequent followers of Kant have sought to argue that one can retain Kant's distinction between the noumenal and the phenomenal without sliding into Schopenhauer's position that reality at the noumenal level is One. See, for example, Henry Allison's 'epistemological' reading of the phenomenal/noumenal distinction in his *Kant's Transcendental Idealism*, revised ed (Yale UP, 2004), arguing that when we refer to a particular thing X we are

Schopenhauer, then, was a *Lumper*; and, as we have just observed, he was a *Pessimistic Lumper*, identifying reality at the noumenal level with a blind, destructive Will. However, there seems no reason why a *Lumper needs* to be pessimistic. As the philosopher Bryan Magee observed of Schopenhauer:

> No general philosophy – no ontology, epistemology or logic – can entail pessimistic conclusions … [I]n this sense [Schopenhauer's] pessimism is logically independent of his philosophy; and so it is. It is true that he was a pessimist; no one more so. And it is true that his pessimism is compatible with his philosophy – but that is only because the two are of necessity, logically unconnected. Non-pessimism is equally compatible with his philosophy.[16]

One of the benefits of giving the noumenal reality that Schopenhauer called 'Will' the name 'Being' instead is to underline Magee's point that there is nothing necessarily pessimistic in Schopenhauer's view of noumenal reality. Calling that reality 'Will' tends to obscure that point as wills *can* be blind, destructive and irrational. Using the term 'Being' instead leaves the point open, for the time being.[17]

## Heidegger

At this stage in the argument, Heidegger would object that it is a mistake to identify Being with some noumenal reality that expresses, or manifests, itself in the form of beings, the split world with which we are familiar. Heidegger thought that instead of adopting this picture of reality:

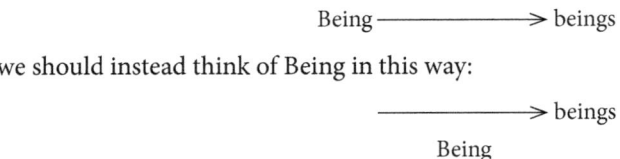

we should instead think of Being in this way:

On this view, Being is no-thing:[18] it is not a *thing* that exists independently of beings, and brings them into existence. Rather, Being is a *process*, a process that involves beings being brought into being: it is 'the Non-being which lets beings be'.[19] As Richard Capobianco explains Heidegger's way of thinking, Being 'is the temporal-spatial flow of all beings: the coming and going, appearing and disappearing, arriving and departing of all beings; the emerging and lingering and passing away of all that is.'[20] To the same effect, George Steiner

---

always referring to the same thing whether we talk about X at the phenomenal or noumenal level. It is just that when we refer to X at the phenomenal level, we are referring to X subject to our ability to cognise it, and when we refer to X at the noumenal level, we are referring to it without that qualification. However, it is hard to see on this view how Kant's view that it is only at the phenomenal level that X can be said to exist in space and time can be sustained. See Van Cleve, *Problems from Kant* (OUP, 1999), 8.

[16] Magee, *The Philosophy of Schopenhauer*, revised ed (OUP, 1997), 12.

[17] See p 76, below, for an argument that Being *cannot* be blind, destructive and irrational.

[18] Cf. Heidegger's endorsement of Hegel's statement that 'Pure Being and pure Nothing are … the same' in Heidegger, 'What is Metaphysics?' in Heidegger, *Basic Writings*, revised ed (Harper, 1993), 108.

[19] Kockelmans, *On the Truth of Being* (Indiana UP, 1984), 49.

[20] Capobianco, *Engaging Heidegger* (University of Toronto Press, 2010), 142. See also Capobianco, *Heidegger's Way of Being* (University of Toronto Press, 2014), 33: '[Being] is not to be confused with any kind of metaphysical entity … "the gleaming of nature" is not a state or condition … but a *happening* …'.

observes that for Heidegger, Being 'is not itself a *being* – or "Idea" or "energy" or "*Ding an sich*" or "Spirit". It is that by which all beings shine forth'.[21] It is this 'shining forth' nature of beings that makes it appropriate to regard beings as *phenomenal* in nature: 'in the word *phenomenon* … Heidegger finds a Greek root [*phainesthai*] meaning "radiance", "self-disclosure".[22] So Being is the 'lighting-process by which beings are illumined as beings.'[23]

In making the move to view Being as no-thing but rather a process, Heidegger makes Being *rootless*. We are not allowed by Heidegger to think of Being as some *thing* that manifests *itself* in the form of phenomenal beings. Instead, Being simply *is* – 'It is It itself'.[24] The result is that there are no rules, no limits, and no guarantees when it comes to Heidegger's Being. For the time being, the 'lighting-process' that is Being lights up the world in the form with which we – there in the middle of Being's lighting process (or, in Heidegger's terminology, *Dasein*) – are familiar. However, there is nothing in the nature of Being that provides us with any assurance that the world will not be lit up in a different way tomorrow.

Heidegger fully acknowledges the point, likening Being 'to a child's play (*Spiel*). Being … is simply the "play" of presencing, of emerging, a play without "why". "It remains simply play," he observes, "but this 'simply' is everything, the one, the only."'[25] On this view, then, Being can be likened – as John Caputo likens it – to 'a child playing a game of draughts with the epochs'[26] that arise out of the varying ways in which Being lights up the world. The result is, as Caputo notes, that 'We are … caught up in a fearful "play" … It is as though the history of Being is playing with us, tantalizing us … The "Being" to which Heidegger invites us to be "released" appears to be a dangerous and destructive force which plays with the essence of man.'[27]

As we have seen, it is precisely this element in Heidegger's thought that Iris Murdoch condemned as 'demonic'. And indeed, Heidegger's insistence that there is no 'why' to the way Being operates does take on a much more sinister aspect when we read Primo Levi's story of what happened to him shortly after arriving at Auschwitz as a prisoner:

> Driven by thirst, I eyed a fine icicle outside the window, within hand's reach. I opened the window and broke off the icicle but at once a large, heavy guard prowling outside brutally snatched it away from me. '*Warum?*' I asked him in my poor German. '*Hier ist kein warum*' (there is no why here), he replied, pushing me inside with a shove.[28]

Furthermore, it is hard to see how Heidegger's view of Being provides us with *any* resources to resist or protest against such thing as the rise of the Nazis and the spread of concentration camps. Instead, someone who adopts Heidegger's view of Being might well regard these developments as representing the latest 'play' of Being[29] – and therefore something that we, the insignificant pawns of Being, simply have to accept.

---

[21] Steiner, *Martin Heidegger* (University of Chicago Press, 1991), 66 (italics in original).

[22] Ibid (italics in original).

[23] Richardson, *Heidegger: Through Phenomenology to Thought*, 4th ed (Fordham UP, 2003), 6.

[24] Heidegger, 'Letter on Humanism' in Heidegger, *Basic Writings* (n 18), 234.

[25] Capobianco, *Engaging Heidegger* (n 20), 122, quoting from Lilly's translation of Heidegger's 1956 lectures on *The Principle of Reason* (Indiana UP, 1991), 113.

[26] Caputo, *The Mystical Element in Heidegger's Thought*, rev'd ed (Fordham UP, 1986), xxiv.

[27] Ibid, 58.

[28] Levi, *If This Is a Man* (trans Woolf) (The Orion Press, 1959), 24.

[29] There is some evidence that Heidegger thought of concentration camps and the rise of the Nazis in exactly this way. On the rise of the Nazis, Heidegger's 1933 address as the newly appointed Rector of the University of Freiburg

None of these things need be true of the *Traditional View of Being* that Heidegger was concerned to attack; that is, the view that Being is some*thing* that manifests *it*self in the form of beings. Obviously, on the *Traditional View of Being*, the nature of Being places limits on how it might manifest itself – and, one would hope that Being's manifesting itself in the form of the Nazi party, or concentration camps, would be beyond it.

But at this point, followers of Schopenhauer would rejoin the fray and argue: 'But what grounds do you have for that hope? The Nazi party did rise, the concentration camps did exist. Surely this shows that the reality that undergirds the split world we live in is indeed a blind and destructive Will, rather than the sanitised "Being" that you are talking about?' The answer to this objection is that if we accept the third postulate of human flourishing – that human flourishing is a good, anywhere and everywhere it exists – then we *cannot* adopt the *Traditional View of Being* and *also* be *Pessimistic Lumpers* like Schopenhauer. This is because if good exists in the world, then on the *Traditional View of Being* that is because Being manifests itself as that good. But the Oneness of Being means that Being cannot manifest itself as good without being *all* good. So a *Pessimistic Lumper* can only remain such by (i) (a) giving up on the idea of human flourishing or (b) denying that human flourishing is a good, *and* (ii) giving up on the idea that there exists any good (outside of human flourishing) of any kind in the universe.

It is doubtful whether there will be many *Pessimistic Lumpers* who will be able to do both (i) and (ii). Given this, a *Pessimistic Lumper* will seek some way of escaping the force of the argument made in the previous paragraph, and may think he has found one in the following counter-argument: 'Your argument could equally well be deployed to establish that Being must be *all evil*. If evil exists in the world – and it obviously does – this is because, on the *Traditional View of Being*, Being manifests itself as that evil. However, the Oneness of Being means that Being cannot manifest itself as evil without being *all* evil. So your argument, suggesting as it does that Being is simultaneously both all evil and all good, has gone wrong somewhere. Where it has gone wrong is that what you are calling "Being" is actually "Will" and "Will" – unlike "Being" – can fluctuate, sometimes doing good and sometimes bad.'

There is a well-known counter to this counter-argument, and it was made by both St Augustine and St Thomas Aquinas.[30] There is no equivalency (the counter-counter-argument goes) between good and evil when it comes to their reality. Good has Being,

('The self-assertion of the German university' in Neske and Kettering (eds), *Martin Heidegger and National Socialism* (Paragon House, 1990)) praised the Student Law, organising students on Nazi lines, as 'the highest freedom' and noted with enthusiasm that 'The much-lauded "academic freedom" will be expelled from the German university'. On concentration camps, in a 1949 lecture on '*Das Ge-Stell*', Heidegger observed that 'farming is now a motorized food industry, in essence the same as the fabrication of corpses in gas chambers and extermination camps, the same as the blockade and starving of the peasantry, the same as the fabrication of the hydrogen bomb'. The lecture was subsequently reworked as the 1955 lecture 'The question concerning technology' (published in Heidegger, *The Question Concerning Technology and Other Essays* (Harper & Row, 1977) and in Heidegger, *Basic Writings* (n 18)). The above sentence was omitted from the 1955 lecture, but the same lecture makes it clear that Heidegger regards the technological age as the latest 'play' of Being, a 'play' in which the 'play' of Being is most hidden and obscured from man. In his 1966 interview with *Der Spiegel*, published posthumously 10 years later, Heidegger remarked that 'only a God can save us' (ie only another 'play' of Being) from this latest and most serious occlusion of Being: Heidegger, '"Only a God can save us": the *Spiegel* Interview (1966)' in Sheehan (ed), *Heidegger: The Man and the Thinker* (Precedent Publishing, 1981).

[30] Augustine, *Enchiridion*, chapter 11 ('What is called evil in the universe is but the absence of good'); Aquinas, *Summa Theologica*, I, q.49, a.1. The argument has its origin in Plotinus, *Enneads*, I.8.

whereas evil does not. So evil, when it is present, is not present because Being has manifested itself as such; the presence of evil is marked by an absence of Being.

More can be said on this, and will be in the third section of this chapter (when we deal with the topic of 'Anti-Being'), but for the time being we will proceed on the basis that the presence of good in the world (including the good of human flourishing) shows that it is impossible for Being to manifest itself in the form of evils such as the rise of the Nazi party or the existence of concentration camps. So the *Traditional View of Being* is what we are looking for – an account of Being that is cleansed of Schopenhauer's pessimism and Heidegger's amorality. However, such an account also needs to be *plausible* before we could possibly rely on it in seeking to see whether there are strong links between (a) the observation that we are the beings that are aware we participate in Being, and (b) the claim that human flourishing consists in QTL-ing. Is it?

## Four Views of Reality

Before addressing this issue, it may be helpful to sum up the discussion so far with the aid of the diagram below, setting out four different views of reality.

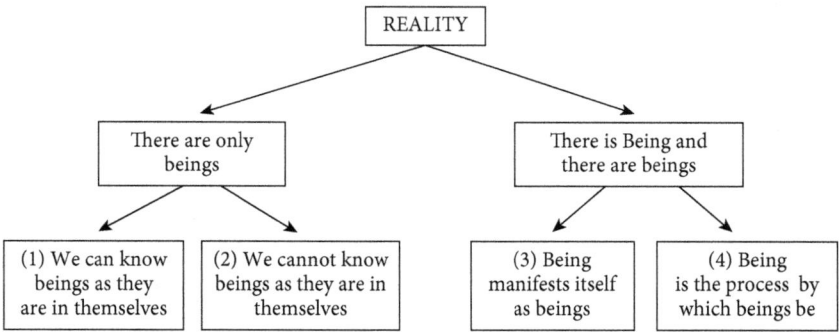

What we have been calling the *Traditional View of Being* is represented by view (3) of reality in the above diagram. This view has the triple advantage of:

(i)    adopting a non-pessimistic view of reality;

(ii)   avoiding the sinister implications of Heidegger's view of Being (represented by view (4)); and

(iii)  transcending the defects in Kant's view of reality (represented by view (2)).[31]

---

[31] Interestingly, Anne Glyn-Jones – whose condemnation of our civilisation as 'morally, aesthetically and spiritually bankrupt' was quoted at the start of this book (p vii) – seems to have adopted the *Traditional View of Being*, arguing that 'Our woes are the direct and logical result of the belief that the physical universe is the only reality that does or can exist; and that truth resides solely in the analysis and understanding of that "reality"' (Glyn-Jones, *Holding Up a Mirror: How Civilisations Decline* (Imprint Academic, 1996), 506). I would agree, insofar as the vision of human flourishing (the RP) that underpins our bankrupt civilisation fails to acknowledge the *Traditional View of Being* and is instead based on the view of reality adopted by *Naïve Splitters*. However, it is beyond the scope of this book to trace the origins of the RP.

However, this leaves the position of a *Naïve Splitter* (represented by view (1)) untouched. Why should a *Naïve Splitter* abandon view (1) and adopt view (3) instead? The question is especially pressing as most readers of this volume will be *Naïve Splitters* and will therefore think that relying on view (3) to arrive at conclusions about the nature of human flourishing is a waste of time. They will further think that no conclusions can be drawn about the nature of human flourishing from the proposition that we are the beings that are aware that we participate in Being, as on view (1) of reality all that proposition can amount to is the claim that we are the beings that are aware that we exist among lots of other beings – and that statement of the obvious could not possibly provide the foundation for an account of the nature of human flourishing.

Readers of this book who are *Naïve Splitters* can be divided up into two camps:

*Camp One:* Those who, having read the previous two chapters, are attracted to the idea that human flourishing consists in QTL-ing; and

*Camp Two:* Those who are unwilling to accept that human flourishing consists in QTL-ing, despite the arguments made in the previous two chapters.

I think most readers in *Camp One* will be persuaded to accept view (3) of reality by the end of the next section, which will be concerned to show that there are strong links between (i) the observation that we are the beings that are aware we participate in Being, and (ii) the claim that human flourishing consists in QTL-ing. By then, it should become clear that view (3), (i) and (ii) comes as a 'package deal' – (i) helps makes sense of why (ii) is true, but only so long as view (3) of reality is correct. So if you are already inclined to accept that (ii) is true, then you will be inclined (at least by the end of the next section) to accept that view (3) of reality is correct because (ii) makes most sense in a universe where view (3) is true.

That leaves *Camp Two*, which is made up of readers who are *Naïve Splitters and* are unpersuaded by anything that has been said so far that human flourishing consists in QTL-ing. It may be that nothing can be said to budge them from that position. However, it is worth pointing out to such readers that Western and Eastern philosophy can be seen as converging on view (3) of reality. (This is something that Schopenhauer himself was keenly aware of, with the result that he was the first major Western philosopher to refer to Eastern philosophical writings.) The story of this convergence would go something like this.

Western philosophy starts off with Parmenides adopting view (3) of reality, and that position is maintained by Plato, the neo-Platonists (in particular, Plotinus), and Christian philosophers such as St Augustine and St Thomas Aquinas. However, after the thirteenth century, Dun Scotus and William of Ockham's 'nominalist' view of reality – which denies the existence of any universals underlying the particular objects of our experience – starts to push Western thought towards view (1) of reality. By the age of Descartes – the seventeenth century – view (1) is firmly in the saddle, and the question becomes what we can know for certain of the split reality that we are in, given that reality *is* split all the way down and there is as a result an unbridgeable gulf between you and me, or between me and the tree outside my window. But starting with Kant and Schopenhauer, the move back towards view (3) begins via view (2);[32] while Heidegger represents an easily-reversed and regrettable overshoot to view (4).

---

[32] The journey back to view (3) is completed by philosophers such as FH Bradley (1846–1921) and TLS Sprigge (1932–2007) (see, for example, Sprigge, *James and Bradley: American Truth and British Reality* (Open Court

Turning to Eastern philosophy, no significant branch of Eastern philosophy seems to have taken the Western turn towards adopting views (1) or (2) of reality.[33] Instead, Islamic or Hindu thinkers have tended to adopt view (3), as does Chinese Taoism and neo-Confucianism.[34] The Zen Buddhist position that the reality of all things is bound up with *mu* (nothingness)[35] has resulted in an ambivalence within Zen Buddhism between adopting view (3) or view (4) of reality. One tradition would have us – through meditating on *mu* – come to comprehend, and accept, the transient nature of all reality. This view of reality seems indistinguishable from view (4).[36] However, another tradition has it that *mu* reflects the ineffable nature of the ground of all reality; that is, our inability to grasp that ground through merely human concepts and language. It is only when we embrace *mu* and give up on trying to grasp the ground of reality intellectually, through words and concepts, that we can *experience* the ground of reality breaking through into our being. This view of *mu* seems much more consistent with view (3) of reality.

It therefore looks like Western and Eastern philosophers are for the most part – to borrow Derek Parfit's wonderful phrase – climbing the same mountain from different sides;[37] the mountain in this case being the mountain of Being. What can account for that, other than that Being does actually exist as a metaphysical entity, and that consequently view (3) of the nature of reality is actually correct?[38] The idea that multiple schools of thought – separated by barriers of geography and language – could independently converge on the same view of the world, when that worldview is fundamentally wrong, seems highly implausible. Much the more plausible analysis is that view (3) is actually correct and the *Naïve Splitters* are wrong.

Enough has now been said, I think, to clear the clouds placed over the notion of Being by Schopenhauer's pessimism, and Heidegger's amoralism. It is possible to take a view of the nature of reality – what we have been calling 'view (3)' in the last few paragraphs and, more generally, the *Traditional View of Being* – that we have good grounds to believe is correct, and that is incompatible with both Schopenhauer's pessimism and Heidegger's amoralism. With these clouds dispersed, we can now turn to the main agenda of this chapter, which is

Publishing, 1993)), and Frithjof Schuon (1907–98) (see, for example, Schuon, *Primordial Meditation: Contemplating the Real* (Matheson Trust, 2015)).

[33] The exception to the rule is the sixth century Indian philosopher Charvaka (or Carvaka), who endorsed view (1) of reality.

[34] For introductory treatments, see Billington, *Understanding Eastern Philosophy* (Routledge, 1997), chs 4, 9–10, 12–13; Adamson, *Philosophy in the Islamic World* (OUP, 2016), chs 17, 26–27, 47–48, 54, 58, 61–62. For more detailed treatments of the relationship between Being and beings: (i) in Hindu thought, *The Upanishads* speak for themselves and provide us with some of the most beautiful affirmations in world literature of what we have been calling view (3); (ii) in Islamic thought, see Nasr and Aminrazavi (eds), *From the School of Illumination to Philosophical Mysticism* (IB Tauris, 2012); and Jambet, *The Act of Being: The Philosophy of Revelation in Mulla Sadr* (Zone Books, 2007).

[35] Cf. the Zen fable – 'A monk once asked Master Joshu: "Has a dog the Buddha nature or not?" Joshu said, "*Mu*!"' (quoted in Kasulis, *Zen Action, Zen Person* (University Press of Hawaii, 1981), 10).

[36] On the links between Heidegger and Zen Buddhism, see Kreeft, 'Zen in Heidegger's *Gelassenheit*' (1971) 11 *International Philosophical Quarterly* 521; Caputo, *The Mystical Element in Heidegger's Thought*, (n 26), 203–17.

[37] Parfit, *On What Matters, Volume One* (OUP, 2011), 25, 419.

[38] Given this point, the life stories of thinkers like Schopenhauer, Thomas Merton, René Guénon, and Robert M Pirsig possess a great deal of fascination as they were all thinkers that were born in the West, and found themselves reasoning from Western premises to conclusions that, they then found, had deep resonances in Eastern thought.

to see whether there are strong links between the observation that we are the beings that are aware we participate in Being, and the claim that human flourishing consists in QTL-ing.

# 2.  Truth and Being

The previous section argued in favour of the *Traditional View of Being*:

(A)   Being manifests itself as beings.

This book takes the view that human nature is defined by the following fact:

(B)   We are the beings that are aware (or are capable of being aware) that we participate in Being.

The question is whether (A) and (B) support the view of human flourishing advanced in the previous two chapters:

(C)   Human flourishing consists in engaging in a quest to lead a truthful life ('QTL-ing').

The beginning of a bridge between (A) and (B), on the one hand, and (C), on the other, is provided by the following sentence from Aristotle's *Metaphysics*:

(D)   'to the extent to which a thing has being, to that extent it has truth.'[39]

Thomas Aquinas made much the same point when he observed that '*ens et verum convertuntur*'[40] – being and truth are convertible. As did Robert Nozick when he argued that 'A thing's truth is its inner being. Its truth is its inner essence, which can shine forth … A thing's truth is its inner light. (This is why truth shines forth.)'.[41] And William Barrett argues that Eastern philosophy endorses (D):

> In the Oriental religious and philosophical tradition, where truth has never been defined as belonging basically to the intellect, the Master is able to discern whether or not a disciple has attained enlightenment from how he behaves, what kind of person he has come to be, not from hearing him reason about the Sutras. This kind of truth is not a truth of the intellect but of the whole man. Strictly speaking subjective truth is not a truth that I have, but a truth that I am … Indian and Chinese sages insisted … that man does not attain to truth so long as he remains locked up in his intellect: a man who located his truth in his mind would have struck these sages as not merely mistaken, but as a human psychological aberration.[42]

---

[39] Aristotle, *Metaphysics*, 993b30–31. The translation is provided by Lawrence Hatab, in his *Ethics and Finitude* (n 8), 113.

[40] Aquinas, *Summa Theologica*, I–II, q.29, a.5. He actually said: '*Bonum … et ens et verum convertuntur*': good and being and truth are convertible; a position which is consistent with that taken above on the impossibility of Being being evil (p 76).

[41] Nozick, *The Examined Life* (Touchstone, 1989), 187.

[42] Barrett, *Irrational Man* (Heinemann, 1961), 171, 231. See also Marcel, *The Mystery of Being, Part II: Faith and Reality* (St Augustine's Press, 2001), 42: 'It is surely impossible for us not to have at any rate a vague assurance that being can only be nominally distinct from a certain fullness of truth.' On the 'convergence of Being, Truth, and Value' in Marcel's philosophy, see O'Malley, *The Fellowship of Being* (Martinus Nijhoff, 1966), 76–77.

The bridge started by (D) can be completed if it is the case that:

(E)   Being manifests itself in beings to a greater or lesser degree.

With the result that:

(F)   Someone who is engaged in a quest to lead a truthful life seeks to have Being manifest itself in him or her to the greatest possible degree.

The use of the word 'participate' in (B) already anticipates (E), as it is possible to participate in something to a greater or lesser degree. So we can restate (F) as:

(G)   Someone who is engaged in a quest to lead a truthful life seeks to participate in Being to the greatest possible degree.

If (G) is true, then we can make out a very strong link between (A) and (B), on the one hand, and (C), on the other. We can say that human beings are not just beings, but the beings that are capable of being aware that they participate in a greater reality – Being – that manifests itself as beings. We can say, further, that our flourishing as human beings consists in our being aware of what sort of beings we are and our seeking, in that awareness, to become *more human* by intensifying as much as possible the connection that we have as human beings with the greater reality in which we participate. (G) claims that what we have been so far calling QTL-ing *is* the process of seeking to intensify one's connection with that greater reality.

The bridge that (G) allows us to build between (A) and (B), on the one hand, and (C), on the other, looks solid. What else could human flourishing consist in, other than a quest to become more human? What could a quest to become more human consist in, other than a quest to become more real? What could a quest to become more real consist in, other than a quest to intensify our connection with the wider reality of which we form part?[43] And what else would we call that quest to become more real, other than a quest to lead a truthful life? However, a lot of work still needs to be done to establish that (G) *is* true, and that there is therefore a strong connection between (A) and (B), on the one hand, and (C), on the other. In order to establish that (G) is true, we need to do four things.

First, we need to show how it is possible to participate in Being to a greater or lesser degree.

Second, we then need to show that someone who seeks to participate in Being to the greatest possible degree is very likely to possess the virtues and engage in the activities that we identified in the previous chapter as lying at the heart of someone's being engaged in a quest to lead a truthful life. If this is the case, then that gives us good reason to believe that (G) is true, as (G) claims that (i) being engaged in a quest to lead a truthful life, and (ii) seeking to participate in Being to the greatest possible degree, *are the same thing*.

---

[43] Cf. Marcel, *The Mystery of Being, Part II* (n 42), 33: 'the more my existence takes on the character of including others, the narrower becomes the gap which separates it from being; the more, in other words, I am.'

Third, we need to consider the objection that, contrary to what (G) claims, any connection between (i) and (ii) is merely contingent rather than necessary. In other words, we need to consider the objection that while someone who seeks to participate in Being to the greatest possible degree may QTL, someone can QTL without seeking to participate in Being to the greatest possible degree.

Fourth, if this objection can be overcome, we then need to solidify the connection that (G) makes between (i) and (ii) by showing how the arguments advanced in the previous chapter in favour of thinking that human flourishing consists in QTL-ing apply equally well, if not better, to the view that human flourishing consists in someone's seeking to participate in Being to the greatest possible degree.

It is to these four tasks we now turn, beginning with the first.

## Modes and Degrees of Participation

We can begin to come to grips with the idea of participating in Being to a greater or lesser degree by thinking about something else in which it is possible to participate to a greater or lesser degree, and which Being is sometimes compared to – a dance.[44] To help us situate our thoughts, let's consider the following passage from Leo Tolstoy's *War and Peace*, describing Count Ilya Rostov and his relative Maria Dmitrievna dancing the 'Danila Kupar' at a society soirée:

> The count danced well and knew that he did, but his partner could not dance at all and had no wish to excel at it. She held her portly figure erect, with her sturdy arms hanging by her sides … It was only her stern but comely face that entered into the dance. What was expressed by the whole rotund person of the count, in Maria Dmitrievna found expression only in her increasingly radiant smile and the puckering of her nose. But if the count, getting more and more into his stride, captivated the spectators by his light-footed agility and unexpectedly graceful capers, Maria Dmitrievna with the slightest of exertions in moving her shoulders or curving her arms … excited no less enthusiasm because of the contrast. … with her size and usual severity of demeanour. The dance grew livelier and livelier … In the intervals of the dance the count, stopping for breath, waved and shouted to the musicians to play faster. Faster, faster and faster, lightly, more lightly, and ever more lightly whirled the count, flying around Maria Dmitrievna, now on his toes now on his heels, until at last he swung his partner back to her place, executed the final *pas*, lifting one fat leg in the air behind, bowing his perspiring head, smiling and making a wide sweep with his right arm amid a thunder of applause …[45]

In this passage, Ilya and Maria were both dancing the 'Danila Kupar' but, clearly, Ilya participated in the dance to a much greater depth than Maria. What marks out the greater depth of Ilya's participation in the dance?

First, Ilya *cared* far more about dancing well than Maria did – Maria 'could not dance at all and had no wish to excel at it.' Second, Ilya was much more *involved* in the dance than Maria was – while it was only Maria's 'stern but comely face that entered into the dance', Ilya's

---

[44] Comparisons between Being and a dance are made by Sir John Davies' poem *Orchestra* (1596); TS Eliot's poem *East Coker* (1940); the final, brilliant (seventeenth) chapter of CS Lewis' novel *Perelandra* (1943); the eponymous first essay in Bringhurst, *Everywhere Being is Dancing* (Counterpoint, 2009).

[45] Tolstoy, *War and Peace* (1867), Book One, Part One, Chapter 17 (trans Edmonds).

'whole' body was thrown into the dance. Third, Ilya took much more *responsibility* for how the dance went than Maria did, urging on the musicians to play their part in making the dance go faster and faster. Fourth, Ilya's actions in the dance were *attuned* to the demands that dancing the 'Danila Kupar' makes on those dancing it and, fifth, Ilya responded *skilfully* to those demands, showing 'light-footed agility and unexpectedly graceful capers' and flying around 'now on his toes now on his heels.' In contrast, Maria was determined to dance the 'Danila Kupar' on her terms, expressing the joy and exuberance of the dance only in 'her increasingly radiant smile and the puckering of her nose.'

The result of Ilya's participating in the dance at a greater depth than Maria is that Ilya *loses himself* in the dance far more than Maria does. His whole person becomes identi-fied with the dance in a way that is simply not true of Maria, who only allows herself to become involved in the dance from the shoulders up. It is only when the dance ends that Ilya re-emerges as himself, lapping up the applause from the crowd. Until then, Ilya is the dance, and the dance is Ilya. But as we have just seen, this loss of self does not result in Ilya becom-ing a passive instrument of the dance. He is just as much responsible for how the dance goes, as the dance is responsible for how Ilya goes.

Can we analogise straight across from someone's participating in a dance to someone's participating in Being? Not quite. We should note first that on the *Traditional View of Being*, Being is (for want of a better word) a thing, while a dance is an activity. So our reflections on what is involved in participating more deeply in a dance can only help us to understand what it is for someone (S) to participate more deeply in an *activity* carried on by Being.

What might that activity be? The question has already implicitly been answered: the activity of Being is to manifest itself as beings. Can S participate in that activity, join that dance? Here is where Heidegger is helpful, precisely because – as we have seen – Heidegger identified Being with a process. And Heidegger had no doubt that humanity's distinctive mission is to contribute to that process, going so far as to say that 'Man is the shepherd of Being.'[46] But what contribution can S make to that process, given S's seeming insignificance in the midst of Being's play? As Heidegger observed, 'Man does not decide whether and how beings appear, whether and how … history and nature come forward into the clearing of Being, come to presence and depart. The advent of beings lies in the destiny of Being.'[47]

For Heidegger, the contribution S *can* make is to *harken* to what Being does – to 'enter into a deep, rich, serene contemplative and mindful comportment towards all beings and things in their temporal unfolding [and upon] awakening to the way of Being … see with fresh eyes the emergence and shining-forth of all beings and things in their "truth".'[48] If we do this – if we 'let beings be as the beings which they are'[49] – then we 'guard the truth of Being.'[50] In doing this – letting Being be – it is particularly important that we respect the essence of language, which Heidegger calls 'the house of Being.'[51] This is because language is the way Being speaks to us as to 'the essence of a thing.'[52] So language is Being's creation – the

[46] Heidegger, 'Letter on Humanism' (n 24), 234.
[47] Ibid.
[48] Capobianco, *Heidegger's Way of Being* (n 20), 96.
[49] Heidegger, 'On the Essence of Truth' in Heidegger, *Basic Writings* (n 18), 125.
[50] Heidegger, 'Letter on Humanism' (n 24), 234.
[51] Ibid, 217, 237.
[52] Heidegger, 'Building, Dwelling, Thinking' in Heidegger, *Basic Writings* (n 18), 348.

way Being enables us to guard the truth of Being – not man's: 'Man acts as though he were the shaper and master of language, while in fact language remains the master of man.'[53]

We can adapt a lot of this to describe how S can participate in the activity of Being's manifesting itself as beings, or, more briefly – to make the distinction from Heidegger's view of Being crystal-clear – Being's manifesting *itself*. Being's doing this would be incomplete, or unfulfilled, if there were no one *to whom* Being manifested itself. So humanity's role is to be the being to whom Being manifests itself.[54]

It follows that S can participate in the activity of Being's manifesting itself by (i) being someone *to whom* Being manifests itself, and (ii) being someone who helps Being manifest itself *to other people*.[55] We can call (i) participation by *contemplation*; and (ii) participation by *witness*. Participation by contemplation involves the 'deep, rich, serene contemplative and mindful comportment towards all beings and things' spoken of above. Participation by witness is carried out by communicating to others 'a kind of piety towards things which detects in them a deeper presence.'[56] And this is done either by (a) being seen by others to be someone who is marked by that kind of piety,[57] or by (b) communicating that kind of piety to others using the resources language affords us to speak of the nature of Being and how it underlies all things.[58] S will participate more deeply in the activity of Being's manifesting itself, the greater the care, involvement, responsibility, attunement, and skill shown by S in contemplating Being's manifesting itself, and in witnessing to Being's manifesting itself.[59]

The last two paragraphs have explained what it would be for S to participate to a greater or lesser degree *in Being's manifesting itself*. However, the task of this section was to 'explain how it is possible to participate *in Being* to a greater or lesser degree.' Can we make a link between the two, so that an S who is a good 'shepherd of Being' in her contemplating, and witnessing to, the reality of Being's manifesting itself can claim to be participating in Being to a greater degree than, say, a *Naïve Splitter* who participates in Being by virtue of the fact that he exists but is – because he is a *Naïve Splitter* – completely oblivious to Being and its works? I think we can, by drawing on the observation made above that someone like Ilya who participates deeply in an activity like a dance *loses themselves* in that activity. An S who is a good 'shepherd of Being' is no longer the S that she was before she became a good 'shepherd of Being'. She has been *taken over* by Being, or at least Being in its active mode of manifesting itself. The need to make that last, slight qualification shows that S cannot claim that by being a good 'shepherd of Being' that she has *become* Being[60] – there is some

---

[53] Ibid.

[54] Cf. King, *Heidegger and Happiness* (Bloomsbury, 2009), 72: 'being itself needs the human essence to manifest itself as itself.'

[55] There is a third way in which S can participate in Being's manifesting itself as beings, a way that is peculiarly appropriate for lawyers and judges (and also educators). This way of participating in Being's manifesting itself as beings is discussed below, at p 165.

[56] Caputo, *The Mystical Element in Heidegger's Thought* (n 26), 244.

[57] Cf. Marcel, *The Mystery of Being, Part II* (n 42), 45: 'I think that we must all, in the course of our lives, have known beings who were essentially creators; by the radiance of charity and love shining from their being, they add a positive contribution to the invisible work which gives the human adventure the only meaning which can justify it.'

[58] 'Language' should be understood *very* widely here, as including music and art.

[59] Cf. Steiner, *Martin Heidegger* (n 21), 32: 'Man is … a privileged listener and respondent to existence. The vital relation to otherness is … a relation of audition. We are trying "to listen to the voice of Being." It is, or ought to be, a relation of extreme responsibility, custodianship, answerability to and for.'

[60] Contrast Robert Oppenheimer's reaction to the first successful trial of the atom bomb: 'Now I am become death, the destroyer of worlds', quoting from the *Bhagavad-Gita*, chapter 11, where the God Krishna appears to

part of Being (if we can talk of something that is supposed to be One as having parts) that will always remain beyond her.[61] But S *can* claim that by virtue of being a good 'shepherd of Being' she is participating in Being as much as a human being can do, and is certainly participating in Being far more than a *Naïve Splitter* does. So we can restate:

(G)     Someone who is engaged in a quest to lead a truthful life seeks to participate in Being to the greatest possible degree.

as:

(H)     Someone who is engaged in a quest to lead a truthful life seeks to be a good 'shepherd of Being'.

The question we now have to address head on is whether this is true. We begin by seeing whether (i) the description of QTL-ing set out in the previous chapter marries up well with (ii) our emerging understanding of what might be involved in someone's seeking to be a good 'shepherd of Being'. If it does, that provides strong evidence that (H) is true, as the most natural explanation of why (i) and (ii) should correspond is that (H) *is* true. Showing that (i) and (ii) *do* correspond is the task of the next section.

## The Good Shepherd

The previous chapter explained that someone (S) who is embarked on a quest to lead a truthful life will be equipped with the following truth-seeking *virtues*: (1) a sense of reality; (2) attention; (3) humility; (4) love of truth. S will also engage in the following truth-seeking *activities*: (5) doing work that places a strong emphasis on developing, and drawing on, a sense of reality; (6) striving to be realistic in viewing the world; (7) striving to be sincere in dealing with others; and (8) striving to be true to oneself – the self one would like to be – in deciding what to do.

The question is whether someone who seeks to be a good 'shepherd of Being' in the way they contemplate, and witness to, Being's manifesting itself as beings will tend to possess virtues (1)–(4) and engage in activities (5)–(8). If so, then we will have made the kind of link between (i) someone's QTL-ing and (ii) someone's seeking to be a good 'shepherd of Being' that would give us good reason to believe the claim made by (H), that (i) and (ii) are actually the same thing.

There are obvious links between some of the truth-seeking virtues and activities listed above and S's seeking to be a good 'shepherd of Being'. Two aspects of QTL-ing, in particular, point to a *very* strong association between S's QTL-ing and S's seeking to be a good

---

the warrior Arjuna in his (Krishna's) most exalted form. That Krishna – 'the destroyer of worlds' – is Being is clear from Arjuna's words in the same chapter on seeing Krishna: 'You are the supreme, changeless Reality, the one thing to be known. You are the refuge of all creation, the immortal spirit, the eternal guardian of eternal dharma. You are without beginning, middle, or end; you touch everything with your infinite power. The sun and moon are your eyes, and your mouth is fire; your radiance warms the cosmos' (trans Easwaran).

[61] Cf. the Zen Buddhist tradition of viewing Being as ineffable (p 79).

'shepherd of Being': (a) the fact that if S is to QTL, she has to be possess the sub-virtue (within the overall virtue of attention) of being open to epiphanies; and (b) the importance of humility to S's QTL-ing.

On (a), if we return to the descriptions of the various epiphanies described in the previous chapter[62] – especially Thomas Merton's experience on the corner of Fourth and Walnut in Louisville, or Ruth Pitter's experience as a 14 year-old, sitting outside a cottage door – what they all seem to involve is a dissolution of the ordinary, split reality that we are familiar with, to reveal an underlying, more unified, reality. In other words, they all involve a revelation of Being's manifesting itself as beings. It follows that an openness to epiphanies is an essential component of someone's becoming, and being, a good 'shepherd of Being'.

On (b), there can be no end to either the breadth or depth of one's contemplating, or witnessing to, Being's manifesting itself as beings. In terms of breadth, there is always more to contemplate, more to witness to; in terms of depth, our contemplating, and our witnessing, can be ever richer, ever more insightful. As Richard Capobianco observes:

> No matter the breadth and depth of our words and meanings, we do not – we cannot – exhaust the manifestation of Nature. The vault of the heavens, Wordsworth reminds us in the poem 'A Night Piece', endlessly 'deepens its unfathomable depth'. For e.e. cummings, 'the mightiest meditations of mankind / cancelled are by one merely opening leaf'. And Hopkins affirms in these lovely lines:
>
> > And for all this, nature is never spent;
> > There lives the deepest freshness deep down things.[63]

Capobianco goes on: 'We take in all that we are able – yet we realize there is more, always more, to manifestation – a richness of showing, a reserve of appearing, that can never be fully tapped. *Physis* endlessly arising and we endlessly astonished.'[64] It follows that if S seeks to be a good 'shepherd of Being' it would be better for her *never* to think that she has achieved her goal. S is more likely to achieve her goal if she simply focuses on constantly expanding her always-too-limited capacities to contemplate, and witness to, Being's manifesting itself as beings. Were she to rest content with the capacities that she has, and think that deploying those capacities is enough to make her a good 'shepherd of Being', she may well be wrong. She is simply in no position (and can never be in a position) to tell whether the capacities she has for contemplating, and witnessing to, Being's manifesting itself as beings make her a Master in performing that task or whether she is still a relative novice. So in terms of her becoming a Master, it would be better for S to cultivate the virtue of humility and always act as though she is a novice,[65] with the result that S will always regard herself as still having a

---

[62] See pp 39–40.

[63] Capobianco, *Heidegger's Way of Being* (n 20), 47, quoting from EE Cummings' 'life is more true than reason will deceive' (1944) and Gerard Manley Hopkins' 'God's grandeur' (1877). Capobianco also refers us (ibid, 110, n 13) to Walt Whitman's poem 'The unexpress'd' (1891) as making the same point: 'All human lives, throats, wishes, brains – all experiences' utterance / After the countless songs, or long or short, all tongues, all lands / Still something not yet told in poesy's voice or print – something lacking'. See also ibid, 42: 'Cézanne painted Mont Saint-Victoire more than sixty times by several accounts, but never once did he think he had exhausted its showing, its manifestation. Similarly, we, in turn, can never say enough about even one of Cézanne's paintings of the mountain!'

[64] Capobianco, *Heidegger's Way of Being* (n 20), 64.

[65] Cf, Marcel, *The Mystery of Being, Part I: Reflection and Mystery* (Harvill Press, 1950), 133: 'There is not, and there cannot be, any global abstraction, any final high terrace to which we can climb by means of abstract thought, there to rest for ever; for our condition in this world does remain, in the last analysis, that of a wanderer, an itinerant being, who cannot come to rest except by a fiction, a fiction which it is the duty of philosophic reflection to oppose with all its strength.'

long way to go in terms of cultivating her capacities to contemplate, and witness to, Being's manifesting itself as beings before she can claim to be a good 'shepherd of Being'.[66]

The connection between certain other aspects of QTL-ing and S's seeking to be a good 'shepherd of Being' is less obvious, but still becomes apparent on reflection. For example, among the truth-seeking activities, we can easily see why (6) striving to be realistic in viewing the world, and (7) striving to be sincere in dealing with others, are strongly associated with someone's seeking to be a good 'shepherd of Being'. One's ability to contemplate Being's manifesting itself as beings will be severely impaired if one does not do (6), and one's ability to witness to Being's manifesting itself as beings will be severely impaired if one does not do (7). But what (if any) is the link between S's seeking to be a good 'shepherd of Being' and, first, (5) S's doing work that places a strong emphasis on developing a sense of reality, and, second, (8) S's striving to be true to the self S would like to be in deciding what to do?

## (i) The Work We Do

Focussing first on (5), and the importance of the kind of work we do, we made a contrast in the previous chapter between physical work and interpretative activities – activities which involve the use and manipulation of concepts. We observed that physical work is far more likely to be compatible with QTL-ing, on the basis that such work inculcates in the person doing the work a lively sense of reality. In contrast, someone whose work consists in some kind of interpretative activity will enjoy a lot more freedom to construct their 'own' reality out of the concepts with which they are accustomed to deal.[67]

Despite this, it might be argued that *Mind*, who works with concepts, will actually be in a better position to seek to be a good 'shepherd of Being' than *Hand*, who engages in physical work. This is because, it might be said, *Mind's* conceptual skills allow them to abstract from the everyday world of beings in which they live and penetrate beyond that world to contemplate, and witness to, Being's manifesting itself as beings. In contrast, the kind of work *Hand* does enmires them so fully in everyday reality that they are given no opportunity to lift their eyes up to, and guess at the existence of, any deeper reality that underlies their daily life.

Such an argument seriously underestimates the resources that *Hand's* work provides *Hand* to contemplate, and witness to, Being's manifesting itself as beings. When *Hand's* work is going well, then *Hand* will usually experience *flow* – in other words, the experience of being so completely absorbed into his work that there is no longer any distinction between *Hand*, the instruments *Hand* is using, and the work that *Hand's* efforts are directed towards doing.[68] All becomes one. When *Hand* comes out of that state and reflects on where they 'were' when they were one with their work, *Hand's* mind will become readily open to the possibility that the oneness that they experienced with the tools and materials they were

---

[66] It seems that, for all his faults, Heidegger did possess this quality of humility, specifying just before his death that the motto 'Wege – nicht Werke' ('Ways – not works') should appear on his Collected Works; in other words, his Collected Works should not be taken as a destination but a way of proceeding. See also Welte, 'Seeking and Finding: The Speech at Heidegger's Funeral' (trans Sheehan) in Sheehan (ed), *Heidegger: The Man and the Thinker* (n 29), 73: 'He was always seeking and always underway. At various times he emphatically characterised his thinking as a path. He travelled this path without ceasing.'

[67] See above, pp 34–35.

[68] On flow, see Csikszentmihalyi, *Finding Flow: The Psychology of Engagement in Everyday Life* (Basic Books, 1997), especially 41, 62–63, 204, 211.

using might represent a more fundamental, a more real, reality than the split reality – where *Hand* is one thing, and the tools and materials *Hand* uses are another – with which *Hand* lives on an everyday basis.

The opposite of flow is *stuckness* – where *Hand* can't get going with the work *Hand* is supposed to be doing either because the tools or materials *Hand* needs to do that work are broken or are missing, or because *Hand* cannot figure how to go about doing the work that they are supposed to be doing. But even stuckness affords *Hand* opportunities to see Being manifesting itself as beings, in a variety of ways corresponding to the variety of ways that *Hand* may experience stuckness.[69]

(1) *Malfunction*. If the source of *Hand*'s stuckness is that a tool he is using no longer works properly, *Hand* will look at the tool in a new, more abstract, way: as no longer something that is ready to hand to allow *Hand* to do certain work, but as something that possesses or lacks certain properties that make it useful for *Hand* to do that work. So, in Heideggerian language, the tool 'shows up' or 'lights up' for *Hand* in a different way when *Hand* is experiencing stuckness, as opposed to when *Hand* is experiencing flow. The fact that the tool 'shows up' or 'lights up' for *Hand* in different ways at different times, and that it is not *Hand* that is responsible for its 'showing up' or 'lighting up' in those ways, should open *Hand*'s mind to the possibility that there is some other, underlying reality that determines how the things around *Hand* 'show up' or 'light up' for *Hand*; in other words, that there is something called Being that manifests itself as beings.

(2) *Absence*. If the source of *Hand*'s stuckness is that the tools or materials that *Hand* needs to do the work they are supposed to do are missing, then two things happen.

First, *Hand*'s attention is drawn to the way in which his ability to work is bound up with the wider world and the resources it provides to do that work. Insofar as *Hand* identifies with the work *Hand* does, *Hand*'s attention is consequently drawn to the way in which *Hand*'s identity is bound up with the wider world and the opportunities it provides for *Hand* to be the sort of person that *Hand* is. In this way, *Hand*'s mind is opened to the reality that they are not wholly responsible for the life they lead – that they are (again, in Heideggerian language) 'thrown' into a world that affords them opportunities to engage with various forms of life, with the result that the life they lead is really one way in which the world into which they have been 'thrown' manifests itself. One can easily see how reflecting along these lines will in turn open one's mind to the possibility that the best way of describing our reality is that we live in a world where Being manifests itself as beings.

Second, *Hand*'s experience of being stuck because of the lack of availability of the tools or materials that *Hand* needs raises an issue for *Hand*: what are you going to do? Are you going to seek out the tools and materials that you need in order to do the work, or are you going to abandon it? This in turn raises questions for *Hand* about the value of the work they do, and ultimately what sort of person they want to be. As we will see when we explore below the links between someone's seeking to be a good 'shepherd of Being' and someone's striving to be true to themselves – the self they would like to be – *Hand*'s reflecting on

[69] In what follows, I've drawn on Dreyfus, *Being-in-the-World* (MIT Press, 1991), 69–83, 88–100; and Crawford, *The Case for Working With Your Hands* (Viking, 2010), 21–28, 72–125. The *fons et origo* of all these observations is Heidegger, *Being and Time* (1927), Part One, Division One ('Preparatory fundamental analysis of Dasein').

these questions of value and identity, and acting on the answers, inevitably results in *Hand*'s seeking to make a deeper connection with Being.

(3) *Ignorance.* Finally, the source of *Hand*'s stuckness may be that *Hand* cannot figure out how to go about doing the work that *Hand* is supposed to be doing. An engine needs to be repaired, but *Hand* cannot figure out what is wrong with it. A machine needs to be built that will perform to certain specifications, but *Hand* cannot figure how to construct the machine to meet those specifications.

*Hand*'s stuckness is an invitation to *Hand* to attend with 'passionate concern'[70] to the reality of the engine or machine (or whatever it is) that *Hand* is working on. It is only by doing this that *Hand* is going to get unstuck and penetrate through to the solution (if it exists) to whatever it is that is obstructing B from making progress.

In attending with such 'passionate concern' to that aspect of reality that *Hand* is supposed to be working on, *Hand* achieves a kind of union with it. This is not the kind of union that comes from flow, but the kind of union that exists wherever love abides. But like the kind of union that comes from flow, the union that *Hand* achieves with whatever it is *Hand* is focussing on may prompt the same kind of openness to the possibility that this union reflects a deeper union undergirding reality, a deeper union that allows *Hand* to connect with the engine or machine (or whatever it is) that *Hand* is working on in such a way that suddenly the solution to *Hand*'s stuckness materialises.

So when *Hand*'s work is going well *and* when it is going badly, the kind of physical work that *Hand* does may well provide *Hand* with opportunities to contemplate, and witness to, Being's manifesting itself as beings. In contrast, the same kind of opportunities are not usually provided by the kind of work that *Mind* does, which involves *Mind*'s using and manipulating concepts.

This is not to say that *Mind*'s kind of work is *incapable* of giving rise to the experiences of flow and stuckness that *Hand* will encounter in their kind of work. However, this tends only to be the case where *Mind*'s work is *already* focussed on contemplating, and witnessing to, Being's manifesting itself as beings – as will be the case where *Mind* is engaged in creating great art[71] or puzzling over scientific questions that go to the heart of our reality. Where *Mind*'s work is not so focussed, then when *Mind*'s work goes well, *Mind* will tend to experience not flow, but *facility*; and when *Mind*'s work goes badly, *Mind* will tend to experience not stuckness, but *boredom*.

And this is not to say either that the kind of work that *Hand* does will *always* give rise to the experiences of flow and stuckness that open the door to *Hand*'s contemplating, and witnessing to, Being's manifesting itself as beings. Physical work that is completely mindless – and is therefore incapable of engaging *Hand*'s whole being – will not give rise to experiences of flow and stuckness, but rather the same experiences of facility and boredom

---

[70] Crawford, *The Case for Working With Your Hands* (n 69), 98. Crawford goes on immediately to observe, 'The truth does not reveal itself to idle spectators.'

[71] Cf. Barrett, *Irrational Man* (n 42), 119: 'Poets are witnesses to Being before the philosophers are able to bring it into thought'; Bringhurst, *Everywhere Being is Dancing* (n 44), 16: 'What poetry knows, or what it strives to know, is the dancing at the heart of being … Poetry is knowing. Knowing is moving in tune with being.' On the relationship between art and Being, see Richardson, *Heidegger* (n 23), 413–15, and Magee, *Confessions of a Philosopher* (Weidenfeld & Nicholson, 1997), 503–04.

that *Mind*'s work will tend to give rise to, where *Mind*'s work is not focussed on contemplating, and witnessing to, Being's manifesting itself as beings.

What the reflections in this section *do* indicate is that the kind of work *Hand* does is likely to be more conducive to their contemplating, and witnessing to, Being's manifesting itself as beings than the kind of work *Mind* does. It follows that there *is* a link between the truth-seeking activity of (5) doing work that places a strong emphasis on developing, and drawing on, a sense of reality and someone's seeking to be a good 'shepherd of Being'.

### (ii)  *The Self We Want To Be*

Can we also make a link between the truth-seeking activity of (8) striving to be true to oneself – the self one would like to be – in deciding what to do, and S's seeking to be a good 'shepherd of Being'? I think we can, but making the link takes a few different stages.

We need first to observe that S's desire to be a particular kind of person (call this kind of person 'P') is not just any desire, like a desire to eat an ice cream. We can follow Harry Frankfurt in distinguishing between 'first-order' and 'second-order' desires, where a first-order desire is 'simply [a desire] to do or not to do one thing or another',[72] such as eating an ice cream. A second-order desire is a desire 'to have (or not to have) certain desires or motives.'[73] So an example of a second-order desire would be a desire not to have a desire to eat an ice cream.

It seems to be the case that second-order desires are rooted in one's desire to be a particular kind of person.[74] This is because the most natural reason you would have a desire not to have a desire to eat an ice cream is that you want to be the kind of person who is indifferent to ice cream (though, sadly, you are not: hence your first-order desire to eat an ice cream). So S's desire to be P shapes the way S evaluates the first-order desires that she has at any one time. She will endorse a particular first-order desire where having and acting on that desire is consistent with S's being P; and she will disown a particular first-order desire (though she may still, through weakness, act on it) where having and acting on that desire is inconsistent with S's being P.

We observed above that the kind of person S desires to be (who we are calling 'P') will be rooted in the thick ethical concepts that S accepts as valid.[75] P will be, first, someone to whom the thick *positive* ethical concepts that S accepts as valid apply. So assuming that S accepts these thick positive ethical concepts as valid, S will want, first, to be the kind of person who can be justly said to be courageous, hard-working, and loyal. P will be, second, someone to whom the thick *negative* ethical concepts that S accepts as valid do *not* apply. So assuming that S accepts these thick negative ethical concepts as valid, S will *not* want to be the kind of person who can justly be said to be shifty, flirty, and boring.

But where do these thick ethical concepts come from? The function they play is to pick out certain types of existence as *qualitatively* higher, or lower, than other types of existence.

---

[72] Frankfurt, 'Freedom of the Will and the Concept of a Person' in his *The Importance of What We Care About* (CUP, 1988), 12.

[73] Ibid.

[74] One might say, then, that a desire to be a particular kind of person is a 'third-order' desire. However, Frankfurt seems to reserve that term for a desire to have (or not to have) a second-order desire to have (or not to have) a particular first-order desire: ibid, 21.

[75] See above, p 46.

So assuming that S accepts the thick ethical concepts of 'courageous' and 'shifty' as being valid, S thereby acknowledges that being courageous is a qualitatively higher form of existence than that involved in not being courageous, and that being shifty is a qualitatively lower form of existence than that involved in not being shifty. And as P combines within herself all the positive thick ethical concepts that S acknowledges as valid and none of the negative thick ethical concepts that S acknowledges as valid, S's desire to be P is a desire to be the kind of person who enjoys the qualitatively highest form of existence that S can envisage. Insofar then as S strives to be the kind of person she wants to be, she strives to enjoy the qualitatively highest form of existence that S can envisage.

The last few sentences help explain the significance of thick ethical concepts for S – but a mystery still hangs over what their significance is. The existence of thick ethical concepts assumes that certain activities and ways of life are qualitatively higher than other types of existence: a life spent on poetry is superior to a life spent playing push-pin.[76] But in what sense is it superior? John Stuart Mill's answer was – (i) the life spent on poetry is superior to (ii) the life spent playing push-pin because someone familiar with both kinds of life would choose (i) over (ii).[77] But why would they make that choice? If the reason for choosing (i) over (ii) is that (i) is a qualitatively higher form of existence than (ii), then we are back where we started in terms of solving our mystery.

Charles Taylor calls what is happening when someone chooses (i) over (ii) because (i) is a qualitatively higher form of existence than (ii), 'strong evaluation'.[78] He suggests that strong evaluation reflects a 'craving that is ineradicable from human life. We have to be rightly placed in relation to the good.'[79] If this is right, then a thick positive ethical concept is a sign, telling us 'This way for a stronger connection to the good!'; and a thick negative ethical concept is a sign that points the other way and says: 'Warning: going this way will weaken your connection to the good!'[80]

Charles Taylor goes on to pick out among the goods that 'I naturally want to be well placed in relation to' a special category of goods that he calls *hypergoods*. These are 'goods which not only are incomparably more important than [other goods] but provide the standpoint from which these [other goods] must be weighed, judged, decided about.'[81] And within the category of hypergoods, there may exist for a given individual (S) an ultimate good, which provides for S:

> the landmarks for what they judge to be the direction of their [life] … It is orientation to [the ultimate hypergood] which comes closest to defining my identity, and therefore my direction to this good is of unique importance to me … Just because my orientation to it is essential to my identity, so the recognition that my life is turned away from it, or can never approach it, would be devastating and insufferable. It threatens to plunge me into a despair at my unworthiness which strikes

---

[76] Bentham is often taken to have asserted the contrary in *The Rationale of Reward* (Hunt, 1825), 206. However, he was actually arguing there that *from one perspective* (its contribution to the total amount of pleasure in society), push-pin could be seen as being a more useful activity than poetry.

[77] Mill, *Utilitarianism* (1863), chapter 2.

[78] Taylor, 'What is Human Agency?' in his *Human Agency and Language: Philosophical Papers 1* (CUP, 1985), 15–27.

[79] Taylor, *Sources of the Self* (CUP, 1989), 44.

[80] Cf. the concept of an 'ethical map' set out in McBride, *The Humanity of Private Law, Part I: Explanation* (n 2), 22–26.

[81] Taylor, *Sources of the Self* (n 79), 63.

at the very roots of my being as a person. Symmetrically, the assurance that I am turned towards this good gives me a sense of wholeness, of fullness of being as a person or self, that nothing else can.[82]

So when you engage in what Taylor calls 'strong evaluation' – choosing poetry over push-pin on the basis that the experience of reading poetry is qualitatively higher than the experience of playing push-pin – your choices are motivated by a desire on your part to maintain, or improve, your connection with the good. Moreover, when you engage in the kind of 'strong evaluation' that is based on your acknowledging a particular hypergood as ultimate for you, your choices are based on your seeking to make, or maintain, the strongest connection with the good that you could possibly imagine enjoying.

In light of this, let's return to S's desire to be P – the kind of person who enjoys the qualitatively highest form of existence that S can envisage. It follows from what has been said in the last few paragraphs that for S, P will enjoy the strongest connection to the good that S can envisage anyone enjoying. So S's desire to be P is a desire to enjoy the strongest connection to the good that S can envisage anyone enjoying.

*If* we can identify 'the good' with 'Being', then whether S knows it or not, in striving to be P, S is really striving to enjoy the strongest connection with Being that S can envisage anyone enjoying. But we have already said that it is the good 'shepherd of Being' who *will* enjoy the strongest connection with Being that anyone can enjoy.[83] So, again, whether S knows it or not, when S seeks to be P, S seeks to be a good 'shepherd of Being'. In this way, there is not just a link between the truth-seeking activity of (8) striving to be true to oneself – the self one would like to be – in deciding what to do, and S's seeking to be a good 'shepherd of Being'. *They are the same thing.* If S 'sells out', and loses integrity by turning her back on the aspiration to be the kind of person that she still acknowledges she 'ought' to be, then we can no longer say that S is seeking to be a good 'shepherd of Being'. But if S keeps faith with her dream to be that kind of person, then S can justifiably claim to be seeking to be a good 'shepherd of Being'.

But can we identify 'the good' with 'Being'? The answer is: within the view of reality that we have been calling view (3) – or the *Traditional View of Being* – and which we are assuming is true for the purposes of seeing whether there is a connection between that view of reality and the proposition that human flourishing consists in QTL-ing, 'the good' *must* be identified with Being.[84] Being is all good, and no good can exist outside Being. So if view (3) of reality – or *The Traditional View of Being* – is correct (and, for the purposes of this section, we are assuming it is) then the truth-seeking activity of striving to be true to the kind of person one wants to be is indistinguishable from one's seeking to be a good 'shepherd of Being'.

## The Unacceptable Implication

Enough has now been said to show – just as (H) told us would be the case – that some-one who seeks to be a good 'shepherd of Being' has to enjoy the truth-seeking virtues

---

[82] Ibid, 62–63.
[83] See above, p 84.
[84] See above, p 76, n 30.

and engage in the truth-seeking activities that we have located at the heart of someone's QTL-ing. However, it might be objected that this does *not* establish that seeking to be a good 'shepherd of Being' is the same thing as QTL-ing, which is what (H) claims. If they were the same thing, then an unacceptable implication would arise, which is that someone who does *not* seek to be a good 'shepherd of Being' could *not* be said to be engaged in a quest to lead a truthful life.

This would mean that exemplary truth-seekers such as the physicist Richard Feynman[85] or the philosopher Karl Popper[86] could not be said to be engaged in a quest to lead a truthful life. This is because both Feynman and Popper were *Naïve Splitters* and as a result did not think there was any such thing as Being and therefore had absolutely no intention of seeking to be good 'shepherds of Being'. Moreover, if we accept that human flourishing consists in QTL-ing and also accept that QTL-ing is the same thing as seeking to be a good 'shepherd of Being', then neither Feynman nor Popper could be said to be exemplars of human flourishing. This seems to be an unacceptable result and points, it might be argued, to the conclusion that, contrary to what (H) claims, QTL-ing and seeking to be a good 'shepherd of Being' are *not* the same thing. While it may be the case that someone cannot seek to be a good 'shepherd of Being' without QTL-ing, it is also the case that someone can QTL without seeking to be a good 'shepherd of Being'.

I think we can avoid this unacceptable implication by distinguishing between (i) *being* a good 'shepherd of Being'; and (ii) *seeking* to be a good 'shepherd of Being'. It may be that (i) is impossible for someone who does not think that there is any such thing as Being.[87] But it is not clear that (ii) is similarly impossible. After all, we just observed that if S strives to be true to the kind of person she wants to be, given the thick ethical concepts that S accepts as valid, then S – whether she knows it or not – is seeking to be a good 'shepherd of Being'.[88] Can we say in the same way that – whether they knew it or not – exemplary truth-seekers like Feynman and Popper were *seeking* to be good 'shepherds of Being'? I think we can. I think we can say that so long as Feynman and Popper were committed to contemplating, and witnessing to, the nature of reality with ever more care and attention, then – whether they knew it or not – they *were* seeking to be excellent contemplators of, and witnesses to, Being's manifesting itself as beings.

An analogy may help to make this point. Children who run about in a garden searching for a treasure that they have been told is there, both know and don't know what they are looking for. They know they are looking for 'treasure' but they don't and can't know what

---

[85] The best example of Feynman's unbending commitment to truth-seeking is his famous observation that if a proposed physical law 'disagrees with experiment it is wrong. In that simple statement is the key to science. It does not make any difference how beautiful your guess is. It does not make any difference how smart you are, who made the guess, or what his name is – if it disagrees with experiment it is wrong. That is all there is to it' (Feynman, *The Character of Physical Law* (MIT Press, 1967), 156). See also Feynman's 1974 Caltech commencement address 'Cargo cult science', reprinted in Feynman, *Surely You're Joking Mr Feynman!* (Vintage, 1992), 338.

[86] Popper's autobiography is entitled *Unended Quest* (Fontana, 1976): the quest in question is undoubtedly a quest for truth. The very first page of Popper's autobiography demonstrates the truth-seeking virtue of humility, saying that his time working for a master cabinetmaker from 1922 to 1924 'taught me not only how very little I knew but also that any wisdom to which I might ever aspire could consist only in realizing more fully the infinity of my ignorance' (ibid, 8). Popper's love of truth is demonstrated later on, when he argues that the value 'of *objective truth, and of its growth*. … is the highest value of all … (Thus I am utterly opposed to those who fear truth – who think it was a sin to eat from the tree of knowledge.)' (ibid, 195 (emphasis in original)).

[87] That was the position taken above, at p 84.

[88] See p 92.

that treasure is until they find it.[89] Similarly, Feynman and Popper both knew and didn't know what they were seeking. They knew they were seeking to be excellent contemplators of, and witnesses to, the nature of reality. But they did not, and could not, know what that involves until they had achieved their goal. If the *Traditional View of Being* is correct, then being an excellent contemplator of, and witness to, the nature of reality involves excellently contemplating, and witnessing to, Being's manifesting itself as beings.

It follows that in leading the lives they did, Feynman and Popper's goal *was* to become an excellent contemplator of, and witness to, Being's manifesting itself as beings. The fact that neither Feynman nor Popper thought that there was any such thing as Being may mean they were always going to fall short of achieving that goal, but it was still their goal – they just did not know that was their goal, because they could not have known that that was their goal all along until they achieved it. So there seems no reason why we cannot say that Feynman and Popper were seeking to be good 'shepherds of Being' even though they did not think that there was any such thing as Being.

In this way, we can agree with (H) that QTL-ing and seeking to be a good 'shepherd of Being' are the same thing while avoiding the unacceptable implication of saying that exemplary truth-seekers like Feynman and Popper were not engaged in a quest to lead a truthful life, and that Feynman and Popper were therefore not exemplars of human flourishing (which they certainly were).

## Revisiting the Four Postulates

Enough has been said by now to show, first, that there is a very strong correspondence between QTL-ing and seeking to be a good 'shepherd of Being', and, second, that identifying QTL-ing with seeking to be a good 'shepherd of Being' does not have any unacceptable implications.

However, this may not convince everyone that (H) is correct in *identifying* QTL-ing with seeking to be a good 'shepherd of Being'. For example, nothing we have said so far *rules out* the possibility that one *can* QTL without seeking to be a good 'shepherd of Being'. But that possibility will look very remote if it can also be shown that the case made in the previous chapter for thinking that human flourishing consists in QTL-ing applies just as well, if not better, to the claim that human flourishing consists in seeking to be a good 'shepherd of Being'. If this is the case, then the claim made by (H) – that QTL-ing and seeking to be a good 'shepherd of Being' are the same thing – will be made out as much as it possibly could be.

Let's see first how well *The Proposition* that human flourishing consists in seeking to be a good 'shepherd of Being' traverses the tightrope set up by our first two postulates of human flourishing, (P1) (that human flourishing is within the reach of any human being, and is not something that can only be enjoyed by a privileged elite) and (P2) (that anyone's flourishing can be harmed by a wide range of different events). The Proposition satisfies both postulates. Taking (P1) first, in principle anyone (including someone suffering from serious disabilities) is capable of seeking to cultivate within themselves an endless wonder

---

[89] Cf. the inherently open-ended and tentative nature of a quest: p 24.

at the world, and to communicate to others a kind of piety towards it, and thereby become a good 'shepherd of Being'.

Moreover, The Proposition makes clear – in a way that was not made clear by the claim that human flourishing consists in QTL-ing – that *children* are capable of flourishing *in exactly the same way* as adults. Under the conception of human flourishing that is dominant in modern Western liberal societies – what we have been calling 'the RP' – what exactly the flourishing of children consists in is a bit of a puzzle. If we insisted that children's flourishing consisted in RP-flourishing, we would have to conclude that flourishing is impossible for children as many of the goods that make up the RP are beyond the grasp of children.[90] However, if The Proposition is correct then children may be the *best* examples available to us of human flourishing.[91] If we seek to become good 'shepherds of Being' we could hardly do better than try to recapture some of the qualities that came to us so naturally as children: the sense of astonishment at the world, the incessant asking of 'why' questions that presuppose there is an ultimate answer to everything, the constant desire to point out things to other people and talk about them ('Look! A tree!').[92]

So if The Proposition is correct, (P1) is satisfied in spades – it truly is the case that flourishing is within the grasp of *anyone* who counts as a member of the human race, including the littlest among us. At the same time, and as we will see in the next section, (P2) is also satisfied by The Proposition – there are plenty of events outside our control that are capable of damaging the natural capacity we enjoy to seek to become a good 'shepherd of Being'.

This leaves our third and fourth postulates about human flourishing: (P3) (that human flourishing is a good thing, everywhere and anywhere it exists) and (P4) (that human flourishing is self-sustaining across time and across persons). Just as with (P1), if The Proposition is correct, we are able to gain a far deeper understanding of how (P3) is satisfied than we were given by the bare claim that human flourishing consists in QTL-ing. Obviously, it follows from everything that has already been said – in particular, the identification of Being with good – that *being* a good 'shepherd of Being' will be a good thing, because being a good 'shepherd of Being' involves maximal participation in the good. However, The Proposition identifies human flourishing with *seeking to be* a good 'shepherd of Being'. In what sense is that seeking, of and in itself, a good thing, everywhere and anywhere it exists?

[90] It may be for this reason that such emphasis is placed on children growing up as quickly as possible in modern Western liberal societies: we seek to solve the puzzle children's flourishing represents by reducing the time-frame within which the issue of their flourishing is a puzzle.

[91] Cf Matthew 18:3 'I am telling you the truth: unless you change and become like little children, you will never enter the Kingdom of Heaven' (my translation).

[92] Cf Matthiesen, *At Play in the Fields of the Lord* (Random House, 1965), 251: 'He blinked, as if just awakened: how unreal everything seemed! How easily, in the absence of children, the whole experience of life became abstracted, a pattern of words and daydreams. Because the life in [his son] was so fresh and immediate, he had served as a reminder of reality'; Salinger, *Raise High the Roof Beam, Carpenters; Seymour-An Introduction* (Little Brown, 1963), 177: 'We're required only to keep looking. Seymour once said … when he was eleven, that the thing he loved best in the Bible was the word WATCH!' (My thanks to Bill Grimstone for bringing both of these quotations to my attention.) Also Capobianco, *Heidegger's Way of Being* (n 20), 26: 'the way remains open to us to take up and take to heart this marvellous matter of *the truth of Being* – Heidegger's distinctive way of calling us back to the experience of Being as manifestation; to the experience of things as they emerge and meet us and, as we say in English, "fill our senses"; to the experience of ourselves "vibrating back" from things, as Walt Whitman put it. The nearness and freshness and vividness of what is, and the astonishment and joy and thanksgiving that this calls forth in us' (emphasis in original).

It is the case, of course, that the process of *seeking to be* a good 'shepherd of Being' is valuable because *being* a good 'shepherd of Being' is valuable. We have already seen that the only reliable way of achieving one's goal of being a good 'shepherd of Being' is to assume that one is *not* a good shepherd, and simply focus on continuing to seek to be a good 'shepherd of Being'.[93] Moreover, the various virtues that are essential to being a good 'shepherd of Being' – one's caring for, attending to, being attuned towards, and feeling responsible for, Being – cannot come into existence overnight. They have to be inculcated and cultivated over time, through seeking to be a good 'shepherd of Being'. However, we are trying to understand how seeking to be a good 'shepherd of Being' is good, not derivatively, but *of and in itself* in the same way that (P3) postulates human flourishing is good, of and in itself.

It was suggested in the previous chapter that the mere fact that we *have* to engage in a quest to lead a truthful life in order to lead a truthful life suggests that 'something important would be achieved by people embarking on such a quest, and that the universe would therefore be a better place for people's embarking on that kind of quest.'[94] But we left it open what that *something* was, suggesting that it would only become clear if and when we engaged in a quest to lead a truthful life. Having undertaken in this chapter a mini-quest to understand better the nature of a quest to lead a truthful life, are we in a better position now to know what that *something* is – the something that accounts for why the universe is structured in a way that the treasure of *being* a good 'shepherd of Being' is hidden from us in the garden of reality, and why we are first required to run about seeking that treasure before we are allowed to find it?

I think we can. The key to unlocking this mystery lies in the observation that what *kind* of connection you, as a good 'shepherd of Being', are able to make with Being is strongly dependent on the story of your life up until now. It is your history that largely determines how Being will 'light up' or 'show up' for you,[95] and therefore your history that largely determines *how* you will contemplate, and witness to, Being's manifesting itself as beings.

It follows from this that each individual can only ever access a narrow and one-sided view of Being; but it also follows that the more uniform the life-stories of people living in a particular community, the more narrow and one-sided will be their *collective* view of Being. From the point of view of Being, this is a problem: if Being would be unfulfilled or incomplete if there were nothing or no-one for it to manifest itself to,[96] then it will also be relatively unfulfilled or incomplete if the people to whom it is manifesting itself are collectively incapable of adopting anything more than a narrow and one-sided view of Being by virtue of the uniformity of their life stories. In contrast, Being will be most fulfilled and complete if it manifests itself to people who are collectively capable of appreciating Being in all its rich and multifarious dimensions by virtue of the diversity of their life-stories.

So for Being to be most fulfilled and complete, it has to manifest itself to people who are all good 'shepherds of Being', *but in different ways*. However, such a diversity of outlook on Being would be impossible to achieve if each of us were not first given the time and

---

[93] See above, pp 86–87.

[94] See above, p 60 (emphasis in original).

[95] This is another Heideggerian insight: see *Being and Time* (1927), II.5. See also Taylor, *Sources of the Self* (n 79), 47–50, 72–73.

[96] See above, p 84.

space to *seek to be* a good 'shepherd of Being', and thereby find our way to Being in our own individual ways. So seeking to be a good 'shepherd of Being' is good, of and in itself, because Being's being most fulfilled and complete crucially depends on our *seeking to be* good 'shepherds of Being'. Without such prior seeking, the value of our *being* good 'shepherds of Being' would not be annulled, but it would be substantially diminished.

Armed with this insight, we can easily see how the various aspects of (P3) are satisfied if The Proposition is correct.[97] A universe without human beings would be one where Being was unfulfilled and incomplete, and therefore less good than one with human beings.[98] And (other things being equal) a universe with more human beings is better than a universe with less because the more human beings there are that contemplate, and witness to, Being in their own way, the more fulfilled and complete Being will be. And, at a personal level, these facts give us reason to take steps, where we are in a position to do so, to ensure that the universe contains more human beings than less.

What about (P4) and the three claims that underpin (P4)?[99] Are they also satisfied if The Proposition is correct? It is hard to see why not. At a personal level, the derivative good involved in seeking to be a good 'shepherd of Being' – the fact that you can only become a good 'shepherd of Being' by constantly seeking to be a good 'shepherd of Being' – will give sufficient meaning to your life that you will never feel suicidal, or wish to give up on seeking to be a good 'shepherd of Being'. And the intrinsic good achieved where a *community* of people all seek to be good 'shepherds of Being' – the existence of the diverse perspectives on Being that their seeking provides – supplies reason for everyone to support the existence of such communities, and, when the chips are down and unpalatable choices have to be made, to prefer the continued existence of one such community over their own continued existence.

If all this is correct, then the four postulates about human flourishing that the RP manifestly fails to satisfy, are amply satisfied – and for much the same reasons – by *both* the claim (made in the previous chapter) that human flourishing consists in QTL-ing *and* the claim (made in this chapter) that human flourishing consists in seeking to be a good 'shepherd of Being'. It seems unlikely that this could be a coincidence, particularly given that we have already seen that the virtues and activities involved in seeking to be a good 'shepherd of Being' are identical to the virtues and activities involved in QTL-ing. Given this, we should accept the claim made by (H), that QTL-ing and seeking to be a good 'shepherd of Being' are the same thing. If this is so, then there exists a clear link between (i) the claim that human flourishing consists in being engaged in a quest to lead a truthful life, and (ii) the claim that human beings are the beings that are aware (or are capable of being aware) that they participate in Being. If (ii) is true, then we can see why (i) would be true, provided we accept (as we should by now) that being engaged in a quest to lead a truthful life is the same thing as seeking to be ever more excellent in the way one contemplates, and witnesses to, Being's manifesting itself as beings.

---

[97] For these aspects, see above, pp 11 and 59.

[98] Cf. King, *Heidegger and Happiness* (n 98), 116–17: 'If human beings were to disappear, it would be a loss for things in general; their being would no longer be fulfilled in its reception by beings capable of both receiving and reflecting on it.'

[99] For these claims, see above, pp 12 and 20.

# 3.  Anti-Being

Identifying QTL-ing with seeking to be a good 'shepherd of Being' not only helps bolster the claim made in the previous chapter that human flourishing consists in QTL-ing. It should also help give us a deeper insight as to what QTL-ing involves than we were provided by the previous chapter. This section explores this possibility, by discussing some of the ways in which someone (S) can be dragged away from seeking to be a good 'shepherd of Being'.

## Vices

First of all, S can be prevented from seeking to be a good 'shepherd of Being' as a result of possessing any one of the following characteristics: (1) pride; (2) hatred; and (3) will to power. We can justifiably designate these characteristics as *vices*: if we identify seeking to be a good 'shepherd of Being' with QTL-ing, and QTL-ing with flourishing as a human being, then it follows that possession of any one of these characteristics will prevent S from flourishing as a human being.

(1) *Pride.* We have already noted that humility is an essential quality to S's seeking to be a good 'shepherd of Being': if S prides herself on *being* a good 'shepherd of Being' then she will, by definition, cease striving to *become* a good 'shepherd of Being'.[100] However, pride can also prevent S getting into the game of seeking to be a good 'shepherd of Being' in the first place, in the same way that Maria Dmitrievna's pride prevented her from properly participating in the 'Danila Kupar' dance described by Tolstoy.[101] Her desire not to be taken over by the dance in the same way that her companion the Count was taken over by it was based on a proud desire to preserve her independence above all else. In the same way, a prideful love of independence can prevent S from seeking to be a good 'shepherd of Being'. When she realises that becoming a good 'shepherd of Being' will result in her being taken over by Being, S may well shy away from seeking to deepen the connection with Being that she has by virtue of her simply existing.

(2) *Hatred.* Any kind of hatred will get in the way of S's seeking to be a good 'shepherd of Being', but for the purposes of establishing the point, we can usefully distinguish between three kinds of hatred: (i) self-hatred; (ii) hatred of Being; and (iii) ordinary hatred.

Self-hatred gets in the way of S's seeking to be a good 'shepherd of Being' in two ways. First, S's hatred for herself saps her of the will to do anything, or focus on anything, other than harming herself. Second, S's self-hatred prevents her seeing anything worthwhile in Being that might make it an appropriate object of contemplation, or witness, as her most immediate experience of Being's manifesting itself is in her own being, which she despises. As a result S's self-hatred may well spill over, if she is so minded, into the second kind of hatred that will prevent S from seeking to be a good 'shepherd of Being', which is hatred of Being.

---

[100] See above, p 86.
[101] See above, p 82.

It seems unlikely that someone who hates Being – like Milton's Satan[102] – would seek to be a good 'shepherd of Being'. That it is possible for mere humans to hate Being is shown by Herman Melville's 'wicked book'[103] *Moby-Dick* (1851), which both depicts Captain Ahab's obsessive hatred of Being, in the form of the whale Moby Dick, and expresses Melville's own hatred of Being.[104] That Ahab's hatred of Moby Dick is no ordinary hatred is made obvious when Ahab's chief mate Starbuck rebukes Ahab for seeking vengeance on an animal that acts purely out of instinct. Ahab's response explicitly draws on Kant's distinction between phenomenal and noumenal reality and makes it clear that Ahab is seeking revenge on noumenal reality – Being itself:

> All visible objects, man, are but as pasteboard masks. But in each event – in the living act, the undoubted deed – there, some unknown but still reasoning thing puts forth the mouldings of its features from behind the unreasoning mask. If man will strike, strike through the mask! How can the prisoner reach outside except by thrusting through the wall? To me, the white whale is that wall, shoved near to me. Sometimes I think there's naught beyond.[105] But 'tis enough. He tasks me; he heaps me; I see in him outrageous strength, with an inscrutable malice sinewing it. That inscrutable thing is chiefly what I hate; and be the white whale agent, or be the white whale principal, I will wreak that hate upon him.[106]

The idea that Ahab, or Melville himself, might seek to become an excellent contemplator of, and witness to, the nature of Being seems risible.

It might be argued, against this, that Ahab/Melville might have sought to become a good 'shepherd of Being' in order to expose Being's wickedness for all to see. However, such an enterprise would seem to be self-refuting in that it assumes that knowing the truth, being clear-sighted, is a good – a good that, because it owes its existence to Being, establishes that Being cannot be all wicked but must (because of the oneness of Being) be all good. A more logical response to Ahab/Melville's hatred of Being – and one that is less damaging than Ahab's response – would be to get out of the business of contemplating, and talking about, Being altogether, and avert one's eyes from it through various diversions.[107]

---

[102] Milton, *Paradise Lost* (1667).

[103] Melville's own description of *Moby-Dick*, in a letter written to Nathaniel Hawthorne in November 1851: 'I have written a wicked book, and feel as spotless as the lamb.'

[104] See Thompson, *Melville's Quarrel with God* (Princeton UP, 2015). It seems that Melville was a Schopenhauerian *avant la lettre*, forming as pessimistic a view of reality as Schopenhauer's before Schopenhauer's works became available in English (1883), and avidly devouring the English translations of Schopenhauer before Melville's death in 1891.

[105] 'Sometimes I think there's naught beyond' is a remarkable anticipation of Heidegger's view of Being (or view (4) of reality), 75 years before Heidegger.

[106] Melville, *Moby-Dick, or The Whale* (1851), chapter 36 ('The Quarter-Deck'). Contrast Job's (eventual) reaction to his misfortunes. On being invited to contemplate Being's manifesting itself as beings (including the sea-dwelling Leviathan: Job 40:15–41:26) Job confesses his inability to comprehend Being and repents his earlier attempts to represent Being's intentions (Job 42).

[107] Cf David Hume's response to the depression induced by his adopting a *Naïve Splitter* view of reality: 'I dine, I play a game of backgammon. I converse, and am merry with friends' (Hume, *A Treatise of Human Nature* (1740), Book One, Part IV, Section VII ('Conclusion of this Book')). It may be worth noting that Melville's last novel (*The Confidence-Man*) was published in 1857, almost a half-century before Melville's death. Hume did not observe a similar period of public silence, but after the above passage did remark that it was difficult to understand why – given his view of reality – he thought it worthwhile to communicate that view of reality to others. However, he put it down to natural inclination that he was 'concerned for the condition of the learned world ... [and felt] an ambition ... of contributing to the instruction of mankind' (ibid).

But what if Ahab's hatred of Moby Dick had been an ordinary hatred – the hatred anyone might well feel for someone or something that had done them a bad turn? Would that have gotten in the way of Ahab's seeking to be a good 'shepherd of Being'? It seems inevitable that it would have, on the basis that 'No man can serve two masters.'[108] We observed above that if S hates X, then S will think that her flourishing is dependent on X's suffering harm or being destroyed.[109] So S will think that her flourishing lies in the direction of X's being harmed or destroyed, whereas it will actually lie (if the arguments made in this chapter are correct) in the direction of her seeking to be a good 'shepherd of Being'. It is hard to see how S can proceed in both directions at once, and as S thinks that her flourishing lies in the direction of X's being harmed or destroyed, then S will proceed in that direction, and will as an inevitable result be taken away from seeking to be a good 'shepherd of Being'.

(3) *Will to power.* CS Lewis observed:

> There is something which unites magic and applied science while separating both from the 'wisdom' of earlier ages. For the wise men of old the cardinal problem had been how to conform the soul to reality, and the solution had been knowledge, self-discipline, and virtue. For magic and applied science alike the problem is how to subdue reality to the wishes of men: the solution is a technique …[110]

It is the desire to 'subdue reality to the wishes of men' that I am referring to as the 'will to power'. An individual, or a society, that has been taken over by the will to power will engage in two characteristic activities: (i) *manipulating* beings to achieve *desired* effects; and (ii) *calculating* what manipulations will most *efficiently*, or *effectively*, achieve those desired effects. Let's follow Alasdair MacIntyre's example and call an individual that engages in these kinds of activities a 'manager'.[111] And let's follow Jacques Ellul's example and call a society that is centred around these kinds of activities 'technological'.[112]

Of course, someone does not have to *be* a manager – in the sense of occupying a role that requires them to do (i) and (ii) – to adopt a managerial mind-set; and one can adopt a managerial mind-set in relation to all areas of one's life. For example, someone who reads *The Game*[113] for tips on how to get women into bed is adopting a managerial mind-set with regard to their relationships with women. Likewise, someone who reads *The Rules*[114] for tips on how to get married to 'Mr Right' may be acting more nobly than someone who pores over *The Game*, but she is still adopting the exact same managerial mind-set as her counterpart who reads *The Game*. In both cases, neither reader can claim to be seeking to be a good 'shepherd of Being' in their relationships with other people. Instead of seeking to think, and talk, about other people with the kind of awe and wonder that befits the beings

---

[108] Matthew 6:24.
[109] See above, p 7.
[110] Lewis, *The Abolition of Man* (1943), ch 3.
[111] MacIntyre, *After Virtue*, 3rd ed (Bloomsbury, 2013), 34–35, 88–89.
[112] Ellul, *The Technological Society* (Alfred A Knopf, 1964) (trans Wilkinson).
[113] Strauss, *The Game: Undercover in the Secret Society of Pickup Artists* (Canongate Books, 2005).
[114] Fein and Schneider, *The Rules: Time-Tested Secrets for Capturing the Heart of Mr Right* (Warner Books, 1995).

that are the most amazing manifestations of Being known to us, the managerial mind-set instead reduces other people to sources of sexual and emotional satisfaction, or physical and financial security.

The same falling away from seeking to be a good 'shepherd of Being' occurs whenever someone adopts a managerial mind-set, and thereby reduces beings to *resources* to be exploited rather than viewing them as manifestations of Being.[115] Heidegger's example is the Rhine, which becomes 'a water-power supplier' by virtue of a 'hydroelectric plant [being] set into the current of the Rhine', with the result that we lose sight of '"The Rhine" as uttered by the *art*work, in Hölderlin's hymn by that name'.[116] Generalising, Heidegger observes that where managerial mind-sets hold sway, 'Everywhere everything is ordered to stand by, to be immediately on hand, indeed to stand there just so that it may be on call for a further ordering. Whatever is ordered about in this way has its own standing. We call it the standing-reserve [*Bestand*].'[117] Other writers on Being[118] invoke the statement 'We must put nature to the rack, to compel it to answer our questions' – a statement that they incorrectly attribute to Francis Bacon[119] – as perfectly summing up the impious way nature is viewed within a managerial mind-set.

A difficult question is whether living in a technological society makes it *impossible* to seek to be a good 'shepherd of Being'. As Heidegger observes, the 'technological revolution in the atomic age could so captivate, bewitch, dazzle, and beguile man that calculative thinking may someday come to be accepted and practiced *as the only* way of thinking.' If this happens, Heidegger warns, 'man would have denied and thrown away his own special nature – that he is a meditative being.'[120] Heidegger thought that this possibility could be evaded. He looked forward to a time when we would 'use technical devices, and yet with proper use also keep ourselves so free of them, that we may let go of them any time.' By doing this, 'Our relation to technology will become wonderfully simple and relaxed. We let technical devices enter our daily life, and at the same time leave them outside, that is, let them alone, as things which are nothing absolute but remain dependent upon something higher.'[121] It is uncertain whether Heidegger's optimism on this score would have survived the technological developments of the twenty-first century, and in particular the invention of devices that are expressly designed to make

---

[115] Cf Marcel, *The Mystery of Being, Part II* (n 42), 55: 'In ordinary life there is nothing to prevent me from behaving to other people in a way which corresponds to [a] quite pragmatic way of looking at them. Servants are an obvious example, But a husband ... can treat his wife as a servant; a father his son, and so on. In these instances we cannot help seeing the real suppression of the value of being'; and at 148: '*The less men are thought of as beings ... the stronger will be the temptation to use them as machines which are capable of a given output*; this output being the only justification for their existence, they will end by having no other reality' (emphasis in original).

[116] Heidegger, 'The Question Concerning Technology' in Heidegger, *Basic Writings* (n 18), 321 (emphasis in original).

[117] Ibid, 322.

[118] See Barrett, *The Illusion of Technique* (n 8), 201; Steiner, *Martin Heidegger* (n 21), 55.

[119] See Pesic, 'Wresting with Proteus: Francis Bacon and the "Torture" of Nature' (1999) 90 *Isis* 81, pointing out that Bacon never said any such thing, and that it is Gottfried Wilhelm Leibniz who, in a letter to Gabriel Wagner in 1696, praised Bacon's experimental method as putting nature on the rack.

[120] Heidegger, *Discourse on Thinking* (Harper & Row, 1966), 56 (trans Anderson and Freund) (emphasis in original).

[121] Ibid, 54.

it extremely difficult to 'leave them outside ... let them alone'. We will have more to say about such devices in the next chapter, when we turn to consider how a system of private law might foster QTL-ing.

There *is* one category of people who seem destined *not* to flourish in a technological society, at least if we identify flourishing with QTL-ing or seeking to be a good 'shepherd of Being'. This is the category of people who *are* managers: that is, people who occupy a role that requires them to engage in the activities of (i) manipulating beings to achieve desired effects, and (ii) calculating what manipulations will most efficiently, or effectively, achieve those desired effects. This is because, as Alasdair MacIntyre points out, 'it is by appeal to his own effectiveness in [doing (i) and (ii)] that the manager claims authority'.[122] In almost all cases, this claim to expertise in doing (i) and (ii) will be completely unjustified: 'effectiveness [is] a quality widely imputed to managers ... both by themselves and others, but [is] in fact a quality which rarely exists apart from the imputation'.[123] As MacIntyre observes, 'all too often, when imputed organizational skill and power are deployed and the desired effect follows, all that we have witnessed is the same kind of sequence as that to be observed when a clergyman is fortunate enough to pray for rain just before the un-predicted end of a drought': 'the levers of power ... produce effects unsystematically and too often only coincidentally related to the effects of which their users boast'.[124]

As a result, in most cases a manager becomes a player in 'a theatre of illusions',[125] making claims for him or herself that cannot be cashed but which still need to be made if the manager is to retain his or her position. A manager is therefore usually *required* to be dishonest as part of their job, with the result that a *Manager* who seeks to be a good 'shepherd of Being' will come under unsustainable psychological pressure. The manipulative, calculative and dishonest nature of *Manager*'s employment means that there will be *nothing* about *Manager*'s worklife that will enable *Manager* to self-identify as being someone who seeks to be a good 'shepherd of Being', and a lot that will be inconsistent with that self-identification. Faced with this tension, *Manager* will either quit their job, or (more likely) be persuaded that it is a mistake to identify their flourishing with seeking to be a good 'shepherd of Being'. Instead, *Manager* will adopt something like the picture of human flourishing provided by the RP, which *Manager* may well be able to live up to while retaining their job. Again, we will have more to say about *Manager*'s quandary, and the position of managers in general, in the following chapter.

## Misfortunes

*Manager*'s example shows that it is not just the possession of vices that can result in someone's failing to seek to be a good 'shepherd of Being'. *Manager* is not taken over by the will to

---

[122] MacIntyre, *After Virtue* (n 111), 89.

[123] Ibid, 89. While MacIntyre does not mention Friedrich Hayek in *After Virtue*, his arguments (at 88–91) as to why managers are usually impotent to achieve their goals seem to have a lot in common with Hayek's critique of the effectiveness of centralised planning: Hayek, 'The Use of Knowledge in Society' (1945) 35 *The American Economic Review* 519.

[124] MacIntyre, *After Virtue* (n 111), 90.

[125] Ibid, 91.

power. *Manager* simply has the misfortune to be a manager in a technological society that has been taken over by the will to power. This result should not surprise us if we identify human flourishing with seeking to be a good 'shepherd of Being' – our second postulate of human flourishing, (P2), holds that someone's flourishing can be affected by a number of events that are outside that person's control. The previous chapter mentioned a number of other events that might get in the way of someone's QTL-ing. Revisiting these events in light of our identifying QTL-ing with seeking to be a good 'shepherd of Being' should give us a deeper understanding of *how* these events impact negatively on our flourishing as human beings.

(1) *Injury*. We observed above that S's being injured may well damage S's capacity to QTL, as S's injury will focus his attention on himself and encourage him to indulge in his all-too-human proclivity to regard himself as the centre of the universe.[126] We can expand on this point via the concept of an 'attention well', as illustrated below.

A is located in a relatively shallow attention well. A's natural preoccupation with herself means she has to make some effort to focus on the beings around her, and to attend to Being's manifesting itself as those beings. However, the effort is not so difficult to make. In contrast, B is stuck in a deep attention well. Climbing out of his attention well and focussing on what's around him will be very difficult for B, if not impossible. As a result, seeking to be a good 'shepherd of Being' will be far easier for A rather than B. Someone who is originally in a relatively shallow attention well like A may find themselves, like B, in a much deeper attention well by virtue of being injured. This is because being injured may well encourage them to turn in on themselves and focus much more of their attention on themselves.

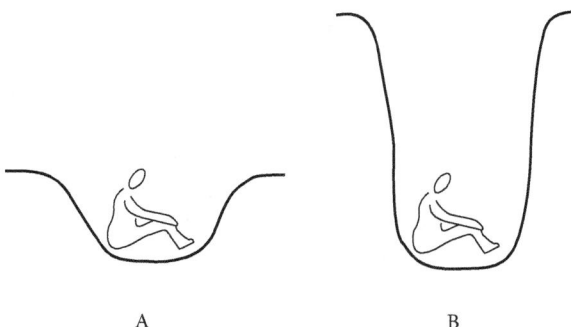

A                                    B

However, it is not just being injured that may make someone turn inwards and deepen the attention well in which they are located. In Part I of this project, we introduced the concept of a 'deadzone' – an experience or activity that, if entered into, 'threatens to shred one's personality so completely that doing so may well amount to a form of suicide' – and gave as an example of someone's entering a deadzone, Sophie's choice in the eponymous William Styron story to sacrifice her daughter and save her son when a Nazi doctor made

[126] See above, p 57.

her choose which of her two children would go to the gas chambers and which would live.[127] We are now in a better position to understand the concept of a 'deadzone' and the devastating impact that Sophie's choice had on her flourishing as a human being.

Someone who enters a deadzone drops into a very deep attention well where it is not possible for them to focus on anything except themselves and/or their past. As a result their capacity to seek to be a good 'shepherd of Being' is completely eliminated, as is – assuming the arguments in this chapter are correct – their capacity to flourish as a human being. We can easily see how a choice like the one Sophie made could have this effect, of destroying her ability to seek to be a good 'shepherd of Being' by causing her to drop into a very deep attention well. Having made her choice, one could expect her to replay that choice over and over again in her mind, always wondering what else she could have done and whether the choice she made was the right one. Her feeling of being irretrievably stuck in the moment where she chose her daughter to go to the gas chambers would be only accentuated by the knowledge that she had made the wrong choice (as I believe she did) – in which case, she would be left stuck in a loop of impossibly wishing over and over again that she could go back in time and make the right choice.

Again, we will have more to say in the next chapter about how private law should deal with cases where one person is in a position to affect the depth of someone else's attention well.

(2) *Disability*. We have already observed that S's being disabled cannot *prevent* S from seeking to be a good 'shepherd of Being'.[128] However, in the previous chapter, we also observed that disability counts as a disadvantage because if S is disabled, S's ability to QTL is a lot more vulnerable to being harmed by other people than would be the case were S not disabled.[129] Identifying QTL-ing with seeking to be a good 'shepherd of Being' helps us see in a lot more detail why this is.

First, the day-to-day experience of coping with a disability can result in S occupying a deeper attention well than would otherwise be the case, with consequences for S's ability to seek to be a good 'shepherd of Being'. Second, if S is treated badly, S may develop the vices of self-hatred or even hatred of Being that will in turn get in the way of S's seeking to be a good 'shepherd of Being'. Third, S's principal experience of Being's manifesting itself as beings will be through the care he receives from those looking after him. If those looking after S have detached themselves from Being (as much as they can do) through indulging the vices of pride, hatred, or will to power, then S will simply be in no position to seek to be a good 'shepherd of Being' in the way S contemplates, and witnesses to, Being's manifesting itself as beings. S's treatment at the hands of his carers means that it will be S's daily lot to contemplate, and witness to, anti-Being, not Being.

(3) *Betrayal*. In the previous chapter, we met Medea and Penelope, who were both possible counter-examples to the thesis that human flourishing involves being engaged in a quest

---

[127] McBride, *The Humanity of Private Law, Part I: Explanation* (n 2), 22.
[128] See above, p 94.
[129] See above, pp 57–58.

to lead a truthful life.[130] Both have been betrayed by their long-term partners: Medea's husband had an affair and left her with two young children to look after; Penelope discovers that her partner has been having an affair behind her back for years. Medea reacts with impotent rage to the situation in which her ex-husband has placed her. On one version of her story, Penelope is dumbfounded at her partner's betrayal and regards her years with him as a 'farce'; the alternative version has her react with amused resignation to the news of her partner's affair. Assuming that human flourishing involves QTL-ing, identifying QTL-ing with seeking to be a good 'shepherd of Being' allows us to provide a more penetrating analysis than we could provide in the previous chapter of what has gone wrong for Medea and Penelope in terms of their flourishing, and how things might go right.

Medea's impotent rage has placed her in a deep attention well that means that seeking to be a good 'shepherd of Being' is simply not a possibility for her. John Kekes recommends that Medea avert her eyes from her situation and pretend that she is a strong, self-confident woman who is able to cope with her situation. However, if the arguments made in this chapter are correct, it is impossible that Medea's adopting such a managerial mind-set in relation to her life could result in her flourishing as a human being. And, indeed, part of Medea's rage may lie in the fact that she has been adopting a managerial mind-set towards her life for quite some time and has had her best laid plans ruined by her husband. Instead, the advice given in the previous chapter was that Medea should try to re-establish contact with the self that she wanted to be when she put her trust in her husband all those years ago. If she does this, then she can say that she is seeking to become the person who has the deepest connection with the good that she can imagine enjoying, and that she is therefore seeking to be a good 'shepherd of Being'.

In the previous chapter, we observed that if human flourishing consists in QTL-ing, then the Penelope who reacts to her partner's affair with amused resignation cannot be said to be flourishing. And, indeed, Penelope cannot be said to have been seeking to be a good 'shepherd of Being' if her reaction to this news was simply to reflect on the 'fun' she and her partner had together. But what about the other Penelope, who is dumbfounded at the 'farce' her time with her partner has been revealed to have always been. If we identify QTL-ing with seeking to be a good 'shepherd of Being', how can this news have any effect on Penelope's flourishing as a human being? She can, after all, still seek right now to be a good 'shepherd of Being' whatever her partner did in the past. Of course she can – but Penelope's partner's betrayal means that Penelope cannot claim to have been seeking to be a good 'shepherd of Being' *while she was with her partner*.

Penelope is in the same position as a child who has been running around in a garden searching for a treasure that they have been told is hidden there, only to be told half an hour later that there is no treasure, and that their parent was simply trying to get the child to wear themselves out and ready to sleep. While the child may have *thought* they were looking for treasure in running around the garden, the absence of the treasure means that is not what they were doing. They were simply wasting their time. Similarly, Penelope may have thought she was contemplating, and witnessing to, Being's manifesting itself as beings in

---

[130] See above, pp 66–67, 69–70.

the relationship she had with her partner. However, the partner's infidelity meant she was doing no such thing: she was simply looking at, and reacting to, one of Melville's 'pasteboard masks'.[131] Penelope is dumbfounded not because her partner's betrayal means she cannot flourish in future, but because it means she was not flourishing in the past when she thought she was.

# 4. Human Flourishing: A Restatement

In this and the last two chapters, we have circled around the topic of human flourishing three times, each time acquiring a more precise understanding of what human flourishing entails.

In Chapter 8, we argued that a Journey Model of human flourishing – which assesses your flourishing by the direction in which your life is going – is far more likely to satisfy our four postulates about human flourishing than a Possessions Model like the RP, which certainly does not satisfy those four postulates.

In Chapter 9, we set out a particular Journey Model of human flourishing, where someone counts as flourishing as a human being if they are engaged in a quest to lead a truthful life (or 'QTL-ing', for short), explained what sort of virtues would be possessed by someone who was engaged in such a quest and what sort of activities they would engage in. We further showed that we have every reason to believe that this model of human flourishing will satisfy our four postulates about human flourishing.

In this chapter, we explained that the proposition that human flourishing consists in QTL-ing is perfectly compatible with the view, advanced at the end of Part I of this project, that what is distinctive about human beings is that they are the beings that are aware (or are capable of being aware) that they participate in Being. This is because QTL-ing is the same thing as seeking to be a good 'shepherd of Being' in the way one contemplates, and witnesses to, Being's manifesting itself as beings. Identifying QTL-ing with seeking to be a good 'shepherd of Being' also allowed us to obtain a more precise understanding of what is involved in QTL-ing. Armed with this more precise understanding, we can improve the table set out on p 53, above. The table overleaf sets out our best understanding of what QTL-ing involves.

Let's say that someone of whom the table overleaf is true is *QTL-flourishing*. That is, they are flourishing, according to the view that human flourishing consists in being engaged in a quest to lead a truthful life. The questions we now have to address, in our project of evaluating English private law, are: how can private law contribute to QTL-flourishing, and if it did, how different would private law look from the way it looks at the moment? If the answer is 'very different' then that suggests private law is currently falling some way short of its vocation to promote human flourishing, and that it is doing so because when it seeks to promote human flourishing, it has a very different – and false – conception of human flourishing in mind: the RP.

---

[131] See above, p 99.

| Body | Mind | Heart | Activities | External Circumstances |
|------|------|-------|------------|------------------------|
| (1) Life and good health. | (2) A sense of reality. <br><br> (3) Not stuck in deep attention well. <br><br> (4) Clear-minded; free of distorting prejudices <br><br> (5) Openness to epiphany. <br><br> (6) Humble: always seeking to improve capacities to apprehend reality, and not insistent on remaining independent of reality. <br><br> (7) Enjoys peace of mind. <br><br> (8) Avoids adopting managerial mind-set in any aspect of life. | (9) Love of truth <br><br> (10) Love of particular fields of activity or inquiry that encourage development and exercise of truth-seeking virtues. <br><br> (11) Bears malice towards none, and no thing. | (12) Does work that places strong emphasis on developing, and drawing on, sense of reality. <br><br> (13) Avoids managerial activities. <br><br> (14) Strives to be realistic in viewing world. <br><br> (15) Strives to be sincere in dealings with others. <br><br> (16) Strives to be true to oneself – the self one would like to be – in deciding what to do. | (17) Lives in community where (a) protected from being placed in deep attention wells; (b) not systematically misled about nature of world or one's place in the world; (c) enjoy a great deal of latitude in terms of freedom of speech and freedom of association; (d) no one is compelled to lie in order to live or make a living. <br><br> (18) Enjoys a reasonable level of income. <br><br> (19) Enjoys the kind of leisure needed to reflect on reality. |

# 11

## Applications and Implications

In this chapter, we address the issue of what a private law dedicated to fostering QTL-flourishing would look like. The difficulty involved in doing this cannot be overstated. As Ivan Illich has observed of the possibility of effecting an analogous change in the law so that society is inverted from being 'a utilitarian society … [into being] a convivial one':

> The law is used to impose a given mind-set on all participants. The resulting content of the law embodies the ideologies of lawmakers and judges. How they experience the ideology inherent in a culture becomes established mythology in the laws they make and apply. The body of laws that regulates an industrial society inevitably reflects and reinforces its ideology, social character, and class structure.[1]

I have found it very difficult to break free of the categories and habits of thought that come all too naturally to me – having spent 30 years thinking, writing and speaking about a private law that is concerned to foster RP-flourishing – in order to try to imagine what a private law that seeks instead to foster QTL-flourishing might look like. So what follows is inevitably merely a preliminary statement of what such a private law might look like, and is doubtless hidebound to a frustrating degree by the constraints that the present has placed on my ability to imagine a very different future. However, I hope that encountering the ideas and approaches advanced in this chapter will make it easier for others to break the mental chains created by the current state of English private law and go much further than I have been able to do in this chapter to articulate what a private law that is concerned to foster QTL-flourishing might look like.

With that said, let's begin our exploration by discussing the area of private law that seems most concerned at the moment with promoting truthfulness among its subjects – the law on fraud.

## 1. Fraud Unravels All

### Sanctions for fraud

Private law, as it currently stands, sanctions the telling of lies in a number of different ways:

---

[1] Illich, *Tools for Conviviality* (Calder & Boyars Ltd, 1973), 94. See also Balkin, 'The Proliferation of Legal Truth' (2003) 26 *Harvard Journal of Law & Public Policy* 5: 'Law has power over people's imaginations and how they think about what is happening in social life. Law in this sense is more than a set of sanctions. It is a form of cultural software that shapes the way we think about and apprehend the world. Law … colonizes the human mind. That is how it proliferates its power over the world' (at 8); 'imagining the world through the eyes of the law, or seeing things in terms of what is true from the standpoint of the law, could have ideological effects on human beings. It tends to push their imaginations in one direction rather than in another' (at 10).

(1)   If A makes a representation to B that is false, knowing that it is false or not caring whether it is true or not,[2] intending for B to rely on that representation, then if B does so rely on that representation and suffers loss[3] as a result, B will be entitled to sue A in damages for *deceit*. Those damages will be designed, at a minimum, to compensate B for all the losses[4] that she suffered as a direct consequence of relying on A's representation, no matter how unforeseeable they were[5] or how unrelated they were to the purpose for which A made his representation.[6] Aggravated and exemplary damages may also be awarded against A.[7]

(2)   The rule in (1) extends to the case where A makes a representation to B, and before B relies on the representation, A finds out the representation is no longer true (if it ever was). If A deliberately fails to correct the misleading impression that he has created in B's mind, with the intention that B should rely on it, then A will be liable to be sued for deceit.[8]

(3)   Other things being equal, B will be able to rescind a contract that A entered into with B, if that contract was entered into by B under the influence of a lie told by A or – to A's knowledge – under the influence of a lie told by a third party. Under the UK Supreme Court's decision in *Zurich Insurance Co plc v Hayward*,[9] B will be held to have entered into the contract with A under the influence of a lie if the lie played some part in B's decision to enter into the contract: the lie does not have to have been believed by B.[10]

(4)   Likewise, a judgment against B and in favour of A that has been obtained by fraud may be set aside by the courts, even though the fraud might have been reasonably discoverable by B before judgment was entered against her.[11]

(5)   It is well-established that statutory provisions that have the object of preventing fraud cannot be relied on to carry out a fraud – as would be the case where B transfers property to A to hold on trust for C and A relies on the fact that B's declaration of trust was not put in writing to argue that A is entitled to keep the property for himself.[12]

---

[2] *Derry* v *Peek* (1889) 14 App Cas 337.

[3] It is beyond doubt that the claimant in a deceit case has to have suffered 'damage' if she is to be allowed to sue (*Pasley* v *Freeman* (1789) 3 TR 51, 56 (per Buller J)).

[4] These can include non-economic losses: *Shelley* v *Paddock* [1980] QB 348 (damages awarded for distress caused by being conned out of £9,400, paid to purchase a house in Spain that was not the defendant's to sell).

[5] *Doyle* v *Olby (Ironmongers) Ltd* [1969] 2 QB 158; *Smith New Court Securities Ltd* v *Citibank NA* [1997] AC 254.

[6] *Smith New Court Securities Ltd* v *Citibank NA* [1997] AC 254, 283 (per Lord Steyn), holding that the so-called 'SAAMCO' limit on the recoverability of damages in a misrepresentation case (where damages can only be recovered in respect of losses related to the purpose for which the representation was made) only applies where the misrepresentation was *negligent*. So in the case where A tells B that he is physically fit enough to go on a mountaineering expedition, when B is not, and B is subsequently injured on the expedition as a result of being caught in an avalanche, B will *not* be able to sue A for damages in respect of his injuries if A was negligent (the purpose of A's representation was to save B from being injured on the expedition as a result of lack of fitness, not to save B from being injured in an avalanche), but B will be able to sue if A was fraudulent.

[7] *Archer* v *Brown* [1985] QB 401.

[8] *With* v *O'Flanagan* [1936] Ch 575; *Briess* v *Woolley* [1954] AC 333.

[9] [2017] AC 142.

[10] Ibid, at [44]–[45] (per Lord Clarke); [67]–[68] (per Lord Toulson).

[11] *Takhar* v *Gracefield Developments Ltd* [2019] UKSC 13.

[12] *Re Duke of Marlborough* [1894] 2 Ch 133; *Rochefoucauld* v *Boustead* [1897] 1 Ch 196, 205–06 (per Lindley LJ).

(6)    Similarly, and as a general rule, if A obtains property from B through a fraud (either by lying to B or a third party who has control of B's property), then A will hold that property on trust – a constructive trust[13] – for B.[14]

(7)    Where B, a bank, has issued a letter of credit to C, and C has handed the letter of credit over to A in return for A's shipping goods to C, if A then attempts to collect on the letter of credit by presenting it (and proof of shipment) to B, B will be entitled to refuse to pay under the letter of credit if it is clear that A, or A's agents, are acting fraudulently (for example, by presenting shipping documents to support A's drawing on the letter of credit that A, or A's agents, know contain untruthful statements).[15]

(8)    Where A has made a claim against B under an insurance contract, if A's claim is affected by fraud in any way, the entire claim is liable to be struck out, and not just the part of the claim that is tainted by fraud.[16] So, for example, if A has a laptop and £200 stolen from his hotel room, and A makes a claim on his insurance policy with B for that and adds in a fraudulent claim for the loss of a Rolex watch, B can apply for A's entire claim to be struck out and not just the claim for the watch.

(9)    Similarly, a court may refuse to grant A – who is suing B – a remedy that is distinctively equitable in character (such as an injunction, or an order of specific performance) if A is found to have engaged in any kind of fraud in bringing his claim against B.[17]

(10)    If A, a trustee, is sued by B, A's beneficiary, A will not be allowed to rely on an exclusion clause in the trust document that purports to exempt A from liability for fraud. This is because A's being allowed to act fraudulently in dealing with assets that he is supposed to hold on trust for B is incompatible with the 'irreducible core' of what a trust is.[18]

(11)    Similarly, a clause in a *contract* between A and B that purports to exempt A from being held liable for defrauding B is unlikely to be valid.[19] In *HIH Casualty and General Insurance Ltd* v *Chase Manhattan Bank*,[20] the House of Lords held that 'the law, on public

[13] Others would prefer to say a 'resulting trust', but the choice between 'constructive' and 'resulting' is always a false one. 'Resulting' refers to the *direction* in which the property is held on trust – the property is held on trust for the person from whom it was obtained. 'Constructive' refers to the *reason* why the trust arises – the trust arises not because it was intended that a trust should be created, but for some other reason.

[14] *Angove's Pty Ltd* v *Bailey* [2016] 1 WLR 3179, at [30] (per Lord Sumption); *Malory Enterprises Ltd* v *Cheshire Homes (UK) Ltd* [2002] Ch 216 (though the finding of a constructive trust over title to registered land that has been fraudulently transferred from B to A is – it may be strongly argued – displaced by the provisions of the Land Registration Act 2002: *Swift 1st Ltd* v *Chief Land Registrar* [2015] Ch 602); *Westdeutsche Landesbank* v *Islington LBC* [1996] AC 669, 716 (per Lord Browne-Wilkinson).

[15] *United City Merchants (Investments) Ltd* v *Royal Bank of Canada, The American Accord* [1983] 1 AC 168.

[16] *Manifest Shipping Co Ltd* v *Uni-Polaris Insurance Co Ltd* [2003] 1 AC 469. For discussion, see Davey and Richards, 'Deterrence, Human Rights and Illegality: The Forfeiture Rule in Insurance Contract Law' [2015] *LMCLQ* 314.

[17] *Armstrong* v *Sheppard & Short Ltd* [1959] QB 384, 397; *J Willis & Son* v *Willis* [1986] 1 EGLR 62; *Gonthier* v *Orange Contract Scaffolding Ltd* [2003] EWCA Civ 873.

[18] *Armitage* v *Nurse* [1998] Ch 241.

[19] For discussion, see Gergen, 'Contracting out of Liability for Deceit, Inadvertent Misrepresentation and Negligent Misstatement' in Neyers *et al* (eds), *Exploring Contract Law* (Hart Publishing, 2009), 239–54.

[20] [2003] 1 All ER (Comm) 349.

policy grounds, does not permit a contracting party to exclude liability for his *own* fraud in inducing the making of the contract.[21] Their Lordships further held that if A wanted to rely on a clause in his contract with B to escape being held liable for his *agent's* fraud, then the clause would have to be 'expressed in clear and unmistakeable terms on the face of the contract … the language used must be such as will alert a commercial party to the extraordinary bargain he is invited to make.'[22]

(12)   If A transfers property to B on the purported basis that that property should be held on trust for C, no such trust will arise if both A and B had no intention that the property should be held on trust for C and intended instead that A should continue to control how the property was disposed of, while hiding the fact of that control behind the veil of a 'sham' trust. Instead, B will be held to hold the property in question on trust for A.[23]

(13)   B will be entitled to sue A in *malicious falsehood* for compensation if A maliciously makes a false statement to C about B or B's property, with the result that B suffers loss.[24] Aggravated and exemplary damages may also be awarded against A.[25] A will be held to have acted maliciously in making his statement if he made the statement knowing that it was untrue, or not caring whether it was true or not, or if he made the statement for a dishonest or improper purpose.[26]

(14)   B will be entitled to sue A in *passing off* if A markets his goods or conducts his business in such a way that people are liable to confuse A's goods or business with B's with the result that either A benefits from the goodwill attached to B's business, or A damages the goodwill attached to B's business.

## The Prevalence of Fraud

This impressive panoply of rules and remedies against fraud is often said to give effect to the precept 'fraud unravels all'. English private law unravels fraud by: (i) making a fraudster make whole the intended victims of his fraud; and (ii) not giving effect to, and undoing, transactions that were procured by fraud, or purport to permit fraud. However, in seeking to unravel fraud, English private law is *not* concerned to promote truth-telling. Instead – I would argue – these fraud-unravelling rules and remedies are in large part a response to the way in which a social order that is based on the promotion of RP-flourishing *encourages* fraud.

---

[21] Ibid, at [16] (per Lord Bingham) (emphasis added).

[22] Ibid.

[23] Conaglen, 'Sham Trusts' (2008) 67 *CLJ* 176.

[24] It was suggested in *Quinton v Pearce* [2009] EWHC 912 (QB), at [86] (per Eady J) that B's loss has to be financial in nature for B to be able to sue, and in *Ajinomoto Sweeteners SAS v Asda Ltd* [2011] QB 497, the Court of Appeal suggested that the central case of malicious falsehood was a lie that damaged business goodwill. *Khodaparast v Shad* [2000] 1 WLR 618 might be taken as supporting a more expansive view of the tort; however, the gravamen of the claimant's complaint in that case – where her ex-boyfriend had falsely represented to others that she was a prostitute – was that she had been sacked from her job as a result of her ex-boyfriend's lies.

[25] Ibid.

[26] *Dunlop v Maison Talbot* (1904) 20 TLR 579.

While fraud will always be with us, there are three aspects of a social order that seeks to promote RP-flourishing that mean fraud can be expected to play a much more significant part in that kind of social order than would be the case in some other social order, such as one that is dedicated to promoting QTL-flourishing.

(1) *Managerial vulnerability to fraud.* As we have already observed, a social order that seeks to promote RP-flourishing will depend heavily on the existence of public and private bodies – *Suppliers* – that produce and distribute the goods on which RP-flourishing depends.[27] These *Suppliers* need to be managed in order to operate, and as a result become vulnerable to fraud, in the following way.

As we have also already observed, managers are generally incapable of possessing sufficient knowledge to do their jobs properly.[28] This lack of knowledge has two consequences in terms of making a *Supplier* vulnerable to fraud. First, most managers will not usually know enough about the *Supplier* they are managing to detect when it is being, or is liable to be, defrauded and take appropriate steps to protect against that danger. Second, some managers will seek to remedy the gaps in their knowledge of the *Supplier* they are managing by relying on other people's advice and expertise – and in doing so will render the *Supplier* in question vulnerable to being defrauded by those same advisers and experts.[29]

(2) *Managerial temptations to commit fraud.* The natural incompetence of managers creates equally natural temptations for them to commit fraud in order to conceal their failures in managing the *Suppliers* on which RP-flourishing depends. The already-mentioned *HIH* case illustrates the potential for managerial incompetence to give rise to temptations to commit fraud.

The litigation in *HIH* was between a *Bank* and an *Insurer*. *Bank* lent money to a Film Production Company (FPC) to assist it to produce a roster of films. This was a risky loan to make because – as the acclaimed screenwriter William Goldman once observed – in Hollywood, 'Nobody knows anything … Not one person in the entire motion picture field knows for a certainty what's going to work. Every time out it's a guess and, if you're lucky, an educated one.'[30] So there was absolutely no guarantee that *Bank* would get its money back from FPC. Knowing this, *Bank* sought to protect its position by taking out an insurance policy with *Insurer*, under which *Insurer* would pay *Bank* back if FPC did not. As it turned out, FPC did not pay *Bank* back and *Bank* sought to enforce its insurance policy with *Insurer*. *Insurer*, in turn, sought to avoid the insurance policy, arguing that *Bank*'s agent, who had arranged the insurance policy, had lied to it about how risky *Bank*'s loan to FPC was. *Bank* argued, in its turn, that *Insurer* was not entitled to rescind the contract of insurance on this ground because the contract of insurance expressly provided that *Insurer* could not

---

[27] See above, pp 18–19.
[28] See above, p 102.
[29] Cf Davies, *Lying For Money: How Legendary Frauds Reveal the Workings of Our World* (Profile Books, 2018), 200: 'The easier something is to manage – the more possible it is to take a comprehensive view of all that's going on, and to check every transaction individually – the more difficult it is to defraud. Vulnerability to crime, in other words, tends to scale with the cognitive demands placed on the management of a business. The more things a manager has to pay attention to, the easier it becomes to carry out a commercial fraud.'
[30] Goldman, *Adventures in the Screen Trade* (Abacus Books, 1996), 40.

rely on any statements (or non-disclosures of relevant information) made by *Bank* or any third parties to rescind the insurance policy.

Leaving aside the vexed question of what actually did happen in the *HIH* case, it's clear how natural managerial incompetence on the part of *Bank* and *Insurer* could[31] have given rise to multiple frauds in this case. First, *Bank*'s managers were incompetent to assess accurately the risk involved in making the loan to FPC. They thought they could avoid the consequences of that incompetence by making *Insurer* carry the can if the FPC loan turned bad. This might have given rise to a temptation to commit fraud – the temptation to lie to *Insurer* about the prospects of the FPC loan going bad. Second, *Insurer*'s managers were as incompetent as *Bank*'s were, in terms of being able to assess accurately what the prospects were of the FPC loan going bad. This might have given rise to a second temptation to commit fraud – the temptation to issue the insurance policy with the intention of resiling from it by alleging it was procured fraudulently should *Bank* seek to enforce it, even though *Bank* anticipated *Insurer* might make this kind of move and secured from *Insurer* a promise that it would not.

These temptations to fraud could have been avoided had *Bank*'s and *Insurer*'s managers recognised their natural incompetence in dealing with the film industry and consequently declined to have anything to do with film financing – but, of course, they could not as there was potentially too much money to be made if everything went well with FPC's film roster. And this might have given rise to the third, and most basic, temptation to commit fraud that might have underpinned everything else in the *HIH* litigation – the temptation on the part of a manager to pretend that they are competent when they are not, and to arrange matters so that their incompetence will never become obvious.

(3) *Societal fraud.* The fact that it is not possible for everyone to enjoy a fair chance of RP-flourishing[32] also gives rise to society-wide temptations to commit fraud within a social order that has set its cap at promoting RP-flourishing. Most obviously, those who do *not* enjoy a fair chance of RP-flourishing within that social order will be tempted to engage in fraud to obtain that which the social order in which they live is incapable of providing them. More insidiously, pretending that it *is* possible to give everyone in a given social order a fair chance of RP-flourishing will give rise to temptations to engage in fraud at all levels of that social order.

At the political level, this pretence leads to politicians lying that this or that reform (which, unaccountably, has not been thought of or implemented until now) is all it will take to create a 'classless society' where everyone will have a fair chance of RP-flourishing. Moreover, and as we have already seen,[33] trying to create a social order where even just a proportion of the population will have a fair chance of RP-flourishing will result in the public finances being run on what used to be called the 'never-never',[34] with devastating

---

[31] I emphasise the word 'could' – the remainder of this paragraph is a reconstruction of how the facts of *HIH* (which were never completely clear in the first place) may have come to pass, rather than a suggestion that that is how they *did* come to pass.

[32] See above, pp 17–20.

[33] See above, pp 19–20.

[34] So-called because purchasing an item on the 'never-never' involved a finance company purchasing the item, giving you possession of the item, and then requiring you to make a seemingly endless series of repayments of the money spent on the item plus interest before allowing you to acquire title to it.

consequences for future generations' abilities to enjoy the same standard of living as the present one; consequences that politicians are forced to ignore or make light of.

At the level of the *Suppliers* that produce and distribute the goods required for RP-flourishing, this pretence involves their lying about the level of worker exploitation required for those goods to be produced. Telling such lies involves a *Supplier* engaging in the activity of *reputation-laundering*. Reputation-laundering takes a variety of forms: (i) using non-disclosure agreements to close down a story about how badly a *Supplier* has behaved; (ii) inserting 'ethical clauses' into the contracts making up a *Supplier*'s supply chain so that the *Supplier* can purport to be requiring the highest standards of behaviour from *its* suppliers in the way those suppliers treat their employees; (iii) enthusiastically endorsing and supporting causes that have, for the time being, become identified as just or righteous in the public eye.

At the personal level, going along with the pretence that, under the right circumstances, everyone can enjoy a fair chance of RP-flourishing involves your entering a fantasy world where you turn a blind eye to the lies you are told at the political level, and you succumb to the reputation-laundering activities engaged in by the *Suppliers* on which (if you are lucky) your RP-flourishing depends. Moreover, you will be inclined to look down on those who do not RP-flourish, attributing their failure to *them* rather than seeing that it may be the case that they never had a fair chance of RP-flourishing in the first place.[35]

These three factors indicate that fraud will be a particular problem in a social order dedicated to promoting the RP-flourishing of its members. The facts on the ground seem to bear out this claim.

Take, for example, the statement that 'fraud unravels all'. The first use of this expression was relatively recent (in legal historical terms). It dates back to the start of the twentieth century: in 1900, Farwell J observed, 'fraud … unravels everything';[36] and in 1912, Farwell LJ remarked, 'fraud unravels all contracts'.[37] The saying was then picked up by Lord Denning[38] and Lord Diplock.[39] Between 1900 and 1983, the phrase 'fraud unravels all' or its equivalent was used by judges eight times – an average of 0.09 times a year.[40] By contrast, between 1983

---

[35] Cf Williamson, 'The Father-Führer', *National Review*, March 28, 2016: 'the white working class that finds itself attracted to Trump has [not] been victimized by outside forces … nobody did this to them. They failed themselves … *Nothing happened to them*. There wasn't some awful disaster … The truth about these dysfunctional, downscale communities is that they deserve to die. Economically, they are negative assets … The white American underclass is in thrall to a vicious, selfish culture whose main products are misery and used heroin needles' (emphasis in original).

[36] *May* v *Platt* [1900] 1 Ch 616, 623.

[37] *London General Omnibus Co Ltd* v *Holloway* [1912] 2 KB 72, 81.

[38] *Lazarus Estates Ltd* v *Beasley* [1956] 1 QB 702, 712 (per Denning LJ): 'fraud unravels everything'; *Campbell* v *Edwards* [1976] 1 WLR 403, 407 (per Lord Denning MR): 'fraud or collusion unravels everything'; *Midland Bank Trust Co Ltd* v *Green* [1980] Ch 590, 625 (per Lord Denning MR, quoting himself in *Lazarus Estates*). The same expression pops up in Viscount Simonds' decision in *Bridge* v *Campbell Discount Co Ltd* [1962] AC 600, at 614. Lord Denning sat in the same case and may have suggested the phrase to Viscount Simonds, which may account for why in Simonds' formulation – 'if there is duress or fraud "which unravels all"' – 'which unravels all' appears within quotation marks.

[39] *United City Merchants (Investments) Ltd* v *Royal Bank of Canada* [1983] AC 168, 184: 'if plain English is to be preferred, "fraud unravels all"'.

[40] In addition to the authorities just mentioned, Megarry J used the phrase 'fraud unravels all' (by then, a 'familiar English phrase') in *Discount Records Ltd* v *Barclays Bank Ltd* [1975] 1 WLR 315, at 319. The law on fraud is discussed by Robert Megarry in chapter 23 ('The Evil of Evils') of his *A New Miscellany-at-Law: Yet Another Diversion for Lawyers and Others* (Hart Publishing, 2005).

and 2019 (when this book is being written), a Westlaw UK caselaw search shows the phrase was used 101 times – an average of 2.8 times a year, and an increase of about 2,816 per cent on its usage before 1983. Some of this increase may reflect a judicial fondness for rolling out a well-turned phrase, but an increase of this magnitude must also reflect a judiciary grappling with a vast increase in fraud.[41]

Hard numbers also support the view that fraud is endemic within our social order. The Annual Fraud Indicator (AFI) estimates how much fraud has cost the UK economy in a given year. In 2010, the AFI stood at £30 billion; in 2011, it rose to £38 billion; and in 2012, exploded to £73 billion. In 2017, the AFI stood at £190 billion – a 533 per cent increase in less than a decade. The figures for the AFI were originally produced by the National Fraud Authority, which was created in 2008 to help co-ordinate the UK government's efforts to combat fraud. The National Fraud Authority was wound up in March 2014, and its functions subsumed within the National Crime Agency, which was charged with combatting 'economic crime' generally.[42] While this move may have been justified on the grounds of efficiency, it is hard to resist the impression that the existence of the National Fraud Authority had become an embarrassment – an open acknowledgement both of a growing problem and the government's inability to deal with it.

If it is the case (as I believe it is) that fraud is an inseparable consequence of living in a social order dedicated to promoting RP-flourishing, it follows that the kinds of sanctions against fraud detailed above can only operate at the margins of our social order: they seek to tamp down on the worst excrescences of fraud while doing nothing to tackle fraud at its roots, for fear that doing so will simultaneously uproot our social order.[43] For example, private law can do nothing about political lies. Lying is so prevalent nowadays among politicians, of all persuasions and political views,[44] that to allow those who have suffered losses as a result of political lies to sue in respect of those losses would be akin (in today's society) to allowing politicians to be sued for breathing. So political lies are usually exempt from the reach of private law as harmful political lies, conveniently, tend not to consist in lies about the claimant, or lies that have been relied on by the claimant to their detriment.

Similarly, we have seen that it is extremely difficult, if not impossible, for a government (G) to pursue the goal of promoting the RP-flourishing of its subjects without running a deficit – the economy will not normally produce enough wealth to enable G to achieve its goal through ordinary taxation. This results in G having to take steps to attract wealth into its jurisdiction, so that that wealth may both be taxed and provide the foundation for increased economic growth and consequently greater tax revenues. In order to attract such

---

[41] A check on the Google Ngram viewer – which tracks the use of words and phrases used in books that are available via Google Books – confirms the point, showing a 929% increase in the use of the phrase 'fraud unravels all' between 1977 and 1999. Given this, it is perhaps no surprise that two journalists called fraud 'the growth industry of the Eighties': Bose and Gunn, *Fraud* (Harper Collins, 1989).

[42] Given this, it is amusing to note that in March 2019, the National Crime Agency had to warn against fraudsters imitating National Crime Agency officers, who would scam people out of their money by warning them that they may have been the victim of a banking fraud and asking to obtain remote access to their computers or their banking details: www.nationalcrimeagency.gov.uk/news/fraudsters-steal-hundreds-of-thousands-of-pounds-posing-as-nca-officers.

[43] Compare the way in which American courts refuse to provide remedies in cases of deceptions within intimate relationships, on the basis that such deceptions are so common that granting a remedy in such cases would overthrow domestic life: Hasday, *Intimate Lies and the Law* (OUP, 2019), ch 6.

[44] See, for example, Oborne, *The Rise of Political Lying* (Simon and Schuster, 2005).

wealth, G has to promise wealth-holders that G will allow the holder's wealth to be used in ways that would usually be regarded as fraudulent – and any unwillingness on G's part to make such a promise would soon be overridden by the realisation that other governments are happy to make that promise, and a 'race to the bottom' is quickly set in motion between G and other governments in terms of what promises they are respectively willing to make to wealth-holders.

So it is that, as we have seen, while 'sham' trusts are regarded as invalid,[45] the position is not so clear when it comes to the sham trust's sibling, the *floating trust*. Under such a trust, A declares that he holds property on trust for B, but reserves to himself the power to dispose of the trust property as he sees fit, including using the trust property for his own benefit. Such a trust is not a sham – A fully intends to hold the trust property in accordance with the terms of the trust – but, if given effect to, the floating trust has the same effect as a sham trust in that it allows A to retain full beneficial control of his property while hiding that fact behind the veil of a trust. The courts have consistently held that an express[46] floating trust is invalid on the ground that it is 'illusory'.[47] In effect, an express floating trust is a contradiction in terms. You cannot purport to settle property on trust and retain full beneficial control of it. As Jersey law used to say, '*donner et retiner ne vaut*' – you can't give and retain at the same time. *Used* to say, however, because in Jersey and other offshore jurisdictions that seek to attract and manage non-residents' wealth, the principle of '*donner et retiner*' has been jettisoned[48] with the result that the walking contradiction of an express floating trust seems now to be allowed to roam about in those jurisdictions.

## The QTL Alternative

A social order that is dedicated to promoting QTL-flourishing should be free of the particular temptations to, and opportunities for, fraud that prevail in a social order dedicated to promoting RP-flourishing. However, as has already been observed, fraud will always be with us. What attitude towards fraud would private law take if it were part of a social order that was dedicated to promoting QTL-flourishing?

In discussing this question, we can adopt the distinction drawn in Part I of this project between the three parts of private law: the part that determines what our *basic obligations* are; the part that governs the law on *transactions*; and the part that is concerned to protect and preserve private law's *legitimacy*. It is unlikely that provisions on fraud that belong to the last two parts of English private law – for example, that terms in a contract or a trust deed allowing fraudulent behaviour by the contracting party or trustee will be invalid – will be very different in a private law that seeks to promote the QTL-flourishing of its subjects.

---

[45] See above, p 111.

[46] The law on mutual wills – which governs the situation where A and B each make wills leaving their assets to the other, and if the other is not alive, C, and promise not to alter those wills – holds that where A dies before B, and B inherits under A's will, B holds all her assets on a *constructive* floating trust for C. This means that on B's death, all of B's remaining assets go to C, no matter what B's final will ends up saying. For discussion, see Sheridan, 'The Floating Trust: Mutual Wills' (1977) 15 *Alberta LR* 211.

[47] The relevant authorities are very well laid out in Russell and Graham, 'Illusory Trusts' (2018) 24 *Trusts & Trustees* 307.

[48] See Trusts (Jersey) Law 1984, Art 9A.

However, as we will see, the law on what basic obligations we owe each other with regard to fraud would have a different set of priorities to those that currently prevail in English private law.

It may be recalled that our basic obligations are obligations that we owe other people without their having to make any special arrangement for our to come under them.[49] They are correlative to – the flip-side of – our basic rights: the rights that we have against other people without our having to make any special arrangement to acquire them. In English law at least, these basic obligations/rights are all geared towards protecting people from suffering significant setbacks to their flourishing as human beings.

As the previous chapter has explained,[50] in a social order that identifies human flourishing with QTL-flourishing, the following events would count as constituting a setback to your flourishing, and therefore *harms*: (1) being placed in a deep attention well; (2) developing a false view of reality; (3) being required to lie or betray your principles; (4) developing hatred for others; (5) being required to do work that does not encourage the development of truth-seeking virtues, or which leaves one no time to enjoy the leisure needed to reflect on reality.

The list is not exhaustive. For example, it does not include the QTL-flourishing-impairing event of developing bad health. That is because we are interested in knowing in what respects a private law that is concerned to promote the QTL-flourishing of its subjects would be *different* from English private law in its current state. There is no reason to think that a private law that was concerned to promote QTL-flourishing would do either more or less than English private law currently does to protect the health of its subjects, under the banner of promoting RP-flourishing. As we will see in the rest of this chapter what is distinctive about events (1)–(5) is that they would all count as harms in a social order dedicated to promoting QTL-flourishing; but they are also events that English private law is not interested in protecting people from because it identifies human flourishing with RP-flourishing, not QTL-flourishing.

A private law that is concerned to promote the QTL-flourishing of its subjects would impose a basic obligation on me, owed to you, not to act fraudulently *if* my acting fraudulently threatens to cause you to suffer one of harms (1)–(5), and imposing such an obligation on me would do more good than harm.[51] The most obvious such harm that you might suffer as a result of a fraud perpetrated by me is (2): developing a false view of reality. We might, following others, call this kind of harm an *epistemic harm*.[52] However, not all cases where A knowingly deceives B should count as cases of B's suffering an epistemic harm at A's hands. Consider the following three scenarios:

(a)   A lies to B that shares in Acme plc represent a good investment, with the result that B buys the shares;
(b)   A creates a painting that he passes off as by Van Gogh, and B buys the painting in the belief that it is by Van Gogh;

---

[49] See McBride, *The Humanity of Private Law, Part I: Explanation* (Hart Publishing, 2018), 40–41.
[50] See above, p 107.
[51] See McBride, *The Humanity of Private Law, Part I* (n 49), 115–17 for an account of the conditions that should be satisfied before a basic obligation is recognised to exist.
[52] See, in particular, Fricker, *Epistemic Injustice* (OUP, 2007).

(c)   A engages in what has come to be known as 'gaslighting',[53] convincing B not to trust her memory or the evidence of her senses by persuading her that she is fundamentally deluded about her situation, and may even be teetering on the brink of insanity.

In all these situations, A knowingly deceives B, but I think as between these three deceptions, (a) does not count as an epistemic harm, (b) arguably does so count, and only (c) clearly counts as an epistemic harm.

(a) does not count as an epistemic harm because while B has been deceived about Acme plc's prospects, B has not thereby developed a false view of reality, if we identify reality – as it was identified in the previous chapter – with Being's manifesting itself as beings.[54] Acme plc's prospects have absolutely nothing to do with that kind of reality, which – for our purposes – is the only reality that counts.

By contrast, A's gaslighting B in (c) counts as an epistemic harm because by making B doubt herself, A undermines what Miranda Fricker calls B's 'epistemic confidence' with the result that she 'literally *loses knowledge* … [she] repeatedly [fails] to gain items of knowledge that she otherwise would have been able to gain.'[55] Furthermore, A's undermining of B has the potential to prevent her 'from developing certain intellectual virtues [such as] the development of intellectual courage, the virtue of not backing down in one's convictions too quickly in response to challenge.'[56] Given this, it is easy to see how A's undermining B will impede her in contemplating Being's manifesting itself as beings, and therefore counts as an epistemic harm.

(b) is a middle case that looks at first sight no different from (a). What makes (b) arguably different from (a) is the significance of Van Gogh's achievement as an artist in acting as a witness to Being's manifesting itself as beings, thereby helping us to contemplate that reality from Van Gogh's perspective. So significant was this achievement that in his 1935 lecture 'The origin of the work of art', Martin Heidegger picked out Van Gogh's 1887 painting *A Pair of Shoes*[57] as an example of how Being discloses itself to us through art: 'Some particular being, a pair of peasant shoes, comes in the work to stand in the light of its Being. The Being of beings comes into the steadiness of its shining.'[58] Heidegger subsequently observed, 'Truth happens in Van Gogh's painting. This does not mean that something at hand is correctly portrayed, but rather that in the revelation of the equipmental being of the shoes beings as a whole – world and earth in their counterplay – attain to unconcealment.'[59]

Given this, it can be argued that forging a Van Gogh inflicts a real epistemic harm on B if B buys the painting thinking that it is by Van Gogh. In looking at the painting, B is not (as B thinks she is) contemplating Van Gogh's take on how Being manifests itself to him – she is looking at something completely different, and something that, given its origins,

---

[53] After the 1938 stage play, the 1940 British film of the play, and the 1944 Hollywood remake of the 1940 film – all called *Gaslight*.

[54] See above, p 77.

[55] Fricker, *Epistemic Injustice* (n 52), 49 (emphasis in original).

[56] Ibid.

[57] #333 in Jacob-Bart's de la Faille's catalogue raisonné of Van Gogh's paintings; #1236 in Jan Hulsker's catalogue raisonné.

[58] Heidegger, 'The Origin of the Work of Art' in Heidegger, *Basic Writings*, rev'd ed (Harper, 1993), 162.

[59] Ibid, 181. As to how Van Gogh's painting does this, see ibid, 159–60.

is incapable of helping her to contemplate Being's manifesting itself as beings.[60] However, what makes (b) merely an arguable case of B's suffering an epistemic harm is that B may well not have bought the Van Gogh in order to contemplate reality through Van Gogh's eyes but as an investment. If this is the case, B suffers as little epistemic harm as she did in (a).

The above arguments show that a private law that is concerned to promote the QTL-flourishing of its subjects will – as between cases (a), (b) and (c) – be *most* concerned to impose a basic obligation on A not to deceive B in case (c), and *least* concerned to impose such a basic obligation on A in case (a). As it happens, English private law has the *completely opposite* set of priorities. So long as B has suffered some kind of loss as a result of investing in Acme plc, she will have no problem establishing that A breached a basic obligation in acting as he did in case (a). In case (b), B will probably only be able to sue A if she bought the forged Van Gogh *from A*. If A sold the painting to a dealer, who then sold the painting to B, there will be no communication between A and B on which B could found an action against A. And in case (c), B will not be able to sue A at all, unless she can show that A's actions caused her to develop a physical or psychiatric illness, in which case she will be able to argue that A committed 'the tort in *Wilkinson v Downton*' in gaslighting her.[61]

That English private law treats as most serious case (a) and as least serious case (c) shows how far English private law is from being a system of private law that promotes QTL-flourishing. More generally, the kind of intentionally told, and intentionally relied-upon, lie that would routinely give rise to a claim for fraud at the moment would *not* normally give rise to a claim under a system of private law that was concerned to promote QTL-flourishing. Whether such a claim could be made would depend on the implications of the lie for the deceived's QTL-flourishing.[62] So it would be a mistake to think that a private law that was concerned to promote QTL-flourishing would recognise as a matter of course that you have an obligation not to lie to me. Any lies you tell me will of course endanger your own flourishing:[63] but any basic obligations you owe me will be designed to protect *my* flourishing and my flourishing will not necessarily be endangered by your lying to me even if we identify human flourishing with engaging in a quest to lead a truthful life.

---

[60] See, to much the same effect, Bowden, 'What is Wrong with an Art Forgery? An Anthropological Perspective' (1999) 57 *The Journal of Aesthetics and Art Criticism* 333, 336–37; Lenain, *Art Forgery: The History of a Modern Obsession* (Reaktion Books, 2011), 234–38.

[61] *Wilkinson v Downton* [1897] 2 QB 57; *O (a child) v Rhodes* [2016] AC 219. In theory, recovery would be easier in the United States where a tort of intentionally inflicting emotional distress is generally recognised. However, if Jill Hasday's *Intimate Lies and the Law* (n 43) is anything to go by, American courts will hardly ever grant relief in 'intimate deception' cases.

[62] Cf Jason Neyers' view that the tort of deceit, in its current form, protects people's rights ('to bodily integrity, property, contractual performance, and parental rights in relation to children') from being interfered with through another's deceit: Neyers, 'Form and Substance in the Tort of Deceit' in Robertson and Goudkamp (eds), *Form and Substance in the Law of Obligations* (Hart Publishing, 2019), 325, quoting with approval Ripstein, *Private Wrongs* (Harvard UP, 2016), 50, fn 32: '[what is] at issue is not ... being lied to, but rather being deprived of what you have through deceit'. This *Kantian* view of the tort of deceit agrees with the view taken in the text that deceit should only be actionable in tort if it interferes with a protected interest of the claimant's but obviously takes a different view as to what amounts to a 'protected interest'. As it happens, I disagree with Neyers that the tort of deceit *currently* takes the form he suggests. For example, suppose A lies to B with the object of getting B not to bid for a painting that A wants for himself, or with the object of persuading B to hang on to shares in a company (in which A has an interest) that B would otherwise sell, thereby depressing the market value of shares in the company. I think B would be able to sue A in deceit for any loss suffered by B as a result of A's deceit; and this is so even though A's lie does not result in B's being deprived of anything that belongs to her (*contra*, Neyers 'Form and Substance', at 328).

[63] See above, pp 44–45.

# 2. Speech and Silence

One very significant difference between (i) English private law in its current state, and (ii) a private law that was geared towards promoting QTL-flourishing, is that (ii) would seek to do far more to protect freedom of speech than (i) does.

## The Silence of Private Law

The truth is that English private law does not regard the protection of freedom of speech as an important priority. This may seem a strange statement given that there *are* aspects of English private law that have the effect of protecting freedom of speech.

For example, there are numerous limits on the law of defamation that have the effect of allowing people to make defamatory statements about others: members of Parliament enjoy a complete immunity from being sued in defamation in respect of statements they make in Parliament;[64] newspapers that carry fair and accurate reports of significant public proceedings cannot normally be sued in defamation if those reports contain defamatory statements about you or me;[65] newspapers also cannot be sued for making defamatory allegations in a story so long as it was in the public interest for the story to be printed;[66] and no one can be sued in defamation for telling the truth about someone else,[67] or for expressing their honest opinion about someone else, so long as that opinion was based (or could have been based) on true facts.[68] The nascent tort of invasion of privacy cannot be invoked against someone who discloses private information about another in the public interest.[69] It is possible, depending on the circumstances, for someone who has been dismissed from their job for statements that they made outside of the workplace to claim that they have been unfairly dismissed.[70]

However, as was observed in Part I of this project, the protections for freedom of speech enjoyed under English private law are not protections for freedom of speech as such, but protections for aspects of RP-flourishing that might be affected were certain types of speech curtailed.[71] That is why, for example, speech that results in someone's being fired from their job attracts a certain limited protection: it is not because private law regards the freedom to speak as being important, but rather because of the importance of one's keeping one's job if one is to RP-flourish. But for the most part, enjoying the freedom to speak one's mind is not

---

[64] Bill of Rights 1688, Art 9.

[65] Defamation Act 1996, s 15, Sched I. The protection from being sued in defamation under these provisions is lost if the newspaper in question acts maliciously in publishing the report; publishing the report was not in the public interest (s 15(3)); and (depending on the nature of the report) if it fails to allow the claimant a reasonable opportunity to correct the impression created by its report.

[66] Now, Defamation Act 2013, s 4; previously, *Reynolds v Times Newspapers Ltd* [2001] 2 AC 127.

[67] Now, Defamation Act 2013, s 2.

[68] Now, Defamation Act 2013, s 3 (replacing the common law defence of 'fair comment', which only applied to statements of opinion on matters of the public interest).

[69] *Campbell v MGN Ltd* [2004] 2 AC 457.

[70] See Mantouvalou, "'I Lost my Job over a Facebook Post – Was that Fair?" Discipline and Dismissal for Social Media Activity' (2019) 35 *International Journal of Comparative Labour Law and Industrial Relations* 101.

[71] See McBride, *The Humanity of Private Law*, Part I (n 49), 138–40.

essential to someone's RP-flourishing;[72] with the result that English private law is normally uninterested in protecting speech *qua* speech. This lack of interest manifests itself in a variety of ways:

(1)   Traditionally, English law thought nothing of holding the press liable for publishing 'blasphemous, immoral, treasonable, schismatical, seditious, or scandalous libels'.[73] As William Blackstone observed, all the 'liberty of the press' required was that the law lay 'no *previous* restraints upon publications'.[74] So in Blackstone's view, the law could damn[75] the press for publishing any of the above types of libel, and 'the *liberty of the press*, properly understood, [would] by no means [be] infringed or violated'.[76] And even this concession to freedom of speech – the rule against prior restraints on publication – has now been jettisoned in privacy cases. Interim injunctions will be routinely awarded by the English courts in such cases (on the basis that should publication occur ahead of a trial of the issues, the claimant's privacy would be irreparably invaded), and the courts have gone so far as to award 'super-injunctions' forbidding anyone from mentioning the fact that an injunction has been awarded (on the basis that reporting that the claimant has obtained an injunction would give rise to unpleasant and possibly accurate speculation as to what the claimant has obtained an injunction about).

(2)   While there is authority that a contractual provision allowing A to dictate how B will lead his life will be invalid,[77] and plenty of authority that a contractual provision that unreasonably allows A to restrain B from plying her chosen trade after she leaves A's employ will also be invalid,[78] it has never been suggested (and no one would dream of suggesting)[79] that the same will be true of a contractual provision between a university (U) and one of its employees (B) that allows U to dictate to B what sort of academic research B will engage in, and set quotas for B as to how many articles B should publish – and in what journals – in a given period of time. The reason for the distinction is that the first two provisions pose a real threat to B's ability to RP-flourish; in particular, B's ability to earn and spend the money B will need to obtain the secondary goods required to RP-flourish. The third type of provision poses no such threat: academic freedom is not a crucial component of RP-flourishing, as is shown by the example of many modern-day academics who enjoy an RP-flourishing existence while not enjoying any kind of academic freedom worthy of the name.

---

[72] Cf Raz, 'Free Expression and Personal Identification' (1991) 11 *OJLS* 303, 303: 'With few exceptions people's interest in … free expression is rather small.'

[73] Blackstone, 4 *Commentaries on the Laws of England* 151 (1753).

[74] Ibid, 152 (emphasis in original).

[75] The language is a reference to the Duke of Wellington's response – 'Publish and be damned' – to the printer Joseph Stockdale, who had offered to keep the Duke's name out of the prostitute Harriette Wilson's memoirs if the Duke paid him enough to do so. Wellington understood the law: he could not obtain an injunction to prevent the memoirs being published, but would be able to bring a claim for libel after publication.

[76] Ibid, 151 (emphasis in original).

[77] *Horwood* v *Millar's Timber and Trading Co* [1917] 1 KB 305.

[78] *Nordenfelt* v *Maxim Nordenfelt Guns and Ammunition Co Ltd* [1894] AC 535.

[79] Though see Cowan, 'Interference with Academic Freedom: The Pre-natal History of a Tort' (1958) 4 *Wayne LR* 205, 221: 'No teacher may surrender [by contract] his constitutional right to academic freedom, not only because it is not alone his, but also because such a surrender is against public policy.'

(3)    We saw in Part I of this project that English private law seeks to promote travel and trade – two important contributors to RP-flourishing – by designating those who offer accommodation to the general public as 'common innkeepers', and subjects 'common innkeepers' to requirements (i) that they offer accommodation to anyone who is ready and willing to pay for it unless they have a good reason not to do so, and (ii) that they insure the property of visitors against its being lost while on the innkeeper's property.[80] However, no similar status exists for those who offer the general public online platforms for the expression of opinions, so that anyone maintaining such a platform would be required not to block someone from using that platform unless they had good reason for doing so. As a result, service providers who provide online platforms for the expression of opinions face no effective legal sanction for preventing people using those platforms to express opinions that are politically unpalatable to the service provider. Nor is it likely that the courts will imply a term into the contract governing the use of the service provider's platform that will provide a user of that platform with any real protection against their being silenced should what they say on that platform prove displeasing to the service provider.[81]

(4)    What Blackstone referred to as 'the sole and despotic dominion' that ownership of property gives the owner 'over the external things of the world'[82] means that a private owner of land is under no obligation to respect the freedom of expression of those using her land with her permission.[83] Any non-contractual licence that they have been given to use the land may be terminated at will[84] by the landowner.[85] As a result, under English law[86] the owner of a privately owned shopping mall is perfectly free to exclude from the mall a campaigner seeking to collect signatures protesting against the only children's playing fields in the area being built over,[87] or a group of youths who have been hanging around the mall because they have nothing better to do.[88] As Kevin and Susan Francis Gray observed of the decision in the latter case:

> a flicker of concern ought to be aroused by the suggestion that the common law allows one private actor, on invoking the threat of indefinite incarceration,[89] to exile a group of citizens permanently

---

[80] McBride, *The Humanity of Private Law, Part I* (n 49), 72, 79.

[81] The question is discussed in detail in McBride, '"All Watched Over by Machines of Loving Grace"? The Inevitable Conflict between Contract Law and Free Speech in Cyberspace' in Davies and Raczynska (eds), *The Contents of Commercial Contracts: Terms Affecting Freedoms* (Hart Publishing, forthcoming).

[82] Blackstone, 2 *Commentaries on the Laws of England* 2 (1753).

[83] It is different where land is owned by a public authority: the authority in question will be bound under both the common law of judicial review (see *Wheeler v Leicester City Council* [1985] AC 1054) and the Human Rights Act 1998 to respect the freedom of expression of those using that land. For discussion, see Feldman, 'Property and Public Protest' in Meisel and Cook (eds), *Property and Protest: Essays in Honour of Brian W Harvey* (Hart Publishing, 2000), 42–50.

[84] *Wood* v *Leadbitter* (1845) 13 M & W 838.

[85] It is different where the licence is contractual in nature. In such a case, the landowner cannot turn those using her land into trespassers by withdrawing their licence to use her land if withdrawing the licence would amount to a breach of contract (*Winter Garden Theatre (London) Ltd* v *Millennium Productions Ltd* [1948] AC 173) and an anticipatory breach of the contractual licence, refusing to allow the claimants into the landowner's premises may be met with an order for specific performance (*Verrall* v *Great Yarmouth BC* [1981] 1 QB 202).

[86] For a very helpful discussion of the law in this area, see Allen, *Property and the Human Rights Act 1998* (Hart Publishing, 2005), 219–23.

[87] *Appleby* v *United Kingdom* (2003) 37 EHRR 38.

[88] *CIN Properties Ltd* v *Rawlins* [1995] 2 EGLR 130; *Anderson* v *United Kingdom* (1998) 25 EHRR CD172.

[89] By virtue of the fact that the shopping mall obtained an injunction against the youths in question 'trespassing' on the mall, with the result that any such trespassing youth would be held to have committed a contempt of court.

from the centre of their home town, thereby endangering their livelihood and severely impairing their freedom to engage in the social and commercial relationships of their choice.[90]

And yet, 'the decision attracted – quite extraordinarily – virtually no comment or criticism of any kind.'[91] The lack of comment or criticism is easily explicable: such is the indifference of English private law to protecting freedom of expression, what would have been extraordinary is if it *had* limited the rights of a landowner to exclude people from his property in order to protect those people's freedom of speech.[92]

If any further confirmation were needed of private law's relative indifference to protecting freedom of speech, it is provided by Thomas Healy's brilliant account of the genesis of Supreme Court Justice Oliver Wendell Holmes' dissent in *Abrams v United States*,[93] which laid the groundwork for the expansive understanding of the scope of the First Amendment to the United States Constitution that eventually prevailed over the course of the twentieth century.[94]

In an earlier free speech case, *Schenck v United States*,[95] Holmes had paved the way for his dissent in *Abrams* by tip-toeing away from the traditional, Blackstone-influenced, understanding of the First Amendment to the United States Constitution – under which the First Amendment was thought only to invalidate prior restraints on the freedom of speech and not punishments for speech that had been uttered[96] – and formulating a 'clear and present danger' standard for what sort of speech could be constitutionally restrained under the First Amendment. Eight months later, in his dissent in *Abrams*, Holmes made his judgment in *Schenck* count by ruling that the 'clear and present' danger standard was not satisfied in *Abrams*,[97] and providing a clear rationale for the First Amendment's limiting the state's ability to interfere with freedom of speech.[98]

Healy recounts how Holmes went about writing his seminal judgment in *Schenck*:

> By this point in his career, Holmes had written about nearly every legal topic under the sun: contracts, torts, evidence, procedure, tax, bankruptcy, criminal law, constitutional law, administrative law. So when he stumbled upon some *new problem, one he had not yet specifically addressed*, his first instinct was to find an analogy in an issue he had addressed. In this way, he had become

---

[90] Gray and Gray, 'Civil Rights, Civil Wrongs and Quasi-Public Space' [1999] *European Human Rights Law Review* 46, 46.

[91] Ibid.

[92] See Rowbottom, 'Property and Participation: A Right of Access for Expressive Activities' [2005] *European Human Rights Law Review* 186, 198: 'The courts are … unlikely to create a right of access [to land for expressive purposes] on their own accord, as can be seen on the various occasions where the courts have been unwilling to develop a licence for the general public to access property', citing the cases at n 85, *Monsanto v Tilly* [2000] Env LR 313, and *Porter v Commissioner of Police of the Metropolis* [1999] 10 WLUK 607.

[93] 250 US 616 (1919).

[94] Healy, *The Great Dissent: How Oliver Wendell Holmes Changed His Mind – And Changed the History of Free Speech in America* (Metropolitan Books, 2013).

[95] 249 US 47 (1919).

[96] A view that Holmes himself endorsed in *Patterson v Colorado*, 205 US 454, 462 (1907).

[97] *Abrams* (n 93), 628. This was something Holmes J was unwilling to do in *Schenck* itself, even though the 'clear and present danger' test was not satisfied in that case either: see Healy, *The Great Dissent* (n 94), 102, 112–14.

[98] *Abrams* (n 93), 630: 'when men have realized that time has upset many fighting faiths, they may come to believe even more than they believe the very foundations of their own conduct that the ultimate good desired is better reached by free trade in ideas – that the best test of truth is the power of the thought to get itself accepted in the competition of the market, and that truth is the only ground upon which their wishes safely can be carried out.'

almost a closed loop, repeating the old formulas over and over again in slightly new contexts. Thinking about the issue of free speech now, Holmes followed the same pattern.[99]

In other words, the great doyen of the common law – the author of classic works on private law such as *The Common Law* (1881) and 'The path of the law'[100] – had had *no occasion* to think about the importance of freedom of speech until 55 years into his career as a legal writer, practitioner and judge.[101] This simply would not have been possible had the protection of freedom of speech been a priority for the private law of Holmes' time; it obviously was not. And as we have seen, the position is not so very different today.

## What Private Law Could Say

What would a private law that was concerned to foster QTL-flourishing do differently? We can discuss this issue under three headings: (1) privacy; (2) inquiry; and (3) access.

(1) *Privacy.* The same considerations that for a long time made English private law ambivalent about protecting people's privacy[102] can be expected also to be taken into account by a private law that seeks to foster QTL-flourishing.

On the one hand, and in favour of protecting people's privacy, is the importance of being able to mix with other people without shame – not only for RP-flourishing, but also QTL-flourishing. It is unlikely that one can effectively seek to be a 'good shepherd of Being' in isolation. Such a search must almost always be conducted in communion with others, with and from whom one can learn to become ever more excellent in contemplating, and witnessing to, Being's manifesting itself as beings. On the other hand, and in favour of *not* protecting people's privacy, is the importance of not being misled about other people's characters – again, not just for RP-flourishing, but also QTL-flourishing. As our discussion of the cases of Medea and Penelope in the previous two chapters show,[103] mixing with someone who is – unknown to you – wearing a 'pasteboard mask' can fundamentally impair your ability to QTL-flourish. As a result, a private law that seeks to foster QTL-flourishing could be expected – as does, to a limited extent, English private law in its current state[104] – to distinguish between damaging (though accurate) statements about you that (i) disclose who you *are*, and (ii) disclose who you *were*. As type (ii) statements do not engage any consideration *against* protecting someone's privacy recognised as valid by a private law that seeks to promote QTL-flourishing, one could expect such a private law to provide generous protection against people's making type (ii) statements about you.

---

[99] Healy, *The Great Dissent* (n 94), 100 (emphasis added).

[100] (1897) 10 *Harvard LR* 457.

[101] Holmes went to Harvard Law School in 1864.

[102] See McBride, *The Humanity of Private Law, Part 1* (n 49), 139–40.

[103] See above, pp 66–67, 69–70, 105–106.

[104] See Rehabilitation of Offenders Act 1974, ss 4(1), 8, making someone who maliciously discloses the fact of someone's having been convicted of a criminal offence liable in defamation so long as the conviction is 'spent'. See also the so-called 'right to be forgotten', recognised by the European Court of Justice in *Google Spain SL v Agencia Española de Protección de Datos (AEPD)* [2014] QB 1022, and given limited effect in the UK by virtue of s 22 of the Data Protection Act 2018 (incorporating, inter alia, Art 17 ('right to be forgotten') of the General Data Protection Regulation into UK law).

So far as type (i) statements are concerned, a private law that seeks to foster QTL-flourishing could be expected to take into account two further considerations in determining whether, and when, to protect people from such statements. First, the age and experience of the claimant. Consider a story that alleges (accurately) that *Producer* requires actresses to sleep with him before he will offer them parts in films, and that *Actress* sleeps with producers in order to obtain parts in films. The revelation about *Actress* is liable to have a devastating effect on her ability to QTL-flourish, as it will isolate her from her peers and also cause her to suffer some of the distinctive harms (being plunged into a deep attention well, or hating others) that are liable to impair someone's QTL-flourishing. The position as regards *Producer* is more complex. In a plea for greater respect for privacy in the modern age, Wendell Berry writes, 'We do not want self-appointed spokesmen for our souls.'[105] But it may well be that disclosing *Producer*'s iniquities to the world is what it is going to take to get *Producer* to confront who he actually is, and put him on the path to QTL-flourishing; clearly, nothing else has worked. So a private law that is concerned to promote QTL-flourishing could be expected, other things being equal, to do far more to protect *Actress*'s privacy than it would to protect *Producer*'s.

But other things may not be equal in *Producer*'s case. The second further consideration that a private law that seeks to promote QTL-flourishing could be expected to take into account in determining whether to protect *Producer* from the type (i) statement about who he is, is how the information was obtained. Berry quotes with approval the writer Janna Malamud Smith's cautious words on the topic of disclosing in one's own writing the details of other people's lives:

> Intimacy … works because you are allowed to do things in a friendship, in a love relationship, that you can't do in public. So when the private things intimacy has allowed you to expose are suddenly made public, that is a legitimate reason for a feeling of profound betrayal … The fact is that betrayals are a real thing.[106]

Intimate relationships are one of the key *loci* in which QTL-flourishing may take place: you encounter Being manifesting itself as beings through revealing oneself to another and allowing them to reveal themselves to you. If the possibility of achieving that kind of intimacy with another is endangered by your fear that you might be betrayed by that other, then your ability to QTL-flourish is also endangered, and one could expect a private law that seeks to promoting QTL-flourishing to protect against that possibility.

So if the information that *Producer* requires actresses to sleep with him before giving them parts in films was obtained through *Producer* admitting to that fact in a setting that provides the opportunity for QTL-flourishing – such as in talking to a loved one, or in a confessional, or in therapy – then a private law that is concerned to promote QTL-flourishing will protect *Producer*'s privacy. But if that information was derived at first hand through an actress being required to sleep with *Producer* in order to get a film part, then *Producer*'s privacy will count for nothing with a private law that seeks to promote QTL-flourishing.

(2) *Inquiry*. Academia is not the only profession that should have truth-seeking as its *telos*, or purpose. Journalists and the police also belong to professions that only make sense if they

---

[105] Berry, *Life is a Miracle: An Essay Against Modern Superstition* (Couterpoint, 2000), 80.
[106] Ibid, 82.

have truth-seeking at their heart. However, it would be naïve to think that these professions cannot be corrupted into becoming trades that have as their *telos* the pursuit of power, or money, or status. For example, in 1880, John Swinton – chief editorial writer on the *New York Times* in the 1860s – attended a banquet thrown in his honour by his peers. He responded to a toast made at the dinner 'to the independent press' as follows:

> There is no such thing in America as an independent press, unless it is in the small towns. You know it and I know it. There is not one of you who dares to write his honest opinion, and if you did you know beforehand that they would never appear in print … The business of the New York journalist is to destroy the truth, to lie outright, to pervert, to vilify, to fawn at the feet of Mammon, and to sell his … country for his daily bread … We are the tools and vassals of rich men behind the scenes … We are intellectual prostitutes.[107]

Wendell Berry fears that academia may be undergoing a similar corruption under the 'man-made evolutionary crisis known in the universities as "publish or perish"':

> If a tree falls in the absence of a refereed journal or a foundation, does it make a sound? The answer, in the opinion of the imitation corporate executives who now run our universities, is no. This academic Darwinism inflicts severe penalties both upon those who survive and upon those who perish. Both must submit to an absolute economic system which values their lives strictly according to their 'productivity' – which is to say that they submit to a form of slavery. Both must submit, at least until tenure, to a university-prescribed regimen of life in which time = work = original discovery = career, thus assuring the ascendancy of professional standards in the minds of the young, and the eclipse of any standard of any other kind. The modern university thus enforces obedience, not to the academic ideal of learning and teaching what is true, as a community of teachers and scholars passing on to the young the knowledge of the old, but obedience rather to the industrial economic ideals of high productivity and constant innovation.[108]

Obviously a private law that seeks to promote QTL-flourishing will seek to protect professions that have (or should have) truth-seeking as their *telos* from suffering the kinds of corruptions identified by Swinton and Berry. But how?

Back in 1958,[109] Thomas Cowan reported that 'Diligent search has failed to disclose a single case holding that a remedy exists in tort law for interference with academic freedom.'[110] He went on to recommend that, given the growing 'belief on the part of college faculties that academic freedom had been violated in critical matters of faculty appointments and

---

[107] Quoted in Boyer and Morais, *Labor's Untold Story* (Cameron Associates, 1955), 81.

[108] Berry, *Life is a Miracle* (n 105), 62–63. See also Alasdair MacIntyre's strictures about the modern university, quoted in McBride, *The Humanity of Private Law, Part I* (n 49), 109, n 103; and Graeber, *The Utopia of Rules* (Melville House, 2016), 134–35: 'There was a time when academia was society's refuge for the eccentric, brilliant, and impractical. No longer. It is now the domain of professional self-marketers.' Interestingly, Paul Campos's article 'Shame' (2008) 17 *Journal of Contemporary Legal Issues* 15 – which describes a number of 'legal academic characters' (15) ('The drone', 'The bully', 'The hack' and 'The fraud') that exemplify how the 'problematic relationship between the requirements of professional training and of pursuing knowledge create special problems for the integrity of the discipline' (22) – finds no room for a fifth character ('The producer'? 'The professional'?) who has sold out completely to the forces that are the subject of Berry's scorn. Maybe such characters are so common that they are now unnoticeable?

[109] It may be no coincidence that the first documented use of the term 'publish or perish' occurred the decade before Cowan's article, in Logan Wilson's *The Academic Man: A Study in the Sociology of a Profession* (OUP, 1942), 197. For the detective work, see Shapiro, 'They Published, Not Perished, but Were they Good Teachers?' (1998) 72 *Chicago-Kent LR* 835, 836.

[110] Cowan, 'Interference with Academic Freedom' (n 78), 223.

promotions at their institutions',[111] the courts should find that a university will commit a tort if it maliciously interferes with a lecturer's academic freedom; that is, his ability 'freely to seek the truth and equally freely to impart it to others by the professional mode of teaching'.[112] Nothing has come of this suggestion, or his already-mentioned suggestion that a term in a contract between a university and lecturer limiting the lecturer's academic freedom should be invalid on grounds of public policy.[113]

Given what has already been said as to private law's indifference to freedom of speech, this should come as no surprise. But even a private law that sought to foster QTL-flourishing could be expected to be cautious about going down such roads in an attempt to protect academia's vocation to seek truth from being corrupted. After all, it is not obvious what 'academic freedom' entails, with the result that the notion of what 'academic freedom' entails is itself very likely to become weaker and weaker as the idea of 'academic freedom' comes under attack.[114] Nor is it obvious how Cowan's proposals could be adapted to protect the journalistic profession from the sort of censorship from above (and self-censorship) that has made eunuchs of the vast majority of journalists working today.

A more promising way forward is suggested by the technique that has been adopted to keep our third truth-seeking profession – the police – in line: the encouragement of 'whistleblowing'.[115] The Employment Rights Act 1996 provides us with a model of how private law can be used to encourage whistleblowing.

Section 43B sets out what kind of disclosures by a 'worker' attract protection under the Act: they have to be disclosures that the work reasonably believed tended to show that a crime or legal wrong has been committed, or that a miscarriage of justice has occurred, or that someone's health or safety, or the quality of the environment, is likely to be endangered, or that one or more of these thing is being concealed.

Sections 43C – H set out to whom the disclosure must be made in order to attract protection under the Act, with section 43H providing that a disclosure to *anyone* will attract protection so long as the worker in question reasonably believed his allegations were correct,

---

[111] Ibid, 224.

[112] Ibid, 225.

[113] See above, n 78.

[114] For example, Robert C Post's statement that 'academic freedom of research can be claimed only by those who participate in the kind of discipline that is capable of advancing knowledge' (Post, 'Academic Freedom and Legal Scholarship' (2015) 64 *Journal of Legal Education* 530, 536) seems tailor-made to be used to deny academic freedom to those who make the sort of 'outside the box' moves that are most likely to result in significant gains in our understanding. And his eye-rollingly hilarious observation (ibid, at 534) that 'Disciplines are ... committed to progress, to the expansion of knowledge. For this reason, disciplines encourage criticism and dissent' seems complacent, at best. See also, to the same enervating effect, Finkin and Post, *For the Common Good: Principles of American Academic Freedom* (Yale UP, 2009), 39 ('Academic freedom ... does not protect the autonomy of professors to pursue their own individual work free from all university restraints. Instead, [it] establishes the liberty necessary to advance knowledge, which is the liberty to practice the scholarly profession'), 149 ('Academic freedom is not the freedom to speak or teach as one wishes. It is the freedom to pursue the scholarly profession, inside and outside the classroom, according to the norms and standards of that profession'). For a different, more bracing, view, see Taleb, *Skin in the Game* (Allen Lane, 2018), 144: 'You can define a free person precisely as someone whose fate is not centrally or directly dependent on peer assessment.' See Haack, *Evidence Matters* (CUP, 2014), 158–72, for a brilliantly skeptical review of the value of peer review, culminating in the conclusion '*the fact that work has passed pre-publication peer review is no guarantee that it is not flawed or even fraudulent; and the fact that work has been rejected by reviewers is no guarantee that it is not an important advance*' (emphasis in original).

[115] See Police Act 2002, Part 2B ('Investigation of concerns raised by whistle-blowers').

did not make them for gain, the allegations made by the worker were 'exceptionally serious' in nature, and it was reasonable for the worker to make those allegations to the person to whom they were made.

Sections 43J and 47B set out how private law will protect a disclosure that qualifies for protection under the 1996 Act. Section 43J provides that a contractual term that purports to preclude a worker from making a protected disclosure will be void. Section 47B effectively makes it a tort for either the worker's employer or someone else working for the employer (either a worker or an agent) to subject the worker to a detriment for making a protected disclosure, with section 49 providing that in such a case the employer will be liable to pay compensation to the victimised worker.

With some adaptations, this model could be used to encourage whistleblowing, not just by police officers who wish to report corruption in the forces for which they work, but also by journalists or academics who wish to highlight interferences with their freedoms to do their jobs properly by the institutions for which they work. To attract protection under a private law that was concerned to promote QTL-flourishing, a disclosure by a journalist or academic would have to – in the reasonable opinion of the journalist or academic in question – indicate that the institution for which they work is failing to respect journalistic/ academic integrity in the way it is operating. And *any* such disclosure to *anyone* would have to be protected, so as to cover the writing of an article for general consumption that exposed some such institutional corruption. Private law would protect such a disclosure in the same way that 'qualifying disclosures' are protected by sections 43J and 47B of the 1996 Act: the disclosure could *not* amount to a breach of contract under any circumstances, and subjecting the person who made the disclosure to a detriment would amount to a tort.

(3) *Access*. The fact that QTL-flourishing almost always involves communion with others means that a private law that is concerned to promote QTL-flourishing will seek to preserve people's access to communal spaces – whether physical, such as a shopping mall, or virtual, online – where they can achieve that kind of communion, or at least make the kind of contact with others that is the indispensable first step to achieving that kind of communion.

Kevin and Susan Francis Gray suggest that such access may be secured in the context of shopping malls by revitalising the already-mentioned law on 'common callings', under which – according to Blackstone – 'if an inn-keeper … hangs out a sign and opens his house for travellers, it is an implied engagement to entertain all persons who travel upon that way; and upon this universal *assumpsit* an action on the case will lie against him for damages if he, without good reason, refuses to admit a traveller.'[116] They suggest that someone who is unreasonably excluded from a shopping mall should be allowed to sue on the same basis:

> in the shopping mall context, the liberality of the property owner's initial invitation to the public is intrinsically aimed at furthering his own (essentially economic) interests rather than those of the community. Having thus fixed the terms of engagement so determinedly in his own favour, the property owner is effectively estopped from making arbitrary or selective derogations from the inclusiveness of the invitation.[117]

[116] Blackstone, 3 *Commentaries on the Laws of England* 165 (1753).
[117] Gray and Gray, 'Civil Rights, Civil Wrongs and Quasi-Public Space' (n 90), 77 (citing *Marsh* v *Alabama*, 326 US 501, 506 (1946) (per Black J)). See also Gray and Gray, 'Private Property and Public Propriety' in McLean (ed), *Property and the Constitution* (Hart Publishing, 1999), 20–31.

Much the same approach could be adopted in respect of companies that provide online platforms for people to communicate with each other. These platforms amount to what Ivan Illich called 'tools for conviviality': 'they can be easily used, by anybody, as often or as seldom as desired, for the accomplishment of a purpose chosen by the user.'[118] However, as has become increasingly clear,[119] the tech companies that provide these platforms regard the 'convivial' nature of their platforms as a bug, not a feature, and want to prevent them being used to express views that the tech companies oppose.

Treating these companies as engaged in a 'common calling', and therefore liable if they unreasonably exclude someone from a platform that they maintain, has the added benefit that doing so would guarantee that English private law could provide effective remedies to litigants whose ability to QTL-flourish has been attenuated through their being kicked off an online platform that is almost certainly hosted abroad (usually in California). Were such a litigant (C) to bring a claim for breach of contract against the platform provider (D) or were they to sue D in tort (for example, in conspiracy (if C has been the subject of co-ordinated action by a number of platform providers) or in defamation (if D purported to justify kicking C off its platform for a reason that is both specious and defamatory)), whether English law applied to C's claim would depend on such things as what the C-D contract said would be the law of their contract, and where the place of any tort committed by D could be said to be.[120] However, an action under the law on 'common callings' is *sui generis* – it is neither an action for breach of contract, nor an action in tort.[121] So long, then, as C resides in England, with the result that C was denied access to D's online platform *in England*, there is no reason why C should not be able to take advantage of the English law on 'common callings' to bring a claim against D (provided, of course, that that area of law extended that far, which it currently does not).

It might be argued that adapting the law on 'common callings' to help secure access to communal spaces goes too far, in two respects. First, it might be argued that it is dispro-portionate to apply the law on 'common callings' to *everyone* who 'hangs out a sign' that a communal space they manage is open to all. Instead, the law should apply *only* to those who occupy such a *dominant position* – either within a town or online – that allowing them to decide who can and cannot use their facilities would severely impact on people's abilities to associate together. There is some support for this more limited approach in the European Court of Human Rights' decision in *Appleby* v *United Kingdom*:

> While … demographic, social, economic and technological developments are changing the ways in which people … come into contact with each other, the Court is not persuaded that this requires the automatic creation of rights of entry to private property … Where however the bar on access to property has the effect of preventing any effective exercise of freedom of expres-sion … the Court would not exclude that a positive obligation could arise for the State to protect

---

[118] Illich, *Tools for Conviviality* (n 1), 22.

[119] Details are provided in McBride, "'All Watched Over by Machines of Loving Grace?'" (n 81).

[120] Ibid.

[121] In *Constantine* v *Imperial Hotels Ltd* [1944] KB 693, a claimant who was unjustifiably turned away from a hotel was simply said by Birkett J to have an 'action on the case' against the hotel owner. In his book on *The Law of Quasi-Contracts* (Sweet & Maxwell, 1952), Percy Winfield said that an action under the law on common callings was an action 'in pseudo-quasi-contract' (26, 30–34), which shows how difficult it is to categorise. My thanks to Robert Stevens for bringing this point to my attention.

the enjoyment of Convention rights by regulating property rights. The corporate town, where the entire municipality was controlled by a private body, might be an example.[122]

However, the nebulous concept of a dominant position is an unsatisfactory hook on which to hang legal obligations: it would be almost impossible for the owners of a shopping mall or online platform to know in advance whether or not they occupy the kind of dominant position that would attract the obligations that attend someone's pursuing a 'common calling'.

Second, it might be argued that a right that one not be unreasonably denied access to privately maintained property that is advertised as being effectively open to everyone 'would put an end to the institution of property as we know it.'[123] However, as Kevin and Susan Francis Gray point out, this seems overstated: in other jurisdictions that recognise a right of reasonable access, such a right has never been extended to the family home, small businesses, hospitals, nursing homes, banks, theatres, or churches.[124] Such a right has only been applied to 'places [that] were the subject of an open invitation to public use' such as 'a community library, a university campus, a ski resort, a [public] racecourse …, a casino, [and] a gasoline service station'.[125]

# 3. Attention Wells

We will now turn, in this and the next two sections of this chapter, to consider the distinctive kinds of harms that a private law that was concerned to promote QTL-flourishing would recognise people as being vulnerable to suffering, and how it might seek to prevent people from suffering such harms.

First up is the harm of being placed in a *deep attention well*.[126] That such an event could count as a harm would count as fantastical within the worldview that identifies human flourishing with the RP. Under the RP, the quality or direction of one's attention is usually irrelevant to whether one can count oneself as flourishing as a human being. Of course, a medical disorder such as ADHD (attention deficit hyperactivity disorder) counts as a disorder among children because it can severely impair their education, and we live in a world where your ability to obtain many of the goods that are essential to RP-flourishing depends on the quality of the education you received when you were growing up. However, we don't concern ourselves so much about ADHD in grown adults as such a disorder is much less threatening to an adult's capacity for RP-flourishing.

So in a world where the RP is accepted as defining what is involved in human flourishing, *we* place little value on the quality or direction of *our* attention, and as a result we tend to be highly promiscuous with our attentions, moving constantly from one concern, fad, interest, spectacle to another. This is not to say, however, that our world places no

---

[122] *Appleby* v *United Kingdom* (n 87), at [47], citing *Marsh* v *Alabama* (n 117).
[123] Honoré, 'Ownership' in Guest (ed), *Oxford Essays in Jurisprudence (First Series)* (OUP, 1960), 114 (quoted by Feldman, 'Property and Public Protest' (n 83), 33, 37).
[124] Gray and Gray, 'Civil Rights, Civil Wrongs and Quasi-Public Space' (n 90), 92–93.
[125] Ibid, 93.
[126] For the concept of an attention well, see above, pp 103–104.

value on the quality or direction of our attention. On the contrary: as books like Tim Wu's *The Attention Merchants*[127] show, our attention is very highly valued in our society. But the value comes from *other people, not us*. Other people want our attention because the ability to hold our attention can be monetised. The monetisation of this ability takes two forms.

The first, and earlier, form is monetisation through advertising. Newspapers, TV stations, and now websites that are successful at getting people's attention are paid by businesses to advertise their products and services in the hope that the advertising business can appropriate for its product or service a bit of the attention that the medium through which they are advertising has gained for itself.

The second, later and much more sinister, form is monetisation through selling products – the most obvious example is a smartphone – that are designed to 'harvest' the attention of the users of those products, keeping the attention of users trained on the product for as long as possible. The commercial success of these products – with 38.1 million iPhones being bought in the UK alone in 2011–17 – suggests that they are attractive to potential buyers because buyers (consciously or unconsciously) *want their attention to be harvested*. Matthew Crawford puts his finger on the ultimate source of that attraction when he speculates that it amounts to a 'death instinct': 'an exhausted response to the … burden of self-regulation that we bear in a culture predicated on freedom.'[128] He detects this 'death instinct' in people who are addicted to playing slot machines, and in particular in players who jam 'a toothpick into the button that initiates a play so that the machine plays itself continuously and the player becomes a mere bystander, watching the credit meter rise and fall (mostly fall).'[129] He also:

> can detect something like a death instinct in myself, for example in those times when I slump in front of the TV and watch whatever is served up. It becomes an occasion for self-disgust as soon as I rouse myself from the couch, and is of no great source of pleasure while I am in this trance, so why do I do it? As someone who is self-employed … the disposition of every hour is a matter of choice, an occasion for reflection and evaluation. Sometimes I just want to stay where I am and watch *Dateline*, because *that's what's next*. Let death come.[130]

Crawford regards this final choice to give up choice and stew mindlessly in front of something that is designed to harvest your attention as the 'dark mirror image' of an 'autotelic activity'. This is 'an activity that has no point beyond its own continuance, because it is not a means to some other end.'[131] But this potentially endless activity is very different from endlessly gambling or watching TV or poking about on your smartphone. Autotelic activities:

> are guided by intimations of something valuable that you are trying to bring more fully into view through your activity. In the course of your repeated efforts, you find what you are aiming at is a moving target, because it reveals itself only in the course of your pursuit.[132]

It is no accident that this language echoes the picture of human flourishing that we have identified with QTL-ing. So we can say that the *telos* of an autotelic activity is life itself,

---

[127] Wu, *The Attention Merchants: The Epic Struggle to Get Inside Our Heads* (Atlantic Books, 2017).
[128] Crawford, *The World Beyond Your Head: How to Flourish in an Age of Distraction* (Viking, 2015), 103, 104.
[129] Ibid, 104.
[130] Ibid, 104–05 (emphasis in original).
[131] Ibid, 105.
[132] Ibid.

flourishing. In contrast, as Crawford observes, 'the gambler … comes to embrace "extinction" as the goal of his activity.'[133]

English private law has been an indifferent spectator to the wars for our attention that have been waged over the course of the twentieth and twenty-first centuries.[134] This, again, is no surprise given that English private law identifies our flourishing with the RP, and under the RP the quality and direction of our attentions tends to have no effect (at least when we are grown-up) on our capacity for RP-flourishing. But things would be very different under a private law that seeks to foster QTL-flourishing. The quality and direction of our attentions would be of paramount importance to such a private law. So important, in fact, that we can propose a very simple test to determine whether a given private law jurisdiction is seriously interested in fostering QTL-flourishing: *does it designate a smartphone as being a defective product?*

A product that is designed to harvest people's attention *would* be regarded as defective under a private law that seeks to foster QTL-flourishing. This is because such a product is, by definition, designed to plunge us into a deep attention well: an attention well that has the effect of preventing us interacting properly with the reality around us. As such, a product that was particularly successful at harvesting attention would be regarded by a private law that seeks to foster QTL-flourishing as being as harmful as cigarettes, and perhaps even more harmful than that. That smartphones – and the apps that run on them – are the most effective attention-harvesting products yet invented can scarcely be doubted. In his book, *Hooked: How To Build Habit-Forming Products*, Nir Eyal reports that:

> Seventy-nine percent of smartphone owners check their device within fifteen minutes of waking up every morning. Perhaps more startling, fully one-third of Americans say they would rather give up sex than lose their cell phones. A 2011 university study suggested people check their phones thirty-four times per day. However, industry insiders believe that number is closer to an astounding 150 daily sessions.[135]

Among a number of features that Tristan Harris – a former 'Design Ethicist' at Google – identifies that make smartphones and smartphone apps so successful at attention-harvesting, two are worth highlighting in particular.[136]

The first is receiving an *intermittent variable reward*. As Harris says, this has the effect of turning every smartphone into a slot machine, where the user's action is linked with a variable reward – 'You pull a lever and immediately either an enticing reward … or nothing. Addictiveness is maximized when the rate of reward is most variable.' James Williams – another former Google employee – agrees: 'This is the underlying dynamic at work behind

---

[133] Ibid, 106. Cf Robert Nozick's description of the choice to live attached to an 'experience machine' (above, p 31) as a 'kind of suicide': Nozick, *Anarchy, State and Utopia* (Basic Books, 1974), 43.

[134] The few private law cases of note that the advertising industry has given rise to have concerned themselves with whether the claims made for a product in an advertisement can give rise to legal liability (*Carlill v Carbolic Smoke Ball Co* [1893] 1 QB 256), and if so, who can be held liable (*Lambert v Lewis* [1982] AC 225). So far as I know, no one has ever sought to sue a manufacturer for *becoming addicted* to using the manufacturer's product. Litigation over cigarettes has focussed not on the fact of addiction, but the harms caused by the addiction – cancer on the part of the users, health-care costs on the part of the state.

[135] Eyal, *Hooked: How to Build Habit-Forming Products* (Penguin, 2014), 1.

[136] All quotes are from Harris' (easily findable) online essay 'How Technology is Hijacking your Mind'.

the high engagement users have with "infinite" scrolling feeds, especially those with "pull-to-refresh" functionality, which we find in countless applications and websites today, such as Facebook's News Feed or Twitter's Stream.'[137]

The second feature is *autoplay*. Harris observes that 'Another way to hijack people is to keep them consuming things even when they aren't hungry anymore. How? Easy. *Take an experience that was bounded and finite, and turn it into a bottomless flow that keeps going*.'[138] This is why, Harris explains, 'video and social media sites like Netflix, YouTube or Facebook *autoplay* the next video after a countdown instead of waiting for you to make a conscious choice (in case you won't). A huge portion of traffic on these websites is driven by autoplaying the next thing.' That so much traffic is driven by autoplay suggests that this feature is tapping into the 'death instinct' identified by Crawford: the all-too-human desire to 'Turn off your mind, relax and float downstream … Lay down all thoughts, surrender to the void.' John Lennon – whose lyrics these are, from The Beatles' *Tomorrow Never Knows* (1966) – assures us that 'It is not dying, it is not dying'. But, in fact, it is[139] – and a private law that was geared towards promoting QTL-flourishing would acknowledge as much and hold the producers of products that rely on such manipulations to harvest people's attentions liable for the harm they do to people's capacities to QTL-flourish.

However, the private law under which we live – a private law that seeks to foster RP-flourishing – would regard the suggestion that smartphones are defective products as just as fantastical as the suggestion that being placed in a deep attention well counts as a harm. Under section 3(1) of the Consumer Protection Act 1987, a product will count as defective if its 'safety … is not such as persons generally are entitled to expect' and a product's safety will be assessed 'in the context of risks of damage to property, as well as in the context of risks of death or personal injury.' Section 45(1) of the 1987 Act provides that '"personal injury" includes any disease and any other impairment of a person's physical *or mental condition*'[140] – but only a very bold spirit would dare to suggest that this phrase covers the case where a product like a smartphone or a slot machine is particularly effective at harvesting people's attention. It is likely that the courts will only find that someone's mental condition has been impaired by a product where it has resulted in them developing a psychiatric illness, while people who find their attention being harvested by a smartphone or slot machine are not suffering from a psychiatric illness but instead a perfectly natural reaction to the manipulations of their attentions that they are exposed to by that product.

The Consumer Protection Act 1987 therefore exemplifies the gulf that exists between English private law as it is now, and a private law that is concerned to foster QTL-flourishing. The gulf exists because of the very different conception of human flourishing – the RP – that English private law has in mind when it seeks to promote the flourishing of its subjects. Were private law to adopt the view that human flourishing consists in QTL-ing, it would at the same time adopt a completely different view of what amounts to a harm.

---

[137] Williams, *Stand Out of Our Light: Freedom and Resistance in the Attention Economy* (CUP, 2018), 35.
[138] Emphasis in original.
[139] As it happens, the lyrics to *Tomorrow Never Knows* are derived from the *Tibetan Book of the Dead*.
[140] Emphasis added.

# 4. Like a Dog

As well as regarding being placed in a deep attention well as a harm, a private law that was geared towards fostering QTL-flourishing would also regard developing a false view of reality as harmful.[141] The particular form of this harm that we will focus on in this section is that of developing the false view that *you are worthless*. The title of this section comes from the conclusion of Franz Kafka's novel *The Trial* (1915), where after a year of ordeals following his initial arrest, K is taken from his flat by two men to a quarry, where he is made to sit on the ground and is executed:

> the hands of one of the gentlemen were laid on K's throat, while the other pushed the knife deep into his heart and twisted it there, twice. As his eyesight failed, K saw the two gentlemen cheek by cheek, close in front of his face, watching the result. 'Like a dog!' he said, it was as if the shame of it should outlive him.[142]

While K is treated at his end 'Like a dog', as though he were worthless, there are suggestions in the novel that he brings this fate on himself, by failing to stand up for himself and insist on his worth as a human being.[143]

In the penultimate chapter of the novel, a priest tells K about a man from the country-side who asks for entry to the law, and on being told by the doorkeeper that the doorkeeper cannot let him in right now, he sits by the *open* gateway to the law, awaiting a permission to go in that is never given. He eventually dies, still waiting. The priest – now revealed to be connected with the court dealing with K's case – also tells K that the court that has been tormenting K 'doesn't want anything from you. It accepts you when you come and it lets you go when you leave.' And in the final chapter, as K is led to execution, he thinks about making a break for it but 'he just became suddenly aware that there was no point in his resistance. There would be nothing heroic about it if he resisted, if he now caused trouble for these gentlemen, if in defending himself he sought to enjoy his last glimmer of life.' And so he allows himself to be led away, like a dog.

K's lack of self-worth deprives him of the ability to be an agent – he waits for things to happen, rather than making them happen himself. This is because only someone who *thinks* they are capable of doing great things, *is* capable of doing great things. As Henry Ford liked to say, 'Whether you think you can, or think you can't, you're right.' And nothing could be greater (within the horizons that we are well-advised to operate within)[144] than QTL-flourishing: of seeking to be an excellent contemplator of, and witness to, Being's manifesting itself as beings. So only those with a well-developed sense of self-worth will be capable of embarking on the quest to be a good 'shepherd of Being'.

It follows that a private law that is concerned to promote QTL-flourishing will be keenly concerned to protect its subjects' sense of self-worth from being undermined as a result of

---

[141] See above, p 41.

[142] Kafka, *The Trial* (1915), chapter 10 ('End') (trans Wyllie).

[143] K is also described in dog-like terms at the end of the first chapter of *The Trial*, as being 'like a thirsty animal lapping with its tongue when it eventually finds water.' As the final chapter of *The Trial*, chapter 10, was written immediately after the first chapter (to give Kafka a determinate idea of where his story was headed), it is not far-fetched to link K's dog-like nature at the end of the first chapter with K's being treated like a dog at the bitter end of the last chapter.

[144] See above, pp 42–43, 86–87.

their being treated 'like a dog'. In what follows, we will discuss how English private law in its current state protects people from being treated 'like a dog' by (i) public officials, and (ii) private actors, in order to get an idea as to how much more would be done in these respects by a private law that was concerned to promote QTL-flourishing.

## Public Officials

In considering the question of how far English private law protects people from being treated 'like a dog' by a public official, we are assuredly not concerned with the situation presented in a case like *Michael* v *Chief Constable of South Wales*,[145] where Joanna Michael was killed by her ex-partner after a police emergency telephone operator fumbled her call for help. Acting incompetently does not equate to treating you as though you are worth nothing.

The case of *Costello* v *Chief Constable of Northumbria Police*[146] fits the bill more closely. In that case, Julie Costello, a police officer, was charged with taking Donna Brannan – a young woman who had escaped from local authority care and had been detained by the police – and locking her in a cell. Costello entered the cell with Brannan and told Brannan to remove her belt and shoes. Brannan then attacked Costello, punching and kicking her. While Costello was being attacked, another police officer, Inspector Bell, stood watching at the entrance to the cell and did nothing to protect Costello from Brannan's attack. In callously allowing Costello to be attacked by Brannan, we can say that Bell treated Costello as though she were worth nothing.

Where A, a public official, treats B as though they are worth nothing by doing something *positive*, like beating B up or locking B up for no reason, then of course A will be held to have committed a tort in relation to B – battery, or false imprisonment – and B will be entitled to a remedy against A for what A did. The special insult involved in A's treatment of B may well be reflected in A's being made to pay B aggravated damages. Exemplary damages may also be awarded against A if he has not been punished for his behaviour under the criminal law and would not be adequately punished in the absence of an award of exemplary damages. However, where as in *Costello*, A treats B 'like a dog' through an *omission* – by failing to save B from danger – the position is more complicated.

The law of negligence will *not* be available to provide B with a remedy for A's (non-) conduct unless the circumstances of the case are such that a private person in A's position would have owed B a duty to take reasonable steps to come to her aid.[147] That requirement was satisfied in the *Costello* case by virtue of the fact that Bell's presence in the cell area had encouraged an officer who was originally helping Costello to lock Brannan up to leave Costello alone with Brannan in the cell area. He assumed that if there were any problems, Bell would help out, and one of the established categories of situation where A will owe B a duty of care to save her from harm is where A has foreseeably discouraged a third party

---

[145] [2015] AC 1732 (discussed in McBride, *The Humanity of Private Law, Part I* (n 49), 3–4).

[146] [1999] 1 All ER 550.

[147] *Michael* v *Chief Constable of South Wales* [2015] AC 1732, at [101], [114]–[116]; *Robinson* v *Chief Constable of West Yorkshire* [2018] AC 736, at [32]–[35]; *Poole BC* v *GN* [2019] UKSC 25, at [28], [74].

from saving B from that harm, or interfered with that third party's being able to save B from that harm. As a result, Costello was able to sue Bell in negligence in *Costello* for failing to protect her from harm. But it would be going too far to say that Costello was able to sue Bell for treating her 'like a dog'. Given that Costello's claim was in negligence, it was a claim against Bell for his failure to *take care* to protect Costello from being attacked by Brannan. Moreover, the insult involved in Bell's standing by and allowing Costello to be attacked would not have been redressable through an award of aggravated damages as such damages are not available in negligence.[148]

So even when it does apply, the law of negligence is not a particularly satisfactory vehicle for dealing with the case where A, a public official, treats B 'like a dog' through an omission. And the law of negligence will frequently not apply to cases like this. Had Costello taken Brannan down to the cells on her own, and then been attacked by Brannan while Bell looked on and watched and did nothing, it would have been hard for Costello to argue that Bell owed her a duty of care to come to her aid. In the case where A simply stands by and allows B to come to harm even though it was A's job to protect B from suffering that harm, the law of negligence will *not* assist B if the circumstances were not such that a private person in A's position would have owed B a duty of care to come to her help. However, two further avenues of recourse might be open to B.

The first is that B might be able to bring a claim against the state agency that employed A under the Human Rights Act 1998, arguing that A's failure to act put the agency in breach of an obligation under the 1998 Act to take reasonable steps to protect B's 'human rights' under the ECHR from being violated when it knew, or ought to have known, that such steps were required.[149] However, such a claim cannot be made against A himself, as individuals are not bound by the 1998 Act. Moreover, the special insult involved in A's failure to lift a finger to help B is not redressable through an award of aggravated damages, or exemplary damages, against A's employer as the European Court of Human Rights has rejected the making of such awards in cases where someone's rights under the ECHR have been violated.[150]

This leaves B's second possible avenue of redress, which is under the tort of misfeasance in public office. As was observed in the *Three Rivers* case, the leading case in English law on misfeasance in public office, there are two different forms of this tort:

> First there is the case of targeted malice by a public officer, i.e. conduct specifically intended to injure a person or persons. This type of case involved bad faith in the sense of the exercise of public power for an improper or ulterior motive. The second form is where a public officer acts knowing he has no power to do the act complained of and that the act will probably injure the [claimant]. It involves bad faith inasmuch as the public officer does not have an honest belief that his act is lawful.[151]

Despite the references in the above quotation to a public officer's 'conduct' or 'act', it is clear that the tort of misfeasance in public office can cover failures to act. As Lord Hobhouse observed in *Three Rivers*, 'If there is a legal duty to act and the decision not to act amounts

---

[148] *Kralj* v *McGrath* [1996] 1 All ER 54, 61.

[149] *Osman* v *United Kingdom* [1999] 1 FLR 193; *Z* v *United Kingdom* [2001] 2 FLR 612.

[150] *Selçuk and Asker* v *Turkey* (1998) 26 EHRR 477.

[151] *Three Rivers District Council* v *Governor and Company of the Bank of England (No 3)* [2003] 2 AC 1, 191 (per Lord Steyn).

to an unlawful breach of that legal duty, the omission can amount to misfeasance for the purpose of the tort.'[152] It is important to note, as did Lord Hobhouse, that 'legal duty' here does *not* mean 'a duty owed in tort to the claimant' – otherwise the claimant could simply sue for breach of *that* duty, and leave the tort of misfeasance in public office alone.[153] It means a duty that the public officer in question owes by virtue of their office.

So in a case where A, a public official, treats B 'like a dog' by failing to go to her assistance, B may well be able to bring a claim against A for misfeasance in public office if: (i) A had a professional duty to go to B's assistance, but A decided not to help B out of malice towards B; or (ii) A knew he had a professional duty to go to B's assistance, but decided to breach that duty, knowing that B would probably suffer harm as a result. So should a claim in negligence not have been available in *Costello*, it seems very likely that a claim in misfeasance in public office would have been: (ii) was certainly satisfied on the facts of *Costello*, and (i) probably was, depending on Bell's motivations for not going to Costello's aid. And unlike a claim in negligence or under the Human Rights Act 1998, a claim for aggravated damages would have been available to Costello had she sued for misfeasance in public office, to mark the special insult involved in Bell's deliberately leaving her to fend for herself, in complete disregard for his obligations as a police officer.[154] Exemplary damages may also have been available, depending on the circumstances.[155]

It seems, then, that the tort of misfeasance in public office is well-suited to provide a remedy to a claimant who has been treated 'like a dog' by a public official who deliberately decided 'to stand idly by'[156] and not help the claimant when it was his duty to do so. However, in a case like this there are two flies in the ointment that the misfeasance tort can spread on any wounds to the claimant's sense of self-worth that might have been inflicted by the official's inaction.

The first is that the tort of misfeasance in public office is not actionable *per se*.[157] In order to sue, a claimant has to show that she has suffered actionable damage as result of the defendant's acts or omissions. And being treated as though she is worth nothing is not enough: it has to be shown that she has suffered 'financial loss or physical or mental injury … an expression [that includes] recognised psychiatric illness but not distress, injured feelings, indignation or annoyance.'[158] As a result, in *Hussain v The Chief Constable of West Mercia Constabulary*,[159] a taxi driver who claimed that the police had – on racial grounds – consistently refused to assist him when he was threatened by his customers was not allowed to sue the police for misfeasance in public office. The only physical harm he could claim to have suffered as a result of his maltreatment by the police was an occasional numbness

---

[152] Ibid, 230.

[153] Ibid, 229: '[the tort of misfeasance in public office] does not, and does not need to, apply where a defendant has invaded a legally protected right of the [claimant].'

[154] *Amin v Imran Khan & Partners* [2011] EWHC 2958 (QB), at [78] (the defendant firm of solicitors were held liable in negligence for not making a claim for misfeasance in public office on behalf of their client; damages were assessed on the basis that 'Such a claim, had it been made in time and not struck out, would have entitled the claimant to aggravated damages …').

[155] *Kuddus v Chief Constable of Leicestershire* [2002] 2 AC 122.

[156] Pogge, 'How Should Human Rights Be Conceived?' in Hayden (ed), *The Philosophy of Human Rights* (Paragon House, 2001), 196.

[157] *Watkins v Secretary of State for the Home Department* [2006] 2 AC 395.

[158] Ibid, at [7] (per Lord Bingham).

[159] [2008] EWCA Civ 1205.

or discomfort in his left leg and arm, usually occurring after a stressful day. The Court of Appeal held that this did not amount to the kind of damage that could ground a claim for misfeasance in public office. The fact that the claimant had (he claimed) been consistently treated in a racist manner by the police was neither here nor there.

The second problem is that almost everyone acknowledges that the tort of misfeasance in public office is an anomaly within the law of tort.[160] It does not seem to exist to vindicate or protect any private law interest of the claimant's. Rather, it seems to exist as a useful check on government maladministration; a check that is made even more useful because it is one that can be activated by a private citizen affected by the maladministration rather than relying on the state to act against itself. As Donal Nolan suggests, the misfeasance tort owes its existence to the need to make 'public demonstration of the fact that deliberate abuse of public office is intolerable behaviour for which an official will be held to account by the courts.'[161] As a result, when a defendant is held liable to a claimant for committing the tort of misfeasance in public office the focus of the court's attention is not on the claimant, but on the defendant. Given this, it is not clear how a finding in favour of a claimant who is suing a defendant for committing the misfeasance tort can have any beneficial effect on the claimant's feelings of self-worth. The claimant seems to be just as objectified and instrumentalised by the law in allowing the claimant to bring a claim for misfeasance in public office as she was by the defendant when he chose to abuse the powers of his office in his dealings with her.

In sum, where A, a public official, treats B 'like a dog', English private law's response is patchy at best. Where A's conduct involves an *act*, then English private law should normally be able to provide B with a remedy that recognises how badly she has been treated by A. But where A's conduct involves an *omission* – where A has callously chosen to stand idly by and not save B from a danger from which he was duty-bound to protect her – B's best hope of gaining an adequate remedy against A for what he did is to sue A for misfeasance in public office. But it may be that that route will be barred to her because she has not suffered 'material damage' as a result of A's inaction; and even if it is not, she may find suing A for misfeasance in public office a less than satisfactory way of restoring her sense of self-worth.

It scarcely needs to be said that a private law that sought to promote QTL-flourishing would suffer from none of these difficulties. It would recognise that A's conduct – whether it involves an act or omission – poses a special threat to an important interest of B's: her sense of self-worth. It would therefore recognise an equally special tort as having been

---

[160] Stevens, *Torts and Rights* (OUP, 2007), 242–43; Aronson, 'Misfeasance in Public Office: A Very Peculiar Tort' (2011) 35 *Melbourne ULR* 1; Nolan, 'Tort and Public Law: Overlapping Categories?' (2019) 135 *LQR* 272. Two dissentients are: Murphy, 'Misfeasance in a Public Office: A Tort Law Misfit?' (2012) 32 *OJLS* 51, arguing that as tort law is so variegated, it is unreasonable to pick on misfeasance in public office as being the odd one out among the range of torts recognised by English law; Chamberlain, *Misfeasance in a Public Office* (Thomson Reuters, 2016), arguing (at 45–59) that it is possible to reconcile the tort of misfeasance in public office with a non-variegated, 'rights-based' view of tort law.

[161] Nolan, 'A Public Law Tort: Understanding Misfeasance in Public Office' in Barker, Degeling, Fairweather and Grantham (eds), *Private Law and Power* (Hart Publishing, 2017), 183, citing in support *Jones v Swansea CC* [1990] 1 WLR 54, 85 (per Nourse LJ): 'The assumptions of honour and disinterest on which the tort of misfeasance in a public office is founded are deeply rooted in the polity of a free society ... It ought to be unthinkable that the holder of an office of government in this country would exercise a power thus vested in him with the object of injuring a member of that public by whose trust alone the office is enjoyed.'

committed by A in such a case, and provide B with remedies designed to reaffirm B's sense of self-worth. If we need a name for this tort (and we would), my suggestion would be the tort of *dishonour.*

## Private Actors

If English private law, in its current state, provides a patchy response to the problem of public officials treating people 'like a dog', it provides virtually no response to the problem of private actors doing the same. And understandably so. The fact that – as we have seen – it is not possible for everyone to enjoy an RP-flourishing existence means that a price has to be paid by someone for others to enjoy that kind of life. As exposés such as James Bloodworth's *Hired: Six Months Undercover in Low-Wage Britain*[162] show, that price is paid by a labouring class that is expected to do punishing work over long hours for low pay with no guarantees of continued employment. As Bloodworth remarks of his time working as a 'picker'[163] in an Amazon warehouse:

> You can, if you like, punch your credit card details into Amazon's website without ever having to see what goes on in this idyllic little corner of Staffordshire. It suits the English to have some anonymous foreign drudge, invisible to the outside world, tucked away in an enormous warehouse carting stuff back and forth with perspiration dripping from his brow. In truth, we want to ignore it as our grandparents turned contentedly away from what went on 4,000 miles away in an Indian sweatshop. It is in some ways easier to wall yourself off from the outside world. You can sit, feet up and kettle on, turn on the computer and order something to arrive the next day with a mere click of the mouse. We have grown accustomed to cheap products that are cheap precisely because they have been produced in conditions such as I have described here. Our standard of living has come to depend on it.[164]

Elizabeth Anderson sums up what life is like working as a 'picker' for Amazon:

> The pace of work is unremitting. Workers are reprimanded for 'time theft' when they pause to catch their breath after an especially difficult job. They are subjected to ever-increasing quotas, constantly yelled at for not making their quotas, threatened daily with discharge, and eventually fired when the required pace gets too high for them to meet – a fate of the vast majority of Amazon's hires.[165]

Bloodworth confirms:

> Dashing around was obligatory if you were to meet the exacting targets set for every worker … water breaks were permitted, but to go off in search of a water dispenser was to run the risk of 'idling', [a] transgression you were often warned about … Most of what was disparagingly called 'idle time' involved things like going to the toilet, yet the wickedness of 'idling' was brought up unfailingly at every briefing, as if the need to perform bodily functions would eventually melt

---

[162] Bloodworth, *Hired: Six Months Undercover in Low-Wage Britain* (Atlantic Books, 2018).

[163] A picker's job is to gather products from the shelves in the warehouse, ready for shipment out to Amazon customers.

[164] Ibid, 75–76.

[165] Anderson, *Private Government: How Employers Rule Our Lives (and Why We Don't Like to Talk About It)* (Princeton UP, 2017),

away in the name of productivity ... Rather than complaining when people had the temerity to go the toilet, productivity-obsessed Amazon might instead have installed more toilets. For those of us who worked on the top floor ... the closest toilets were down four flights of stairs.[166]

Anderson concludes that 'workers' interests count for nothing in Amazon's eyes.'[167] And nor do they have to: as Bloodworth reports, the employment agencies that supply Amazon with pickers 'constantly drum it into workers ... that if they kick up a fuss about the conditions at work there is a vast reserve army of their fellow countrymen ready to take their place.'[168] Though 'fellow countrymen' may be a mistake: Bloodworth observes that 'a growing number of British people are unwilling to be treated like animals' and that this 'ought to be considered a sign of progress. British workers have minimum standards with respect to what they will put up with – standards that many of the precarious and poorly paid jobs our economy now relies upon fail to satisfy.'[169]

Two points should be made about all of this. First, Amazon's high-profile – and the ease with which Amazon's warehouses can be infiltrated by investigative journalists – makes it an obvious target for critiques such as Bloodworth's and Anderson's. But the problems identified by those critiques are far more widespread. After leaving Amazon, Bloodworth got a job as a home care worker and reports that the nature of his job made him 'desperate to [quit] in a way I had not been [working for Amazon], trying though the work at Amazon had been. What seemed to make it worse as a home carer was the way the treatment meted out to us had the potential to rebound on the people we were charged with looking after.'[170] Nor did things get any better when he worked later on at a call centre, or as a driver for Uber.

Second, there is no reason to think that employers who end up treating their employees like animals ever consciously made a *choice* to do this. Anderson puts her finger on the ultimate reason for why employees are treated badly when she observes of the American company Walmart:

> A leading complaint of Walmart workers is rude and abusive managers, who scream at and harass them to get them to work harder. This abusiveness may be due to the fact that lower-level managers themselves are assigned work goals without any consideration of what it takes to meet them, and are constantly harassed by upper management for not working hard enough.[171]

So it may be that the primary driver behind the maltreatment of workers detailed by writers like Bloodworth and Anderson is the incompetence of the managerial class to achieve the goals they are set by their superiors through anything but the most crude methods of closely monitoring workers' behaviour and putting them under pressure to achieve more and more. And, as we have seen, this incompetence is not something for which the managerial class should be blamed: it is inherent in the status of a manager that you will usually be incompetent to manipulate the resources available to you to achieve anything more than the simplest targets.[172]

---

[166] Bloodworth, *Hired* (n 162), 48–50.

[167] Anderson, *Private Government* (n 165), 129.

[168] Bloodworth, *Hired* (n 162), 23.

[169] Ibid, 57.

[170] Ibid, 119.

[171] Anderson, *Private Government* (n 165), 136–37. See also Bloodworth, *Hired* (n 162), 16, 46.

[172] See above, p 102. See also Sandelands, *Being at Work* (University Press of America, 2014), at 85–86, quoting 'Dennis Bakke of AES' describing the 'conventional image of "managing"' as resting on the following

The existence of the managerial class is also probably the best explanation for a quite different form of drudgery that is peculiarly associated with the modern workplace – working in what the anthropologist David Graeber calls a *bullshit job*.[173] Graeber defines a bullshit job as 'a form of paid employment that is so completely pointless, unnecessary or pernicious that even the employee cannot justify its existence even though, as part of the conditions of employment, the employee feels obliged to pretend that this is not the case.'[174] Graeber goes on to identify five categories of bullshit job: 'flunkies, goons, duct tapers, box tickers, and taskmasters.'[175]

'Flunky jobs are those that exist only or primarily to make someone else look or feel important.'[176] Goons are 'people whose jobs have an aggressive element, but, crucially, who exist only because other people employ them.'[177] Examples of goon-like bullshit jobs, for Graeber, are jobs in 'marketing or PR' or call centre jobs that involve 'tricking or pressuring people into doing things that [aren't] really in their best interest.'[178] 'Duct tapers are employees whose jobs exist only because of a glitch or fault in the organization; who are there to solve a problem that ought not to exist.'[179] But they don't solve the problem by removing it; they solve it by providing some way of working around it or coping with its existence. The fact that the problem could easily be solved by removing the problem is what renders the duct taper's job a bullshit job. 'Box tickers' are employees 'who exist only or primarily to allow an organization to be able to claim it is doing something that, in fact, it is not doing.'[180] Finally, 'taskmasters' are either people 'whose role consists entirely of assigning work to others' when that role is unnecessary, and the taskmaster knows it; or people 'whose primary role is to create bullshit tasks for others to do, to supervise bullshit, or even to create entirely new bullshit jobs.'[181]

Graeber notes how odd it is that bullshit jobs should exist in a capitalist economy: 'under our current economic system, this is precisely what is not supposed to happen ... the fact that so many people are being paid to do nothing in the first place defies all our assumptions about how market economies are supposed to work.'[182] Graeber goes on to observe that 'If the existence of bullshit jobs seems to defy the logic of capitalism, one possible reason for their proliferation might be that the existing system *isn't* capitalism ...'.[183] The political scientist James Burnham would have agreed with Graeber's analysis. Writing as far back as 1941, Burnham argued in his book *The Managerial Revolution* that the capitalist social

assumptions: (1) workers are lazy; (2) workers work primarily for money; (3) workers are selfish; (4) workers perform best when they have one, simple repeatable task to accomplish; (5) workers are not capable of making good decisions about important matters; (6) workers are irresponsible; (7) workers need to be monitored; (8) workers should be compensated according to how much work they do; (9) workers are interchangeable; (10) workers need to be told what to do and how to do it. Bakke concludes that 'leadership is not about managing people. People are not resources or assets to be managed.'

[173] Graeber, *Bullshit Jobs: A Theory* (Allen Lane, 2018).
[174] Ibid, 9–10.
[175] Ibid, 28.
[176] Ibid.
[177] Ibid, 36.
[178] Ibid, 37, 39.
[179] Ibid, 40.
[180] Ibid, 45.
[181] Ibid, 50.
[182] Ibid, 146.
[183] Ibid, 190 (emphasis in original).

order was on its way out and was being replaced by a managerial order, where managers 'will be the ruling class in society'.[184] It is the rise of managerialism that Graeber sees as crucial to the proliferation of bullshit jobs in the modern economy.[185] 'Flunkies' are 'feudal retainers' that help to underline a manager's importance and status within an organisation.[186] 'Goons' exist to strong-arm people into falling in line with managerial objectives, or 'wash' the reputation of the manager in order to legitimate his control. 'Duct tapers' exist to make up for the natural incompetence of management at achieving its goals. 'Box tickers' are, like 'goons', also engaged in reputation-washing.[187] And 'taskmasters' are either managers themselves, or are charged with monitoring the bullshit jobs on which the managerial class depends.

The fact that bullshit jobs seem to be the reverse image of the jobs we began discussing in this section – well-paid as opposed to low-paid, involving very little work as opposed to involving punishingly hard work – should not blind us to the fact that bullshit jobs are just as degrading and enervating as the jobs we were initially discussing. Graeber observes that:

> Such jobs are likely to be not waged but salaried. There may not be an actual boss breathing down one's neck – in fact, usually there isn't. But ultimately, the need to play a game of make-believe *not of one's own making*, a game that exists only as a form of power imposed on you, is inherently demoralizing … It's no wonder the soul cries out. It is a direct assault on everything that makes us human.[188]

So when we think about how private actors treat others 'like a dog' in the workplace we need to acknowledge that there are different ways in which workers might be dehumanised by the work they do. They might be dehumanised by (1) being required to do work that grinds them into the ground; or by (2) being required to do work that they know is pointless while having to pretend that it is meaningful. The first kind of work breaks your body; the second kind breaks your soul. Either involves your being treated 'like a dog', as though you are worth nothing.

What, then, does English private law in its current state do about protecting people from being made to do work of either type (1) or type (2)? So far as type (2) is concerned, the answer is 'nothing'. As David Graeber observes, a 'right to meaningful employment' would be an entirely 'new, unfamiliar, right' in the firmament of rights currently recognised in the West.[189] The concern that English private law feels for safeguarding the physical welfare of its subjects – as part of its general agenda of promoting their RP-flourishing – means that English private law *does* take *some* steps to protect workers from being harmed as a result of doing type (1) work. However, the limited focus on protecting workers' physical health, combined with the necessity for type (1) work to be done if anyone is to RP-flourish, means that English private law will always fall well short of completely protecting workers from being treated 'like a dog' by being made to do type (1) work.

---

[184] Burnham, *The Managerial Revolution* (Greenwood Press, 1972), 72.

[185] Graeber, *Bullshit Jobs* (n 173), 176–89.

[186] Ibid, 30–34, 174–75.

[187] Ibid, 170–73.

[188] Ibid, 98–99 (emphasis in original).

[189] Ibid, 128. He cites, in support of this point, Article 23 of the UN Universal Declaration of Human Rights, which states that 'Everyone has the right to work, to free choice of employment, to just and favourable conditions of work and to protection against unemployment.' He notes that 'It also guarantees equal pay for equal work, compensation adequate to support a family, and the right to form labor unions. It says nothing about the purpose of the work itself' (ibid, 306, fn 12).

For example, in *Johnstone v Bloomsbury Health Authority*,[190] the issue was for how long the defendant health authority could lawfully require the claimant doctor, a senior house officer, to work. The claimant's contract specified that he would work a 40 hour standard work and on top of that be on call to work up to an average of an extra 48 hours a week. The claimant was made ill as a result of working for some weeks more than 88 hours (an average of 12.5 hours a day, seven days a week).

The judges who decided *Johnstone* in the Court of Appeal disagreed as to what the claimant's contract meant for how long the defendant could require the claimant to work. The majority thought that the defendant's right to require the claimant to work up to 88 hours a week was limited by the defendant's obligation as an employer to take reasonable steps to protect the claimant's health. But they disagreed as to in what way that right was limited. Browne-Wilkinson VC took the narrow view that the defendant could require the claimant to work up to 40 hours a week (the standard amount) regardless of the effect on the claimant's health, but had to take the claimant's health into account in determining how much overtime (up to an extra 48 hours) the claimant would be required to work. Stuart-Smith LJ took the wider view that the defendant *always* had to take into account the claimant's health in requiring him either to work his standard hours or overtime. Leggatt LJ, dissenting, took the view that if the claimant had contractually agreed to give the defendant the option of making him work up to 88 hours a week, then the defendant was entitled to exercise that option regardless of the effect on the claimant's health.

All of the judges *agreed* that the terms in the claimant's contract regarding how long the claimant could be required to work for the defendant should not be struck out as contrary to public policy; indeed, they regarded the point as being 'unarguable'.[191] Presumably, the judges would have regarded it as not just unarguable, but completely bizarre, to think that *regardless of the effect on the claimant's health*, a term that required the claimant to work up to (on average) 12.5 hours a day, seven days a week, made too great a demand on the claimant's *time*, and should therefore be struck down as unconscionable or contrary to public policy.

The limited developments in English private law that have occurred since *Johnstone* in terms of protecting workers' time from being monopolised by their employers have owed nothing to the courts, and everything to the UK's membership of the European Union, as a result of which the UK government was forced to pass the Working Time Regulations 1998, which implemented the Working Time Directive 1993.[192]

The Regulations provide for: (i) maximum working hours of 48 hours per week;[193] (ii) an entitlement to rest for 11 hours continuously in every 24 hours while working for an employer,[194] and to rest for 24 hours in every week working for an employer;[195] (iii) rest breaks of not less than 20 uninterrupted minutes every six hours,[196] and a general entitlement to 'adequate rest breaks' where 'the pattern according to which an employer organizes

---

[190] [1992] QB 333.

[191] Ibid, 346–47, 349.

[192] The five year gap between the Directive being issued and its being implemented in UK law speaks for itself as to the UK's hostility towards imposing legal limits on how long a worker can be required to work.

[193] Reg 4.

[194] Reg 10.

[195] Reg 11.

[196] Reg 12.

work is such as to put the health and safety of a worker ... at risk, in particular because the work is monotonous or the work-rate is predetermined'.[197] However, the Regulations also provide that provision (i) can be excluded by written agreement between a worker and their employer,[198] that the Regulations do not apply in the transport sector, or to work at sea, or 'to the activities of doctors in training',[199] and that entitlements (ii) and (iii) will not apply in special cases where a 'worker's activities involve the need for continuity of service or production' or where 'there is a foreseeable surge of activity' affecting a worker involved in agriculture, tourism or the postal services.[200]

So what would a private law that sought to foster QTL-flourishing do differently? It is unlikely that the problem of protecting workers from being made to do type (1) or type (2) work can be tackled head-on by giving workers rights not to be made to do such work. While the concept of being made to work 'like a dog' is perfectly comprehensible within the confines of a book like this, as a legal concept it would leave a lot to be desired in terms of its clarity and predictability of application. And trying to define more precisely what sort of work workers would have a right not to be made to do would create the danger of under-definition – not capturing all examples of the kind of work we wish to protect people from being made to do – and manipulation, where unscrupulous employers arrange their affairs so as to artificially avoid the definitions we use.

Instead, a private law that sought to foster QTL-flourishing would seek to address the root cause of workers being made to do type (1) or type (2) work. That root cause has been identified above as the existence of the managerial class, and in particular the need for that class to resort to very crude measures to achieve its goals and the need for that class to cover up for its failures to achieve those goals by surrounding itself with 'bullshit jobs'. This suggests that the most effective way private law can protect workers from being made to do type (1) or type (2) work is for private law to provide that: *a manager cannot be lawfully dismissed for failing to achieve a target.* Giving managers security of employment in this way would: (i) remove the incentives that managers have to make people do type (1) or type (2) work; and (ii) encourage companies to explore whether they can operate effectively without managers.[201] As a result, the number of instances of people being made to do type (1) or type (2) work could be expected to be radically reduced. Of course, it follows from what was said at the start of this section[202] that a price would have to be paid for the reduction in the numbers of people doing type (1) work, in terms of people's capacities to RP-flourish. However, this becomes less of a concern if (as I think we should) we disown the RP as a reliable guide to what human flourishing consists in, and instead identify human flourishing with QTL-ing.

---

[197] Reg 8.
[198] Reg 5.
[199] Reg 18.
[200] Reg 21.
[201] This is something that tech companies have experimented with. See Wu, *The Attention Merchants* (n 127), 261 fn ('As Google's first CEO, [Larry] Page once fired all of Google's managers, reasoning that they were not only useless, but interfered with engineering, what with all their meetings, planning sessions, and so on ...'); and McCord, 'How Netflix Reinvented HR' *Harvard Business Review*, January – February 2014. My thanks to Isabel Haskey for bringing the flatter nature of the Netflix corporate structure to my attention.
[202] See above, p 139.

# 5. The Hate You Make

The third distinctive harm that a private law that was concerned to foster QTL-flourishing would both recognise, and seek to protect us from suffering, is that of coming to hate someone else. In order to understand how this might happen, we have to understand the nature of *anger*, and how anger at someone else can mutate into hatred for that person.

Anger seems to be the natural concomitant of *caring* for something. If I care about X and you damage X in some way, then I will – on learning of what you have done – feel anger towards you. My anger will be justified if I am justified in caring about X. So if you run over my wife then the anger I feel towards you will be justified; less so, if I see you swatting a fly.

Martha Nussbaum takes the view that anger is *never* justified, because it always involves something that the previous paragraph omits to mention. She argues that if I feel anger towards you, I desire to see you suffer some kind of harm for what you have done.[203] This harm either takes the form of *payback* or *downgrading*. The desire to see you suffer payback is irrational – Nussbaum argues – because your suffering cannot bring back the thing that I cared about and that you damaged.[204] The desire to see you downgraded exists in the case where I care about my status relative to you, you have angered me by acting in a way inconsistent with that status relationship, and making you suffer in some way will put you back in your rightful place. Nussbaum thinks that the desire to see you suffer harm in this kind of case is intelligible but 'normatively problematic' because our relative status is not something I should care about.[205] Nussbaum therefore argues that anger is always unjustified and that in the case where you have harmed some X that I care about, the better route is to enter into a 'Transition' state where I move away from indulging my natural impulse to feel angry with you and instead entertain 'more productive forward-looking thoughts, asking what can actually be done to increase either personal or social welfare.'[206]

In identifying anger with a desire to see the person with whom we are angry suffer some kind of harm, Nussbaum follows Aristotle, who observed in his *Rhetoric* that 'Anger may be defined as an impulse, accompanied by pain, to a conspicuous revenge for a conspicuous slight directed without justification towards what concerns oneself or towards what concerns one's friends.'[207] However, it may be doubted whether this is correct. As Amia Srinivasan notes, 'anger without the desire for revenge is something many of us know well. Suppose my friend betrays me, and I am angry with her. I might want revenge. But might I not want – have we not all wanted – the friend to recognise the pain she has caused me, the wrong she has done me?'[208] Moreover, on the Aristotle-Nussbaum view, it should be impossible for someone to feel angered about some historical event that is so far in the past that any possibility of payback for those responsible for that event is long gone. But it would be an odd sort of person who did *not* feel anger on reading Frederick Douglass's account of the

---

[203] Nussbaum, *Anger and Forgiveness* (OUP, 2016).
[204] Ibid, 5.
[205] Ibid, 5–6.
[206] Ibid, 6.
[207] Aristotle, *Rhetoric*, II.2.1387a30.
[208] Srinivasan, 'The Aptness of Anger' (2018) 26 *The Journal of Political Philosophy* 123, 129. My thanks to Sandy Steel for bringing Professor Srinivasan's writings on anger to my attention.

murder (approximately 200 years ago) of a 15 year old slave-girl, the cousin of Douglass's wife, by the wife of the slave-girl's 'owner':

> [The girl] had been set that night, and several preceding nights, to mind Mrs Hicks's baby, and having fallen into a sound sleep, the baby cried, waking Mrs Hicks, but not the slave-girl. Mrs Hicks, becoming infuriated at the girl's tardiness, after calling several times, jumped from her bed and seized a piece of fire-wood from the fireplace; and then, as she lay fast asleep, she deliberately pounded in her skull and breast-bone and thus ended her life.[209]

So if my being angry with you does not, of and in itself, involve a desire to see you suffer harm, what does it involve? In his *On the Soul*, Aristotle offered an alternative, physical, definition of anger to the philosopher's definition of anger as 'the appetite for returning pain for pain'. The physicist, Aristotle said, would define anger as 'a boiling of the blood or warm substance surrounding the heart'.[210] If I am angry with you, you make my blood boil. As such, my anger towards you is a condition that is akin to sexual excitement.[211] It is not like an illness in that it is a normal human condition, but at the same time it is like an illness in that no one could bear to live in such a state perpetually and it consequently requires some kind of relief.

Relief from feeling angry may come in a number of different ways.[212] First: *distraction*. I simply focus on something other than the source of my anger, and my anger gradually subsides. Second: *recharacterisation*. I reduce my anger with you at what you did by reframing what happened to deny your responsibility for damaging X. *You* weren't to blame for damaging X: it was the fault of the situation you found yourself in, or your upbringing, or you just made a good faith mistake in the heat of the moment. Third: *reconciliation*. You acknowledge what you did, and find some way of making up for it that allows us both to move on with much the same relationship as we enjoyed before you did what you did. Fourth: *forgiveness*. I do not allow the fact that I care about X and the fact that you damaged X to get in the way of my caring about you. I therefore put aside, without ignoring or forgetting, what you did and choose not to allow it to affect our relationship. Fifth: *payback*. Far from being irrational, as Nussbaum supposes, payback teaches you a lesson, at least when it involves damaging something (Y) that you care about in the same way I care about X.[213] The lesson is the Golden Rule: don't treat others in ways you would not like to be treated. After Y is damaged, I can take some satisfaction from thinking, 'Now you know how it feels'. The hope that that thought inspires, that you may learn your lesson and abide by the Golden Rule in future, may be enough to allow my anger with you to subside. Sixth: *reconstruction*. This is Nussbaum's preferred route away from anger and in the case where I am angry with you, it seems to involve my exercising a God-like power to bring good out of evil, with my

---

[209] Douglass, *My Bondage and My Freedom* (1855), ch 8 ('A chapter of horrors').

[210] Aristotle, *De Anima*, I.I.403a30.

[211] Cf Achilles' statement that anger is 'sweeter than dripping honey' (*Iliad*, 18.109). On comparisons between anger and sexual excitement, see Allen, 'Angry Bees, Wasps, and Jurors: The Symbolic Politics of ὀργή in Athens' in Braund and Most (eds), *Ancient Anger: Perspectives from Homer to Galen* (CUP, 2003), 82.

[212] We are considering here how someone who *is* angry might be helped. The alternative – of being the kind of person who *never* gets angry – is only available to someone who has given up caring about anything. Aristotle rightly condemned such a person as 'foolish' and 'slavish': *Nicomachean Ethics*, IV.5.1126a1–7.

[213] It is no accident that payback is almost always accompanied by the thought, 'That'll teach him.'

turning your damaging X into a *felix culpa*[214] that allows me to build some good on top of the ruins of what you did to X.

But what if no relief from my anger with you is available? I cannot think of anything else but what you did, and cannot deny that you did it. You feel no contrition for what you did, and I can't forgive you for it. Any payback would be inefficacious to teach you the errors of your ways. And no good can humanly come of what you did. This is where, I believe, hatred comes in: hatred is the child of an anger that cannot be relieved.[215]

Hatred, recall, involves the belief that my flourishing is dependent on your not-flourishing.[216] In the case where I suffer unrelievable anger towards you, we can see why I might end up believing that my flourishing is dependent on your not-flourishing and therefore end up hating you. You make my blood boil and none of the treatments outlined above will help cool things down. Faced with this reality, it would be natural for me to think that given that it is *you* who are making my blood boil and nothing else will help, the only remaining measure that could relieve me of my anger towards you and allow me to resume living a flourishing life is for you not to exist anymore – or, at least, for your life to amount to a living death where your continued existence is a burden to you, rather than a blessing.

Given the above, I can legitimately say that you *made* me hate you if: (1) you damaged some X that I cared about; (2) it was reasonable for me to care about X; (3) what you did was so serious that I could not be reasonably be expected to forget or forgive what you did, or to try to make some good come out of what you did; and (4) your attitude towards what you did makes remote any prospect of our reconciling, or your learning anything from receiving any payback for what you did. If all these conditions are fulfilled then I could be expected to be unrelievably angry at you for what you did, and it is not my fault but your fault that I am in this state.

A private law that was concerned to promote my QTL-flourishing would seek to save me from your making me hate you by:

(a)   imposing a duty on you, for my benefit, not to do *x* if your doing *x* is likely to result in conditions (1), (2), and (3) being satisfied; and

(b)   attempting – in the event that you breach a duty not to do *x* imposed under (a) – to ensure that condition (4) will not also be satisfied by threatening to impose special sanctions on you if you stubbornly insist that you were justified in doing *x* or if you make it clear that you are indifferent to the consequences that your doing *x* had for me.

English private law has all the tools it needs to do both (a) and (b). In particular, awards of *aggravated damages* seem wonderfully well-adapted to performing function (b), as they may be awarded against a defendant who has acted in an arrogant and high-handed

---

[214] Literally 'happy fault', *felix culpa* is a Christian theological term, used to describe how Adam and Eve's sin in disobeying God might be said to have produced more good than would have been the case had Adam and Eve not sinned.

[215] If this is right, then Melville's hatred of Being (above, p 99) will have had its roots in an unrelievable anger at Being's manifesting itself as beings. Given that Melville was a Schopenhauerian *avant la lettre*, it would not be surprising if (i) Melville was angry at Being for manifesting itself as beings (including him), and (ii) that anger was unrelievable because none of the ordinary remedies for anger were available.

[216] See above, p 7.

way either in committing a tort,[217] or in the way he has treated the victim of his tort *after* committing it.[218] However, true to form, English private law in its current state shows little to no interest in doing (a). In fact, the notion of a *relational wrong* – a wrong that involves harming me by damaging something or someone that I have some kind of relationship with – has become increasingly alien to English private law over time.

So where you carelessly injure or kill someone with whom I am in a 'close and loving relationship', I will only be entitled to sue you if (i) I suffer a psychiatric illness as a result of what you did, and (ii) my psychiatric illness was caused either by my witnessing my loved one being killed or injured, or seeing them in the 'immediate aftermath' of their being killed or injured.[219] The fact that your conduct – if compounded by your wilful refusal to recognise you did anything wrong – threatens to make me hate you is neither here nor there. As the Court of Appeal observed in *Reilly* v *Merseyside Health Authority*, 'The sound policy of the law is that the excitement of a normal human emotion … is not compensatable.'[220] As hatred is a normal human emotion – a normal reaction to suffering unrelievable anger (another normal human emotion) – it does not count as something that English private law in its current state seeks to save someone from suffering.

This impression is confirmed by other areas of English private law. The English version of what is known in the United States as an 'anti-heart balm' law – a law abolishing people's rights to sue in respect of conduct that has left them with a broken heart[221] – is the Law Reform (Miscellaneous Provisions) Act 1970. Section 1 of that Act abolished people's abilities to sue for breach of a promise to marry, while section 5 abolished people's rights to sue a defendant in tort for: (a) inducing the claimant's spouse to leave them; (b) depriving a parent of the services 'of his or her child by raping, seducing or enticing that child'; and (c) harbouring the wife or child of the claimant.

Under section 1A of the Fatal Accidents Act 1976, a claimant will be entitled to sue for damages for bereavement in a case where the defendant caused the death of the claimant's spouse or child by committing a tort in relation to that spouse or child. However, the amount the claimant (together with anyone else entitled to sue under section 1A) will be entitled to sue for is fixed at just below the not very princely sum of £13,000. Moreover, where the claimant's child was killed as a result of the defendant's tort, no claim for bereavement can be made by the claimant under section 1A if the deceased child was married or over 18 – a limit that resulted in an equivalent claim being made, and allowed, under the Human Rights Act 1998 where the claimant parents' 24 year old child was negligently allowed to commit suicide by the defendant health authority.[222]

Finally, in *In Re Organ Retention Group Litigation*,[223] Gage J dealt with a number of cases where parents of deceased children wished to sue the defendant hospitals after they learned

---

[217] See, for example, *Thompson* v *Hill* (1870) LR 5 CP 564 (deliberately committing tort of private nuisance by blocking off light) and *McMillan* v *Singh* (1984) 17 HLR 120 (wrongfully ejecting tenant in order to make more money from renting premises).

[218] *Ley* v *Hamilton* (1935) 153 LT 384; *Alexander* v *Home Office* [1988] 1 WLR 968; *Sutcliffe* v *Pressdram Ltd* [1991] 1 QB 153.

[219] *McLoughlin* v *O'Brian* [1983] 1 AC 410; *Alcock* v *Chief Constable of South Yorkshire Police* [1992] 1 AC 310.

[220] (1995) 23 BMLR 26, 30 (per Mann LJ).

[221] For an account of the dubious politics underlying the wave of 'anti-heart balm' laws adopted in the United States in the 1930s, see Hasday, *Intimate Lies and the Law* (n 43), 103–09.

[222] *Rabone* v *Pennine Care NHS Foundation Trust* [2012] 2 AC 72.

[223] [2005] QB 506.

that those hospitals had extracted body parts from their child for the purposes of carrying out a post mortem and had then failed to replace those body parts in the child's body before returning the child's body to the child's parents for burial. Gage J acknowledged that 'many families … have been deeply distressed and angered by the revelation that a major organ or organs have been removed and retained from their child's body without their consent or knowledge.'[224] Despite this, Gage J held that as 'the claimants have no right of burial and possession of organs lawfully removed at post mortem' they could have 'no action for wrongful interference with the body of the child'.[225] Any claims that the claimants could bring against the defendant hospitals had to be brought in negligence, on the basis that the claimant had suffered a psychiatric illness as a result of either (a) the defendant's failing to treat the claimant with reasonable skill and care as the defendant's patient, or (b) the defendant's failing to give back organs extracted from the claimant's child's body when it had 'assumed a responsibility' to the claimant that it would do so.

A private law that sought to foster QTL-flourishing would adopt a very different approach to all these kinds of cases. It would recognise the danger that A's losing a loved one at B's hands poses for A's ability to QTL-flourish if B disdains or makes light of A's loss, and in such a case would allow A to sue B for significant damages. Such damages would normally be far in excess of the £13,000 that is the most A could obtain under section 1A of the Fatal Accidents Act 1976. Moreover, the availability of such damages would not be conditional on A's showing that he has suffered a psychiatric illness as a result of B's conduct: a private law that sought to foster QTL-flourishing would regard placing such a limit on A's ability to sue B in this kind of case not as 'sound policy', but as bizarrely irrational.

# 6. The Burden of the Past

This concludes our discussion of the distinctive harms that a private law that sought to foster QTL-flourishing would seek to protect us from suffering. But such a private law would also seek to relieve us of certain burdens from our past that can get in the way of our QTL-flourishing. At first sight, the suggestion that our past can have this effect seems counter-intuitive. According to a Journey Model of human flourishing, the past is always another country. Our flourishing depends on where our lives are heading *now*, not on where they have been in the past. However, our past may cripple our ability to move our lives forward in a flourishing direction, in a couple of different ways.

First, a past *betrayal* may impair our ability to put our trust in, and achieve intimacy with, other people in future – when forming such trusting and intimate relationships with other people is a vital cog in our ability to QTL-flourish.[226] Second, *regrets* over how things went for us in the past might result in our living in the past, thinking over and over about how things might have been for us, with the result that we become incapable of going forward with our lives and instead go round and round our regrets.[227]

---

[224] Ibid, at [114].
[225] Ibid, at [161].
[226] See above, p 105.
[227] This describes the predicament of person f, in the figure on p 24.

We will discuss below what might be done by a private law that is concerned to foster QTL-flourishing to address the way someone's past might blight their ability to QTL-flourish. But we can note immediately that such a private law will be very different from the private law under which we live now. Consistently with *that* private law's adopting a Possessions Model of human flourishing – the RP – English private law in its current state does not seek to help us *overcome* or *transcend* our past. Rather, it seeks to ensure that there exists a *continuity* between our past and our future so that we are able to carry forward into the future the goods that we have been lucky enough to secure in the past. It does this, among other things, by doling out to us what John Gardner called 'security rights': 'rights which, if they go unviolated, will help to keep [the right-holder's] life on its existing track'.[228] While not in any way disdaining the importance of such security rights, a private law that seeks to promote QTL-flourishing will also seek to endow us with rights and powers that will enable us, where necessary, to make a fresh start in our lives, free from the burdens of past betrayals and regrets about the past.

## Betrayal

The kind of betrayal I am talking about is well-illustrated by the cases of *AKJ v Commissioner of Police of the Metropolis*[229] and *DIL v Commissioner of Police of the Metropolis*.[230] Those cases concerned police attempts to spy on environmental, anarchist and other activist groups by infiltrating them with undercover police officers. In order to preserve their cover, these officers would engage in long-term sexual relationships with other members of the group they were infiltrating.

For example, an undercover officer using the name 'Marco Jacobs' infiltrated the 'Cardiff Anarchist Network'. One of the members of the group, ARB, claimed that 'Jacobs' started a sexual relationship with her, 'purported to be a confidante, empathiser and source of close support ... including in relation to deeply personal aspects of their lives: he attended, for example, the funeral of ARB's father after his death from cancer'.[231] ARB would later tell the press that 'Jacobs' had become one of her best friends over three years before she started having sex with him and that 'for him to come along and lie to us and get that deep into our lives was a colossal, colossal betrayal.'[232]

Many other activists claimed to have suffered the same treatment.[233] RAB, a member of 'Anti-Fascist Action', had a five year sexual relationship, from 1995 to 2000, with an undercover officer operating under the name 'Mark Cassidy'. In 2000, 'Cassidy' suddenly disappeared. RAB eventually found out his true identity and sued the police for damages. She told a Parliamentary inquiry that her treatment by Cassidy 'has impacted seriously on

---

[228] Gardner, *From Personal Life to Private Law* (OUP, 2018), 183.

[229] [2014] 1 WLR 285.

[230] [2014] EWHC 2184 (QB).

[231] *AKJ v Commissioner of Police of the Metropolis* [2013] 1 WLR 2743, at [43] (per Tugendhat J).

[232] 'Third undercover police spy unmasked as scale of network emerges' *Guardian*, 15 January 2011.

[233] For full accounts, see Evans and Lewis, *Undercover: The True Story of Britain's Secret Police* (Faber and Faber, 2013); the House of Commons Home Affairs Committee's *Undercover Policing: Interim Report*, 26 February 2013; and the ongoing Undercover Policing Inquiry, conducted by Sir John Mitting (www.ucpi.org.uk).

my ability to trust, and that has impacted on my current relationship and other subsequent relationships … It has also distorted by perceptions of love and my perceptions of sex.'[234]

Helen Steel – a Greenpeace activist famous for her campaigning against the burger chain McDonald's[235] – was deceived into conducting a two-year sexual relationship from 1990 to 1992 with an undercover officer calling himself 'John Barker'. In 1992, 'Barker' faked a mental breakdown and disappeared, and Steel spent years discovering what had really happened. She was unable to have a relationship with anyone else until 2004: as she observed, 'The field of people you can trust is very small.'[236] When Steel and other activists sued, trying to take advantage of our RP-centric private law to seek some redress for what had happened to them:

> Steel and her fellow litigants were required to undergo psychological assessment. This, she says, felt like adding insult to injury. 'You couldn't just say, "This was upsetting and wasted this many years of my life"', Steel explains. 'You had to demonstrate either financial loss or a diagnosable psychological injury. If you've lost the opportunity to have children or the opportunity to form loving relationships, that's not counted as a loss because you can't put a value on it. So you have to relive everything, you have to see it all written down, all intensely personal. You have to focus on everything that's gone wrong and you end up feeling that you've made a failure of your life.'[237]

How would a private law that sought to foster QTL-flourishing handle cases such as these? Not by looking backwards to see if any of the claimants' 'security rights' have been violated and, in case they have been, seeking to restore to those claimants what they would have had had those rights not been violated. Instead, it would look forwards and do what needs to be done to prevent the betrayal that the claimants have suffered from damaging their capacities to QTL-flourish in future.[238]

The mere fact of entering a judgment in favour of the claimant and against the defendant who betrayed the claimant would help, by making it clear that the claimant's treatment by the defendant was abnormal, and does not reflect on how the claimant might be expected to be treated by others in future. What form the judgment would take, would depend on the circumstances. Some sort of punitive and preventative element would normally be required, to help reassure that this sort of betrayal will not re-occur in the future; where

---

[234] 'Police spies: in bed with a fictional character' *Guardian*, 1 March 2013.

[235] *McDonald's Corporation v Steel and Morris* [1997] EWHC 366 (QB); *Steel and Morris v United Kingdom* (2005) 41 EHRR 22.

[236] 'Helen Steel and John Dines: the spy who loved me' *Sydney Morning Herald*, 19 March 2016.

[237] Ibid.

[238] In the terminology adopted in Part I of this project, any liability incurred by the defendant will be 'free-standing' in that it does not give effect to a duty owed by the defendant to the claimant, and 'not wrong-based' in that it is not predicated on the defendant's having breached a duty owed to the claimant in acting as he did: McBride, *The Humanity of Private Law, Part I* (n 49), 55–58. As such, there are strong links between the putative liability discussed here, and liabilities that arise under the law on proprietary estoppel where C has relied on an assurance by D that she will be given some kind of interest in D's land in the future. These liabilities can be seen as forward-looking, as intended to ensure that C's acts of reliance do not prevent her flourishing in future. For the opposite argument, that these liabilities are backward-looking, intended to provide C with some kind of recompense for the loss she has suffered as a result of relying on D's assurance, see McFarlane, 'Proprietary Estoppel: The Importance of Looking Back' in Davies and Pila (eds), *The Jurisprudence of Lord Hoffmann* (Hart Publishing, 2015).

the 'preventative element' would involve enjoining[239] individuals like 'Cassidy', 'Jacobs' and 'Barker', and those who 'managed' them, from any involvement in police work in the future.[240]

Any judgment would also cover the cost of any counselling that is required to help the claimant overcome, so far as she can, her feelings of betrayal and consequent distrust of intimate relationships. As for a more general compensatory award, it is hard to see what purpose would be served by it. While it is true – as our discussions above of Penelope and Medea show[241] – that the claimant's capacity to QTL-flourish, her capacity to contemplate and witness to Being's manifesting itself as beings through her relationships with others, was fundamentally impaired for as long as she was in a relationship with the defendant, no amount of money is going to restore that capacity to her. So a general compensatory award – compensating her for that loss of capacity – can only perform the same symbolic function as is performed by the overall judgment in favour of the claimant: of emphasising to the claimant that what happened to her should not have happened to her and should not be expected to happen again.[242] As such, a general compensatory award may do some good, so long as its symbolic nature is acknowledged and it is not suggested that it can make up in any way for what happened to the claimant.

## Regrets

A private law that was concerned to foster QTL-flourishing could be expected to be less concerned about other betrayals *qua* betrayals, where those betrayals do *not* have the effect of damaging someone's ability to form intimate relationships in future.

For example, consider the case where *Adam* and *Eve* entered into a sexual relationship, *Eve* got pregnant and falsely represented to *Adam* that *Adam* was the father of the child, with the result that *Adam* supported *Eve* and the child for many years before discovering that he was not, after all, the child's father.[243] Or consider the case where *Eve* tricks *Adam* into getting her pregnant, with the result that *Adam* incurs legal responsibilities to look after the child that is the fruit of *Eve*'s trickery.[244]

---

[239] Such an injunction could not currently be awarded under Australian law as injunctions in that jurisdiction must be (in the terminology of McBride, *The Humanity of Private Law, Part I* (n 49), 55) 'duty-supporting'; in other words, give effect to a duty that the defendant is subject to: *Australian Broadcasting Corporation v Lenah Game Meats Pty Ltd* (2001) 208 CLR 199, at [60], [105]. However, such an injunction could be awarded under English law: Senior Courts Act 1981, s 37(1) (creating power to award an injunction 'in all cases in which it appears to the court to be just and convenient to do so').

[240] 'Barker' – real name John Dines – started working in 2011 as a director of police graduate training courses at Charles Sturt University in Sydney, Australia, where he was confronted by Steel, who was 'very concerned about what tactics [course participants] were being trained in and whether they were going to be trained in many of the discredited tactics that were used in the UK, which have now been acknowledged to be human rights abuses': 'Helen Steel and John Dines: the spy who loved me' (n 236).

[241] See above, pp 105–06.

[242] Cf John Gardner's explanation of awards of general damages as 'reparative' but as being 'unusual in [having] no reparative value independently of the thought, on the part of the recipient, that it has such value … The payment … [has] reparative value thanks to the thought it does. It can make people feel better about themselves, about their lives, or about each other': Gardner, *From Personal Life to Private Law* (n 228), 154.

[243] England: *P v B* [2001] 1 FLR 1041; *A v B (damages: paternity)* [2007] EWHC 1246 (QB); Australia: *Magill v Magill* (2006) 226 CLR 551.

[244] Canada: *PP v DD*, 2017 ONCA 180. (My thanks to Jason Neyers for drawing this case to my attention.) An unusual example of such a case is provided by the English case of *B v IVF Hammersmith Ltd* [2018] EWCA

In both cases, *Eve* is guilty of betraying *Adam*'s trust in her, but it is not a betrayal that is likely to impair *Adam*'s capacity to QTL-flourish in the future. *Eve*'s betrayal is not likely to result in *Adam*'s becoming wary of forming intimate relationships in the future – having been fooled once by *Eve*, he is hardly likely to be fooled again by a future sexual partner – and, indeed, it could be argued that *Eve*'s betrayal has opened up some possibilities for QTL-flourishing on *Adam*'s part for which *Adam* should be grateful: the opportunity to form a bond with *Eve*'s child in the first case (whoever happens to be the true father of the child), and the opportunity to form a bond with his own child in the second case. So a private law that was concerned to foster QTL-flourishing could be expected to be just as wary of affording *Adam* a remedy in these kinds of cases as private law in its current state has proved to be.[245]

However, what *might* motivate a private law that seeks to foster QTL-flourishing to be concerned about these kinds of betrayals is if they result in the kind of regret that prevents *Adam* moving on with his life, and results in *Adam* instead endlessly circling in his memory the moment where *Eve* turned his life upside down, contemplating over and over again what might have been had *Eve* not played that part in his life.

For example, suppose that in the first kind of case, *Eve*'s lie that her child was *Adam*'s resulted in *Adam* and *Eve* no longer trying to have a child together, on the basis that they had already succeeded – so that *Adam* ended up forgoing the chance to have a child of his own. This is one of the regrets that afflicts one of the activists who was targeted for a sexual relationship by an undercover police officer called Mark Kennedy:

> Lisa … lost her chance to have children. She and Kennedy were together for most of her 30s and so, I suggest to her, he effectively stole her childbearing years. 'Yes, and I feel very angry,' she says. 'Who knows who I might have met, what decisions I might have made, but those choices were taken from me by the state.'[246]

This is the kind of a loss of a chance that is most likely to produce paralysing regrets in your life: where you know you have been deprived of a chance of a different life, but can have no idea – because that different life represents a road not taken in your life[247] – what that chance amounted to, good or bad. As a result, you can only wonder how your life would have been and as that wondering can never be satisfied or find a conclusion, it can be impossible to move on from it and think instead about what you will make of the road your life *has* taken.

It may come as no surprise by now that this kind of loss of a chance – the kind of loss of a chance that has the most potential to have a debilitating effect on your capacity to QTL-flourish – is of little concern to our RP-centric private law. Under English private law

---

Civ 2803, where a number of embryos were produced from A and B's genetic material in the course of their undergoing in vitro fertilisation treatment at D's clinic. The embryos were then frozen, and it was agreed they could not be unfrozen and planted in B without A's consent. After A and B's relationship broke down, B falsely represented to D that A had consented to one of the embryos being used to make B pregnant, and as a result the embryo was thawed, planted in B's womb, and produced a daughter in due course. A sued D for breach of contract, but was unsuccessful.

[245] Claims in these kinds of cases have generally proved unsuccessful in all common law jurisdictions. The English courts have gone furthest in indicating a willingness in principle to afford the claimant a remedy (usually in deceit), but in practice have declined to allow the claimant to claim for damages for the cost of bringing up a child that he was deceived into thinking was his, or was tricked into producing: *A v B (damages: paternity)* [2007] EWHC 1246 (QB), at [61]–[63]; *B v IVF Hammersmith Ltd* [2018] EWCA Civ 2803, at [39].

[246] 'Helen Steel and John Dines: the spy who loved me' (n 236).

[247] Cf Frost, 'The road not taken' in his collection of poems *Mountain Interval* (Henry Holt, 1916).

as it currently stands, damages for a loss of a chance are only recoverable by a claimant against a defendant who is potentially liable to the claimant for causing the claimant to suffer *economic loss*. So whether or not a claimant (C) can sue a defendant (D) for causing her to lose a chance of obtaining some benefit or avoiding some harm turns not on how bad the effect of C's losing that chance will be for her, but on whether C and D's case is the kind of case where C would normally be entitled to sue D for causing her to suffer economic loss.[248]

For example, an employer who negligently fails to provide his employee with a safety harness while the employee is working high above the ground will not be held liable for any injuries suffered by the employee as a result of falling to the ground if it is more likely than not that the employee would still have fallen even if he had been provided with a safety harness.[249] And if the chance the employee would not have fallen was 35 per cent, the employer will not be held liable for depriving the employee of that 35 per cent chance of not falling.[250] The requirement to provide the employee with a safety harness was designed to safeguard the employee's health and not the employee's economic welfare; as a result, the failure to provide a safety harness is not something that could give rise to liability for economic loss.

If, on the other hand, the failure to provide the employee with a safety harness *was* the cause of the employee's falling to the ground and being injured – in the sense that it would not have happened but for that failure – then, if the employee's injuries mean that there is a 10 per cent chance the employee will develop arthritis in the future, the employer will be held liable for that loss of a chance of avoiding developing arthritis: one of the situations in which a tortfeasor is routinely liable for economic loss suffered by the victim of his tort is where that tort caused the victim to suffer foreseeable physical injury, and the victim suffered economic loss as a result of that injury.

Given this, it might be possible for *Adam* to sue *Eve* for the loss of a chance of having children if he gave up the chance of having children because of *Eve*'s lies, as economic loss is easily recoverable in a deceit case. However, *Adam*'s claim would probably fail on the basis that a claimant can only sue a defendant in deceit for economic loss if that loss results from the claimant's relying on the defendant's lies in a way that the defendant *intended* the claimant to rely when the defendant lied to the claimant. And it is unlikely that *Adam* will be able to show that *Eve* intended that *Adam* should forgo the chance of having children when she lied to him.

A private law that sought to foster QTL-flourishing would not allow the question of whether or not *Adam* can sue *Eve* for suffering a loss of the chance to have children to turn on such footling technicalities. Instead, where *Eve* is clearly to blame for *Adam*'s suffering paralysing regret over how his life has gone, a remedy will be provided to *Adam*. But what remedy? It must be a remedy that will allow *Adam* to be reconciled with the way his life has gone. In other words, it must be a remedy that enables *Adam* to stop thinking about the road not travelled, and instead continue down the path that his life has taken.

Here, a handsome award of compensatory damages can do a lot of good. Such damages will *not* be assessed in the backward-looking way that damages for a loss of a chance are

---

[248] McBride and Bagshaw, *Tort Law*, 6th edition (Pearson Education, 2018), 281–82.
[249] *McWilliams v Sir William Arrol & Co Ltd* [1962] 1 WLR 295.
[250] *Rothwell v Chemical & Insulating Co Ltd* [2006] EWCA Civ 27.

currently assessed. Under that approach, we put a money value on the good that one has lost a chance of obtaining and then award a proportion of that value equivalent to the chance of obtaining that good that the claimant lost.[251] Instead, a private law that sought to foster QTL-flourishing would adopt a forward-looking approach, asking how much money would the claimant need to be given to reconcile them to losing the chance that they lost. It is a mistake to think that this will yield the same result as the backward-looking approach. Under the backward-looking approach, a claimant who loses a 0.01 per cent chance of winning £100 million will be awarded £10,000. But it is unlikely that £10,000 will be enough to allow the claimant to stop ruing – and ruining her life over – the fact that she missed out on a chance (no matter how small) to win a life-changing amount like £100 million.[252] On a forward-looking approach, the claimant would need to be awarded enough to change her life in a way that she *appreciates* enough to reconcile herself to losing the chance of changing her life that winning £100 million would have given her. £10,000 is not enough to bring about such an appreciable change in someone's life if they are living in the UK – probably at least five times that amount would be required.

# 7. The Perils of Litigation

Much more could obviously be said as to how private law might foster QTL-flourishing, and how different that private law would be from English private law in its current state.[253] However, the thought occurs and should now be addressed: Would a society that was focussed on the promotion of QTL-flourishing have a place for private law at all? Would it not, rather, rid itself of private law and all its accoutrements, in the cause of promoting QTL-flourishing? What motivates this thought is the undoubted dangers for people's capacities to QTL-flourish that are inherent in allowing a claimant to sue a defendant. These are dangers that are courted by everyone involved in private litigation: the claimant, the defendant, their lawyers, and judges alike. The dangers are fourfold in nature.

## Deception

The first danger is the standing temptation on the part of claimants and defendants to lie, either in order to advance a private law claim or in order to evade being held liable to a claimant. For example, concerns on the part of the insurance industry about the rate of

---

[251] See, for example, *Chaplin v Hicks* [1911] 2 KB 786.

[252] The point becomes clearer when we ask whether anyone would volunteer to run a 0.01% chance of *losing* £100m in return for a one-off payment of £10,000. The answer is clearly 'no'.

[253] Two subjects for future research may be picked out. (1) How an individual's built environment can affect their capacity to seek to be a good 'shepherd of Being' and how private law can afford individuals protection against their built environment being degraded by architects, developers, and the government. (2) Given the crucial role that language plays in enabling an individual to be a good 'shepherd of Being' (see above, p 83), what private law can do by way of endowing people with language rights that would have the effect of protecting the right-holder against being deprived of their language, or having their language degraded through speech codes. A good starting point for research on (1) would be Gorringe, *A Theology of the Built Environment: Justice, Empowerment, Redemption* (CUP, 2002); on (2), Sokolowski, *Presence and Absence: A Philosophical Investigation of Language and Being* (Catholic University of America Press, 2017).

fraudulent whiplash claims – usually when the claimant was involved in a car accident caused by the defendant's fault – led to the enactment of the Civil Liability Act 2018, which sought both to limit how much could be awarded by way of damages for whiplash injuries, and to ban settlements of claims for whiplash injuries in the absence of medical evidence of those injuries.

The temptation to lie and deceive obviously goes beyond claimants and defendants and extends to their lawyers; so much so that the identification of lawyering with lying is now well entrenched in the popular imagination.[254]

The shocking case of *Spaulding v Zimmerman*[255] illustrates the temptation at work. In 1956, David Spaulding was involved in a car accident caused by the negligence of John Zimmerman, in whose car Spaulding was a passenger. Spaulding suffered concussion and multiple rib fractures in the accident, and brought a claim for damages against Zimmerman. Zimmerman's lawyers had a doctor examine Spaulding and the doctor diagnosed Spaulding as suffering from an aortic aneurysm (an abnormal bulge in one of the blood vessels supplying blood to Spaulding's heart) which in all likelihood was caused by the car accident. Spaulding's own doctors – who examined Spaulding in the immediate aftermath of the accident – had not spotted the aneurysm. Zimmerman's lawyers failed to tell Spaulding about the aneurysm – despite the fact that they well knew that should it rupture, Spaulding would probably die – and settled Spaulding's claim for damages for $6,500. Had Spaulding known about the aneurysm, his claim would obviously have been settled for a far higher figure.

The settlement in the *Spaulding* case was set aside when the fact of Spaulding's aneurysm was discovered.[256] However, in other cases there is no sanction for deceptive conduct by lawyers conducting civil litigation. Indeed, Daniel Markovits goes as far to argue that 'lawyers are *professionally obligated* to lie and to cheat'.[257] Most obviously: 'adversary advocates [have a] professional duty to make, and to try to persuade courts to accept, statements about the law that they privately think mistaken.'[258]

Finally, not even judges are immune from the temptation to deceive. Lord Radcliffe advised that when deciding private law cases, 'judges will serve the public interest better if they keep quiet about their legislative function'[259] and maintain what Lord Reid would later call the 'fairy tale'[260] that judges who decide private law cases merely declare what the law says and do not make or change the law.[261] EW Thomas stigmatises this suggestion

---

[254] See, for example, Hodes, 'Truthfulness and Honesty Among American Lawyers: Perception, Reality, and the Professional Reform Initiative' (2002) 53 *South Carolina LR* 527.

[255] 116 NW 2d 704 (1962) (discussed, Cramton and Knowles, 'Professional Secrecy and its Exceptions: *Spaulding v Zimmerman* Revisited' (1998) 83 *Minnesota LR* 63).

[256] The aneurysm was discovered as part of a routine medical check-up in 1959, and Spaulding immediately had surgery to repair it, surgery that resulted in the side effect of Spaulding suffering major damage to his power of speech: ibid, 71.

[257] Markovits, *A Modern Legal Ethics: Adversary Advocacy in a Democratic Age* (Princeton UP, 2008), 67 (emphasis in original).

[258] Ibid, 53.

[259] Radcliffe, 'The Lawyer and his Times' in Sutherland (ed), *The Path of the Law* (Harvard UP, at 14–15, quoted in Thomas, *The Judicial Process: Realism, Pragmatism, Practical Reasoning and Principles* (CUP, 2008), 26–27.

[260] Reid, 'The Judge As Law Maker' (1972) 12 *Journal of the Society of Public Teachers of Law* 22, 22.

[261] Radcliffe, *The Law and Its Compass* (Faber & Faber, 1961), 39.

as 'utterly unthinkable ... a basically dishonest device in that it seeks to perpetuate a false process by a pretence that cannot survive public scrutiny.'[262] but observes that:

> While Lord Radcliffe's sentiments might not be voiced out loud in respectable legal circles today, however, they retain an unspoken force in the innate desire of judges to distance themselves from personal responsibility for their decisions or from the criticism that they are setting themselves above the law.[263]

This innate desire of judges is well-evidenced in any number of modern-day leading private law cases that have changed the law in significant ways but where the judges who decided those cases refused to acknowledge that that is what they were doing in their decision.

For example, in *Lister* v *Hesley Hall Ltd*[264] – a decision that has had the effect of transforming the law on vicarious liability in England and Wales – the leading judgment of Lord Steyn, holding the defendants vicariously liable for acts of sexual abuse committed by their employee: (i) claimed to be rooted in 'legal principle'[265] and free of the kind of 'conceptualistic reasoning' that might lead to 'absurd results' in a case where an employee has intentionally committed a tort, (ii) argued that the state of authorities meant that while 'Our law no longer struggles with the concept of vicarious liability for intentional wrongdoing', the traditional test for determining when an employer would be vicariously liable for an employee's tort did not 'cope ideally with such cases',[266] and (iii) concluded that that the traditional, 'simplistic'[267] test for vicarious liability could be discarded in favour of a test focussing on 'the relative closeness of the connection between the nature of the employment and the particular tort.'[268]

Similarly, in *Lipkin Gorman* v *Karpnale Ltd*[269] – a decision that had the effect of making it legitimate for claimants to bring claims under English private law simply on the basis that the defendant had been 'unjustly enriched at the expense of' the claimant – there was no acknowledgement of the major (and, in the view of many commentators 30 years on, fateful)[270] ramifications that that decision would have in terms of altering English private law. Instead, Lord Goff's judgment simply asserted that cases in which a third party recipient of stolen money was held liable to the owner of that money were 'not usually founded upon any wrong by the third party, such as conversion' but were instead 'founded simply on the fact that, as Lord Mansfield said, the third party cannot in conscience retain the money – or, as we say nowadays, for the third party to retain the money would result in his unjust enrichment at the expense of the owner of the money.'[271] In just six lines (and with

---

[262] Thomas, *The Judicial Process* (n 259), 27.

[263] Ibid.

[264] [2002] 1 AC 215.

[265] Ibid, [13].

[266] Ibid, [20].

[267] Ibid, [20].

[268] Ibid, [24].

[269] [1991] 2 AC 548.

[270] Watts, '"Unjust Enrichment" – The Potion that Induces Well-Meaning Sloppiness of Thought' (2016) 69 *Current Legal Problems* 289; Stevens, 'The Great Unjust Enrichment Disaster' (2018) 134 *LQR* 574. See also McBride, *The Humanity of Private Law, Part I* (n 49), concluding (at 198): 'we have a law of restitution, but no law of unjust enrichment.'

[271] Ibid, 572.

the agreement of his fellow Law Lords), Lord Goff changed the law in a way the courts are still struggling to come to terms with[272] – but without a word of acknowledgement that he was changing the law in such a fundamental way.

## Antagonism

The second danger for QTL-flourishing that is created by private law litigation is that the relationship between defendant and claimant is almost always antagonistic in nature,[273] and the antagonism between defendant and claimant is liable to give rise to feelings of anger and, where that anger cannot be relieved, QTL-flourishing-impairing feelings of hatred.

It is for this reason that, as Nathan Oman observes, 'Litigation is an un-Christian activity.'[274] So, immediately after having delivered His teaching on the nature of human flourishing – the Beatitudes – Jesus enjoined His followers, 'Love your enemies, do good to those who hate you, bless those who curse you, pray for those who abuse you. To him who strikes you on the cheek, offer the other also; and from him who takes away your coat do not withhold your tunic either.'[275] On another occasion, a member of the crowd he was teaching called out, 'Teacher, tell my brother to divide the inheritance with me.' But Jesus was uninterested in upholding whatever legal rights and duties that might have existed between the two brothers: 'Man, who made me a judge or arbitrator over you? … Take care, and be on your guard against all covetousness, for one's life does not consist in the abundance of his possessions.'[276] St Paul was to the same effect, instructing the members of the Church in Corinth: 'To have lawsuits at all with one another is already a defeat for you. Why not rather suffer wrong? Why not rather be defrauded?'[277]

It is likely that these warnings would only be redoubled in today's society, where the mutual feelings of ill-will that may be stirred up by litigation are likely to be fanned into a raging fire through the involvement of lawyers, who can be expected to take their cues from Lord Brougham's famous statement of the 'first and only duty' of an advocate, which is to 'save [his] client by all means and expedients, and at all hazards and costs to other persons …' Lord Brougham insisted that 'in performing this duty [the advocate] must not

---

[272] See above, n 270, and also below, pp 180–81.

[273] For an exception, see *Hunt v Severs* [1994] 2 AC 350, where a wife sued her husband in negligence for compensation for injuries suffered by her in a motor bike accident for which her husband (at that time, her boyfriend) was at fault, and the claim for compensation included a claim for a reasonable sum for the services her then boyfriend and had provided looking after her while she was recovering from her injuries. However, even this litigation was rendered adversarial by the fact that the husband's insurer would ultimately pay the compensation bill and successfully fought to knock off the claim for the reasonable sum, on the ground that as soon as it was paid over by the defendant to the claimant, the claimant would have to pay it back to the defendant.

[274] Oman, 'John Calvin's Quarrel with Civil Recourse Theory' in Cochran and Moreland (eds), *Christianity and Private Law* (CUP, forthcoming). Oman thinks that only the picture of civil litigation supplied by civil recourse theory – where litigation is designed to provide the claimant with a way of delivering payback to a defendant who has seriously wronged her – explains the Biblical warnings against engaging in litigation. However, those warnings are adequately explained by the potentially adverse consequences of the antagonism inherent in civil litigation, whatever may be the basis of the power to bring a civil claim against another.

[275] Luke 6:27–29 (ESV).

[276] Luke 12:13–15 (ESV).

[277] 1 Corinthians 6:7.

regard the alarm, the torments, the destruction which he may bring upon others … he must go on reckless of consequences …'[278]

The legal ethicist David Luban supplies a 'particularly egregious example' of a defendant's lawyer fulfilling Lord Brougham's mandate by engaging in tactics that could only inspire hatred for the defendant and its lawyer among those seeking to sue the defendant.[279] The defendant manufactured 'the Dalkon Shield, an intrauterine contraceptive device that [was] marketed during the 1970s to over three million women. Because of a design flaw, the Dalkon Shield caused an estimated 66,000 miscarriages and sterilized thousands of women by infecting them with pelvic inflammatory disease (PID).' The defendant's lawyer adopted a number of tactics in order to discourage women affected by the Dalkon Shield from suing the defendant:

> One tactic acquired the nickname 'the dirty questions list.' Defense lawyers taking depositions asked plaintiffs very specific, very graphic questions about intimate details of their personal hygiene and sexual practices … [The defense] lawyers argued that the 'dirty questions' were relevant to the lawsuits because they might reveal alternative sources of PID infection. The questions mainly served, however, to intimidate plaintiffs into dropping their lawsuits or settling them for inadequate amounts. The message was clear that they might have to answer the same questions in open court. Among other things, defense lawyers asked plaintiffs for the names of all their past and present sexual partners ('besides your husband'), with the clear implication that the partners' names might be revealed and their testimony elicited for purposes of impeaching plaintiffs' answers to the 'dirty questions' about what they liked to do in bed.

## Stasis

Another hate-inducing tactic adopted by defence lawyers in the interests of their client is that of using 'procedural delays to exhaust their opponents' funds.'[280] But even in the absence of such artificial delays, any civil litigation is likely to take time[281] and any human being involved in that litigation is likely to feel that their life is 'on hold' while they wait for that litigation to be resolved, one way or the other. It is for this reason that Lord Steyn thought that English private law was justified in taking a restrictive stance on allowing claimants to sue for compensation for psychiatric illness: 'where there is a prospect of recovery of [such] compensation … psychiatric harm is repeatedly encountered and often endures until the process of claiming compensation comes to an end … The litigation is sometimes an unconscious disincentive to rehabilitation.'[282]

A social order that identifies human flourishing with QTL-flourishing, and consequently seeks to foster QTL-flourishing, will be disturbed at the prospect of anyone feeling that their life is 'on hold' and that they cannot move on with their life until they are clear of some event

---

[278] Nightingale (ed), *The Trial of Queen Caroline, Volume 2* (Albion Press, 1821), 8.
[279] Luban, 'The Adversary Trial Excuse' in Luban, *Legal Ethics and Human Dignity* (CUP, 2009), 35–36.
[280] Ibid, 35.
[281] As of the time of writing (August 2019), the latest *Civil Justice Statistics Quarterly* for England and Wales, covering January to March 2019, reports that 'In January to March 2019, it took an average of 36.9 weeks between a small claim being issued and the claim going to trial' while 'For multi/fast track claims, it took on average 58.5 weeks to reach a trial.'
[282] *Frost v Chief Constable of South Yorkshire* [1999] 2 AC 455, 494.

that will happen at some uncertain time in the future. But it is not just the human parties to litigation who are likely to suffer QTL-flourishing-sapping feelings of being stuck in limbo. Increasingly, lawyers feel the same way.

The time-consuming routine of dealing with private law litigation – whether as a lawyer representing a party to that litigation, or as a judge hearing arguments in a case and deciding the case in light of those arguments – means that, as Anthony Kronman observes, 'To the ultimate question of life's meaning, it is now unthinkable that one can find even the smallest part of an answer by choosing a legal career. This might be sought instead, *in pianissimo*, in the world of love and friendship that begins where the world of work leaves off.'[283] But, as Kronman also observes, those involved in practising private law enjoy very little time free from the world of work. So while many private lawyers today see their work merely as a 'means of making a living … [they] find this a hard view to accept and continue to demand fulfilment from their work even as it offers less and less.'[284]

As a result, those who practise private law – as solicitors, barristers or judges – increasingly resemble Sisyphus, trapped in a cycle where their hopes of fulfilment from their work are inevitably followed by the disappointment of those hopes, and nothing fundamentally changes for them until they are spat out by the cycle on retirement. Given this, it is no wonder that 'a growing number of (mostly American) studies of law students and practitioners … [show] lawyers as anxious, depressed and de-motivated by their experiences of training and practice' and that 'as regards the English legal profession … there is extensive comment on stress and the deteriorating work-life balance in the national and trade press …'[285] It is also little wonder that the question of whether the work traditionally done by lawyers – including deciding cases – could be done by an artificial intelligence (AI) instead should be seriously discussed at this time.[286] If lawyers themselves feel like lifeless drones in doing their work, it is hardly surprising that the idea of replacing them with *actual* lifeless drones should have started to gain traction.

## Privilege

One of the attractions of the idea of law work being done by AIs is the prospect that the expense of running and accessing a system of private law might thereby be substantially reduced.[287] That expense is one of the reasons why the protections and benefits afforded by English private law are increasingly inaccessible to ordinary people.

Hazel Genn's *Paths to Justice* survey[288] was carried out in 1996, and attempted to estimate what proportion of the population would have suffered a non-trivial 'justiciable' problem

---

[283] Kronman, *The Lost Lawyer: Failing Ideals of the Legal Profession* (Harvard UP, 1993), 370.

[284] Ibid, 373.

[285] Webb, 'Being a Lawyer/Being a Human Being' (2002) 5 *Legal Ethics* 130, 146 fn 101, citing, *inter alia*, Benjamin, Darling and Sales, 'The Prevalence of Depression, Alcohol Abuse, and Cocaine Abuse among United States Lawyers' (1990) 13 *International Journal of Law & Psychiatry* 233.

[286] For recent discussions, see Markovic, 'Rise of the Robot Lawyers?' (2019) 61 *Arizona LR* 325; Surden, 'Artificial Intelligence and Law: An Overview' (2019) 35 *Georgia State University LR* 1305; Sourdin, 'Judge v Robot? Artificial Intelligence and Judicial Decision-Making' (2018) 41 *University of New South Wales LJ* 1114.

[287] See Susskind, *Tomorrow's Lawyers: An Introduction to Your Future*, 2nd ed (OUP, 2017), chs 9–11.

[288] Genn, *Paths to Justice* (Hart Publishing, 1999).

(a problem 'for which a legal remedy exists'),[289] and to study how those problems were resolved. Genn estimated that 'Over a five year period about 40% of the general population experienced one or more problems or events for which a legal remedy is available.'[290] A study of 1,134 adults who had suffered such problems showed that 5 per cent took no steps at all to resolve those problems. Half of that 5 per cent 'had an annual income of less than £10,000' and that 5 per cent were likely to have 'no educational qualifications.'[291] Most of those surveyed who had considered contacting a solicitor about their problems but who failed to do so had been deterred from seeking legal advice by the cost of doing so.[292] Of those who did use a solicitor to help deal with their problems, *no one* in the £32,000–£40,000 income bracket agreed with the proposition 'Lawyers' charges are reasonable for the work they do.' This figure, Genn observed, 'lends some support to the contention that only the well-off and the poor (through legal aid) can afford legal services.'[293]

Of the survey population, 14 per cent had their problems resolved by going to court. Genn again: 'This suggests that court and other legal proceedings play a very minor role in the resolution of justiciable problems afflicting ordinary members of the public as private individuals.'[294] That 14 per cent included survey members who were claimants in legal proceedings *and* survey members who were defendants, and the split between them was roughly 50:50.[295] But only about 12 per cent of the survey members 'reported that their justiciable problem involved them being the subject of action rather than the initiator of action.'[296] So of that 12 per cent about *half* ended up having the complaint against them resolved by a court, while of the remaining 88 per cent only about *one-tenth* ended up having their complaint about someone else resolved by a court. Given this, 'as far as private individuals are concerned, it appears that their exposure to legal proceedings is more likely to be as a defendant than as a plaintiff.'[297] Genn estimated that as a result of the greater propensity for private individuals to be sued under private law, rather than to sue, 'cases were about 57% more likely to be resolved when the respondent was a defendant than when the respondent was a plaintiff.'[298]

Genn's survey is now almost a quarter of a century old, but it is impossible that the figures produced by her survey will have improved over that time. Quite the opposite: it is virtually certain that since Genn carried out her survey, private law will have become *less* useful as a tool to be used *by* ordinary people and proportionately *more* useful as a tool to be used *against* ordinary people. This is because since the mid-1990s UK governments, of whatever political hue, have reacted to their inability to generate sufficient tax revenues to cover the cost of providing basic public services[299] by attempting to *cut* the cost of running a system of private law and to *shift* the remaining cost of running that system onto private individuals and law firms.

---

[289] Ibid, 5.
[290] Ibid, 65.
[291] Ibid, 69.
[292] Ibid, 80.
[293] Ibid, 237.
[294] Ibid, 150.
[295] Ibid, 218.
[296] Ibid, 152.
[297] Ibid, 151.
[298] Ibid, 172.
[299] See above, p 19.

Efforts to *cut* the cost of running a system of private law have principally taken the form of trying to ensure that as many private law disputes as possible are resolved through alternative dispute resolution such as mediation, rather than by going to court.[300] The Ministry of Justice has also instituted a programme of court closures, with 49 county courts (which hear small claims cases) being closed in 2010 alone. It has also been assiduously exploring the possibility that virtual courts that operate online may provide a cheaper method of doling out civil justice.[301]

Efforts to *shift* the remaining costs of running a system of private individuals onto private individuals and law firms have taken a couple of different forms. First, claimants wishing to sue for damages in respect of a personal injury are now almost always barred from seeking legal aid to bring their claim,[302] and must instead – if they are impecunious – find a firm willing to represent them on a 'no win, no fee' basis, where no firm will be so willing unless they are convinced that the claimant is more likely than not to win their case.

Second, the traditional position was that 'the civil courts were financed jointly by the taxpayer – who paid for judges and court buildings – while the rest of the cost of civil justice was met out of court fees.'[303] However, since 1992 there has been an attempt to finance the costs of running the civil courts entirely out of court fees. This has triggered a seemingly unstoppable rise in such fees in relation to all private law claims, so that now – for example – the fee for starting proceedings in the High Court to a recover a debt between £10,000 and £20,000 equals 5 per cent of the value of the sum claimed,[304] and attempting to recover one's costs after winning a case in the UK Supreme Court will cost 2.5 per cent of the sum claimed.[305]

Given these developments, the impression that private law exists for the benefit of the interests of companies and the comfortably off, and not for the benefit of ordinary people, can only have grown over the last 25 years since the *Paths to Justice* survey was being carried out. However, it is not only the expense of accessing private law that creates (or should create) that impression. Marc Galanter's now classic work on 'Why the "Haves" Come Out Ahead'[306] explains that as between 'claimants who have only occasional recourse to the courts (one-shotters or OS) and repeat players (RP) who are engaged in many similar litigations over time',[307] the repeat players enjoy an obvious systematic advantage over the one-shotters in moulding private law in their favour over time.[308]

---

[300] See, for example, *PGF II SA v OMFS Co I Ltd* [2014] 1 WLR 1386, imposing a sanction on a defendant when making an order for costs because the defendant failed to respond to the claimant's invitation to see if they could settle their differences via mediation.

[301] See the Ministry of Justice Policy Paper 'Transforming our justice system' (September 2016) and the report of the Online Dispute Resolution Advisory Group, 'Online dispute resolution for low value civil claims' (February 2015).

[302] This is the combined effect of the Access to Justice Act 1999 (which abolished the availability of legal aid in personal injury cases except for medical negligence cases) and s 9 of the Legal Aid, Sentencing and Punishment of Offenders Act 2012 (which abolished the exemption in favour of granting legal aid in medical negligence cases, except in cases involving children).

[303] Genn, *The Hamlyn Lectures 2008: Judging Civil Justice* (CUP, 2010), 45–46.

[304] Civil Proceedings Fees Order 2008 (SI 2008/1053), Sched 1.1.

[305] Supreme Court Fees Order 2009 (SI 2009/2131), Sched 4.1.

[306] Galanter, 'Why the "Haves" Come Out Ahead: Speculations on the Limits of Legal Change' (1974) 9 *Law & Society Review* 95.

[307] Ibid, 97.

[308] Ibid, 98–103.

Repeat players: (1) 'having done it before, have advance intelligence' as to how the courts will deal with a given transaction in future; (2) 'develop expertise and have ready access to specialists'; (3) 'have opportunities to develop facilitative informal relations with' the courts that will deal with their cases; (4) can build up a record that establishes their credibility when bargaining with others; (5) 'can play the odds ... over a long series of cases' to maximise their position at the end of those cases; (6) can forego an immediate material gain from the way a particular case is decided in favour of that case being decided in a way that might favourably 'influence the disposition of the decision-maker next time round'; (7) will possess the 'experience and expertise' that enables them to know what rules are most likely to be advantageous to them in the long run and 'to concentrate their resources on rule-changes that are likely to make a tangible difference' and to devote resources on making sure those rule-changes work for them.

Galanter acknowledges that not all repeat players 'are to be equated with "haves" (in terms of power, wealth and status)' while not all one-shotters count as "have-nots" but it is the case that 'In the American [and British] setting most RPs are larger, richer and more powerful than are most OSs, so these categories overlap ...'[309] The result is that the 'position of advantage' possessed by repeat players 'is one of the ways in which a legal system formally neutral as between "haves" and "have-nots" may perpetuate and augment the advantages of the former.'[310]

In light of these reflections, it seems that private law is always destined to bring into being, and govern over, the kind of social order that was given the name 'Classica' in Part I of this project.[311] Classica is a class-ridden society where the 'Lucky Ones' at the top enjoy various goods associated with human flourishing, and have very little to do with the 'Unlucky Ones' at the bottom who do not enjoy those goods. The flaw in Classica's set-up is that the Lucky Ones are likely to fall prey to systematic delusions about both who they are and who the Unlucky Ones are as a result both of their privilege and their isolation from the Unlucky Ones.[312] If we are interested in living in a social order that promotes QTL-flourishing that flaw is a fatal flaw: it ensures that no one living in Classica is likely to be leading a life that is QTL-flourishing. But if the operation of private law guarantees that the social order it governs will, over time, resemble Classica, why would a social order that seeks to foster QTL-flourishing make any room for private law?

## Saving Private Law[313]

Despite these dangers, private law could be expected to form a central part of a social order that seeks to foster QTL-flourishing.

Our starting point in seeing why this is, is provided by a meeting Louis C Brandeis – at that time, a New York lawyer, and later to become a Justice of the US Supreme Court – took

---

[309] Ibid, 103.
[310] Ibid, 103–04.
[311] McBride, *The Humanity of Private Law, Part I: Evaluation* (n 49), 105.
[312] Ibid, 106; also, above pp 52–53.
[313] With apologies to Sandy Steel, whose title 'Saving Private Wrongs' (in (2016) 14 *Jerusalem Review of Legal Studies* 1) I have borrowed/adapted for this heading.

with James Lennox, who co-owned with his father a business that ran a tannery, and counsel for one of Lennox's creditors. The business was effectively insolvent, and Lennox and his father also had many personal debts. In the course of the meeting, Brandeis suggested that Lennox assign the tannery to his firm on trust. Brandeis' firm would then administer the tannery for the benefit of everyone to whom the Lennox business, and Lennox and his father personally, owed money. This suggestion was acted upon, and Brandeis' firm was able to ensure that the creditors of the Lennox business recovered 100 per cent of the money they were owed, and that the personal creditors of Lennox and his father recovered 40 per cent of their money. When Brandeis was later asked by Lennox's lawyer 'for whom [Brandeis] was counsel when he advised the assignment, Brandeis replied, "I should say that I was counsel for the situation."'[314]

John P Frank stigmatises Brandeis' remark as 'one of the most unfortunate phrases he ever casually uttered … Lawyers are not retained by situations, the adversary system assumes that they faithfully represent one interest at a time.'[315] However, I think Brandeis' phrase provides us with a fruitful way of thinking about the roles both of the lawyers who represent parties to a private law case, and of the judge who decides that case.[316] All of them are ultimately focussed on making sense of the situation that has given rise to the case in question.[317] The claimant's lawyers will argue that: (1) we have a problem here, (2) this is what we have done in the past when this kind of problem has occurred, and (3) in light of that, this is how we should deal with this problem. The defendant's lawyers will dispute one or more of the claims made by the claimant's lawyers, and the judge will decide which view of the situation is better.

What counts as a problem will obviously depend on the nature of the private law jurisdiction that the case is being heard in. In a private law jurisdiction that is focussed on fostering RP-flourishing, C's feelings of betrayal on learning that her lover over the last few years was actually a police spy will not count as a problem that anything needs to be done about. By contrast, if that jurisdiction were instead concerned to promote QTL-flourishing, C's feelings of betrayal would be regarded as a problem that would need to be addressed in a way that ensures those feelings of betrayal do not poison C's future relationships with other people. And in a Kantian private law jurisdiction that was not concerned with fostering human flourishing at all, but was instead concerned to maintain and uphold relationships of mutual independence between its subjects, C's feelings of betrayal would not be a problem, but the use to which C's body was put to by the spy might be.

So in a jurisdiction that seeks to foster QTL-flourishing, the lawyers involved in a private law case will inevitably be engaged in reflecting together on the questions: (1) what sort of events get in the way of someone's QTL-flourishing? and (2) how should the law respond to those events? What I want to suggest is that engaging in a joint effort to answer these

---

[314] Frank, 'The Legal Ethics of Louis D Brandeis' (1965) 17 *Stanford LR* 683, 702.

[315] Ibid.

[316] Also in praise of Brandeis' observation, though in the limited context of lawyers representing groups, see Shaffer, 'The Legal Ethics of Radical Individualism' (1987) 65 *Texas LR* 963, 979–81.

[317] Cf Kronman, *The Lost Lawyer* (n 283), 362: 'What lawyers are particularly trained to do and can generally do better than philosophers and economists is think about cases – imaginary future cases … but real past ones too. The ability to fashion hypothetical cases and empathically to explore both real and invented ones is the lawyer's professional forte.'

questions is itself a form of QTL-flourishing, so that the participants in that effort can justifiably claim that they too are engaged in a quest to lead a truthful life. This is because when we argue together over the answers to questions (1) and (2), we seek to gain and give effect to an ever-clearer understanding of what it would be for a people to live together on terms that enable those who wish to do so, to seek to achieve the closest connection to Being that anyone can achieve. In seeking to gain and give effect to that understanding we seek to participate in the activity of Being's manifesting itself as beings. We do this not – as others do[318] – by contemplating or witnessing to Being's manifesting itself as beings, but by helping to imagine and create what Heidegger called 'the clearing',[319] where Being's manifesting[320] to human beings can take place. In seeking to help create and maintain that clearing, private lawyers who operate in a jurisdiction that seeks to foster QTL-flourishing deserve the title of seeking to be good 'shepherds of Being' as much as anyone does. Such private lawyers can therefore truly be said to be engaged in a quest to lead a truthful life.

Private lawyers working in a jurisdiction that seeks to foster QTL-flourishing will therefore have no reason to share the despondency that seems to afflict those who work in the field of private law in today's common law jurisdictions. They will find in their work the kind of meaning that today's private lawyers cannot seem to find in theirs. Moreover, their role in doing that work will be indispensable. Just as an AI is incapable of achieving the kind of connection with Being that human beings are capable of – because an AI is unaware that it is a being that participates in Being – an AI is incapable of reflecting on what the answers to questions (1) and (2) are.[321] It can only be told what those answers are, and instructed to give effect to those answers. It follows that an AI will never be capable of doing the work that private lawyers would do in arguing and deciding cases in a jurisdiction that seeks to foster QTL-flourishing,[322] and the widespread adoption of AIs to determine the outcome of private law cases would mark the death of private law as a forum for reflecting on what the answers to questions (1) and (2) might be.

These points indicate that a social order that sought to foster QTL-flourishing would *not* dispense with private law on the ground that operating a system of private law will have adverse effects on the QTL-flourishing of the lawyers who help to run that system. There would be no such adverse effects. Quite the opposite: working as a private lawyer within such a social order would be a way of achieving a QTL-flourishing existence. But would that social order still dispense with private law because of the way civil actions: (i) encourage the telling of lies, (ii) foster harmful antagonisms between the parties to litigation, (iii) will tend,

---

[318] See above, pp 83–85.

[319] On the 'clearing' see Dreyfus, *Being-in-the-World* (MIT Press, 1991), ch 9. Interestingly, Dreyfus points out that in Heidegger's thought, 'situation is another name for the clearing' (ibid, 168), so that 'The shared situation is called *the clearing*; being-in-the-clearing is *being there*' (ibid, 165, emphasis in original). So if a private lawyer is (as I contend they should think of themselves as being) 'counsel for the situation', they are 'counsel for the clearing'.

[320] We omit here the words 'itself as beings' out of respect to Heidegger, who thought that there was no 'it' to Being: see above, pp 74–75.

[321] It is no accident that the author of *What Computers Still Can't Do: A Critique of Artificial Reason* (MIT Press, 1992) is Hubert Dreyfus – the same Dreyfus whom we have just been quoting as an authority (indeed, a world authority) on the interpretation of Heidegger's work.

[322] Cf Koenig, Oseid and Vorenberg, 'OK Google, Will Artificial Intelligence Replace Human Lawyering?' (2019) 102 *Marquette LR* 1269, arguing that 'The lawyer's craft goes beyond what AI can do because we listen with empathy to clients' stories, strategize to find the story that might not be obvious, thoughtfully use our imagination and judgment to decide which story will appeal to an audience, and creatively tell those winning stories.'

because of economic inequalities in society, to be used as a weapon against ordinary people far more often than they work to protect ordinary people, and (iv) help entrench deceptive divisions between the 'haves' and the 'have-nots' in society?

It could be expected that (i) and (ii) would be less of a problem in the kind of social order we are discussing. Certainly, a lawyer who thought of themselves as 'counsel for the situation' would not be tempted to lie on behalf of their client in civil litigation, or engage in the kind of hate-inducing tactics seen in the Dalkon Shield litigation. And a judge who made it clear that her first loyalty is to finding a satisfactory solution to 'the situation' before her would have no need to pretend that her solution has many precedents when it is in fact a novelty for which the judge should be congratulated (provided it does in fact represent a satisfactory solution). The claimant or defendant in civil litigation might still be tempted to lie and feel hate-encouraging anger towards their counterpart on the other side of the litigation. However, it seems likely that dispensing with private law in order to avoid these temptations would do far more harm than good. Not least among the harms done by dispensing with private law is that of depriving people of the opportunity to forgive their enemies – how am I supposed to indicate that I have forgiven you some wrong you did me if I had no means of taking recourse against you for that wrong in the first place?

As to harms (iii) and (iv), it seems likely that a social order that sought to foster QTL-flourishing would be marked by far less inequality in terms of the distribution of wealth than the social orders in Western liberal societies, precisely in order to avoid the fatal flaw for QTL-flourishing that is inherent in societies such as Classica. So the economic policy of a social order dedicated to fostering QTL-flourishing would be distributist in nature, seeking to ensure that the wealth of society was widely spread, rather than concentrated in a few hands.[323] We can therefore be hopeful that such a social order would not see a system of private law give rise to effects (iii) and (iv).

It seems, then, that the harms that the processes of the system of private law inflict on people's capacities to QTL-flourish are not the fault of those processes, but rather the fact that those processes take place within a social order that is not interested in fostering QTL-flourishing, but seeks instead to foster RP-flourishing. So yet another difference between English private law as it is now, and English private law as it would be if it sought to foster QTL-flourishing, is that many of the harms to people's capacities to QTL-flourish that arise out of the *way* private law in its current state operates would disappear or be radically attenuated under a system of private law that sought to promote QTL-flourishing.

## Making the Turn

It follows that a social order that sought to foster QTL-flourishing would both have a system of private law, and that there would exist significant differences between that system of private law and English private law in its current state, both in terms of the respective systems' rules and doctrines and in terms of how those systems operate.

---

[323] On distributism, see Pope Leo XIII's papal encyclical *Rerum Novarum* (1891); Belloc, *The Servile State* (1913); Chesterton, *The Outline of Sanity* (1927); Belloc, *An Essay on the Restoration of Property* (1936).

If it is the case – as was argued in Part I of this project – that English private law currently seeks to help us lead lives that are RP-flourishing (flourishing according to the account of human flourishing provided by the RP), but it is also the case – as has been argued in Part II of this project – that human flourishing is better identified with QTL-flourishing rather than RP-flourishing, then it seems obvious that English private law is defective and that we would be better off if English private law turned away from seeking to promote RP-flourishing and sought to foster QTL-flourishing instead.

Given this, the question we now need to consider is: can anything be said *against* the proposition that those responsible for English private law should change its rules and doctrines in the ways canvassed in this chapter so that English private law does a better job of fostering QTL-flourishing than it does at the moment? Of course, those who believe that private law should not be in the business of encouraging human flourishing at all would have plenty to say against this proposition. But in the final chapter of this project, I will consider a different kind of objection to English private law's turning away from encouraging RP-flourishing and turning towards fostering QTL-flourishing. According to this objection, the fact that almost all of English private law's subjects currently identify their flourishing with RP-flourishing presents an insurmountable obstacle to English private law's undergoing a change of direction from promoting RP-flourishing to fostering QTL-flourishing.

# 12

## The Limits of Democracy

The title of this chapter is ambiguous. It could be read as referring to the limits that should be placed on the ability of majorities to determine the shape of the society they live in. A book on public law would probably refer to 'the limits of democracy' in that first sense.[1] However, as a private lawyer, I intend my chapter title to be read in a second way: as referring to the limits that democratic considerations place on how far unelected judges can go in developing private law, and as asking whether those limits would be breached by a judiciary that sought to develop private law so that it fostered QTL-flourishing, rather than RP-flourishing.

A simile will help explain the concern of this chapter. We can compare private law to a ship that is currently bound in a certain direction – that of promoting RP-flourishing. The passengers aboard the ship – the subjects of private law – are largely happy with where the ship is going. This is because the RP is 'the RP' – it is the picture of human flourishing that is widely endorsed in our society. However, suppose that the ship's captain and crew – the judges – are convinced by the arguments in this book that the ship is currently bound in the wrong direction: the RP is a false picture of what human flourishing involves, and human flourishing actually consists in QTL-ing. Should they override the wishes of their passengers and alter the direction of the ship towards the goal of promoting the passengers' QTL-flourishing? Or should they allow the passengers to dictate the ship's course? – even though doing so is likely to result in the ship's continuing on its current direction, a direction that the captain and crew now believe to be profoundly misguided.

The answer I will offer is a complex one, undemocratic in theory but democratic in practice. The ship's captain and crew should do what *they* – and not the passengers – think is best in steering the ship. However, what happens to be best is that they continue on the course that the passengers currently want, which is in the direction of promoting RP-flourishing. Any change of course must wait on a general change of heart among the passengers: to change course any earlier than that would be unwise.

## 1. Six Positions

Let's begin by considering how we might evaluate whether or not the judges should change private law in one way or another. Suppose that the courts are invited to develop

---

[1] See, for example, Ely, *Democracy and Distrust: A Theory of Judicial Review* (Harvard UP, 1980); Allan, *The Sovereignty of Law* (OUP, 2013), ch 8; Lemieux and Watkins, *Judicial Review and Contemporary Democratic Theory* (Routledge, 2018).

private law in a particular way – let's call that development, δP. In judging whether or not the courts should δP, there are a number of different positions we might adopt:

(A)    The courts should δP if that would make things go best.[2]

(B)    The courts should δP if that would make things go best, but only if a majority of the subjects of private law would support the courts' doing this.

(C)    The courts should δP if that would make things go best, but only if doing so would not violate anyone's rights.

(D)    The courts should δP if that would make things go best, but only if doing so would be consistent with the subjects of private law thinking that they are being treated with equal concern and respect.

(E)    The courts should δP if that would make things go best, but only if δP represents an incremental change in the law.

(F)    The courts should δP if doing so would enhance the protection private law gives to its subjects' rights.

This is not, and is not meant to be, an exhaustive list of the positions that might be adopted when evaluating whether the courts should δP. However, this list seems representative of the positions that might realistically be adopted in evaluating whether the courts should δP.

In considering these positions, two points should be noted. First, it might be a matter of some controversy whether a given condition on the courts' δP-ing is satisfied. For example, (A) specifies that the courts should δP if that would make things go best – but who decides whether δP-ing will make things go best? In order to resolve this issue, let's stipulate that every 'if' in the above formulae is followed by 'the courts think'. Of course, some other viewpoint could be adopted. (A) could be read as saying that the courts should δP if the Vinerian Professor of English Law at Oxford University thinks that would make things go best. But this does not seem to be a position that might realistically be adopted. The only viewpoint that it seems to make sense to adopt in determining whether any of the above conditions on the courts' δP-ing are satisfied is that of the courts themselves.

Second, it should be noted that (B), (C) and (D) all place some kind of *democratic constraint* on the courts' δP-ing. The different constraints that they place on the courts' ability to δP reflect differing views as to what it means to live in a democracy. On one view, in a democracy, the majority should have the final word on issues about how the power of the state is to be deployed.[3] On another view, in a democracy, individual rights limit how state

---

[2] The phrase 'make things go best' is borrowed from Parfit, *On What Matters: Volume One* (OUP, 2013), 22.
[3] Hayek, *The Constitution of Liberty* (University of Chicago Press, 1960), ch 7; Waldron, *Law and Disagreement* (OUP, 1999), ch 11.

power may be deployed.[4] On a third view, in a democracy, everyone must be treated in a way by the state that enables them to think that they are being treated with equal concern and respect.[5] It should also be noted that while (E) does not place any kind of democratic constraint on our judgment as to whether or not the courts should δP, (E) is still *democratic in nature*, because it takes the view that radical changes to private law should be reserved to a democratically-elected legislature. By contrast, each of (A) and (F) are *undemocratic*. Neither (A) nor (F) places any kind of democratic constraint on when the courts should δP, and neither provides that certain changes in private law should only be made by a democratically-elected legislature.

So which position should we adopt in determining whether or not the courts should δP? I will argue in favour of position (A), which we can now rename 'the *Simple Formula*'. I will argue that the *Simple Formula* is superior to any of its rivals when it comes to providing a basis for evaluating a proposed judicial development in private law. If this is right, then the question of whether the courts should change private law so that it no longer promotes RP-flourishing but instead promotes QTL-flourishing along the lines proposed in the previous chapter falls to be determined by application of the undemocratic *Simple Formula*. If this is right, then the charge that changing private law in this way would be 'undemocratic' is irrelevant to the issue of whether the courts should effect such a change of direction in private law: the courts should simply do whatever they think would make things go best.

However, the question still remains whether changing private law so that it is concerned to foster QTL-flourishing rather than RP-flourishing *would* make things go best. I will answer that question in the negative: until there is a general change in social views as to the nature of human flourishing, away from identifying human flourishing with the RP and towards identifying human flourishing with QTL-ing, there is little point (and much to be said against) changing private law so that it fosters QTL-flourishing. I will then conclude by reflecting on the prospects of such a general change occurring in the foreseeable future.

## 2. The Superiority of the Simple Formula

Before we compare the *Simple Formula* with its rivals, we should say something about how the *Simple Formula* works. In applying the *Simple Formula*, the courts would be well-advised to employ what we can call the *no sacrifices heuristic*,[6] which says that promoting

---

[4] Rawls, *A Theory of Justice*, revised ed (Harvard UP, 1999), 53, and Rawls, *Justice as Fairness* (Harvard UP, 2001), 42, explaining that the first principle of justice governing the basic structure of a democratic society requires that the members of that society equally enjoy certain 'basic rights and liberties' such as freedom of thought, liberty of conscience, and freedom of association.

[5] Dworkin, *Freedom's Law: The Moral Reading of the American Constitution* (OUP, 1996), 17, and Dworkin, *Is Democracy Possible Here?* (Princeton UP, 2006), ch 5; Christiano, *The Constitution of Equality: Democratic Authority and its Limits* (OUP, 2008), ch 3.

[6] A heuristic is a quick device for finding a reasonable solution to a problem where finding the optimal solution to that problem would be impossible or take far too long. An example of a heuristic is the 'Lindy' heuristic popularised by Nassim Nicholas Taleb – and named after the New York deli where it was discovered – that a Broadway show that had run for 200 days could be expected to run for 200 days more, a show that had run for 100 days could be expected to run for 100 days longer, and so on. Taleb consequently dubs as 'Lindy' something that ages in reverse: the longer it lives, the longer it can be expected to live. See Taleb, *Skin in the Game* (Allen Lane, 2018), 141–43.

X's flourishing at the expense of Y's will be self-defeating; in other words, you can't promote one person's flourishing at the expense of another's. The *no sacrifices heuristic* may break down in certain extreme cases – all heuristics do – but the courts are much more likely to go right in giving effect to the *Simple Formula* if they apply the heuristic than if they don't.[7] Employing the *no sacrifices heuristic* allows us to say a given change in private law – δP – will *only* make things go best if: (i) δP will enhance the capacities of some individuals to flourish as human beings and (ii) δP will not damage any other individuals' capacities to flourish as human beings.[8]

In light of this, let us match the *Simple Formula* for evaluating whether the courts should δP against each of its rivals, beginning with position (B), which says that the courts should δP if the courts think that would make things go best, but only if the courts think a majority of the subjects of private law would support the courts' doing this.

## The *Simple Formula* versus (B)

In order to see whether we should prefer the *Simple Formula* to (B), or *vice versa*, we need to construct an argument as to when political power should be exercised in accordance with the wishes of the majority, and see whether that argument applies to the kind of exercise of political power that δP represents. Such an argument should not rest on, or appeal to, the ideas that people have certain basic political rights, or that people should be treated with equal concern and respect by those who govern them, as we will be testing the *Simple Formula* against ideas such as those when we come to positions (C) and (D). Can such an argument be made? I believe it can, and it goes as follows:

(1) *The durability of political power.* The first step in the argument observes that however political power is acquired – at the point of a gun or through popular acclaim or through the accident of birth – political power is not likely to endure for very long unless the fact of its location is generally accepted by the subjects of that power. This was Gandhi's insight: 'even the most powerful cannot rule without the co-operation of the ruled.'[9]

(2) *The inevitability of disagreement.* At the same time it is virtually inevitable that the subjects of political power will disagree among themselves as to how that power should be exercised. Diversities of background, upbringing, education, status, and taste, combined

---

[7] The *no sacrifices heuristic* makes sense against the background of: (1) the first postulate of human flourishing, which holds that under reasonably favourable circumstances there should be no need to sacrifice anyone's flourishing to promote another's flourishing; (2) arguments (laid out in McBride, *The Humanity of Private Law, Part I: Explanation* (Hart Publishing, 2019), 100–07; also above, pp 52–53) for thinking that it would be difficult for anyone to flourish in a political community that did not seek to promote the flourishing of all of its members; (3) the dismal record, when it comes to promoting human flourishing, of governments that thought the saying 'you can't make an omelette without breaking eggs' was a useful guide to public policy.

[8] In the language of the economists, δP will make things go best if δP represents a Pareto improvement.

[9] Gandhi, 'Russia and India' *Indian Opinion*, 11 November 1905; *The Collected Works of Mahatma Gandhi, Volume 5: 1905–1906* (The Publications Division, Ministry of Information and Broadcasting, Government of India, 1961), 132.

with natural human weaknesses (in particular, the all-too-human tendency to identify what is in my interests with what is in the general interest) will inevitably result in different people adopting different views as to how political power should be exercised.

(3) *Preserving power through disagreement.* Confronted with subjects who disagree on how he should exercise the powers he holds over them, the holder of those powers (call him *Rex*) has a problem: however *Rex* exercises his powers, a significant number of those subjects will disagree with his choice and as a result – given point (1) – *Rex*'s continued hold on his powers will be endangered. How, then, can *Rex* exercise his powers without losing them?

(4) *Democracy as a solution.* One solution to *Rex*'s problem is to make it clear that he will exercise his powers in a way that is approved of by the majority of the subjects over whom *Rex* exercises those powers. Provided *Rex* proceeds fairly to ascertain the majority opinion among those subjects – and even better if *Rex* encourages those subjects to delib-erate among themselves before expressing their opinion[10] – *Rex* will be able to exercise his powers without endangering his continued hold on those powers. The majority of *Rex*'s subjects will obviously be happy that *Rex* has exercised his powers in accordance with their wishes; but, much more crucially, the minority who thought that *Rex* should have exercised his powers in some other way will *also* be happy that *Rex* exercised his powers in the way he did.[11] This is because they will think they had a fair chance of forming a majority them-selves and winning *Rex* over to their side of the argument; and fair play dictates that they should accept their loss gracefully, just as they would have wanted the other side to have done if they had formed the majority – and which they may well still do, sometime later on down the line.[12]

(5) *Expertise as an alternative.* This democratic solution to *Rex*'s problem has its downsides. The first is that it makes *Rex* a cipher for the views of the majority of his subjects, thus diminishing his agency as the holder of political power. Second, the democratic solution will prove to be no solution at all if a significant number of *Rex*'s subjects are destined permanently to be in the minority. They will not think that they had a fair chance to form a majority themselves and therefore have no reason to feel happy with *Rex*'s giving effect to the wishes of the majority. Given this, *Rex* may cast around for a different solution to his problem of how to exercise his powers without endangering his continued hold on them. The alternative solution will be for *Rex* to persuade his subjects that he is in a better posi-tion than they are to determine how his powers should be exercised. If he is successful in persuading his subjects of his superior expertise in exercising his powers, those subjects could be expected to accept *Rex*'s decision to exercise his powers in a certain way, even though had they been in his shoes they might have exercised those powers differently.

---

[10] Along the lines recommended in Gutmann and Thompson, *Democracy and Disagreement* (Harvard UP, 1996), ch 2; and Gutmann and Thompson, *Why Deliberative Democracy?* (Princeton UP, 2004), chs 1–4.

[11] Richard Wollheim identified this as 'A Paradox in the Theory of Democracy' in Laslett and Runciman (eds), *Philosophy, Politics and Society* (Blackwell, 1962), when it is in fact of the essence of democracy's value in ensuring political stability.

[12] Cf. Bickel, *The Morality of Consent* (Yale UP, 1977), arguing (at 15) that democracy functions 'not merely as a sharer of power, but as a generator of consent.'

(6) *Excursus: Burke's address to the electors of Bristol.* Edmund Burke's famous address to the electors in his Bristol constituency[13] illustrates the two solutions to *Rex*'s quandary. Burke's opponent opts for the first solution to preserving political power: 'My worthy colleague says, his Will ought to be subservient to yours.' But Burke opts for the second solution, the way of expertise, observing of the electors' representative that 'his unbiassed opinion, his mature judgment, his enlightened conscience, he ought not to sacrifice to you … Your Representative' owes you, not his industry only, but his judgement; and he betrays, instead of serving you, if he sacrifices it to your opinion.' Burke goes on to attempt to vindicate his claims of superior expertise in deploying the political power entrusted him by the electors of Bristol: 'what sort of reason is that, in which the determination precedes the discussion; in which one sett of men deliberate, and another decide; and where those who form the conclusion are perhaps three hundred miles distant from those who hear the arguments?'

(7) *Conclusion.* If *Rex* wants to continue holding the political powers he currently holds over his subjects, he would be well-advised to make it clear that he will exercise those powers in a way consistent with the majority's opinion as to how those powers should be exercised *unless* he can convince his subjects that he enjoys a superior expertise to them in deciding how those powers should be exercised.

Applying this conclusion to the issue of whether (B) is a superior yardstick to the *Simple Formula* for determining whether the courts should δP, (B) should be preferred to the *Simple Formula unless* the courts can convince the subjects of private law that they possess a superior expertise to those subjects in determining how private law should be developed.[14] Can they? The answer is 'Of course they can – and in fact, they already do.'

It is a striking fact of our current political order that there is virtually no general public interest in the state of private law or the question of how private law should be developed.[15] This lack of interest is most easily accounted for on the ground that the public is convinced that the courts know best when it comes to private law, and there is little need for them to take an interest in the courts' performance in developing private law. It is easy to identify a number of reasons for this.

First, private law is very *technical*, and it is hard for a layperson to master its technicalities as a preliminary to taking a position on what private law should say. Second, private law is made up of a lot of *interlocking* rules and doctrines, with the result that it is hard to form a view of how private law should develop without first having spent a lot of time

---

[13] Burke, 'Speech at the conclusion of the poll, 3 November 1774' in Elofson and Woods (eds), *The Writings and Speeches of Edmund Burke, Vol III: Party, Parliament and the American War 1774–80* (OUP, 1996), 68–70.

[14] Lord Reid took the same position in 'The Judge as Law Maker' (1972) 12 *Journal of the Society of Public Teachers of Law (New Series)* 22, 23, arguing that 'we must play safe [and] decide the case on the preponderance of authority [when it comes to] issues which the ordinary man regards as controversial. On many questions he will say: "That is the lawyers' job, let them get on with it." But on others he will say: "I ought to have my say in this. I am not going to accept dictation from the lawyers."' The corollary of this position is that on issues which the 'ordinary man' does not regard as controversial, and as 'the lawyers' job' to get on with, the courts do not have to play safe at all, but can do what they think is best *à la* the *Simple Formula*.

[15] It is even more striking that when political philosophers discuss the relationship between judges and democracy, their attention focuses exclusively on judicial controls on government action via judicial review; there is, so far as I can see, no discussion by a political philosopher of whether the judges should be more democratically accountable in developing private law.

and effort tracing the connections between the different parts of private law and how they interact. Third, private law is *long-standing*, with the result that the courts' claims to superior expertise in developing private law have been vindicated by prescription – ordinary people will feel that the courts must be doing something right if they have been allowed to develop private law for so long without noticeable disaster.[16] Fourth, the costs of private law are *not obvious*. Obviously, in every private law case there are winners and losers, but it is not obvious that anyone or any class of individuals loses out overall as a result of the existence of private law. As a result, private law is viewed by ordinary people as a force for good, and therefore not something that they should concern themselves with.[17]

By contrast, when it comes to *public* law, the courts have a much harder time of it in terms of convincing ordinary people of their superior expertise in determining how public law should be developed, and consequently come under much more pressure to respect the majority of public opinion in developing public law.[18] All of the features of private law that make private law a matter of little interest to members of the public are absent from public law; indeed, the precise opposite features figure large in public law and make the operation and development of public law something that members of the public feel able to have a view on.

First, public law is not technical. It consists in the repeated application of well-worn formulae derived from the common law and the European Convention on Human Rights to judge the legality of governmental action. It is therefore not difficult for a layperson to understand public law and form a view on it. Second, public law cases are fairly discrete – housing cases are not social security cases are not immigration cases. As a result, a layperson does not have to keep their eye on a lot of different moving parts within public law in order to form an intelligent view as to how public law is operating in a particular area of interest to them. Third, public law is very new – the modern common law of judicial review is only of about 50 years' standing, and the law on judicial review for violation of human rights standards is only about 20 years old – with the result that public law has simply had no chance to prove its worth in the public eye. Fourth, the costs of public law are obvious, in terms of the way public law – as it has been developed – hampers the government's ability to pursue its vision (which also may be the majority's vision) of the common good.

These features of public law mean that the courts may be well-advised to adhere to something like (B) in developing public law; otherwise, they may well be stripped of their powers to develop public law at all. By contrast, there is no need for the courts to adhere to (B) in developing private law. The courts' claims to superior expertise in developing private law are acknowledged by general public opinion, with the result that the courts' adhering to the *Simple Formula* in developing private law will not endanger the courts' continuing to have the power to develop private law.

---

[16] Private law is a good example of something that is 'Lindy', in Nassim Nicholas Taleb's terms (n 6): the fact that it has been around for so long gives us reason that it will be around for a long time in the future.

[17] Confirmation of this is provided by the fact that when private law is perceived by the public as being in danger of causing harm – such as when it is seen as encouraging a 'compensation culture' that discourages people from engaging in valuable activities for fear of being sued – then suddenly the public becomes very interested in private law, and measures such as s 1 of the Compensation Act 2006 have to be passed to address that public concern.

[18] Cf the concerns about the state of English public law articulated by Sumption, 'The Limits of Law' and Finnis, 'Judicial Law-making and the "Living" Instrumentalisation of the ECHR', both in Barber, Ekins and Yowell (eds), *Lord Sumption and the Limits of Law* (Hart Publishing, 2016).

## The *Simple Formula* versus (C)

(C) says that the courts should δP if that would make things go best, but only if doing so would not violate anyone's rights. Ronald Dworkin's inspired characterisation of 'rights as trumps'[19] might be taken as supporting (C) – that where making things go best comes into conflict with someone's rights, then that person's rights 'trump' our desire to make things go best.[20]

However, we should recall that under the *no sacrifices heuristic* δP will only make things go best if (i) δP will enhance the capacities of some individuals to flourish as human beings and (ii) δP will not damage anyone else's capacities to flourish as human beings. If (i) and (ii) are true, it is hard to imagine that anyone could have a right that the courts not δP or – in other words – that the courts δP-ing would violate anyone's rights.[21] If δP will do some people some good, and do no harm to anyone else, how could someone say that they have a right that such good not be done? Who could this 'someone' be? Clearly not, one would have thought, someone who belongs to the group of people who will suffer no harm as a result of the courts' δP-ing. So if someone has a right that the courts not δP, it must be someone in the group of people who will be *benefited* from the courts δP-ing. *Can* someone have a right not to have a benefit conferred on them?

The idea that there can be such a right seems to run up against the idea that the rights we have exist to protect our interests.[22] If this is correct, the idea of your having a right that I *not* act *in* your interests seems paradoxical. However, what is normally called the 'Interest Theory' of rights is not the only game in town; it is opposed by the 'Will Theory' of rights, according to which your having a right against me involves my having a duty to act in a particular way and your having the power to control whether or not that duty exists.[23] On this view, your having a right that I not act in your interests boils down to my having a duty not to act in your interests unless you want me to do so. This seems less paradoxical.

For example, suppose that I discover that you are in financial trouble and owe £10,000 on your credit card, and you are £15,000 in the red on your current account (a sum that is far in excess of your overdraft limit). As I have money to burn (and also know your bank details), I sit down at my computer and with a few strokes on the keyboard I pay off your debts to the bank, and pay an extra £5,000 into your current account to give you a bit of a financial cushion. You react angrily to what I have done: 'It was very nice of you to pay off

---

[19] Dworkin, *Taking Rights Seriously* (Harvard UP, 1977), xi; Dworkin, 'Rights as Trumps' in Waldron (ed), *Theories of Rights* (OUP, 1984).

[20] Note, however, that Dworkin himself did not mean for his phrase 'rights as trumps' to be read in this way, but rather saw people's rights as constraining the *kinds of reasons* that the government could act on, and in particular as constraining the government from failing to treat its subjects with equal concern and respect. So Dworkin's conception of 'rights as trumps' was meant to support (D) rather than (C). See Waldron, 'Pildes on Dworkin's Theory of Rights' (2000) 29 *Journal of Legal Studies* 301.

[21] Indeed, as we have seen, the dramatic change in private law that is contemplated in this book – private law's fostering QTL-flourishing rather than RP-flourishing – might bring about *greater* protection for traditional political rights such as freedom of speech: above, pp 120–30.

[22] Raz, *The Morality of Freedom* (OUP, 1986), 166; Kramer, 'Rights Without Trimmings' in Kramer, Simmonds and Steiner (eds), *A Debate Over Rights: Philosophical Enquiries* (OUP, 1998).

[23] Hart, 'Legal Rights' in his *Essays on Bentham* (OUP, 1982), 184.

my debts, but you shouldn't have. My business is my business and if I had wanted your help I would have asked for it. Here is the extra £5,000 you paid into my account: I cannot accept it. Obviously, I can't afford to give you back the £25,000 you paid my bank, but I will try to repay it when I can.' This seems like an intelligible reaction to what I did, and supports the idea that you had a right (in the 'Will Theory' sense of the term) that I not act in your interests, at least on this occasion.

What might motivate such a furious reaction to my doing you a favour? What seems to underlie it is the threat to your independence that my paying the money into your bank account seems to pose. This threat seems to take two forms. First, it seems like I am treating you like a child. You have gotten into trouble and rather than allowing you to fix your own problems (or learn from the mistakes you have made), I have sorted them out for you without even asking for your say-so. Second, now that I have paid off your debts (and given you an extra £5,000 on top) you may feel that you now owe me in some as yet indefinable way – and that feeling of obligation may constrain you in your future dealings with me from treating me as you would if you owed me nothing.

So we can make sense of the idea of your having a right that I not act in your interests where my doing so would threaten your independence, either by treating you like a child, or by making you feel that you owe me something with knock-on effects on how you are able to relate to me in future. But does this support the idea that the courts' $\delta$P-ing – where $\delta$P will enhance some people's abilities to flourish as human beings, while not harming other people's abilities to flourish – might violate the rights of the group of people (call the group 'G') whose capacities to flourish are *enhanced* by the courts' $\delta$P-ing? It is hard to see that it does.

First, if the courts' $\delta$P-ing does have the effect of enhancing the capacities of the members of G to flourish as human beings, the members of G might well feel grateful to the courts for doing this, but it is hard to imagine that this sense of gratitude would threaten the future independence of the members of G. It is hardly likely that they will have any future dealings with the judges that were responsible for $\delta$P; and even if they did, it is hard to imagine that sense of gratitude as seriously impinging on the way they relate to those judges.

Second, it is hard to see that the members of G are being treated like children if the courts' $\delta$P-ing enhances their capacities to flourish as human beings. This is particularly the case where the *only* way to enhance their capacities to flourish as human beings is through the courts' $\delta$P-ing. This case would be analogous to the situation where there has been a computer glitch at your bank and you are now *wrongly* accounted as owing £10,000 on your credit card and as being £15,000 in the red on your current account. You have tried to get the bank to remedy the error, but they are being obstructive. I learn from a mutual friend what has happened, and as I have some influence with the bank, I make representations on your behalf without your knowing about it. The bank responds to those representations by correcting the error in your accounts. I further suggest that the bank pay £5,000 in your account as compensation for your inconvenience, and the bank accedes to this suggestion. It is hard to imagine you would react furiously to my intervention in your case – and if you did, most reasonable people would think you were in the wrong to do so.

In light of these arguments, it seems like (C) adds nothing to the *Simple Formula*. If $\delta$P-ing would make things go best, $\delta$P-ing will not violate anyone's rights. It follows that we have no reason to prefer (C) to the *Simple Formula*.

## The *Simple Formula* versus (D)

(D) says that the courts should δP if that would make things go best, but only if doing so would be consistent with the subjects of private law thinking that they are being treated with equal concern and respect. At first sight, it seems like (D) falls foul of the same problem as (C) – if the courts' δP-ing would make things go best, then it is hard to see how the courts' δP-ing would involve them in failing to treat the subjects of private law with equal concern and respect. As such, (D) seems – like (C) – to add nothing to the *Simple Formula*.

However, it may be that (D) comes into its own if and when the courts contemplate the kind of δP that is the concern of this book – that of altering the rules and doctrines of private law so that it no longer fosters RP-flourishing, but instead fosters QTL-flourishing. Let's assume that such a change will make it harder for people to enjoy an RP-flourishing life, and easier for people to QTL. Would such a change involve treating individuals who identify human flourishing with RP-flourishing with less concern and respect than individuals who identify human flourishing with QTL-ing? Ronald Dworkin thought that it would:

> Government must treat those whom it governs with concern, that is, as human beings who are capable of suffering and frustration, and with respect, that is, as human beings who are capable of forming and acting on intelligent conceptions of how their lives should be lived. Government must not only treat people with concern and respect, but with equal concern and respect. It must not distribute goods and opportunities unequally on the ground that some citizens are entitled to more because they are worthy of more concern. It must not constrain liberty on the ground that one citizen's conception of the good life is nobler or superior to another's. These postulates, taken together, state what might be called the liberal conception of equality ...[24]

In Dworkin's view, the kind of δP contemplated in this book would not necessarily involve a failure of concern, but it would involve a failure of *respect*. It would involve the courts in showing a preference for one kind of life over another, and distributing private law rights and duties, powers and liabilities in order to facilitate the preferred lifestyle at the expense of people's abilities to lead the disfavoured lifestyle. But does doing this actually involve a failure of respect, and if so is that something that should concern us?

Dworkin says that (1) 'Governments must treat those whom it governs with ... respect, that is, as human beings who are capable of forming and acting on intelligent conceptions of how their lives should be lived' and (2) a government's treating its subjects with *equal* respect means that it 'must not constrain liberty on the ground that one citizen's conception of the good life is nobler or superior to another's.'[25] However, (2) does not seem to follow from (1).

(1) seems to suggest that treating A and B with *equal* respect means acknowledging that *both A and B* are *capable* of 'forming and acting on intelligent conceptions of how their lives should be lived.' But if I am capable of doing $x$ then – by definition – I am also capable of failing to do $x$.[26] Moreover, if the issue of how to live one's life is something that can be the

---

[24] Dworkin, 'What Rights Do We Have?' in Dworkin, *Taking Rights Seriously* (n 19), 272–73.

[25] Ibid.

[26] Cf an analogous point about law made by John Gardner: that law cannot *aim* to be morally justified if law *is* morally justified, because aiming entails the possibility of failure. See Gardner, 'Law's Aims in *Law's Empire*' in Hershovitz (ed), *Exploring Law's Empire: The Jurisprudence of Ronald Dworkin* (OUP, 2008), 216.

subject of intellectual reasoning – as Dworkin suggests it is, by acknowledging that conceptions of how one's life should be lived can be 'intelligent' – then it is possible for someone to reach a conclusion on that issue that is both intelligent, in that they reached that conclusion by engaging in intellectual reasoning, and *wrong*, in that that conclusion was arrived at through a process of intellectual reasoning that went awry somewhere along the way.

So a government that acknowledges that both A and B are capable of 'forming and acting on intelligent conceptions of how their lives should be lived' will acknowledge that (R) is true, where (R) says:

(R) It is possible that A will (i) succeed in forming and acting on an intelligent conception of how his life should be lived; but it is also possible that A will (ii) fail to form and act on an intelligent conception of how his life should be lived. And even if A does (i), A's intelligent conception of how his life should be lived may be right, but it may also be wrong. And everything that is true of A will also be true of B.

What does a government's acknowledging (R) is true entail for how it treats A and B? Nothing at all, so far as I can see, when it comes to treating A and B with *equal respect*. Certainly, there is no reason why a government that acknowledges that (R) is true would end up concluding that it must not 'constrain liberty' on the ground that A's conception of the good life 'is nobler or superior' to B's. But a government that acknowledges that (R) is true may well conclude that so far as treating A and B with *equal concern* is involved, it is required to do what it can to help maximise the chances of both A and B's succeeding in forming and acting on an intelligent and accurate conception of how their lives should be lived.

So a government treats its subjects with equal respect when it acknowledges that human fallibilities and frailties are such that *all* of its subjects need all the help they can get to flourish as human beings; and it treats its subjects with equal concern when it provides *all* of its subjects with the help they need to flourish as human beings. Given this, it is hard to see how giving effect to a δP that will enhance people's chances of succeeding in flourishing as human beings could involve a failure to treat the subjects of private law with equal concern and respect.

Is there some other way of establishing that a δP that involves private law seeking not to foster RP-flourishing but fostering QTL-flourishing instead shows a lack of respect for those who identify human flourishing with RP-flourishing? One way might be to argue that such a δP suggests that those who identify human flourishing with RP-flourishing are *stupid*. There is therefore an element of insult involved in the kind of δP we are currently considering. However, this argument does not work. To suggest that someone's position on a particular issue is wrong, and to proceed on that basis, is *not* to suggest that that person is stupid.[27] Dworkin himself acknowledged this to be the case when he observed that 'My understanding of human dignity might be defective. You must judge for yourself and, if necessary, correct my account'.[28] Intelligent people – and they do not come much more intelligent than Dworkin – can be wrong, and no insult or disrespect is involved in making that observation.

---

[27] Cf Christiano, *The Constitution of Equality* (n 5), 225: 'one does not treat another person as inferior merely by thinking that some or even many of their ideas are less defensible than one's own. Indeed, one can think of another as superior ... while rejecting their particular views.'
[28] Dworkin, *Justice for Hedgehogs* (Harvard UP, 2011), 338.

Second, it might be argued that the kind of δP we are considering *will* – whether we like it or not – have the effect of causing those who identify human flourishing with RP-flourishing to feel disrespected by their government, in that they will feel like they are second-class citizens in their own country. Whatever one's conception of human flourishing, this must count as a significant harm. As Joseph Raz observes:

> the very ability to identify with one's society is an independent background good, and feeling alienated from it is a significant handicap. They have a considerable, often imperceptible impact on people's ability to engage in activities involving relations with other people, or contributions to their well-being or to the common good.[29]

Let's call the harm of feeling like a second-class citizen in one's own country, *alienation*. The fact that a δP that involves private law seeking to foster QTL-flourishing rather than RP-flourishing may result in people who identify human flourishing with RP-flourishing suffering the harm of alienation does *not* require us to endorse (D) in relation to this kind of δP. This is because the fact that people may suffer the harm of alienation as a result of this kind of δP is something that can and should be taken into account under the *Simple Formula* in judging whether or not that δP will make things go best. After all, under the *no sacrifices heuristic* a δP will *not* be judged to make things go best if it promotes some people's capacities to flourish as human beings at the expense of harming other people's capacities to flourish.

So even in relation to a major δP – such as private law's switching from seeking to foster RP-flourishing to fostering QTL-flourishing – (D) adds nothing to the *Simple Formula*, just as it adds nothing to the *Simple Formula* in cases where a minor δP is adjudged to make things go best. Given this, we should prefer the *Simple Formula* to (D), while at the same time acknowledging that our reflecting on (D) has resulted in a warning flag being posted in relation to the major δP discussed in this book – it may be that such a δP will not make things go best because bringing it about will cause people to suffer the harm of alienation. This is a topic that we will return to in the next major section of this chapter. But for the time being, we continue to evaluate the *Simple Formula* against its rivals.

## The *Simple Formula* versus (E)

(E) says that the courts should δP if that would make things go best, but only if δP represents an incremental change in the law. Some judges support (E), but equally other judges do not. Lord Reid observed that:

> [In the] Appeal Court ... broadly speaking you will find three lines of approach. There are those who used to be referred to as black letter lawyers; careful men who like to go by the book or, if you like, Lord Denning's 'timid souls'.[30] Then there are those who want to press on, by the nature

---

[29] Raz, 'Free Expression and Personal Identification' (1991) 11 *OJLS* 303, 314. See also Christiano, *The Constitution of Equality* (n 5), 61–63 (on people's interest in 'being at home in the world').

[30] This refers to Denning LJ's judgment in *Candler v Crane, Christmas & Co* [1951] 2 KB 164, 178: 'This argument about the novelty of the action does not appeal to me in the least. It has been put forward in all the great cases which have been milestones of progress in our law and it has always, or nearly always, been rejected. If you read the great cases of *Ashby v White*, *Pasley v Freeman* and *Donoghue v Stevenson* you will find in each of them the

legal reformers. And lastly there are those who are impatient with technicalities and who are not content unless common sense prevails.[31]

Judges in the first group could be expected to support (E), while judges in the second or third group would not – they would support the *Simple Formula*.

Of the judges who have recently sat in the UK Supreme Court, Lord Reed serves as a model of a judge who seems to support (E), while Lord Toulson seemed to reject (E) in favour of the *Simple Formula*.[32] For example, in *Robinson v Chief Constable of West Yorkshire*,[33] Lord Reed rejected the idea that the courts could or should determine whether or not a defendant owed a claimant a duty of care by simply asking whether it would be 'fair, just and reasonable' to find that such a duty of care was owed. Instead, he argued that in cases where 'it has clearly been established that a duty of care is or is not owed' the courts should simply give effect to the established position and refuse to consider 'whether the existence of the duty is fair, just and reasonable' unless the case is being heard in the UK Supreme Court and the court is being 'invited to depart from an established line of authority'.[34] In novel cases where it has not been established whether or not a duty of care is owed, Lord Reed recommended that the courts adopt 'the characteristic approach of the common law in such situations [which is] to develop incrementally and by analogy with established authority'.[35]

Writing extra-judicially about the law of restitution, Lord Reed observed that 'academic scholarship which adopts an abstract and universalising approach to legal problems seems to me to be less useful to a judge than scholarship which demonstrates an awareness that legal problems are situated at a particular time and place and that they require an approach to their resolution which is concrete and particular'.[36] As a result, he counselled against attempting to reduce down the law of restitution to a set of mechanical formulae that could be applied across the board to all cases involving a claim for restitution,[37] endorsing instead Lord Walker's observation in *Deutsche Morgan Grenfell Group plc v Inland Revenue Commissioners* that 'it is of the nature of the common law to develop slowly, and attempts at dramatic simplification may turn out to have been premature and indeed mistaken'.[38]

Lord Reed's incremental approach to the law of restitution is well-demonstrated by his judgments in *Investment Trust Companies v Revenue and Customs Commissioners*[39] and *Prudential Assurance Co Ltd v Revenue and Customers Commissioners*.[40] In the *ITC* case,

---

judges were divided in opinion. On the one side there were the timorous souls who were fearful of allowing a new cause of action. On the other side there were the bold spirits who were ready to allow it if justice so required. It was fortunate for the common law that the progressive view prevailed.'

[31] Lord Reid, 'The Judge as Law Maker' (n 13), 22–23.

[32] As of the time of writing (August 2019), Lord Reed is poised to become President of the UK Supreme Court. Lord Toulson served on the UK Supreme Court for just over three years, retiring from the court on 22 September 2016. He tragically died while having heart surgery less than a year later, on 27 June 2017.

[33] [2018] AC 736.

[34] Ibid, [26].

[35] Ibid, [27].

[36] Reed, 'Theory and Practice' in Dyson, Goudkamp and Wilmot-Smith (eds), *Defences in Unjust Enrichment* (Hart Publishing, 2016), 313.

[37] Ibid, 316.

[38] [2007] 1 AC 558, at [156].

[39] [2018] AC 275.

[40] [2018] UKSC 39.

Lord Reed observed that 'A claim based on unjust enrichment does not create a judicial licence to meet the perceived requirements of fairness on a case-by-case basis'[41] and that 'the adoption of the concept of unjust enrichment ... does not provide the courts with a tabula rasa, entitling them to disregard all authorities pre-dating'[42] the case that adopted that concept as a ground of liability.

In *Prudential Assurance*, Lord Reed (together with Lords Hodge and Mance) departed from the House of Lords' decision in *Sempra Metals Ltd v Inland Revenue Commissioners*,[43] which decided – only 10 years before *Prudential Assurance* – that compound interest could be awarded against a defendant who was liable to make restitution of money paid by mistake to the defendant. Lord Reed assailed the decision in *Sempra Metals* as illustrating 'the risks of effecting major changes to the law of restitution through judicial decision'[44] and as inconsistent 'with a long-established understanding of, first, the nature of the cause of action based on a mistaken payment, and secondly, the basis on which interest is payable.'[45] Lord Reed also quoted with approval from Lord Mance's dissenting judgment in *Sempra Metals*, where Lord Mance 'cautioned against a radical reshaping of the law, observing ... that "we must navigate using the reference points of precedent, Parliamentary intervention and analogy, and we should bear in mind the limitations of judicial knowledge and the assistance provided by a series of Law Commission reports."'[46]

Lord Toulson was altogether more swashbuckling in his approach to developing private law, no more so than in *Patel v Mirza*,[47] where he pushed the doctrine of precedent to its absolute limit (and some would say beyond its limits) not only in seeking to reformulate the law on when a claimant's illegal act would bar the claimant from bringing a claim in the case at hand – a claim for restitution of money paid for a consideration that failed – but also in seeking to use his decision to reformulate how the defence of illegality would apply in *all* private law cases.

Lord Toulson ruled that a 'court which is considering the application of the common law doctrine of illegality [should] have regard to the policy factors involved and to the nature and circumstances of the illegal conduct in determining whether the public interest in preserving the integrity of the justice system should result in denial of the relief claimed.'[48] Lord Toulson rejected the criticism that this 'relatively flexible approach' to the defence of illegality 'would create unacceptable uncertainty' on the basis that he was 'not aware of evidence that uncertainty has been a source of serious problems in those jurisdictions which have taken' the same approach, and that while 'there are areas where certainty is particular important' the law on when a defence of illegality to a private law claim can be raised is not one of them.[49]

---

[41] [2018] AC 275, at [39].
[42] Ibid, at [40].
[43] [2008] AC 561.
[44] [2018] UKSC 39, at [63].
[45] Ibid, at [75].
[46] Ibid, at [53], quoting from [2008] AC 561, at [205].
[47] [2017] AC 467.
[48] Ibid, at [109].
[49] Ibid, at [114].

The same bold approach to developing private law is evident in Lord Toulson's judgments in *Willers v Joyce*,[50] *AIB Group (UK) plc v Mark Redler & Co Solicitors*,[51] and *Mohamud v Wm Morrison Supermarkets plc*.[52]

In *Willers*, Lord Toulson recognised a new tort of maliciously instituting civil proceedings against another, in the teeth of objections that doing so was 'unwarranted by authority, unjustified in principle and undesirable in practice.'[53] Lord Toulson recognised this new tort because 'It seems instinctively unjust for a person to suffer injury as a result of the malicious prosecution of legal proceedings for which there is no reasonable ground, and yet not be entitled to compensation for [that] injury' and because he was not convinced there existed any 'countervailing factors such that [the tort of malicious prosecution's] applicability to civil proceedings should be limited ...'.[54]

In *AIB*, Lord Toulson ruled that where a trustee paid out money to another in breach of trust pursuant to a commercial transaction, the trustee should not – as traditional equitable principles might suggest – be held liable to restore the misallocated money to the trust fund, but instead 'the extent of the equitable compensation [payable] should be the same as if damages for breach of contract were sought at common law.' This was because 'the fact that the trust was part of the machinery for the performance of a contract is relevant as a fact in looking at what loss the [claimant] suffered by reason of the breach of trust ...'.[55] As a result, the trustee would only be held liable for any loss that would not have happened had he applied the trust money correctly.

In *Mohamud*, Lord Toulson – in, effectively, only one paragraph of his judgment and without citation of any supporting authority – extended the scope of an employer's vicarious liability for the torts of his employee to the case where there was 'an unbroken sequence of events'[56] between the employee's doing something he was supposed to do for his employer (in *Mohamud*, serving a customer) and the employee's tort (in this case, following the customer into a car park and subjecting him to a vicious and racist assault). The result of the decision in *Mohamud* was an extension of the scope of the law on vicarious liability far beyond its previous bounds, under which an employer could be held vicariously liable for an employee's tort not only where the employee did something he was employed to do by committing that tort, but also where the nature of the employee's employment created a 'special risk' that he might commit that kind of tort.[57]

However, it may be over-simplistic to pigeonhole Lord Reed as a cautious incrementalist and Lord Toulson as a reforming 'bold spirit'. After all, it was Lord *Toulson*'s adoption in *Michael v Chief Constable of South Wales* of an incremental approach to finding a duty of

---

[50] [2018] AC 779.

[51] [2015] AC 1503.

[52] [2016] AC 677.

[53] [2018] AC 779, at [174] (per Lord Sumption, dissenting). Lords Neuberger, Mance and Reed also dissented. In his brief judgment, Lord Reed argued that 'major steps in the development of the common law should not be taken without careful consideration of the implications, however much sympathy one may feel for the particular claimant' (ibid, at [184]).

[54] Ibid, at [43]; also [57].

[55] [2015] AC 1503, at [71].

[56] [2016] AC 677, at [47].

[57] *Lister v Hesley Hall Ltd* [2002] 1 AC 215.

care in negligence[58] that underpinned Lord Reed's later endorsement of that approach in the *Robinson* case. And it was Lord *Reed* who delivered the *extremely* bold decision of the UK Supreme Court in *Armes* v *Nottinghamshire County Council*,[59] to find a local authority vicariously liable for tortious acts of physical and sexual abuse carried out by foster parents with whom the defendant local authority had placed the claimant victims of those acts of abuse. The decision in *Armes* has been widely criticised, with one commentator claiming that the decision 'affirms that the law of England and Wales concerning vicarious liability is long on policy, and short on principle'[60] and is 'now no more than a blunt tool for giving effect to judicial instincts for social justice.'[61]

The fact that judges who instinctively give effect to the *Simple Formula* sometimes act as though they endorse (E), and judges who are temperamentally inclined to endorse (E) sometimes find themselves giving effect to the *Simple Formula* in developing private law, suggests that (E) and the *Simple Formula* are not so opposed as might first appear.

Rather, it could be argued (and I would argue) that (E) adds nothing to the *Simple Formula*. Instead, (E) represents a check on the application of the *Simple Formula*: (E) reminds the judges that when they are considering effecting a major development in private law, their capacity to determine whether such a change will make things go best is limited and advises them that that kind of change in private law would be better made by Parliament or a law reform body, which will be in a better position than they are to evaluate the consequences of that change. Some judges, like Lord Reed, usually heed the advice (E) gives them and steer clear of making major changes in private law; but they occasionally disregard that advice, as Lord Reed did in *Armes*. Other judges, like Lord Toulson (or Lord Denning), are bolder and usually are not deterred by (E)'s advice from relying on their own judgment to decide whether a major development in the law will make things go best. But sometimes they will heed the advice given them by (E), as Lord Toulson did in *Michael*,[62] and leave a proposed major change in private law to Parliament.

If (E) adds nothing to the *Simple Formula*, but merely represents advice as to how the courts should give effect to the *Simple Formula*, we have no reason to prefer (E) to the *Simple Formula*. This now leaves only (F) as a potential rival to the *Simple Formula* for providing us with a basis for determining whether or not the courts should δP.

## The *Simple Formula* versus (F)

(F) says that the courts should δP if doing so would enhance the protection private law gives to its subjects' rights. In trying to make sense of (F) we immediately run into the problem of determining what is meant by the *rights* of the subjects of private law. However,

---

[58] [2015] AC 1732, at [102] ('The development of the law of negligence has been by an incremental process rather than giant steps. The established method of the court involves examining the decided cases to see how far the law has gone and where it has refrained from going. From that analysis it looks to see whether there is an argument by analogy for extending liability to a new situation, or whether an earlier limitation is no longer logically or socially justifiable.')

[59] [2018] AC 355.

[60] Dickinson, 'Fostering Uncertainty in the Law of Tort' (2018) 134 *LQR* 359, 359.

[61] Ibid, 363.

[62] For an example of Lord Denning doing the same, see *Combe* v *Combe* [1951] 2 KB 215.

the definitional work done in Part I of this project[63] allows us to make short work of this question. *Rights* could mean, in relation to the subjects of private law:

(1) Those subjects' *interests* that are currently protected under private law, and which result in some people saying that the subjects of private law have a 'right to …' liberty, or personal security, or their possessions, and so on.

(2) The things that those subjects have a 'right to …' in a *Kantian way*.[64] In other words, the means that Kantians think belong to a subject of private law (such as her body and her property).

(3) The legal 'rights that …' those subjects have under private law that other people act in particular ways.

(4) The *Kantian* 'right that …' those subjects have under the Kantian Doctrine of Right that other people not violate their independence as persons.

Of these possible meanings, we should instantly dismiss (3). Under meaning (3), (F) says that the courts should δP if doing so would enhance the protection private law gives to its subjects' private law rights (whatever they currently happen to be) that other people act in particular ways. It is very hard to see why the courts' powers to δP should be limited in this way. In fact, virtually any proposed δP would be ruled out on this version of (F).

This leaves us with three possible versions of (F). Under two of those versions (those supplied by meanings (2) and (4) of the word *rights*), the courts should only δP where their δP-ing would develop private law in a way approved of by Kantians. Under meaning (2), the courts should only δP when doing so would enhance the protection private law gives to those things that Kantians think belong to a subject of private law, such as their body or their property. Under meaning (4), the courts should only δP when doing so would enhance the protection private law gives to people's 'rights to independence'.

It is hard to imagine these versions of (F) appealing to anyone but Kantians. The version of (F) supplied by meaning (2) would rule out a δP that would enhance the protections private law gives to people's privacy (unless a Kantian argument can be made that people's privacy belongs to them). The version of (F) supplied by meaning (4) would rule out a δP that would impose a duty of easy rescue on people who are well placed at no inconvenience to themselves to save a stranger from harm. Instead of asking and debating – as we would under the *Simple Formula* – whether such developments in private law would make things go best, such developments would simply be forbidden to the courts under these versions of (F).

Quite right too, would be the response of the Kantians. But if the arguments made in Part I of this project are correct, and Kantian explanations do not in fact provide the most satisfying and perspicuous explanations of English private law in its current state, then accepting either of these versions of (F) would have the effect of rendering English private law deeply incoherent. If, as Ronald Dworkin argued, the common law in any jurisdiction can be compared with a 'chain novel' where each generation of judges attempts to develop the law in a way that is continuous with the efforts of their predecessors,[65] then requiring

---

[63] See McBride, *The Humanity of Private Law, Part I* (n 7), 43–54.

[64] For this use of the term 'right to …', see ibid, 51–54.

[65] Dworkin, *Law's Empire* (Harvard UP, 1986), 229.

the courts *now* only to develop private law in ways that are stamped with the Kantian seal of approval would be akin to George Eliot's turning Dorothea Casaubon into a vampire halfway through *Middlemarch*.[66] Private law could no longer claim to amount to a body of law that treats everyone's cases alike under a coherent set of rules and principles. As a result, private law's legitimacy and therefore its effectiveness would come into question.

In light of this, the already unappealing Kantian versions of (F) become appalling and should be rejected. This leaves only the version of (F) that is produced by meaning (1) of the word *rights*, under which the courts should only δP if doing so would enhance the protection that private law gives to the interests of its subjects that it already protects. It is hard to see this version of (F) as having any intelligible appeal – if private law is currently failing to protect some acknowledged interest of one of its subjects, why shouldn't the courts develop private law so that it protects that interest? – but even if we think it does, (F) still adds nothing to the *Simple Formula*. If the arguments made in Part I of this project are correct, then the ultimate interest of its subjects that private law protects is their interest in flourishing as human beings. So – according to this version of (F) – the courts should only δP if doing so will enhance the protection private law gives to its subjects' flourishing as human beings. But that is exactly what the *Simple Formula* says.

## Conclusion

The *Simple Formula* has triumphed over all its rivals. When it comes to a proposed development in private law – δP – the courts should δP if doing so would make things go best, where δP will make things go best if (i) δP would enhance the capacities of some of its subjects to flourish as human beings, and (ii) δP would not damage the capacities of anyone else to flourish. The first hurdle in the way of private law's being developed so that it promotes QTL-flourishing rather than RP-flourishing can be surmounted. The possibility that such a change in the law – occurring as it would at a time when most people identify their flourishing with RP-flourishing rather than QTL-ing – would be 'undemocratic' is neither here nor there. The only question is whether developing private law in this way would make things go best. It is to that question that we now turn.

## 3. The Need to Choose

Ronald Dworkin distinguished between 'two types or classes of political decisions: those involving mainly what I shall call *choice-sensitive* issues, and those involving mainly *choice-insensitive* ones.'[67]

Choice-sensitive issues, he explained, 'are those whose correct solution ... depends essentially on the character and distribution of preferences within the political community.'[68] He offered the question of 'whether to use available public funds to build a new sports center

---

[66] At least in Seth Grahame-Smith's *Pride and Prejudice and Zombies* (Quirk Books, 2009), the existence of zombies in Regency England is acknowledged in the very first line of the book.

[67] Dworkin, *Sovereign Virtue: The Theory and Practice of Equality* (Harvard UP, 2000), 204.

[68] Ibid.

or a new road system' as an example of a choice-sensitive issue, on the ground that 'information about how many citizens want to use or will benefit directly or indirectly from each of
the rival facilities is plainly relevant, and may well be decisive'[69] to the issue of how the public
funds should be used. By contrast, a choice-insensitive issue is one whose correct solution
does not depend on people's preferences. So 'the decision whether to kill convicted murder-
ers or to outlaw racial discrimination' is choice-insensitive because the right decision on
these issues does not depend on 'how many people want or approve of capital punishment
or think racial discrimination is unjust.'[70]

Dworkin went on to suggest that allowing political issues to be resolved by majority
vote makes most sense in relation to choice-sensitive issues, and that if we allow choice-
insensitive issues to be similarly resolved that is because of the symbolic, negative impact
that denying people a vote on those issues would have.[71]

I want to suggest in this section that the issue of whether developing private law so
that it fosters QTL-flourishing rather than RP-flourishing will make things go best is
choice-sensitive, in this way: it depends on how many of the subjects of private law identify
human flourishing with QTL-flourishing rather than RP-flourishing. For ease of discussion,
let's call the $\delta P$ that involves private law's seeking to foster QTL-flourishing rather than
RP-flourishing, '$\Delta P$'. And let's consider five cases, set out in the following table.

| CASES | Percentage of private law's subjects who identify human flourishing with | |
|---|---|---|
| | RP-flourishing | QTL-flourishing |
| (1) | 100 | 0 |
| (2) | 70 | 30 |
| (3) | 40 | 60 |
| (4) | 10 | 90 |
| (5) | 0 | 100 |

As in the previous section, we will apply the *no sacrifices heuristic* and proceed on the basis
that $\Delta P$ will make things go best if and only if: (i) $\Delta P$ will enhance some people's capacities
for flourishing as human beings, and (ii) $\Delta P$ will not damage other people's capacities for
flourishing.

We begin by focussing on Case (1), which describes our current situation: all (or as good
as all) of private law's subjects identify their flourishing with RP-flourishing. The discussion
in the previous section gives us a couple of reasons for thinking that (ii) will not be satisfied
if $\Delta P$ occurs in Case (1).

First, such a $\Delta P$ is likely to result in private law's subjects suffering the undoubted harm
of *alienation*, of feeling that they are being treated as second-class citizens in their own
country. Alienation is an undoubted harm because it counts as a harm whatever one's

---

[69] Ibid.
[70] Ibid.
[71] Dworkin, *Sovereign Virtue* (n 67), 205–07.

conception of what human flourishing involves. It counts as a harm if human flourishing is identified with RP-flourishing, because being able to mix with other people without shame is an important secondary good that one has to enjoy in order to enjoy the primary goods that make up RP-flourishing.[72] It counts as a harm if human flourishing identified with QTL-flourishing because alienation impairs someone's ability to form productive relationships with other people, and threatens to cause the alienated individual to adopt a falsely negative view of him or herself.

Second, if ΔP occurs in Case (1), when private law's subjects identify their flourishing with RP-flourishing, then private law would become as politically controversial as public law is at the moment. The result would be that the courts' abilities to develop private law so as to make things go best would come under threat when the nature of private law – its technicality and the fact that its different parts interlock – means that only the courts have, or will ever have, the expertise to develop private law in a way that will make things go best. Should that threat materialise and the courts be permanently prevented from further developing private law by legislation that provides, for example, that no new torts will be recognised and that all validly made contracts will be given effect to in full unless doing so offends against some statutory provision, private law would quickly lose what effectiveness it has to make things go best and would become an irrelevant relic of the past.

So we have good reason to think (ii) would not be satisfied in respect of ΔP in Case (1). It is therefore likely that under the *no sacrifices heuristic* such a ΔP will not make things go best. And even if we dispense with the *no sacrifices heuristic*, we will reach the same conclusion. This is because (i) will not be satisfied: there will be *no benefits* from ΔP, in terms of enhancing people's capacities for human flourishing.

The reason why ΔP would yield no benefits in Case (1) is rooted in the fact that human flourishing is like eating or sleeping or reading. No one can do it for you: you have to do it yourself. This is why no government can *make* its subjects flourish as human beings: all it can do is *assist* them to flourish by creating the right conditions within which people can do what they need to do to flourish as human beings. This point is sometimes obscured by Possessions Models of human flourishing, which tend to suggest that flourishing is simply a matter of having the right goods in one's life. However, even under a Possessions Model of human flourishing, you cannot be counted as flourishing unless you *hold on* to the goods that are constitutive of your flourishing: and that holding on is something only you can do yourself. And the point that human flourishing is something that you have to do yourself is obvious if we adopt a Service Model or Journey Model of human flourishing. So, for example, if it is the case (as I have contended) that the essence of human flourishing is being engaged in a quest to lead a truthful life, you cannot be said to be engaged in such a quest unless you have chosen to engage in that kind of quest. You cannot engage in a quest by accident.

The implication is that if I identify my flourishing as a human being with RP-flourishing, I will be *incapable* of QTL-flourishing. You can, of course, try to assist me in all sorts of ways to engage in a quest to lead a truthful life, but unless I believe that my flourishing depends

---

[72] See McBride, *The Humanity of Private Law, Part I: Explanation* (n 7), 98, 124.

on my engaging in such a quest, the idea of engaging in such a quest will never occur to me, or if it does, the idea will strike me as literally *quixotic*.[73] If this is right, it is futile for the courts to ΔP in Case (1). The assistance private law will provide those subjects to QTL-flourish will be of no assistance at all until those subjects begin to identify their flourishing with QTL-flourishing.

How many subjects of private law would need to undergo this change of heart before we can say that ΔP will make things go best? To deal with this question, let's move on to consider Cases (2), (3) and (4). Applying the *no sacrifices heuristic* may lead us to conclude that ΔP will not make things go best in *any* of these cases. This is because in all these cases it could be argued that ΔP will damage the flourishing of those who identify their flourishing with RP-flourishing by alienating them from the society they live in. As a result, we will be unable to find that ΔP will make things go best in Cases (2), (3) or (4). We can only be confident that ΔP will make things go best in Case (5), where 100 per cent of private law's subjects identify their flourishing with QTL-flourishing.

This position is so extreme that it casts doubt on the validity of the argument that has led to its being adopted. The fault lies not in the *no sacrifices heuristic* but in the fact that the blame for the feelings of alienation suffered by those who identify their flourishing with RP-flourishing is laid at the door of ΔP in *each* of Cases (2), (3) and (4). This seems unreasonable.

For example, suppose that *Linus* and *Lucy* are siblings, and they both live in their parents' house. *Linus* wants to listen to death metal music in his room, turned up to 11. *Lucy* wants to practise playing the tuba for her school band and orchestra. Their parents forbid *Linus* to listen to death metal music unless he uses headphones (which he complains may result in his hearing being damaged), but they encourage *Lucy* to practise as much as possible on the tuba. Faced with this difference in treatment, *Linus* may well feel alienated from his parents and find it harder to identify with his home as *his* home. If it's *his* home, he may think, how come *Lucy* gets to do what she wants to do, when he isn't allowed to do what he wants to do? The reality is, he might conclude, that it's really *Lucy*'s home, and he's just staying in it until he can afford to get out and get his own place. While *Linus*'s feelings of alienation are understandable, they are also unreasonable. They fail to take into account the reasons why the parents might discriminate between listening to death metal music and playing the tuba, and that failure is something for which *Linus* can justly be blamed. So any feelings of alienation *Linus* experiences are *his* fault, not his parents' fault.

In light of this, let's now return to our three cases. In Case (2) the feelings of alienation that will be experienced by the 70 per cent who identify their flourishing with RP-flourishing when ΔP occurs will be both understandable and reasonable. General faith in the 'wisdom of crowds' – another heuristic – will mean that the 70 per cent will have no reason to think that their conception of human flourishing is defective in anyway. As a result, it will be reasonable for them to experience ΔP as an unwelcome and unwarranted judicial coup; and

---

[73] The eponymous hero of Miguel de Cervantes' novel *Don Quixote* (1605–15) engages in a quest to become a knight errant at a time that had outgrown such *folies de grandeur*. Cf. Unamuno, *Tragic Sense of Life* (Macmillan, 1921), 329: 'What, then, is the mission of Don Quixote, today, in this world? To cry aloud, to cry aloud in the wilderness. But though men hear not, the wilderness hears, and one day it will be transformed into a resounding forest, and this solitary voice that goes scattering over the wilderness like seed, will fructify into a gigantic cedar, which with its hundred thousand tongues will sing an eternal hosanna to the Lord of life and death' (trans Crawford Flitch).

their resulting feelings of alienation will be something for which ΔP can justly be blamed. In Case (4) the position is reversed. The 10 per cent who still identify their flourishing with RP-flourishing have every reason to question whether their conception of human flourishing is correct and to search out arguments – such as those made in this book – that establish that it is not. Their failure to do so is something for which they can be blamed, with the result that the feelings of alienation that they experience when ΔP occurs cannot be laid at the door of ΔP. Case (3) is obviously more marginal, and my view is that it is more akin to Case (2) than Case (4), with the result that the 40 per cent's feelings of alienation from private law after ΔP occurs are the fault of ΔP, and are not due to the failings of the 40 per cent.

It follows that if ΔP is not to cause any flourishing-impairing feelings of alienation for which ΔP can rightly be blamed, there must first exist a super-majority of subjects of private law (around 75 per cent?) who identify their flourishing with QTL-flourishing. If such a super-majority exists, there will also be little likelihood of ΔP bringing private law into such political disrepute that a flourishing-impairing threat to future judicial control over the development of private law will be created. So ΔP will make things go best – in the sense of enhancing people's capacities to flourish as human beings without at the same time being responsible for other people's capacities to flourish being damaged – when there exists a super-majority of subjects of private law who identify their flourishing with QTL-flourishing. But before that moment is reached, ΔP will have flourishing-impairing effects (principally, creating feelings of alienation) that will make it hard to say ΔP will make things go best under the *no sacrifices heuristic*.

How likely is it that that moment will ever arrive? That is the question we will address in the following section, the final section of this project exploring the humanity of private law.

## 4. The Future of Politics

2016 seems destined to join 1066, 1215, 1535, 1649, 1688, 1776, 1815, 1833, 1914, 1945 and 1979 as a momentous year in the history both of British politics, and world politics generally. For it was in 2016 that what Robert Nozick called 'the zigzag of politics'[74] came to an end.

What that phrase of Nozick's referred to was the way the electorate in both the United Kingdom and the United States would zigzag between different political parties, first voting for a left-wing party, then for a right-wing party, and then going back to the left. Nozick explained that this zigzag arose out of the fact that 'there are multiple competing values that can be fostered, encouraged, and realized in the political realm' and that it 'is *impossible* to include all of those goals in some consistent manner' in a given party's political programme.[75] As a result, the electorate has no choice but to zigzag between parties in order to ensure that none of the politically important values are neglected:

> Goals and programs have been pursued for some time by the party in power, and the electorate comes to think that's far enough, perhaps even too far. It's now time to right the balance, to include

---

[74] Nozick, *The Examined Life* (Simon & Schuster, 1990), ch 25.
[75] Ibid, 292, 293 (emphasis in original).

other goals that have been, recently at least, neglected or given too low a priority, and it's time to cut back on some of the newly instituted programs, to reform or curtail them.[76]

'The electorate wants the zigzag,'[77] Nozick confidently asserted. 'Sensible folk, they realize that *no* political position will adequately include all of the values and goals one wants pursued in the political realm, so these will have to take turns.'[78]

What may have been true of the electorate in 1990, when Nozick was writing, was no longer true in 2016, when a very large number of people in both the United Kingdom and the United States made it clear they were no longer willing to zigzag between the conventional positions adopted by the established left-wing and right-wing parties, but wanted something different. What underlay the breakdown of the zigzag is still a controversial question, but my diagnosis is that it was triggered by a loss of faith that the zigzag was heading in a progressive direction, towards a social order where *everyone* could enjoy a greater than 50:50 chance of RP-flourishing. Instead, there was a growing realisation among a significant number of the electorate in both the United Kingdom and the United States that (i) they were living in a social order where very large numbers of people – unprecedented in world history – were enabled to RP-flourish, but (ii) at the same time, equally large numbers of people living in that social order enjoyed no realistic prospects of RP-flourishing, and (iii) there was no realistic prospect that further zigzagging between the established parties of the right and the left would bring about the kind of social change that would enable everyone living in their society to RP-flourish. Hence the desire to abandon the zigzag in favour of something different.

Three years on from the momentous events of 2016, it is clear that what has replaced the zigzag is a four-way political fight between the following groups. First, the *Populists*. This group is made up of people who believe that it is possible to live in a social order that will enable *everyone* living in that order a reasonable chance of RP-flourishing – hence the term, 'populist'. But the populists believe that such a social order will have to look very different from the sort of order that has so far prevailed in modern Western liberal societies: less cosmopolitan, less infatuated with free markets, more conservative in the old-fashioned, Burkean, sense of that term.[79] The *Populists* are opposed by the *Cosmopolitans* – those who have managed to achieve an RP-flourishing lifestyle under the social order prevailing in modern Western liberal societies and see the populist push for changes in that social order as (i) a threat to their own personal position and livelihood, and (ii) potentially disastrous, in that they threaten to throw away the very real gains achieved by modern Western liberal societies in enabling RP-flourishing on a historically unprecedented scale.

The two-way fight between the *Populists* and the *Cosmopolitans* is turned into a three-way fight by the *Gnostics*. 'Gnosticism' is a term derived from the Greek word for 'knowledge',

---

[76] Ibid, 294.

[77] As did Nozick: 'given a choice between permanently institutionalizing the particular content of any group of political principles ... – I mean the types of principles meant to specify what goals should be pursued *within* a democracy, not the ones that underlie a democracy itself by providing its rationale and justification – and the zigzag process of democratic politics, one where the electorate can have been presented with those same principles too among others, I'll vote for the zigzag every time' (ibid, 296, emphasis in original).

[78] Ibid, 295 (emphasis in original).

[79] In his *Dictionary of Political Thought*, 3rd ed (Palgrave Macmillan, 2007), 69–70, Roger Scruton identifies the elements of Edmund Burke's thought as consisting in: (i) defending social continuity; (ii) criticising individualism; (iii) viewing society as a partnership not between members of that society but across generations and as including the dead and yet to be born; (iv) recognising inequality as inescapable, (v) in favour of private property, and (vi) defensive of tradition and custom against abstract reason.

*gnosis. Ancient* gnosticism was characterised by the belief, or knowledge, that the universe is evil, and the earth is nothing but a miserable prison for human beings.[80] Salvation from the grim plight in which human beings find themselves could only come from a benevolent God, who is not responsible for the evil state of the universe but has the power to intervene to create a new universe and, within it, a new earth that will provide a happier home for human beings. Ancient gnosticism was killed off by the rise of Christianity, but has been replaced by a modern (or secular) form of gnosticism.[81] Like their ancient counterparts, modern gnostics believe that there is something wrong with the world, but unlike ancient gnostics, modern gnostics believe that it is possible for *human beings* to recreate the world in a way that will eliminate the evils that currently afflict it. So for modern gnostics, the salvational role played by God in ancient gnosticism is instead played by human beings – or at least the select group of human beings who are 'in the know' as to what's wrong with the world, and what can be done to set things right and create a 'heaven on earth'.

In the political realm, *Gnostics* tend to be the children of *Cosmopolitans* – people who have grown up enjoying an RP-flourishing lifestyle, but who have come to reject the RP as an authentic vision of human flourishing and have instead adopted a Service Model of human flourishing instead. The particular form of Service Model that they have adopted is one which identifies their flourishing with their serving the goal of eliminating one or more of the evils that afflict the world. There are as many strains of gnosticism as there are evils that people see themselves as existing to defeat, but two strains in particular have given rise to important political movements, not least because the evils they seek to address are very real. The first strain is *green gnosticism*, which targets the evil of environmental degradation. The second strain is *liberal gnosticism*, which dedicates itself to ridding the world of the evil of cruelty. Originally focussed on creating a world that would be free of the cruelty of *brutality*,[82] liberal gnosticism now focusses much more on the cruelties of *exclusion* and *humiliation*, where the cruelty of exclusion exists whenever someone is excluded from some valuable opportunity or activity by virtue of who they are, and the cruelty of humiliation exists whenever someone is made to feel that they are second-rate.

So the *Populists* and *Cosmopolitans* agree in identifying human flourishing with RP-flourishing but the *Populists* think much more can be done to encourage universal RP-flourishing, whereas the *Cosmopolitans* seek to defend what has been achieved so far by way of encouraging RP-flourishing from being undermined by the *Populists*. By contrast, the *Gnostics* reject any kind of Possessions Model of human flourishing like the RP, and instead endorse a Service Model of human flourishing centred around serving the cause of ridding the world of evil.

Joining this now three-way fight are the *Liberty Lovers*. While the *Populists* can be seen as having overthrown the original zigzag of politics and the parties of the *Cosmopolitans*

---

[80] For discussion, see Rudolph, *Gnosis: The Nature and History of Gnosticism* (Harper & Row, 1987); Jonas, *The Gnostic Religion*, 3rd ed (Beacon Press, 2001).

[81] On which see, in particular, Eric Voegelin's *The New Science of Politics* (Univ of Chicago Press, 1952) and his *Science, Politics, and Gnosticism* (Regnery Gateway, 1968).

[82] The liberal views of Judith Shklar (*Ordinary Vices* (Harvard UP, 1984), ch 1, and 'The Liberalism of Fear' in Rosenblum (ed), *Liberalism and the Moral Life* (Harvard UP, 1989)), Annette Baier ('Moralism and Cruelty' (1993) 103 *Ethics* 436) and Richard Rorty (*Contingency, Irony, and Solidarity* (CUP, 1989), ch 4) were all explicitly rooted in the need to live in a world free of the cruelty of brutality, and claimed to draw inspiration for those views from Montaigne and Montesquieu (Shklar), David Hume (Baier), and Orwell and Nabokov (Rorty).

and the *Gnostics* can each be seen as having arisen in an attempt to command the political space created by the zigzag's overthrow, the *Liberty Lovers* were an integral part of the zigzag and regard its overthrow with some bemusement. This is because for the *Liberty Lovers*, politics is much less about promoting human flourishing as it is about defending human freedom. So the *Liberty Lovers* will have nothing to do with the fights between the *Populists*, *Cosmopolitans* and the *Gnostics* over how our politics should promote human flourishing. Instead, they continue to do as they did before 2016: speak in favour of a politics that is much more limited in its ambitions, as attempting to secure for everyone some measure of liberty, while debating among themselves how to define that measure of liberty, whether in terms of freedom from harm, or freedom from one's rights being violated, or some form of positive liberty to pursue the life one wishes to pursue.

How will it all turn out? – is the question that everyone living in the aftermath of the zigzag's overthrow wants answered. The arguments made in this book allow us to make some educated guesses.

First, if the arguments made in this book are correct, the *Populists'* hope that it will be possible to create a new social order which will do a much better job of promoting RP-flourishing than the one that tends to prevail in modern Western liberal societies is destined to be disappointed: no such order is on offer to us, and the fact that no such order is on offer to us is one of the biggest reasons we have for thinking that the RP is not an authentic vision of what human flourishing involves.[83]

To that extent, then, the *Cosmopolitans* are right: what we have at the moment is the best we can hope for by way of promoting RP-flourishing. However, while this position may be right, there is also a very real ugliness involved in the *Cosmopolitans'* maintaining it. The ugliness lies in the fact that there is only one way in which someone can identify human flourishing with RP-flourishing while at the same time asserting that modern Western liberal societies are the best we can hope for by way of promoting RP-flourishing – and that is by rejecting the first postulate of human flourishing, which is that human flourishing is within the reach of every human being, and is not the preserve of a privileged elite.

If, to borrow the language of Sellar and Yeatman, the *Populists* are 'Wrong but Wromantic' while the *Cosmopolitans* are 'Right but Repulsive',[84] the *Gnostics'* adoption of a Service Model of human flourishing centred on fighting evil makes them positively dangerous, both to themselves and to others.[85] This gnostic conception of human flourishing eats away at anyone who adopts it: no one can maintain a sense of personal integrity and decency for very long when they enter into a symbiotic relationship with evil, needing evil to exist in order for them to think that they are leading a flourishing life by fighting it.[86] Moreover, where the evil that the gnostic pins their flourishing on eliminating finds its roots not in capitalism or the class system or historic inequalities, but rather humanity itself,[87]

---

[83] See above, pp 19–20.

[84] Sellar and Yeatman, *1066 and All That* (Methuen & Co Ltd, 1930), 71.

[85] Cf. the doubts raised above about Service Models of human flourishing in general, at pp 3–4.

[86] Cf. Burkart, 'From the Economy to Friendship: My Years of Studying Ivan Illich' in Hoinacki and Mitcham (eds), *The Challenges of Ivan Illich: A Collective Reflection* (State University of New York Press, 2002), 158: 'When people asked me, "How's work going?" I would answer, "Never been better. Families are falling apart, so there is plenty of divorce and juvenile delinquency; arrests are up, so I have a lot of criminal trials; auto accidents and injuries at work are high, so my personal caseload is huge. Business is good." In a strange way all of us in the [social] service economy are feeding off social decay, a kind of cannibalizing of society.'

[87] Cf Solzhenitsyn, *The Gulag Archipelago* (1958–68), Volume II, Part IV, Chapter 1: 'the line separating good and evil passes not through states, nor between classes, nor between political parties either – but right through every

the gnostic ambition to eliminate evil can mutate into a terrifying ambition to eliminate humanity itself.

If, then, the aftermath of the overthrow of the zigzag saw just a three-way fight for political control between the *Populists*, the *Cosmopolitans*, and the *Gnostics*, the future would be depressing indeed. We would effectively be faced with a choice between living in a reheated version of the Soviet Union (should the *Populists* gain control and seek fundamentally to re-order society in order to enhance people's general capacities for RP-flourishing), the Holy Roman Empire (should the *Cosmopolitans* prevail, casting aside all pretence that the (neo-feudalist) social order that will be controlled by them exists for the benefit of anyone but them), or Maoist China (should the *Gnostics* come to power). However, the *Liberty Lovers* are also in the post-zigzag fight for political control and it seems that our hopes for a decent future are dependent on that party winning out. However, such an outcome, while less depressing, is hardly inspiring (as well as being extremely unlikely to boot). As has already been observed,[88] human flourishing is fragile and is unlikely to prosper within a legal order that leaves it alone to fend for itself.[89]

It may be, then, that the four-way fight that has succeeded the overthrow of the zigzag simply represents the playing out of an endgame that will inevitably culminate in checkmate for the prospects of human flourishing in the West. Certainly, that analysis would be consistent with Anne Glyn-Jones' conclusion, quoted at the start of this book, that we live in a civilisation 'which has run its course ... which is bankrupt.'[90] However, I think we still have grounds for hope.

The very fact that three of the four parties in our four-way fight owe their existence to the stance they take on the nature of human flourishing should give us hope that they will be open to listening to the arguments made in this book to the effect that the accounts of human flourishing that they currently endorse are intellectually unsustainable and that they should instead take the position that their flourishing consists in their being engaged in a quest to lead a truthful life (QTL-ing). Should they listen to, and accept, those arguments then enough of a majority would coalesce around the view that human flourishing consists in QTL-ing to make it justifiable for English private law to be transformed in the ways canvassed in the previous chapter. This would in turn strengthen people's capacities to QTL, and help kick-start the widespread adoption of the kinds of activities and attitudes that would make QTL-flourishing self-sustaining across persons and time, in line with our fourth postulate of human flourishing. Should this happen, then far from portending an imminent collapse, the overthrow of the zigzag and the travails ushered in by that momentous event will prove to have been indispensable first steps towards our living in a social order that truly fosters our flourishing as human beings; a flourishing that will take on as many different forms as there are human beings but will always involve our being moved by, and towards, the Love that moves the sun and the other stars.

---

human heart – and through all human hearts. This line shifts. Inside us it oscillates with the years. And even within the hearts overwhelmed with evil, one small bridgehead of good is retained. And even in the best of all hearts, there remains ... an unprooted small corner of evil' (ellipsis in original).

[88] See above, pp 8–9, 177–78.

[89] For a glimpse of what English private law would look like in the aftermath of a victory for the *Liberty Lovers*, see Atiyah, *The Damages Lottery* (Hart Publishing, 1997); Epstein, *Simple Rules for a Complex World* (Harvard UP, 1995); Morgan, *Contract Law Minimalism* (CUP, 2013).

[90] See above, p vii.

# INDEX OF NAMES

# INDEX OF SUBJECTS

CPSIA information can be obtained
at www.ICGtesting.com
Printed in the USA
LVHW101641231020
669661LV00007B/217